USING COMMUNICATION

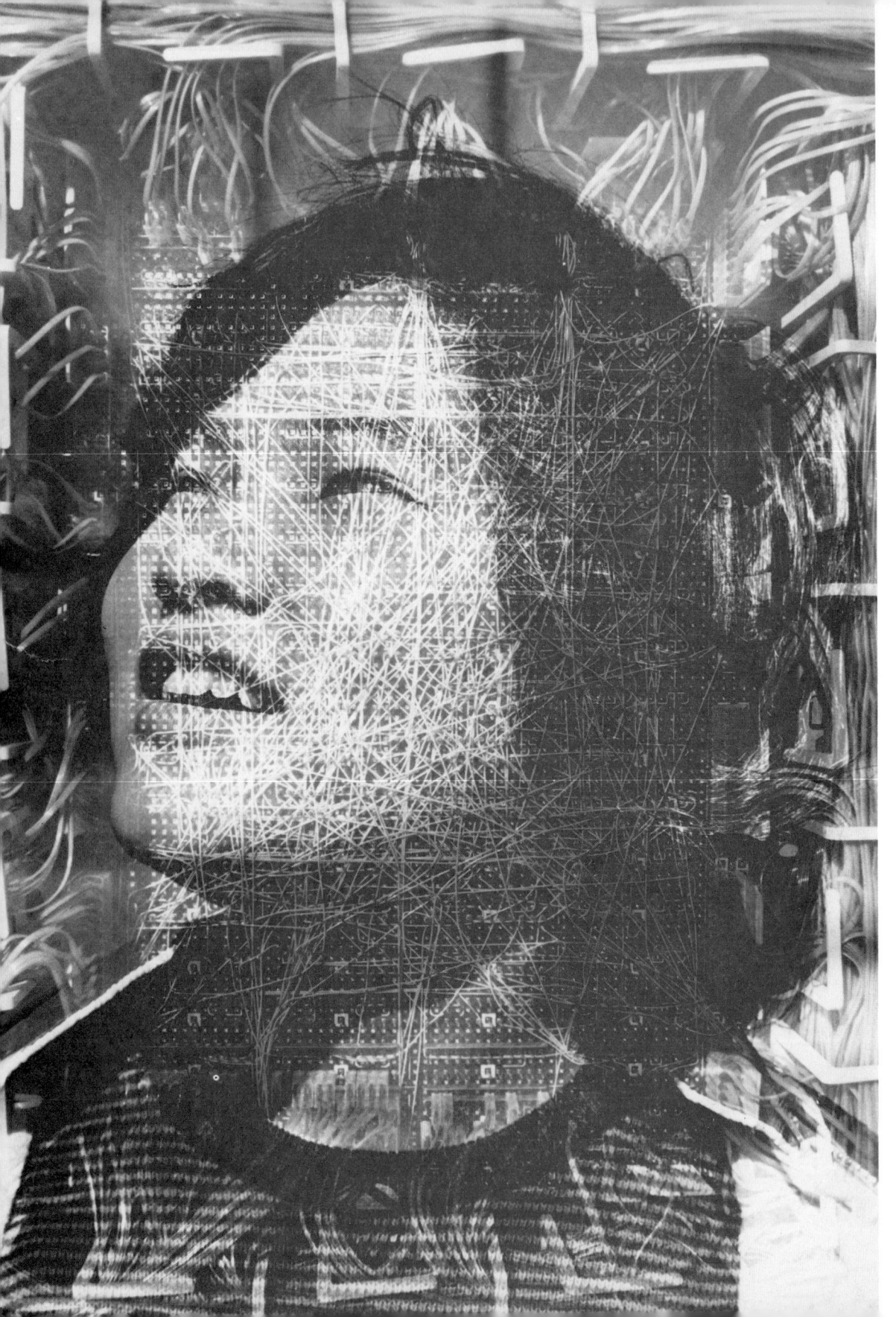

USING COMMUNICATION

RICHARD E. CRABLE
Purdue University

ALLYN AND BACON, INC.

Boston • London • Sydney • Toronto

Photo Credits

Pages ii, 1, 11, 25, 40 (lower right), 62, 78, 86, 216, 304, and 312, Talbot D. Lovering (Allyn and Bacon Staff Photographer); page 28, Webster-Dick Photography; page 114, Donald Wright Patterson, Jr., Stock, Boston; page 124, (top), John Running, Stock, Boston; (bottom), Peter Vandermark, Stock, Boston; page 138, Ellis Herwig, Stock, Boston; page 149, ABCD; page 152, Hays/Monkmeyer; page 182, M.I.T. Historical Collections; page 216, Boston University Photo Service.
Allyn and Bacon Photo Collection—page 40 (upper left), Bill Semick, (upper right), Courtesy of Dow Chemical, (lower left), Courtesy of International Harvester; pages 52 and 288, Phil Carver & Friends; page 87, Courtesy of the Occupational Health and Safety Administration; page 211, Photo by Bobbi Carrey; page 238, Action Office by Herman Miller, Inc; page 250, Courtesy of Gulf Oil Corporation/Lois M. Weissflog; page 274, David Kelley; page 304, Courtesy of WBZ–TV (Talbot D. Lovering)

Copyright © 1979 by Allyn and Bacon, Inc., 470 Atlantic Avenue, Boston, Massachusetts 02210. All rights reserved. No part of the material protected by this copyright notice may be reproduced or utilized in any form or by any means, electronic or mechanical, including photocopying, recording, or by any information storage and retrieval system, without written permission from the copyright owner.

Library of Congress Cataloging in Publication Data

Crable, Richard E.
    Using Communication.

    Bibliography: p.
    Includes index.
    1. Communication. I. Title.
P90.C7   001.5   78-27818
ISBN 0-205-06558-9

Printed in the United States of America.
Second printing . . . November, 1979

*For my mother and father, Mary and Kermit
— They gave me their understanding, their
valuing of education, and their love.*

CONTENTS

Preface   xiii

PART 1

  1 Communication as Mediation: An Orientation to Using Communication   3

    Conflict and Compatibility   4
    Mediation: Especially by Communication   5
    The Relevance of Mediation   7
    Chapter Summary   8

  2 Communication as a Process   11

    General Features of Communication   12
    Elements of a Communication Model   14
    Phases in the Communication Process   18
    Chapter Summary   20
    Exercises   21

PART 2 Introduction   25

  3 Intrapersonal Conflicts as Problems   29
    The Self in Conflict   29

The Self and Role Conflicts 31
The Self and Decisions 32
  Information Processing 32
  Behavior Decisions 33
  Value Formation 34
Conflicts Among Selves, Information, Behaviors, and Values 35
Intrapersonal Conflict, Acceptance, and Mediation 36
  Acceptance of the "As-is" Self 36
  Acceptance of the "Becoming" Self 37
Chapter Summary 38

4 Perceiving: an Intrapersonal Strategy 41

Perception is Active 42
Perception is Selective 43
Perception is Inductive 44
Perception is Context-Bound 45
Perception is Motivated 45
Perception is Personal 46
Perceiving and Intrapersonal Conflicts 47
Exercises 49

5 Language and Verbal Self-Analysis: an Intrapersonal Strategy 53

Language and Labeling 54
Language as Arbitrary and Rational 55
Language and Perception 56
Language and Abstraction 56
Language and Stereotyping 57
Verbal Self-Analysis and Intrapersonal Conflicts 57
Exercises 60

6 Nonverbal Self-Analysis: an Intrapersonal Strategy 63

Types of Nonverbal Symbols 64
The Meanings of Nonverbal Symbols 64
The Functions of Nonverbal Symbols 66
Commonly Found Meanings of Nonverbal Symbols 67
  Kinesics 67
  Proxemics 68
  Haptics 69
  Oculesics 69
  Objectics 70
  Chronemics 70
  Vocalics 71
  Environmental Factors 71
  Physical Appearance 72

Nonverbal Self-Analysis and Intrapersonal Conflict   72
Exercises   75

7 Intrapersonal Decisioning   79

The Nature of Argumentation   79
Decisions, Argumentation, and Intrapersonal Conflicts   81
Exercises   85

PART 3 Introduction   87

8 Interpersonal Conflicts as Problems   91

Conflicting Perceptions of the Other   92
Conflicts Over Roles   94
Conflicts Over Relationships   97
    Conflicts Over Liking and Distance   97
    Conflicts and Similarity   98
    Conflicts and Dominance   100
    Conflicts and Climate   101
Conflicts in Ethics   103
    Conflicts and Ethical Standards   104
    Conflicts and the Application of Ethical Standards   105
Chapter Summary   106
Applying What You Know in New Ways (How to Apply Intrapersonal Strategies in Interpersonal Situations)   108

9 Listening as an Interpersonal Strategy   115

Listening/Interpersonal Problems   116
Strategies for Listening   118

10 Feedback as an Interpersonal Strategy   125

Feedback and Mediation   126
Specific Strategies of Feedback   128
Feedback Games   133
Using Feedback for Mediation   135
Exercises   136

11 Interviewing as an Interpersonal Strategy   139

The Nature of Interviewing   140
Goals of Mediation in the Interview   140
Questions as Tools for Mediation   142
General Strategies of Interviewing   144
Exercises   147

PART 4 Introduction 149

12 Small Group Conflicts as Problems 153

The Nature of Small Group Communication 153
Group Participation Conflicts 155
    Intra/Interpersonal Problems in the Small Group 156
    Problems Involving Status 156
    Problems of Representation 157
    Conflicting Memberships 158
People-Task Balancing Problems 158
    Task and Interpersonal Conflicts 159
    Personal and Group Goal Conflicts 159
    Leadership and Membership Conflicts 160
Problems in Climate 160
Problems of Group Decision-Making 161
Problems of Dysfunctional Roles 163
Chapter Summary 165
Special Feature: Applying What You Know in New Ways (How to Apply Earlier Strategies in the Small Group Setting) 167

13 Consensus and Win-Win Gaming as Group Strategies 173

Various Types of Games 173
The Win-Win Strategy 175
Quality Versus Acceptance 177
Exercises 179

14 Decision-Making Processes as Group Strategies 183

Information Analysis 184
Dewey's Steps to Reflective Thinking 186
Creativity and Decision Making 189
    Brainstorming 190
    Synectics 190
Argumentation and Group Decision-Making 192
Exercises 197

15 Role Enactments as Group Strategies 201

Task Roles 202
Maintenance Roles 203
Organizational Roles 204
Leadership Roles 205
Exercises 208

Contents

PART 5 Introduction   211

16 One-to-Many Communication Conflicts as Problems   217

The Context of One-to-Many Communication Conflicts   218
    The Organization of Organizations   218
    The Individual in the Organization   224
    Organizations and Systems   227
Problems in the One-to-Many Setting   228
    Problems of Communicating *through* the Organization   228
    Problems of Communicating *to* the Organization   230
    Problems of Speaking *for* the Organization   231
Chapter Summary   232
Special Feature: Applying What You Know in New Ways (How to Apply Earlier Strategies in the One-to-Many Situation)   235

17 Serial Communication as One-to-Many Strategies   239

Select Your Communication Purpose   240
Realize Sources of Distortion   243
Decide How to Communicate   245
Decide When to Communicate   245
Beware of the Interrelationships Among Messages Presented Serially   246
Exercises   247

18 General Strategies of Speaking   251

Improving Credibility   251
Controlling Anxiety   253
Adapting Delivery   255
    Credibility-Enhancing Delivery   256
    Communicative Delivery   257
    Appropriate Delivery   258
Supporting with Visual Aids   261
    What Sorts of Visuals Can Be Used?   262
    When Should Visual Aids Be Used?   263
    How Should Visual Aids Be Used?   265
Adapting Language   268
    Language Should Be Nondistracting   269
    Language Should Be Appropriate   270
Chapter Summary   271

19 Strategies of Presentational Speaking   275

Creating the Proposal   275

Reasoning and Persuasive Analysis 276
  Reasoning Analysis 277
  Persuasive Analysis 278
Organization and Reasons 281
Preparing for the Presentation 283
Adapting to the Process of Presentational Speaking 284
Chapter Summary 286
Exercises 286

20 Strategies of Public Speaking 289

Analyzing the Audience 290
  Demographic Variables 290
  Psychological Variables 291
Creating the Specific Purpose 292
  The Audience and You 292
  General Purpose 292
  The Handling of Topics 292
  Organizational Guidelines 293
  Factors in Selecting the Specific Purpose 293
  Selecting the Specific Purpose 294
Organizing the Speech 294
Adapting General Speaking Strategies in Public Speaking 297
Chapter Summary 298
Exercises 299

PART 6 Introduction 301

21 Mass Communication Conflicts as Problems 305

Types of Media Influence or Efforts 306
The Problem of Potential Effects 307
The Problem of Monopolized Channels 308
The Problems of Freedom and Control 308
The Problem of Media Interrelationship 309

22 Strategies for Mass Media Conflicts 313

Being Critical; Being Fair 313
Realize the Media's Responsibility 314
Realize that You Can Affect the Media 315
Realize that Strategies of Mediation Interrelate 315
Exercises 318

Index 321

PREFACE

More than anything else, this book is intended to be useful.

I am one of those people who would study communication because it is an exciting, dynamic process. Most people who enroll in basic communication courses, however, do not plan to spend the rest of their lives researching and teaching communication. The book has been written for them.

Communication is not actually the focus of this text: the *use* of communication is its primary emphasis. Twentieth century life means that everyone will be faced with problems in an increasingly complex and organized world. Individuals will be faced with problems involving dissatisfaction with themselves, with other individuals, with groups, with organizations, and with mass media. Some of these problems or conflicts require the help of professionals of one kind or another. Other problems can be helped by the individual knowing how to use communication to solve problems. This book discusses some of the problems faced by people all the time; it also discusses strategies that can help with those problems.

Why, then, should a student take a basic course in communication? Because such a course can be personally useful in "coping" with the world.

MAJOR GOALS OF THE TEXT

Though there are dozens of specific goals for the text, four major goals are of overriding importance:

1. Readers of the text should be able to understand fully the process of communication as a tool for solving problems.

What I mean here is that some things are valuable for *what they are:* a painting, a sunrise, a child's grin. Other things are more important because of *what can be done with them:* a hammer, a toothbrush, an umbrella. Some things are important for both reasons: a beautiful, but economical automobile. When two different people look at the automobile, both may realize its beauty and its economy; yet, one may stress the excellence of the car because of what it is, while the other may stress the functional aspects of the auto. Communication, similarly, can be appreciated for the exciting process that it is *and* for its value in doing something. I appreciate communication from both standpoints, but the text is written to accentuate the potential of communication for *doing.* Specifically, that doing involves the solution, or "mediation" of human problems.

2. Readers of the text should be able to understand how human problems are often based upon communication problems, or "conflicts."

As our world becomes beset with problems of all kinds, certain explanations become popular. In ancient times, general and specific human problems were explained as being the results of angry gods. In modern times, nearly every problem seems to be explained as a "communication problem." A candidate loses an election? A communication problem. A school levy is defeated? A communication problem. A marriage disintegrates? A problem of communication. An organization acquires an unfavorable image? A communication problem. The problem with one explanation for all problems may be that it is not any explanation at all. Surely, some human problems *are* communication problems. Surely, also, not all human problems are simply matters of communication. The text attempts to describe the sorts of human problems that are in fact related to communication.

3. Readers of the text should be able to understand how communication "strategies" (concept-based skills) can be used for resolving or "mediating" communication conflicts—and, thus, some human problems.

The text unself-consciously deals with the sorts of skills that may help people deal with problems related to communication processes. The skills discussed are based upon a firm understanding of the communication process and things that can improve such processes. Even though not all problems are communication problems, an amazing range of human problems are less severe when communication becomes more effective. The strategies discussed in the text are based upon the common goal of helping make communication more effective.

4. Readers of the text should be able to use communication strategies for mediation.

The ultimate test of the book is how well readers begin actually *using* communication. Communication is such a consistent part of everyone's world that everyone *will use* communication. That is not the issue. The question is *how well* communication is used to deal with human problems. The entire text is aimed at improving the readers' use of communication.

These four goals are meant to be dependent upon one another. The fourth goal is really the culmination of the others. The extent to which readers achieve the goal of using communication to help with their problems is the extent to which the text has been successful.

INTENDED CHARACTERISTICS OF THE TEXT

Books, like people, are seen in different ways by different observers. Perhaps it would be helpful here to describe how I have intended to have the book be perceived by its readers.

First, I have intended the book to be useful, something I have already discussed. I have tried to deal with a wide range of possible problems and situations that occur in everyday life. I have tried to describe these situations and problems in enough detail to allow readers to envision them. Strategies of using communication have been explained with the goal of having each reader see something in a chapter that is new and important. The greatest compliment I could receive from a reader is for that person to decide to keep the text as an addition to his or her personal collection of helpful books.

Second, I have intended the book to be comprehensive. The book describes the communication problems encountered by the individual in dealing with everyone from him or herself to the television industry. Communication problems occur in one-to-one settings, groups, organizations, and the individual's exposure with the mass media. I have tried to take that into account. The text was not conceived as a survey of communication settings, but it has become that simply because of the nature of humans: they become involved in every conceivable sort of communication setting. The text became a survey of communication settings simply because of the diversity of the problems human beings face.

Third, the text is intended to be clear and easily understood. Examples, illustrations, and case studies are used to complement the prose of the chapters which follow. The text will be most helpful to those without earlier experience in communication studies. Consequently, I have written the text with these people in mind. Complex language and sophisticated vocabulary that might hinder the learning process have been avoided. Each student should be able to read and comprehend the main points of the discussion.

Fourth, the text is intended to be integrated. Human problems seldom seem related to only one communication "setting." In the text, I have tried continually to stress how *a* communication problem may actually be *several* communication problems. In the same way, strategies of communication that can be learned in relation to one communication setting may be helpful in other settings. The text is written to explain how both communication problems and strategies interrelate.

Finally, I have tried to make the text as flexible as possible. A course based upon the text may be primarily theory-oriented or practice-oriented, or fit anywhere in between. Chapters within a unit may be treated in different orders if that seems desirable. The special sections and case studies in the text may be used extensively as class activities or as outside-of-class activities. In essence, the text can be used for a variety of teaching emphases.

In my effort to have the text exhibit the qualities mentioned above, I have benefited greatly from the teachers who taught me, from my experience in teaching the basic course, from the advice of my editors, and from the suggestions made by my excellent reviewers. It is my hope that the reader finds those qualities in the completed text.

INSTRUCTIONAL FEATURES

The text has been prepared with the student uppermost in mind. It is my belief that a text should be more than a descriptive book; it should serve some of the functions of a "handbook" or "lab" book. One way to describe this is to say that the text should be a "learning package." In writing the book for students I have included a number of specific features which should make the process of education more efficient:

1. *Chapter-beginning examples.* Many of the chapters begin with examples or brief illustrations of the sorts of problems which will be dealt with in the chapter. The examples may prove to be interesting, but they are positioned primarily to create a frame of reference for the reading. Readers are instantly introduced to the problems at hand which are discussed in detail in the chapter.

2. *In-text examples and illustrations.* The text contains numerous examples and illustrations. Experience—and my reviewers—helped me provide examples when and where they were most needed. Since the text is intended to be as useful as possible, these examples and illustrations help ensure that the text remains concrete and practical.

3. *Strategy summaries.* Toward the end of the chapters that deal with strategies is a summary that does more than list the material in the text. These summaries provide a convenient and concise statement of how the strategies can be used most effectively and efficiently. In a sense, they become "checklists" for review and later reference.

4. *Case studies.* Most of the "strategies" chapters end with case studies rather than summaries. My belief in taking this approach is that readers can benefit immensely from having the opportunity to put their new knowledge into practice immediately. Generally, the first of several cases are "worked through" for the reader as a method of illustration. Other cases in the chapter demand more thought and input from the reader. The result, I hope, is an immediate sense of the practicality and usefulness of the text's discussion.

5. *End-of-chapter exercises.* Where appropriate, exercises are included in the text. These may be conducted in class and orally, used as out-of-class assignments, or used simply to stimulate thought. However they are used, they can add greatly to the practicality of the text.

6. *Introductions to text parts.* With graphics and descriptions, these brief sections are designed to help create a frame of reference for the complete unit, whether it is interpersonal conflicts and strategies or one of the other units. The introductions allow the specific kind of communication in the unit to be related always to the general notion of a communication process.

7. *"Applying What You Know In New Ways."* These special features are designed to keep the reader aware that strategies learned in one section of the text are generally applicable to later sections. For example, one of the sections deals with how to apply strategies learned in the intrapersonal unit to the problems discussed in the interpersonal unit. The constant reapplication of strategies is intended to make the discussion of such strategies as integrated as it should be.

The special instructional features of the text are designed to provide readers with the tools to help them learn to use the concepts and skills in the text.

A FINAL WORD

The factors I have discussed are ones I felt you should know about before reading the text. One of the greatest challenges to a writer, perhaps, is communicating to a diversified audience. My task here has been to explain something about the nature and goals of the text. I hope that the material contained in the following pages is a help to those who have the need of *using communication* more efficiently and more effectively.

R. E. C.
January 1979

ACKNOWLEDGMENTS

In an undertaking of this scope, many people are influential—and, invariably some will be left out of the acknowledgements. Still, there are those who must be named specifically. I wish to thank students at Ohio State University, Drake University, and Purdue University because they truly affected the direction of the text; Frank Ruggirello of Allyn and Bacon for his initial encouragement of the project; and Bill Barke of Allyn and Bacon for his excellent help in the concluding stages of the project.

For their comments and evaluations, I wish to thank the people who reviewed the manuscript at various stages of its preparation. They are (in alphabetical order) Professors Gwenn Danielson, Portland Community College; Maurine Eckloff, Kearney State College; Isa Engleberg, Prince George Community College; Bonnie Johnson, Pennsylvania State University; Gerald Miller, Michigan State University; Larry Miller, Indiana University; Janice Rushing, University of California at Los Angeles; Joan Shields, Arapahoe Community College; and Dwayne Van Rheenen, University of Maine at Orono.

I wish to thank members of my family; the Crables of Ohio, the Bachs of Kentucky, and the Crables of Indiana. Two of the last—Bryan and Audrey—put up with more than their share of "Shhhh . . . Daddy's working!" Their love in part was demonstrated by their tolerance.

Finally, I am most indebted to my wife Ann. She is an astute critic of my work and has helped provide much of the insight in the following pages. For that, I could easily consider her a co-author. In addition, she has taught me more about communication and intimacy than all the studies I have ever read—or done. For that, I consider her the most important person in my world.

USING COMMUNICATION

PART 1

1
COMMUNICATION AS MEDIATION: AN ORIENTATION TO USING COMMUNICATION

You have been wondering lately about the courses you are studying in school. You look at the latest figures on unemployment and you are not sure you are well prepared for the job market. You think about your experience, your interests, and your academic background. Exactly how well prepared are you? What kind of employee will you be?

It is your first job interview. You have sat for half an hour outside the personnel director's door. You have your credentials with you and you are anxious to create a favorable impression. Finally, the door opens and the personnel director calls your name. What are you going to do now?

Now, you have a job. One of the things you learn is that you are assigned to work with several other employees on a company problem. When a decision is reached, you will have the responsibility for presenting the group's findings in a meeting of senior executives. How will you become a helpful and important member of the group? What will you do when you have to present the group's findings at the meeting?

The situations above are hypothetical problems. Still, I suspect that you will face problems like them in the years ahead, if you have not already done so. How do you understand these problems? More importantly, what do you do about them? This text is written to help answer those questions.

Students should expect to gain two important things from this book: first, an understanding of various kinds of communication problems; and second, skills and guidance in how to handle those problems. The book is not written primarily as an introduction to theory in communication. It is not meant to be a survey of all the areas included in the study of communication. It is instead a practical guide for the understanding and possible solution of everyday communication problems. The focus will always be upon *mediation: the process of settling or reconciling undesired differences between people or unwanted problems in human life.*[1]

Usually, *mediation* is used to describe what happens in situations such as labor-management negotiations. The people who try to settle contract issues are called *mediators*. When you face problems in your everyday life, you usually cannot call upon the services of a professional mediator. What you can do is to learn to use certain knowledge and skills to mediate your own problems. You, in a way, can become your own mediator. Whether an individual is in the role of student, employee, wife, husband, parent, or friend, that individual frequently will sense the need to make the world (or people in it) more like he or she wishes it to be. That individual will feel the need to *mediate the situation* or to do something about the problem.

CONFLICT AND COMPATIBILITY

The terms *compatibility* and *conflict* are crucial to understanding the nature of human problems and attempts at mediation. Whatever else human beings are, they are social animals who tend to group together for protection, for love, and for convenience. One of the most important factors that allows people to group together is *compatibility: the state of being comfortable or satisfied: or a sharing of characteristics.*[2] Just as cave dwellers found enough in common to allow them to live in groups, modern society is based upon people sharing similar interests or goals. For every individual who decides to live on a mountaintop or in a forest to escape society, there are millions who cluster together into families, tribes, communities, and corporations. People are truly social animals and their compatibility with others allows them to group together.

Humans discover that their clustering together is not without problems. They discover *conflict: situations where people are incompatible or competitive with one another.*[3] They find that those around them have beliefs and desires which are different from their own. They find that in their search for love and security they often confront antagonism and jealousy. They find that their quest for political and economic convenience is often frustrated by their fellow humans. To understand the nature of human problems, the idea of conflict is crucial.

One of the ways of understanding conflict better is to realize that it can arise in several general forms in human problems. The conflict might be *differences over the goals* in some activity.[4] The student who wants to be a writer and the parent who wants him or her to be a lawyer demonstrate conflict over goals. Other conflict can occur over ideas, facts, or information. This *conflict over substance, information or content,* as researchers call it, exists when my friend argues that a Republican should be elected senator and I argue that the Democratic candidate should be elected. Conflict also arises at times over *differences of procedures,* or the method of getting something done. Conflict over procedures exists when one student in an organization wants to take a roll-call vote, while another wants the voting to be by secret ballot. Still another sort of conflict emerges over *interpersonal differences.* When two people simply cannot get along because they dislike one another—or even when only one dislikes the other—interpersonal conflict has arisen. Human conflict becomes more understandable when it is seen as disagreement or differences in goals, content, procedures, or personality.

Though compatibility and conflict are important in understanding human problems, the popular assumption that the first is always good and the second is always bad needs to be discussed. Compatibility is usually explained in positive, if not glowing, terms. Compatibility in marriage, friendships, and international relations is certainly positive. Yet frequently, the effects of compatibility are not so positive: I assume that the leaders within both Hitler's hierarchy and organized crime (whatever that is) are compatible, but I question the benefits of their compatibility. On the other hand, conflict is normally treated in negative terms. Conflict, it is said, must be avoided or overcome in marriages, businesses, and student organizations. Modern researchers, however, are beginning to point out that conflict—if handled properly—can lead to better decisions and higher creativity.[5] The business which is staffed by "Yes-people" probably would prosper better with some higher degree of conflict over goals or procedures. Conflict, like compatibility, should be considered as neither good nor bad until a particular situation is studied. *Either can be constructive and helpful or dysfunctional and harmful.*[6] Both are natural ingredients in human problems.

People do not always agree upon whether a certain instance of conflict is beneficial or not. They may not even agree that conflict exists in the situation. A problem does not simply arise; rather, it is created when someone says, "Well, it's a problem to *me!*"[7] What is a major problem to you may be unimportant to another. When you find yourself in a situation that seems uncomfortable, that needs solution, you should be able to understand the nature and significance of that situation. Human beings are social animals and social animals confront problems.

MEDIATION: ESPECIALLY BY COMMUNICATION

Just as social beings have always confronted problems and social conflict, they have always felt the need for various methods of solution or mediation. The most obvious method of mediation is by *physical acts of force.* To make the world as they want it, humans intimidate, steal from, and kill one another and create a history of crime and war. Another method of mediation is *spiritualism.* Humans appeal for help to the gods, to God, or to the forces of the cosmos, and create a history of religion and prayer. Another method of mediation is formal *counseling*, where a third party of some kind is called upon to mediate the situation. In order to get help with personal problems or problems with others, people seek the professional services of marriage counselors, psychologists, or psychiatrists, and create a history of therapy. Another method of mediation is *communication with others immediately involved* with the problem. People persuade, argue with, or relate to one another, and create a history of communication.

I hesitate to speculate whether individuals mediate their conflicts more by spiritualism, physical acts of force, counseling, or communication with others. A person's use of these or any other means of mediation depends upon such factors as training, experience, and preference—in addition to the nature of the problem. I would guess that rabbis mediate more problems with prayer than I do. I assume babies mediate more problems with physical acts than counseling, and I suppose that psychiatrists mediate more of other people's conflicts with counseling than others might. Generally, most people use all these methods and more at one time or another. They may perhaps try one method and then another if the problem continues. The important point is not what I might guess, but rather that an individual in a complex world probably should know something about all these possible methods of problem solution. This text is aimed at helping people use communication strategies as a method of solving certain of their problems.

The idea of approaching communication as mediation is hardly novel. The history of such an approach really begins with its use by Corax in 476 B.C. in Sicily. As Aristotle and others tell us, the problem then was controversy over land titles and distribution.[8] Corax is said to have been instrumental in teaching people to persuade others in courts of law. These acts of persuasion resulted in the mediation of problems without resort to force. That tradition of communication and persuasion—called *rhetoric*—was carried to Greece and was effective in helping the Greeks solve the problems of early democracy.[9] Communication scholars such as Aristotle relied upon systematic observation of people to understand the nature of problems and why various communication strategies (not just persuasion) worked. With the rise of social science, contemporary communication researchers since the 1930s have borrowed and applied insights from psychology, sociology, anthropology, and linguistics—and generated their own findings.[10] Today communication research and scholarship involves critical analysis, laboratory experiments, and field research in classrooms, business organizations, and mass media markets.

Throughout this long development of communication studies, the major thrust of the effort has been both *to understand the nature of human communication problems and to use appropriate strategies to help solve or mediate those problems.* Those are the related goals of this text. The thinking and writing of ancient scholars of rhetoric will be combined with the latest thinking and research from contemporary scholars so that the student can understand communication problems that arise and methods that may aid the mediation of those problems.

THE RELEVANCE OF MEDIATION

Contemporary studies of communication involve a wide variety of communication problems that are of concern to the contemporary student. Some scholars and researchers focus upon *intrapersonal*—within the self—communication. How do your feelings about yourself influence how you communicate with others? How many *selves* make up what *you* are? How can the *self-concept* be changed through communication? These are questions related to intrapersonal communication. Other scholars study *interpersonal*—between two or more people—communication. How can you really tell another person the way you feel? How do you handle that first employment interview? What are the most important things to remember when you are part of a group working on a task? These and other matters will be dealt with when interpersonal communication is discussed. Still other scholars have delved into the public speaking situation. What do you need to do to deliver an acceptable speech to the Kiwanis Club? How does that differ from the sort of presentation you would make as an engineer or marketing specialist in a modern organization? These and similar *public communication* ideas will be of interest. Finally, because virtually no contemporary individual lives outside the influence of organizations and the mass media, you need to know something about those communication situations. Contemporary scholars ask such questions as: How does information flow in an organization? What can you do to affect it? How are organizations affected by the mass media? What influence can the individual have with the mass media? This view of the range of communication as mediation is wide simply because communication can be such a vital tool in your efforts to make the world more like you would like it to be.

It is crucial here to note that these different "areas" of communication situations and problems are very much related to one another. Problems that arise in a group of several people who must perform a task are always related to issues of another kind. A group of students, for example, who assume the task of improving the course in which they are enrolled will soon find out how their problem is complicated by the views of the academic department as an organization, the university or college as an organization, or the instructor as an individual with concerns of his or her own. Groups and individuals learn that one communication problem is probably several communication problems. An effort will be made throughout this text to look at several of the many potential problems in the one situation. Communication problems, like their solutions, are seldom simple and easy.

Just as it is important to know that the study of communication as mediation can involve all sorts of situations, it is crucial also to realize that not all mediation attempts will have the same goal. In one situation, for instance, the goal may be to win the affection and respect of a person who has been unfriendly. On another occasion, the goal may be to increase the amount of affection that is already displayed, or to cool off a relationship that is not wanted. In still another instance, the goal may simply be to maintain or continue the sort of relationship that already exists. Whether the goal is to increase, decrease, change, or maintain elements of a particular situation, individuals need an understanding of the problem and guidelines on how to communicate; they need, that is, to know how to mediate a situation.

CHAPTER SUMMARY

The focus of this book, then, is not upon the study of communication simply because communication happens to be an exciting and challenging area of human knowledge. The focus is upon the study of communication as a way of helping *you* to understand everyday communication problems and the methods that *you* may use in dealing with them.

The remaining five parts of the book are designed to help you with various problems in your life. Chapter 3, the first chapter of Part 2, is a study of *intra*personal problems which may become conflicts for you. The remaining chapters in Part 2 are devoted to communication strategies that may help you mediate those conflicts. Part 3 is arranged similarly: a chapter on *inter*personal conflicts and several chapters on communication strategies. Part 4 is a study of small group conflicts and strategies. Part 5 deals with the conflicts and strategies in "one-to-many" communication. Finally, Part 6 deals with conflicts and strategies in the mass communication setting. Before we begin to look at specific communication strategies, you need to understand the process of communication itself. That is the task of Chapter 2.

NOTES

[1] This concern for *mediation* can be found also in Richard E. Crable, "What Can You Believe About Rhetoric?" *Exploration in Speech Communication*, ed. John J. Makay (Columbus, Oh.: Charles E. Merrill Publishing Co., 1973), pp. 28–38.

[2] Other terms can be used for somewhat the same idea. I prefer the term compatibility because it *may* imply similarity, but it always implies satisfaction in the situation. Sometimes, for instance, people can be satisfied with their differences. My wife and I are very different in some ways, but the differences are mostly characteristics that *complement one another* rather than clash. In this sense, we can be both different and compatible.

[3] For an excellent and readable discussion of conflict, see Robert J. Doolittle, *Orientations to Communication and Conflict* (Chicago: Science Research Associates, Inc., 1976).

[4] For discussions relevant to these ideas, see D. Johnson and F. Johnson, *Joining Together: Group Theory and Group Skills* (Englewood Cliffs, N.J.: Prentice-Hall, Inc., 1975), p. 171.

[5] See, for example, Doolittle, *Orientations to Communication and Conflict*, pp. 3–5.

[6] We shall see conflict and compatibility as both constructive and unconstructive in virtually every situation we examine.

[7] This view of how we largely *construct* the world we live in will be continually referred to in our study. For an introduction to this view, see David Swanson and Jesse Delia, *The Nature of Human Communication* (Chicago: Science Research Associates, Inc., 1976).

[8] For a brief discussion of the tradition, see Edward P. J. Corbett, *Classical Rhetoric for the Modern Student*, 2nd ed. (New York: Oxford University Press, 1971), pp. 594–96.

[9] For a discussion, see Richard McKeon, "General Introduction," Aristotle, *Introduction to Aristotle,* ed. by Richard McKeon (New York: The Modern Library, 1947), pp. ix–xxix.
[10] The influences from all these modern sciences will become evident as chapter topics are developed.

2
COMMUNICATION AS A PROCESS

You sit alone in your room trying to decide whether to go out for the evening or whether to study for the math exam. You seem to be communicating with yourself.

You walk to class the next day with a friend and classmate. As you walk, you discuss the exam you are about to take. Again, you seem to be communicating.

You enter the classroom and your instructor begins to explain the nature of the exam and the grading procedure that will be used. Earlier, you were sitting amid a group of class members wondering what the exam would be like and how the grading would be done. In each case, communication seemed to be occurring.

You leave class at the end of the exam and pick up the campus newspaper. The newspaper seems also to be a kind of communication device.

If communication seems to be all these things, then what, exactly, is communication? The question is crucial. You cannot hope to use communication as a tool for mediation unless you understand the nature of communication. As you become familiar with the ideas and concepts related to communication, you will find the use of communication as a tool easier; but, the question remains, What is communication?

There are nearly as many definitions of communication as there are people who write about it. You will not benefit from a lengthy list of definitions, but you will need to have some understanding of communication as I use the term.

Let me describe the major features of communication as I see them. From these features, a usable and helpful definition of communication can be built, and with the addition of some details, you will understand enough about the process of communication to understand later discussions about its use as a tool.

GENERAL FEATURES OF COMMUNICATION

One of the general features or components of communication is the idea of *meaning: an importance or significance that a person attaches to something.*[1] You may treasure a high school letter sweater or a well-worn stuffed animal because it has *meaning* or significance to you. Communication involves the same concern for importance or significance. A casual "That's pretty good artwork" from your father may once have meant more to you than all the praise in the world from your art teacher. Sometimes the meaning of a statement is less clear. You may be wearing a new pair of slacks and a friend says, "Well, those are interesting." You may not know whether the comment is a compliment or an insult. You may not know what the statement meant. In all those situations and in all other communication situations, meaning is an important feature.

In communication studies, *things that someone attaches meaning to* are called *symbols,* the second important feature of the communication process.[2] Spoken words and written words may mean something since someone can attach significance or importance to them. Words, whether they are spoken or written, are called *verbal symbols.* But many symbols—in fact, most symbols—are not words so they are called *nonverbal symbols.* Hand gestures, eye winks, and head nods are all nonverbal symbols, since they may mean something to a person in a particular situation. Less obvious nonverbal symbols include clothing and appearance, the amount of space that you keep between you and another person, and the way you may someday arrange the chairs in your office. All those are things that can mean something to people. Verbal and nonverbal symbols will be discussed more later, but for now it is important to know that symbols are a crucial feature of communication.

What connects the concerns for meaning and symbols is the third major feature of communication. Communication is a *process: an ongoing, dynamic activity.*[3] Communication is not the act of making a statement. It is a dynamic, lively activity where *symbols* are used to get others to share *meanings.* An individual will use verbal and nonverbal symbols in order to let the other person know what he or she means. That is activity and it is highly dynamic. It is not enough to speak words to someone. You will try to say what you mean again and again until the listener says, "Yes, I see what you mean." Communication is a process and the more you learn of it, the more you will appreciate how dynamic it is.

This discussion of sharing meanings through symbols introduces a fourth main feature of communication. Communication involves the idea of *re-*

created meaning: the creation of a meaning that is similar to yours in the mind of another.[4] My feeling is that if you have not succeeded in making the other person understand fairly exactly what you mean, you have not communicated. Symbols may have been used and some sort of meaning may have been created in the other person, but to me, that is not necessarily communication. Let me explain. You may have enjoyed a piece of pumpkin pie and turned to a friend. "That was *some* piece of pie," you say. If the friend says, "I agree. It was great," then you have communicated. If the reply is, "I agree. That was probably the worst pie I ever had," then you have failed to re-create your favorable reaction to the pie. I might call that *miscommunication,* but I would not call it communication. The same is true in a different situation. I look down and see a rock that I identify as being from a glacial era. I attach all sorts of importance to the glacial marks and the rock has meaning to me. Did the rock communicate to me? I think not, since rocks, as far as we know, can have no meanings that they try to re-create in others. You are free to disagree with me, but my point is that for communication to occur, there must be some meaning that exists for one individual, and is *re-created* in the mind of someone else.

This notion of re-created meanings is related to a fifth feature of communication: *intent or purposefulness in the re-creation of meaning.*[5] The phrase, *You cannot not communicate,* has become popular in communication studies.[6] It means that people can attach some significance or meaning to everything you do. If you wear a green shirt, that can mean something. If you get a new hairstyle, that can mean something. The green shirt example can be used to show why I disagree that *You cannot not communicate.* Let us say that you wear a green shirt because you look good in green and you want to have another person notice you. You have *intended* to wear the shirt as a symbol. You think that you look attractive in green and you want to re-create that meaning in a certain other person. If that person says, "Well, you look nice today," then you have communicated the meaning with your symbol. On the other hand, let us say that you wear the green shirt because that was the only clean one that you have. If you get the same compliment, you have *accidentally* created a meaning in someone's mind; you have not re-created a meaning that you intended. Again, you are free to disagree, but I think the first compliment was communication—and the second one was a pleasant miscommunication. Intent or purposefulness is to me a major feature of communication.

Communication involves one other feature that I want to discuss. Communication is a *transaction: a process in which changes or exchanges occur.*[7] When you have communicated a meaning to another person, that person is changed because of the new idea or insight. You also have changed because you now think you know the person shares a meaning or idea with you. In addition, the meaning you had may have changed because of the response that the other person had to your idea. Whether the changes are in the people, the ideas, or in the meaning you have, communication will involve ongoing change for as long as the process continues. Communication will always be a transaction; changes of some sort will always occur because of it.

With the addition of the notion of transaction, you know something of the major features of communication: meaning, symbols, re-created meanings, process, intent, and transaction. Those features can be combined to create a usable definition of communication. As I shall use the term, *communication is the process of symbolic transaction aimed at the re-creation of meaning.*[8] You know now what that means. In order to communicate, you have a meaning which you put into symbols so that another individual can re-create your meaning for him- or herself. This is a transaction because you, the other person, and perhaps your own meaning are changed and exchanged in the intended process of getting the other person to understand what you mean. The rest of the book will provide details to show how you can make the re-creation of meaning more successful and more beneficial in mediating the kinds of problems you have.

Knowing a definition of communication based upon its general features is usually not enough to understand communication fully. Communication is easier to understand if its specific elements are explained. The specific people and things needed to re-create intended meanings in the process of communication are our next concern.

ELEMENTS OF A COMMUNICATION MODEL

The most basic elements of the communication process as I shall use the term are people. When communication is discussed, two or more people are usually involved, and I shall call *the people participating in communication* the *communicators*. Communicators are *people* who have meanings that they wish to share, or *people* who wish to have a meaning shared with them. I am fascinated with the possibility of people communicating with machines or computers, or people communicating with animals—and vice versa. The narrowing of concern to people is prompted mostly by the need to retain focus upon the student and his or her problems. More intriguing is the idea of one person communicating with him- or herself—and I shall discuss later how that seems possible. The point to remember is simply that for our purposes, communicators are people, whether one, two, several, or many.

Our discussion must take into consideration that people have different abilities, viewpoints, and strengths. I shall call factors such as levels of knowledge, kinds of past experiences, and various beliefs *conceptual screens: the factors that give the individual somewhat unique characteristics.*[9] Various political and social viewpoints, different cultures, biases of any form, and amounts of education are all factors that help explain who the communicators are. The factors explain also how information is *filtered* or affected in different individuals. Conceptual screens affect sent and received messages, and will be discussed in detail later. For now, it is enough to realize that communicators are different. One of the ways of describing why they are different is to recognize that they *screen* ideas and information differently depending upon their *conceptual screens.*

Communicators and conceptual screens are only the first two elements of the communication process. When communicators attempt to re-create meaning, they put symbols into some sort of form which we will call a *message: the oral statement, written comment, facial expression, or nonverbal activity that is created by the communicator who wishes to have a meaning re-created.* Closely related to this third element of communication is the fourth element. *Feedback is the response that the other individual(s) makes to the original message.*[10] Feedback can take the form of any set of symbols that the second communicator uses to respond to the message; an oral statement, a written comment, or any type of nonverbal symbol such as a smile, a frown, or a gesture. To understand communication as a process and a transaction, feedback is crucial. The initial communicator is not the only active member of the process. *Senders* of messages (first communicators) are important because they create symbols about their meanings, but *receivers* of messages (second or other communicators) are also important: they are the ones who must attempt to understand the symbols, to re-create the intended meaning, and to make a response (feedback). When the feedback is offered by the original receiver of the message, that person becomes the sender, and the process continues for as long as the communicators continue. Perhaps more importantly, the sending and receiving of messages can be done at the same time: we make a comment while we look for nonverbal feedback from a friend. Messages and feedback response are important elements of the communication process.

In order that messages re-create meanings they must be sent through a *channel or medium: something that can carry or allow the sending of symbols.* Channels or media in communication function the way that river beds or water pipes do: they allow the passage of things through them.[11] Television is a medium or channel since it permits the transmission of verbal and nonverbal symbols. A letter and the postal service serve as media to allow written messages to be sent. The air between two people functions as a medium since without air molecules, sound waves could not be produced. Light allows nonverbal symbols to be seen and so it too functions as a medium. Whenever there is a message sent, some medium is present to allow the sending of it.

Once the importance of communicators, conceptual screens, messages, feedback, and channels is realized, one final element of the communication process must be discussed. *Interference* is a term I shall use to mean *the factors in any part of the communication process that hinder successful meaning re-creation.*[12] Interference can be a function of the communicators. If a person with whom you wish to communicate is absent, communication may be impossible. Sometimes conceptual screens cause the interference. Biases, ignorance, or differing attitudes may be responsible for miscommunication. Interference is related to the message or feedback if handwriting is illegible, a word is unfamiliar, or a different language is spoken. Interference can also be in the channel. A poor telephone connection, a lost letter, or a room full of noise can all cause the failure of communication to occur. Communication is sometimes impossible and usually difficult. Interference of some sort is an important reason why.

We have discussed such things as messages and media being elements of a communication *model*. When all these elements are pictured as they interact during communication, they represent a model of the communication process. Figure 2.1 is a pictorial summary of the discussion of elements.

Once a communication model is established, it is easier to visualize communication as the process of symbolic transaction aimed at the re-creation of meaning. Still, all communication processes occur within a *system:* people and factors *outside* the process are affected by and affect the communication of two or more people. When you and a friend are involved in a discussion about campus housing, for example, you may be remembering an article in your student newspaper on the subject. You may be recalling what your roommate told you about his or her struggle to find an apartment. At the same time, your friend may be thinking of other problems he or she has heard about the housing situation. Whether there are just the two of you talking or a whole group, the communication process will be affected by other communications that you or others know about. You will be *receiving* messages even from sources not present at the time.

Your communication with a friend may also affect other things beyond the present discussion. He or she may repeat what you say to another friend. Someone may be overhearing your discussion. You may even become involved later in an interview by a student reporter where you will discuss again what you are discussing now. The point is that the friend before you is not the only receiver who may be influenced by your message. You may find yourself *sending* messages even to people not present at the time.

The informal communication that you have with a friend or a co-worker, then, can affect other things—and can be affected by other individuals or groups. Communication, we say, is part of a *system: a large, dynamic network that affects and is affected by communication.*[13] The idea of *system* is important as a way of keeping you aware that any single communication process is part of a much broader human activity. As I said in Chapter 1, any single communication problem that you wish to mediate will probably be a whole series of problems. Now you know why: because any single communication will be affected by so many other people and factors. Figure 2.2 shows the complexity of the factors and messages that may affect your communication. Note that all communicators affect themselves as well as others—and they are affected by themselves and their conceptual screens as well as by others.

An understanding of the major features and elements of communication will take you far in appreciating the complexity of the communication process. What may help you further is to understand that the communication process has several phases or *sub-processes*. These phases or sub-processes are the next topic.

Communication as a process

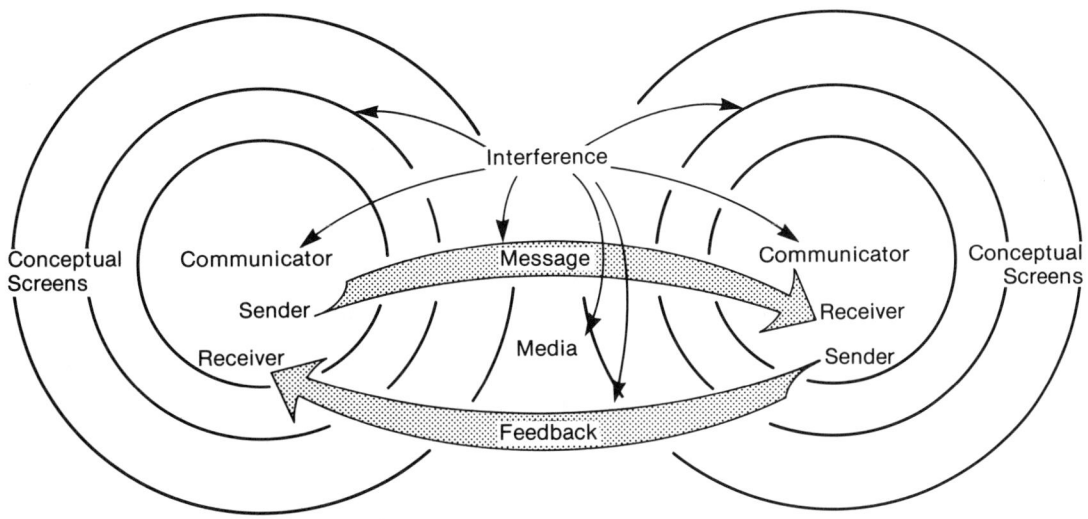

Fig. 2.1 Elements of a communication model (Note that interference—the smaller arrows pointing to each of the other elements—can occur in each of those elements.)

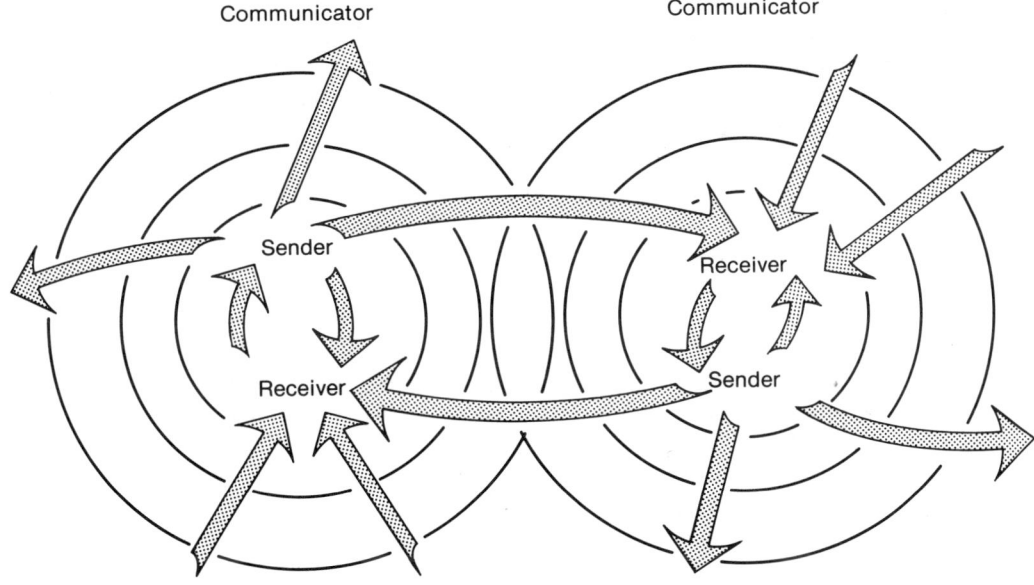

Fig. 2.2 Communication as a system (Note that while the two communicators are sending messages and feedback to one another, each is sending messages to him- or herself and others—and each is receiving messages from these same other sources.)

PHASES IN THE COMMUNICATION PROCESS

Our introductory discussion has suggested that there are several phases in the communication process. Each of these activities or phases can help you to understand the difficulty of using communication as a kind of mediation tool.[14]

The starting point in the process of communicating what you mean to someone else is when you physically receive some sort of stimulus. The stimulus may be a sound, a sight, or some other factor. *Reception*, the first phase of the communication process, is *the simple process of sensing something in the environment by sight, taste, smell, hearing or touch—or of sensing your own thoughts or ideas.* Before you send a message to someone, you receive some stimulus from your brain or environment. That reception of sensation, in turn, is followed by the second phase of the process, *interpretation: the giving of meaning or significance to what has been sensed.* When a food is tasted, some significance is attached to it. You may say the food is great, or terrible. When you hear a voice, you may interpret it as being important to you—or irrelevant. The process of reception or sensing things is probably not so important as the meaning or significance that is attached to it.

The phases of reception and interpretation are so closely related that sometimes a single word is used to describe them. *Perception* can be viewed as the composite act of sensing something and giving it significance. Some researchers and writers argue that people really don't sense anything that is not significant:[15] you may have heard a car horn, but only recall that you did when someone asks you about it. Your interpretation of it was so insignificant that you really didn't know you had sensed it. Similarly, some researchers say that to talk of interpretation of meaning without talking about what was sensed is unproductive. My point here is simply that the processes of reception and interpretation are closely related. You will understand the whole communication process better if you understand that reception and interpretation can be spoken of separately—or as a single process called *perception*.

Another point which should be made here relates to the earlier discussion of conceptual screens. Since people differ in the way they screen information and stimuli, it is no surprise that the interpretation of anything sensed will be different for different people. The same sound or sight may mean different things to different individuals. People perceive different things primarily because of their different interpretations of the thing sensed.

Added to the two processes of reception and interpretation is a third phase in the communication process, *choice: the process in which an individual decides what, if any, action to take.* When someone enters into communication with another, that act is a choice made because of an interpretation. I may listen to a political speech and decide to tell a friend about it. The decision not to engage in communication is a choice also; I may have heard and interpreted the speech, but decided not to respond vocally.[16] The choice of response will vary according to the interpretation. If someone calls you a name that questions your ancestry, you may respond angrily—and with violence. If the same comment is interpreted as a joke by a friend, your response may be far different. The choice of response and whether you make one depends upon your interpretation of the stimulus.

When a choice has been made as to what response you wish to make, you search for a way to express yourself. The fourth phase of communication is *symbolization: the process of translating responses into meaningful symbols.* If you have chosen to respond angrily to some interpretation, you may symbolize the feelings in angry verbal symbols. Or, you may frown at the person or walk away in an effort to nonverbally translate your choice of response. Sometimes the symbolization is difficult. Common ways of expressing this difficulty include, "I can't find the right words," "I have no words to tell you how angry I am," "Those were not the best things to say," or, "What could I do to show her how I felt?" Your problem may be that you do not know how to respond—what choice to make. Your problem may also be that once you have decided how to respond, you can't symbolize what you mean.

A final phase in the communication process is *transmission: the process of sending the set of symbols to another.*[17] Once a person has decided to respond angrily or lovingly to something, the symbolized message must be somehow sent to the other person. If the symbols are verbal, a decision must be made about whether to transmit the message orally, by letter, by note, by telephone, or some other means. If the choice has been to respond with anger nonverbally, the person must decide whether to frown, to walk away, or to simply ignore the other individual the next time they meet. The question is simply, How do I send this message? In deciding, you might take factors of interference into consideration. A letter might be too slow or a telegram might have more impact. As we shall see, the factors in determining how the message is to be transmitted may be crucial to the communication.

Figure 2.3 attempts to add an understanding of the phases of the communication process to factors already discussed. Note that these phases of the process are important for both or all of the participants involved in communication. The message that finally results from the sender's reception, interpretation, choice, symbolization, and transmission becomes something the receiver receives as a stimulus. The receiver receives the verbal or nonverbal stimulus, and then must interpret the message. A choice is made, and the chosen response is symbolized and transmitted to the person who first sent the message. The result is feedback, and the original sender now acts as receiver. The activities can be viewed as a process since they can go on indefinitely and simultaneously; they can be viewed as a transaction because both or all the participants are affected and changed by the process that occurs.

This overview of the process of communication was intended as an introduction to the terms and ideas that will be applied in the rest of the book. My goal is not that you know everything about the communication process, but that you know enough about it to understand later discussions.

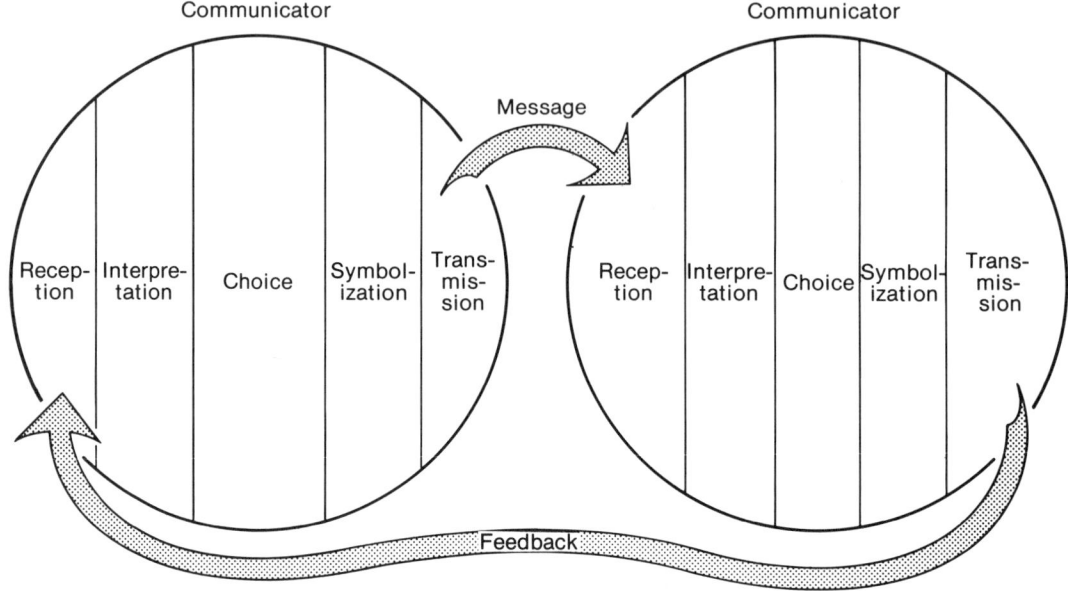

Fig. 2.3 Phases in the communication process

CHAPTER SUMMARY

To understand how to use communication as a tool, you must understand communication as a process. We began by describing the general features of communication: meaning, symbols, process, re-created meaning, intent, and transaction. These features of communication, as the term will be used in this book, can be combined to form a usable definition of communication: the process of symbolic transaction aimed at the re-creation of meaning.

In order to make the definition more clear, we examined the more specific elements of communication as they can be visualized. The importance of communicators acting as senders and receivers made sense in terms of the messages and feedback that are other essential elements of the process. The notion of conceptual screens was introduced as a way of explaining different means of filtering information. People differ from one another and conceptual screens is one way of explaining the differences. Messages, we found, must have some sort of channel or medium that allows the messages and feedback to be sent. Perhaps most importantly, it became clear that factors which we called interference can hinder the communication of what you mean.

To make the discussion of communication more realistic, we noted that communication always occurs as a whole system of factors. Things and people outside the immediate situation can affect—and be affected by—what goes on in the communication setting. Finally, we looked at the various phases of

Communication as a process

communication as a way of realizing the complexity of communication. Communication problems—and other problems that you want to mediate with communication—may be affected by what happens when communicators are receiving stimuli, interpreting stimuli, choosing how to respond, symbolizing their meanings, or sending their messages.

Once the process of communication is understood, its use as a tool is easier to appreciate. The study of communication as a process has provided the terms and perspectives that can aid your understanding of communication as mediation. In Part 2 of the text, we shall discuss conflicts and strategies in the *intra*personal situation.

EXERCISES

All the concepts and ideas in the chapter will become more clear to you if you can apply them to concrete communication situations. The chapter began with descriptions of several communication situations; the situations are reviewed below (numbers 1–5). Refresh your memory concerning them and then respond to *all* the questions in regard to *each* situation.

1. You were alone trying to decide whether to study or socialize.
2. You were walking with a friend discussing the exam you were about to take.
3. You were in class where a whole group of you pondered the nature of the exam and the grading procedures.
4. Your instructor stood at the front of the room and described the exam and the grading procedure.
5. You began reading the campus newspaper on your way home from class.

None of these situations is unusual. Try to put yourself in the situations and then answer the following questions about them.

a) In terms of the general features of communication:
   i) What sorts of meanings might you as a communicator have had?
   ii) What sorts of nonverbal and verbal symbols might you have used to express those meanings?
   iii) How is it that the activity of using symbols was a process?
   iv) Why, in each case, was someone concerned about re-creating his or her meanings?
   v) Why might you have been concerned with intent in each situation?
   vi) In what ways would each process have been a transaction?

b) As you envision the situations, think about the specific elements of communication:
   i) Who probably served as sender? receiver? Did the roles change?
   ii) What do you think the messages and feedback might have been?
   iii) In what ways might the various communicators have had different conceptual screens?
   iv) What would have been the channels or media for the communication?
   v) What might have been the sources of interference in the situations?

c) Consider the idea that communication occurs within a system:
   i) What might have been other parts of the system in each situation?
   ii) How did each of the situations serve as a part of the system of each of the other situations?
d) Think of the various sub-processes or phases of the communication process in each situation:
   i) Why was the reception important in each situation? *Whose* reception was involved?
   ii) Why was interpretation important? *Whose* interpretation was in-involved?
   iii) Why was choice important in each situation? *Who* was called upon to make choices? What might they have been?
   iv) Why was symbolization important? Who was involved in it?
   v) Why was transmission important in each situation? How do you think it occurred?

NOTES

[1] For a discussion of the significance of meaning in communication, see Dean C. Barnlund, "Toward a Meaning-Centered Philosophy of Communication," *Journal of Communication* (1974), 197–211. Much of the discussion concerning the features of communication is based on Richard E. Crable, "What Can You Believe About Rhetoric?," *Exploration in Speech Communication*, ed. John J. Makay.(Columbus, Oh.: Charles E. Merrill Publishing Co., 1973), pp. 28–38.

[2] More specifically, symbols mean something beyond themselves. A tooth mark on a chair in my parents' house is a symbol to them. Beyond the flaw in the chair, it evokes a time when my son was teething—sometimes on furniture. For a discussion of the nature of symbols—as opposed to signals—see Wallace C. Fotheringham, *Perspectives on Persuasion* (Boston: Allyn and Bacon, Inc., 1966), pp. 57–61.

[3] See, for instance, David K. Berlo, *The Process of Communication* (New York: Holt, Rinehart and Winston, Inc., 1960).

[4] This idea of *re-created* meanings is explained further in Crable, "What Can You Believe About Rhetoric?," but it also relates to the idea of intent, as you will soon see.

[5] I do not mean here that what was intended will always be clear. I simply mean that the sender of a message, in my opinion, communicates only when he or she has successfully accomplished the re-creation of meaning in the receiver, regardless of whether the sender has made the purpose clear to the receiver.

[6] This view was popularized by Paul Watzlawick, Janet Beavin, and Don Jackson, *Pragmatics of Human Communication: A Study of Interactional Patterns, Pathologies, and Paradoxes* (New York: W. W. Norton, 1967).

[7] For a discussion, see Kenneth Sereno and Edward Bodaken, *Trans-Per: Understanding Human Communication* (Boston: Houghton Mifflin Co., 1975), pp. 8–10.

[8] The conception is consistent with the definition found in Richard E. Crable, *Argumentation as Communication: Reasoning with Receivers* (Columbus, Oh.: Charles E. Merrill Publishing Co., 1976), chap. 4.

[9] The idea is consistent with that in Crable, *Argumentation as Communication* and with the notion of *fields of experience* in Wilbur Schramm, "How Communication Works," *The Process and Effects of Mass Communication*, ed. Wilbur Schramm. (Urbana, Il.: Univ. of Illinois Press, 1954), pp. 3–10.

[10] The idea of feedback seems to have arisen from electronics, where sound can feed back into a system and create the high-pitched noise heard sometimes when a microphone is used.

[11] The analogy of the water pipe or river bed is limited in the sense that river and water generally flow only one way. Messages, of course, can flow both ways simultaneously through the same medium or channel.

[12] The term *noise* is used by Claude Shannon and Warren Weaver, *The Mathematical Model of Communication* (Urbana: Univ. of Illinois Press, 1949), p. 5 to discuss problems that develop in the channel. Since the same sorts of problems can be related to all other parts of the process, I will use the word *interference* as the general term for these problems.

[13] See Sereno and Bodaken, *Trans-Per*, pp. 8–10 for a brief discussion.

[14] This discussion is based upon that found in Crable, *Argumentation as Communication*, chap. 4.

[15] Some of these studies will be cited later; for now, it is only important that you understand the issue.

[16] In some instances, the decision not to respond verbally will be highly important, as we shall see in later discussions.

[17] What is most important here is that people transmit symbols, not meanings. Meanings can only be re-created through the process of sending symbols that are constructed in ways others will find meaningful.

PART 2

INTRODUCTION

Part 2 is a study of *intrapersonal conflicts and strategies.* In Chapter 3, the focus is upon you as an individual. As an individual in an organized society, you experience many different kinds of problems: values that come into question, decisions about behaviors, and ideas about who *you* are. Problems that you have as an individual can be termed *intrapersonal conflicts,* the subject of Chapter 3.

When you experience intrapersonal conflicts, the problems center upon you and how you feel, primarily about yourself. In intrapersonal communication, you serve both as sender and receiver of the same message. True, you will be influenced by factors other than your own message: that is one reason com-

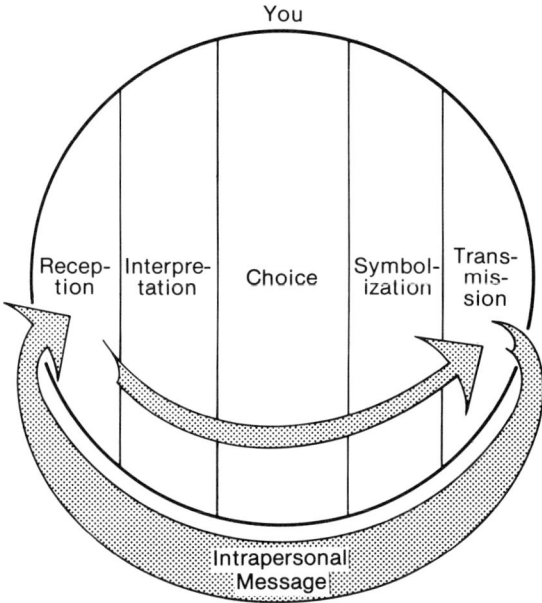

Fig. 1. The intrapersonal setting

munication must be viewed as a system. Still, our intrapersonal focus remains largely upon you.

For problems that can be labeled *intrapersonal,* there are communication approaches which can be useful as strategies of intrapersonal mediation. These strategies can help you mediate the problems which you experience with yourself. Chapters 4 to 7 are devoted to various strategies for intrapersonal mediation: perceiving, verbal self-analysis, nonverbal self-analysis, and intrapersonal decisioning.

Part 2 is designed to help you gain insight into intrapersonal conflicts and their mediation through communication strategies.

3
INTRAPERSONAL CONFLICTS AS PROBLEMS

Communication, as the term was discussed in Chapter 2, always begins with people. More specifically, communication begins with *a single person* who has some meaning that he or she wishes to share by means of symbols. Two or more people are usually involved in communication, but it would be a mistake to overlook the importance of each single communicator. All communicators have sets of meanings with regard to who they are, what they are, and what they would like to be. These sets of meanings are generally referred to as the *self-concept: the image or impression that a person has about him- or herself.* The understanding of people in pairs or groups may be easier if we understand them as individuals. Similarly, as an aid in understanding *inter*personal conflicts, we can try to understand *intra*personal conflicts. To achieve that goal, conflicts among *selves,* roles, information, values, and behaviors must be discussed.

THE SELF IN CONFLICT

One of the major reasons for conflict within an individual is that the self-concept is made up of a variety of factors. For convenience, we can discuss these as different *selves* which contribute to the whole self-concept. The concept of *actual self* can be described as *who you are—really.*[1] My belief about the actual self is that if it does exist, no one will ever know. What we think of ourselves—of others—will always be matters of interpretation. I think that it would be impossible for us ever to know once-and-for-all *who we are*. Instead, what we develop are ideas or impressions of who we are: one or several *perceived selves*.[2] All of us have some idea of who we are and what we are. These perceptions may not be accurate. They may be inconsistent with what other people perceive. Still, our perceptions of who we are have much to do with the development of the self-concept.

In addition to our *perceived self*, most of us probably have some idea of what we would like to be: our *desired self*.[3] You may want to be more popular, more successful, more athletic, or more intelligent. These refer to wishes and desires, rather than to what you actually perceive; they may also become goals or objectives that you pursue as you exercise, study, or interact with others. It is probably also true that most people have some idea of the things that they wish *not* to be: the *feared self*.[4] You may display your feared self by beginning a "bit of news" with the words, "Well, you know how I hate gossiping, but did you hear that . . . ?" You may reveal your feared self by deciding not to do something because "People like me don't do that." However the feelings are expressed, they are important. They reveal that self-concept is affected both by what you wish you were and what you want to avoid being.

Another dimension of the self relates, not to the perceived self, the desired self, or the feared self, but rather to your perceptions of how others react to you: *perceived perceptions or metaperception of self*.[5] Here, what you think of yourself is less important than what you think others think about you. I have heard people say that they do not care how others react to them, but I have never judged that to be the case. Someone, somewhere, is important to each of us, and the perceptions of that someone are important. It may be true that in a given situation you may not care what someone thinks about you and what you have done. In everyone's life, though, there are *significant others*—people whose opinions matter; our perceptions of how these people perceive us are important to the self-concept.

Clearly, other kinds of selves could be discussed, but even these few illustrate the need to understand communicators as individuals. A communicator's perceived self might be generally the same as the desired self. If that is the case, the communicator may be satisfied with who he or she is. That is especially true if the communicator thinks that others perceive him or her similarly. This situation of intrapersonal compatibility, however, does not always occur. Most people probably feel the conflict of falling short of their desired selves; at times, they may even feel that they are more nearly their feared selves than they would like to admit. Even when that is not the case, an individual may experience conflict by believing that others have the wrong impression; that they perceive him or her inaccurately. Situations like that can be termed instances of *intrapersonal conflict*. Intrapersonal conflict, or conflict about your self, can be personally unsatisfying as well as interpersonally troublesome.

THE SELF AND ROLE CONFLICTS

What makes the situation worse is that these selves that have been discussed change from time to time. Instead of having *a* self-concept, you have many conceptions of yourself based upon the situations you are experiencing. In different situations you may feel that you must play different *roles.* Sometimes expectations about who you *should* be affect how you perceive yourself. In different situations, you may find that your desired self and your feared self are creating conflict—but in contrasting ways. At home, for example, you may experience conflict because you fear you are too aggressive. You want to be more reserved. With strangers, in contrast, you may experience conflict because you fear you are too reserved. You want to be more aggressive. Particular situations can easily change what you think you are, should be, and should not be; particular situations mean changes in what you think others think about you.

Such intrapersonal conflicts are not unusual. In my life, for example, I find myself in extremely varied situations. These situations call for me to act in different ways. What we can say is that the situations prompt me to act *different roles: different patterns of behavior and expectations.* During a single day, I may play the role of husband, father, neighbor, teacher, department administrator, friend (to several different people), writer, handyman, lawn worker, first-aid administrator, and son to my parents. Some of these roles call for highly different attitudes and behaviors. I am not being dishonest when I switch behavior patterns from one role to another—and sometimes back again. My problem is one that everyone faces: human beings are faced with different situations. They are expected to shift from one role to another. The change in role behavior may be completely compatible. I normally can play the role of father without creating conflict with my role as husband. Sometimes, however, the change in role causes intrapersonal conflict. As a department administrator, I sometimes have to make decisions which, as a teacher, I do not like. When I am involved in writing and research, I sometimes have trouble playing well the role of father. Those are among the times when intrapersonal conflict is prompted by the change in role: I perceive myself playing a role that conflicts with another role. My feared self in one situation may be my desired self in another situation.

Though I have discussed examples from my own life here, little of the discussion has to be changed to have it relate to yours. You play the role of student (often in a wide range of classes), son or daughter, roommate, worker at a part-time job, and perhaps spouse, parent, and full-time employee. You may play the role of friend, socialite, athlete, sorority or fraternity member, and so on. What all that should mean to you is that these various roles probably bring changes in who you think you are, who you want to be, who you do not wish to be, and what you think others think about you. Any shift between roles can make for a compatible idea of the self; but any of them may also bring a part of you into conflict with another part. The result of a shifting of roles may be intrapersonal conflict.

THE SELF AND DECISIONS

The conflict among selves and roles may become completely obvious to you when you must make some sort of decision. When you must decide what you will do, you will frequently have to examine carefully all the various factors that make you—you. Let us look at the potential problems in information processing, behavior choice, and value formation.

Information processing

One of the delights of being a parent is realizing how simple education can be—for awhile. When a child begins to use language to process information, to coordinate or make sense of it,[6] education is still easy: "Whatz dat?" "It's a snake." "Oh, nake!" The unquestioned discussion goes on . . . and on . . . and on. The child never really has to decide whether to believe the information. Children simply believe and learn. Then, on some dark day, the child learns to ask "Why?" Suddenly, he or she begins to make decisions about whether to believe and to learn. The child slowly begins to have enough information so that connections are made between things. Once my son learned that ears were those things that stuck out on the sides of people's heads, he began finding ears everywhere. For the lack of the term *handlebars*, he decided that motorcycles must have "ears"; after all, they stuck out on the side of the cycle's "head."

The passage of years only increases the complexity of information processing. During elementary and high school years, you may have learned that in time of war all Americans volunteer to fight for their country. Later, you may have learned that every war has had significant numbers of people against it, from the Revolutionary War to the War in Vietnam. On the basis of new learning, what do you do with the old learning? the old information? You may be familiar with Patrick Henry's "Liberty or Death" speech. Did you know that he almost certainly did not say the words of that speech? What do you do with this information? Do you continue to believe as you have, and assume I am joking (which I am not)? Or do you modify your earlier belief? My point is that an individual learns (or should learn) at an early age that much information requires a decision. Instead of accepting daddy's word that a dandelion is a weed, you begin to challenge him, saying that it might be a flower. Instead of simply accepting what I say about Patrick Henry, you ask yourself whether it is true, and how it fits with earlier beliefs.

When information-processing decisions are being made, you must expect the possibility of intrapersonal conflict. The child in you believes that Patrick Henry made his speech; the realist in you believes that I would not be silly

Intrapersonal conflicts as problems   33

enough to lie. Which will you believe? The idealist in you believes that America is the land of equality; the cynic in you believes that some people are "more equal" than others. Which will you believe? You may not care about Henry's speech—or equality for that matter. For you, then, no conflict arises. Despite that, you probably find instances of conflicting information that do matter. When they matter a great deal, the intrapersonal conflict of information processing can be severe. The feeling that information is compatible can suddenly become lost, and you ask, "Wait, how does this new idea fit into what I already know?"

Behavior decisions

At times, you will confront situations where your behavior—not information—is in conflict. The police officer who tickets a citizen for speeding and then drives away at a speed above the legal limit illustrates the point. The person who buckles up for safety, and then drives while under the influence of alcohol further illustrates the point. The term *behavior* includes so many human actions that conflicting behaviors should be expected to occur sometimes. In one situation, playing one role, you may do something entirely inconsistent with what you might do in another situation: the bank teller may cheat a bit on his or her income tax, but would not consider embezzlement. The wild party which you freely attend might be considered inappropriate in your family's living room.

Frequently, conflicting behavior is based upon the difference between verbal and physical behavior. I have found myself warning my children not to slam a door—for what seemed like the ninety-ninth time. In my anger, I have then slammed the door as I left the room. People sometimes speak strongly about an upcoming election or a city council issue, but do not vote or attend the council session. You may tell a fellow student what you think of an instructor's exam, but fail to ever speak to the instructor about it. You might criticize sexism at the counter where you are buying this month's issue of a magazine that is . . . just a little sexist. In these situations, the conflict may well be between what you say and what you do.

Again, some conflicts may be primarily matters of shifting roles. In a job interview, you may find yourself saying that Saturday work is fine, even when getting out of bed on Saturday is the last thing you want to do. In church, you may discover that talking about loving your neighbor is easier than actually loving the guy upstairs with the loud stereo. It may be far easier to write about the importance of learning history on a test paper than it would be if you were discussing the same issue with a roommate. As the situations change, your role may change; as the expected role changes, so might your behavior. This is not to say that all of your behavior will be in conflict with all the others, but that behavioral conflict is something you may frequently experience.

Sometimes behavioral conflicts are unconscious: you do not even know when they occur.[7] At other times, the conflict will seem more severe simply because you have been forced to make a decision about two or more behaviors. You may have promised not to repeat something that has been told to you in confidence. Suddenly, however, you feel that you can help a friend more by betraying the confidence than by keeping the secret. What do you do? You may have criticized an instructor's test in conversations with friends, and then find that in the next class period the instructor asks for comments about the test. What do you decide to do? You may have argued aloud that the right to participate in elections is a responsibility of all citizens. What do you do when you have the chance to distribute campaign materials—at the same time that three class papers are due? Situations like this put the individual in the position of having to choose between alternative behaviors. Either alternative can put you at odds or in conflict with yourself. You can be faced with all sorts of questions: I know what I did, but now what should I do? I know what I said, but what should I say now? When verbal and physical behaviors are somehow incompatible, intrapersonal conflict may well be the result.

Value formation

Sometimes individuals are faced with problems that involve *values: generalized principles or evaluations.*[8] Conflict about the various selves and about behaviors may really be problems that have their roots in values. Values tend to be basic biases or approaches that are developed slowly over years of parental upbringing and education. Parents may teach the values of friendship, understanding, and love for other people. In addition, various religious values and political values may be learned. Formal schooling may teach the values of intellectual curiosity, of cooperation, and so forth. Values are also learned through experiences of many kinds. Needing a new bicycle may help teach the value of thrift and saving. An unfortunate experience with a friend may teach you a great deal of the value of true friendship or love. Job experiences on a part-time basis may teach some values of education and preparation for a career. Whatever the source of these principles and generalized evaluations, everyone undergoes the process of *value formation.*

One of the sources of conflicting values is that values sometimes simply seem inconsistent. Since values are so general, one value may frequently collide with another. You are taught, for example, the values of success and of cooperation. What happens when your desire to succeed means that you must take advantage of someone else? In job settings, only one of several people working at the same job may be promoted. Do you cooperate as well as you can with the others, or do you concentrate upon your own advancement? In certain situations, most of us are called upon to make choices between the expectations of our families and our desire to do what we want with our life. In that kind of situation, is the value of family desires more or less important than the value of personal freedom? In the long process of value formation, some conflict between values will probably occur. At such times, the familiar questions arise, What is most important to me? How do I decide between the things that I value?

Frequently, intrapersonal conflict over values occurs when a new value confronts an established one. For years you may have valued marriage as the only legitimate way in which couples could live together. What happens when you see more and more individuals accepting cohabitation as a perfectly acceptable alternative to marriage? For years you may have believed in the basic value of fair play in American politics. When you read and hear of Watergate, foreign payoffs to members of congress, and political dirty tricks, do you begin to feel that success and personal gain are more important than fair play? In my own experience, I once unquestioningly placed loyalty to country—right or wrong—high in my sense of values. As an undergraduate during the Vietnam War years, I became disturbed by American actions there. My value of patriotism came into direct conflict with my value of international honesty and integrity. For me, the conflict was severe. In my case, and in these others, the individual suddenly finds him- or herself in a situation of intrapersonal conflict. What do we do when some of those basic values come into conflict with one another?

CONFLICTS AMONG SELVES, INFORMATION, BEHAVIORS, AND VALUES

The discussions about selves, information, behaviors, and values have focused upon the ways in which these can create conflict. I do not mean to imply that these will always be in conflict. There is no way to prove it, but I suspect that most often our selves, information, behaviors, and value frameworks are more or less in agreement. In most cases, I suspect, there is no intrapersonal conflict. The point is that at one time or another, everyone will experience conflicts of the type described. When the individual as a communicator suffers from these conflicts, contact with others is affected, so the first consideration in our study of communication problems and strategies probably should be the individual and his or her problems.

One other point should be mentioned again: problems and conflicts are *creations* rather than *occurrences*. Your values, behaviors, and selves can be said to conflict only when you perceive that to be the case. At times, you may be fully aware that what you have just said conflicts with what you have just done. At other times, something that appears to someone else to conflict may seem no conflict at all to you. I have heard students discuss at different times the value of life and the value of individual rights. When I ask about something like the abortion issue as a way of pointing out a possible conflict, I get interestingly different responses. To the question, If a woman has the right to an abortion, how can a child in the womb have the right to life? I tend to get two different answers. One is, I never thought about that . . . I don't know what to say. Another answer is, Well, the child is really not born yet, so it doesn't have the right to life . . . you see? In the first answer, the person understands for the first time that there might be a conflict in values. The result may be intrapersonal conflict about the values—for the first time. In the second answer, the speaker has found a way to reconcile the potential conflict, or to reason in such a way that the values do not seem to him or her to be in conflict. The result is this speaker's perception of intrapersonal compatibility.

These two situations illustrate the important point that intrapersonal conflict is indeed *intrapersonal*. You yourself determine what is conflicting and what is compatible even though other people, such as instructors or parents, may see a different kind of conflict or no conflict at all. You are the one who decides whether the conflict exists. You are the one who decides if the conflict is severe enough to make you want to mediate it, and, finally, you are the one who decides *how* the conflict is to be approached.

INTRAPERSONAL CONFLICT, ACCEPTANCE, AND MEDIATION

One of the ways that you can approach intrapersonal conflicts is *self-rejection: the spurning or disdaining of who or what (you think) you are.*[9] In milder forms, self-rejection may mean that you simply come to dislike certain things about yourself. In my own case, I perceive myself as a "workaholic." At the same time that I enjoy my work, I feel guilty sometimes about the amount of time I spend on it. I suspect that there are certain things about who or what you are that are equally dissatisfying. In certain cases, though, self-rejection becomes severe. A person may become so totally dissatisfied with him- or herself that there is a complete rejection of the self. Such complete rejection of the self might require psychological or psychiatric counseling.

An alternative to self-rejection is *self-acceptance: the liking or approval of who and what (you think) you are.*[10] In a society that continually analyzes itself it is not surprising that self-acceptance has become a popular topic of discussion. With everyone analyzing and trying to understand everyone else, it is far too easy to simply find fault with who you are. It is far too easy to decide that the conflicts that make up who you are make you an unworthy person. Because of such factors, many people need to learn to accept themselves as individuals. Self-acceptance can be of two rather different kinds.

Acceptance of the as-is self

Often, items for sale in antique or junk shops are marked *as-is*. What that means is that the object being sold has some flaw, imperfection, or problem.

When you buy something as-is, you have no right to complain if you eventually find the imperfection because you knew you were buying an imperfect product.

Our discussions of intrapersonal conflicts make it clear that in one sense or another all of us are in as-is condition. Most of us do not perceive our self as being the *ideal* self. Anyone who does not see a difference between the perceived self and the ideal is probably blind to his or her shortcomings. Skills in perception, verbal self-analysis, and nonverbal self-analysis should help you in two ways. First, they should help you to understand the conflicts in your selves, your behavior, and your values. Second, the skills and the understanding behind them should help you to improve your perception and your verbal and nonverbal communication. One result should be that you understand some of the reasons for your perceptions of conflict. Secondly, you should be able to alter your verbal and nonverbal behavior so that you and others perceive you in a more favorable light.

Despite all this, you may find that you are "better, but not well yet." You may find that you are still in a somewhat as-is condition. It is at that point that you must strive to accept yourself—complete with all your flaws, imperfections, and problems. The rejection of who you are can become a tremendously important problem. Rejection affects not only all your intrapersonal perceptions and decision making, but also your relationships with everyone else with whom you transact. Open and straightforward communication with others requires that you first establish open and straightforward communication with yourself. In a real sense, you must accept yourself in the as-is condition just as you must accept others in their as-is condition.

Acceptance of the becoming self

In another sense, however, you cannot afford to be completely satisfied with your self. Complete self-acceptance would not encourage you to improve as a communicator or as a person. As you sharpen your skills in perception, language, and nonverbal symbol use, you ought to sense progress and development in who you are. Your acceptance of yourself must be accompanied by an acceptance of who you are *becoming*. As you mediate those conflicts among selves, behaviors, and values, you may develop a positive feeling about who you are becoming. Even if you are dissatisfied with your as-is condition, you can work hard intrapersonally and begin to be satisfied with your development as a communicator and as a person. Whatever your intrapersonal conflicts may be, they did not develop overnight, and they will not be mediated overnight either. Communication strategies, and skills of perception, symbol use, and decisioning can help you to mediate the normal, or expected levels of intrapersonal conflicts, but those strategies and skills are not magic. The development of what you want to be should be considered a lifelong task. As you make those small gains, you must intrapersonally reward yourself. You may never become completely satisfied with who you are, but you can learn to take satisfaction from self-improvement. You can learn to accept the becoming self.

The acceptance of the becoming self differs from both self-rejection and acceptance of the as-is self. You accept and recognize that you are in the process of becoming more like who and what you want to be. One of the ways to begin accepting your becoming self is to use communication strategies for the mediation of your intrapersonal conflicts. Certainly, some intrapersonal conflicts are so severe that an outside mediator such as a minister, a social worker, or a psychologist may be needed, but in some cases communication strategies can help you to mediate your own problems. First, you can learn strategies which will help you identify and understand sources of intrapersonal conflict. Second, you can learn certain strategies which can help mediate those conflicts once they are understood. Communication begins with one person. If you as that person can better understand and mediate your intrapersonal conflicts, other communication activities will be easier.

CHAPTER SUMMARY

The chapter began as it ended, with a concern for you as an individual involved with others in communication. In describing intrapersonal conflicts, we looked first at the ways in which the selves of an individual can be in conflict. Most people have perceived selves, desired selves, feared selves, and perceptions of how others interpret these selves. Though these perceptions of self can be compatible, at times they are in conflict. One of the primary ways of explaining the conflict is by noting the effect of roles and expectations upon the self.

Another way in which the selves of an individual can come into conflict is when the individual must make decisions about information, behaviors, and value formation. These were discussed as potential areas of conflict. The chapter included a discussion of how conflict is a creation of an individual's perception: only the person him- or herself can experience intrapersonal conflict.

Finally, the chapter explained certain ways to respond to intrapersonal conflict; self-rejection, acceptance of the as-is self, and acceptance of the becoming self. The acceptance of the becoming self depends upon the individual's progress toward becoming more the kind of person he or she wants to be. Communication strategies can help this process, as well as the understanding and mediation of some kinds of intrapersonal problems and conflicts. Chapters 4 through 7 deal with helpful methods of intrapersonal mediation.

NOTES

[1] In a later section of this chapter entitled, "The Self and Role Conflicts," we shall find that one of the factors in who you are is the context or situation in which you find

yourself. As the situation changes, who you are will also change. In Chapter 4, the discussion of perception will make reasons for doubting the existence of an *actual* instead of a *perceived* self even more clear.

[2] I do not mean here that your perceptions of yourself are not related to what others think about you. In fact, scholars and researchers generally agree that how you perceive yourself may be a *reflection* of how you think others see you. Your self-perception, as Cooley has said, may be a *looking-glass* self. See Charles H. Cooley, *Human Nature and the Social Order* (New York: Schocken Books, 1964; c. 1902), p. 184.

[3] Don E. Hamachek, *Encounters with the Self* (New York: Holt, Rinehart and Winston, 1971), p. 230.

[4] Whereas the ideal self may imply a self with maximum self-respect, the feared self may imply a self for which you would have no respect. Respect is a matter of self-esteem—how highly you regard yourself. See Nathaniel Brandon, *The Psychology of Self-Esteem* (Los Angeles: Nash, 1969), especially pp. 106–107.

[5] For a complete discussion of *metaperception* of self, see R. D. Laing, H. Phillipson, and A. Russel Lee, *Interpersonal Perception: A Theory and Method of Research* (London: Tavistock Publications, 1966).

[6] For a helpful discussion of information processing generally, see Gerhard J. Hanneman and William J. McEwen, *Communication and Behavior* (Reading, Ma.: Addison-Wesley, 1975), pp. 38-42.

[7] I am thinking of times when you are aware that you somehow—in some vague way you cannot express—feel dissatisfied with yourself.

[8] For a complete treatment of the relationships among beliefs, attitudes, and values, see Milton Rokeach, *Beliefs, Attitudes, and Values* (San Francisco: Jossey-Bass, 1968).

[9] Self-rejection is perhaps more familiar as the feeling that, "I'm not OK." See Thomas A. Harris, *I'm OK—You're OK* (New York: Harper & Row, 1967).

[10] An excellent discussion of self-acceptance is David W. Johnson, *Reaching Out: Interpersonal Effectiveness and Self-Actualization* (Englewood Cliffs, N.J.: Prentice-Hall, 1972), chap. 8.

4
PERCEIVING: AN INTRAPERSONAL STRATEGY

You see a man walk toward your campus in a well-tailored suit. He walks straight and tall. The man takes large strides, and carries a briefcase in one hand. You feel you already know what sort of person this is. Why?

You and a friend attend a campus-sponsored meeting on the pros and cons of abortion. You think that once your friend has heard the arguments in favor of allowing abortions, he or she will agree with you and your position. You find, however, that your friend does not even seem to have heard some of the arguments. Why?

You have come to know a particular student in one of your classes fairly well. One day you stop at the corner drugstore. You are reaching for your wallet before you realize that the cashier is the person from your class. Why didn't you recognize him or her at once?

You sit in class listening and idly doodling in the margin of the text. The person sitting next to you says, "Say, you're a pretty good artist!" You respond that you have never given it any thought. Why might you not have noticed it before?

The four situations have to do with how or what you see in the world around you. They have to do with ideas you get and interpretations you give to the things about you. In short, they have to do with *perception*.

To understand the nature of perception, a step backward may be helpful. Two important elements in the communication model we discussed earlier are reception (the sensing of stimuli) and interpretation (the giving of significance to the sensed stimuli). These two processes together can be called perception. Perception, then, is how people sense things and *make sense* of things. Perception is the basic way in which people understand themselves and the world around them. Perception is the basic way you understand your self and the selves around you. You can increase your understanding of perception by realizing that perception is (1) active, (2) selective, (3) inductive, (4) context bound, (5) motivated, and (6) personal. Once you understand the nature of perception, you can use perceptual strategies for intrapersonal mediation.

PERCEPTION IS ACTIVE

One of the misconceptions about perception is that things perceived by a person simply come into the brain, much as light rays enter the lens of a camera and get transformed into a picture. Perception is frequently misunderstood as a passive activity in which people act as sponges which soak up the stimuli around them. Actually, perception is a highly active process.[1] Your perception of yourself is not something that just happens to exist. It is created as you actively try to make sense out of who you are—really. The perceptions of you that others have are formed in the same way: they are creations of other people who are in the process of perceiving. Interpretation was defined earlier as a *giving or attaching of significance or meaning to what has been sensed.* When stimuli are received, they are (probably simultaneously) given some degree of importance and some kind of meaning. If things and symbols already *had* meanings, perception might be passive. You would perceive things as they are: as a camera does. Instead, things and symbols *are given* meanings and degrees of importance by people through the process of perception. Perception is an active process.

In intrapersonal conflict specifically, knowledge of the active nature of perception is crucial. When you have a perception of yourself, you must realize that you have created that perception. The perceptions of your selves are not what you *are*; they are meanings and significances that you *have placed* upon yourself. You have actively created your own perceptions of self. Your ideas of the desired self or the feared self are created in much the same way. They are meanings about yourself that you would like to attach to yourself—or that you hope you will never have to attach to yourself. Your perceptions of what others think about you are also your creations. They are related to the meanings that you attach to the meanings that you think others attach to you. As you can see, the whole situation becomes more complicated. Perceptions about your selves and conflicts with regard to information, behavior, and values are based upon the same idea: perceptions are active creations of people.

Knowing that perception is active is not enough to fully understand how to mediate intrapersonal conflict. Among other things you need to realize that perception is selective.

PERCEPTION IS SELECTIVE

In the active process of creating perceptions about yourself and your intrapersonal conflicts, you attach meaning and significance to information about yourself. The amount of information you use for this purpose probably is far less than you might suppose. The reason for this is that the general process of perception is selective: a great deal of information is used, but much more is ignored.[2]

Perception is selective, first, because of what is called *selective exposure: the human tendency to avoid some information.* Republican voters may consciously avoid listening to Democratic politicians and ideas. Atheists may consciously avoid religious discussions. The boss may avoid asking for feedback from employees so that he or she will not have to hear disturbing ideas. In these situations and countless others, people avoid certain stimuli. This causes their perceptions to be selective; to occur on the basis of incomplete information.

Selective exposure is not necessarily evil. In fact, it is unquestionably necessary. As a contemporary individual, you are bombarded with hundreds and hundreds of messages a day—and thousands and perhaps millions of stimuli such as colors, sounds, non-speech noises, and odors.[3] Even if you wanted to expose yourself to everything there is to see, hear, taste, smell, and feel, it would be impossible. So, consciously or unconsciously, you select those things to which you will expose yourself.

Just as you will not expose yourself to all the information available to you, you also will not pay attention to every part of all the information to which you are exposed. Perception is selective, second, because of *selective attention: the singling out of certain parts of something.* Just as you cannot expose yourself to everything, you cannot pay attention to every part of the things you experience. If you go to a play, there is no way that you can pay attention to the sound effects, orchestra, lighting, stage set, directing strategies, costumes, props, theatre facilities, blocking, all the characters, and the script. If you are interested in all these factors, your attention will rotate among all of them. Your attention will shift. The selectivity of your attention will not occur on purpose, but simply because you cannot pay attention to everything at once.

In everyday encounters, selective attention is just as important. When you meet your friend George and begin to talk, your attention may shift. You may see that his hair has been trimmed recently, that his clothes do not match, that he seems depressed, that his teeth are nicely white, that he has something important to say, that you love his Boston accent, and that he is trying to grow a beard. You may pay attention to all these factors, but you cannot do all that at the same time. We often experience situations in which we admire a person's appearance instead of paying attention to what he or she is saying. Perception is selective partly because of selective attention.

Even those things to which you pay attention are subject to different kinds of meaning attachment. Perception is selective, third, because of *selective inter-*

pretation: the attachment of significance and meanings in particular ways.[4] Two people, for example, may attend to the same aspect of a situation and yet see two very different things occur. Eyewitness accounts are extremely popular with juries—after all, the witness saw the robbery suspect. Yet, judges and attorneys are all too aware that eyewitnesses give one of the least dependable kinds of evidence. Two eyewitnesses may have seen the same robbery take place from virtually the same angle and from the same distance, but lawyers and judges are not surprised to find that the descriptions of the suspect vary widely in terms of height, weight, and clothing. What someone interprets as tall may seem short to someone over six feet in height. A fair complexion might be interpreted in terms of the average (whatever that is) complexion. Perception is selective, then, partly because people select the meanings that they will attach to something.

Perception is selective in yet one more way. *Selective retention refers to the idea that people forget much of what they perceive.* Even if you have attended to and interpreted something, you may still forget it with the passage of time. You may have a tendency to remember the best of childhood—or the worst. You may remember your successes more than your failures—or vice versa. You may recall the times when you have been strong—or when you have been your weakest. Whatever the case and whatever the reason, your recall or retention is selective. You remember only a (sometimes small) part of what you attend to and perceive.

When you are actively creating your self, you must remember that your self-perception is based on selected information. As a human being, you cannot perceive your self on the basis of all the available information. Some of what you are may remain hidden forever. Some of who you are will not be perceived because you refuse to pay attention to it. Some of who you are is lost because of the meanings you choose to give to yourself. And finally, some of who you are is lost because you have forgotten important experiences, qualities, and behaviors. When you are trying to understand the perception of yourself that you have created, remember that the perception is made up of bits and pieces that have been consciously or unconsciously selected.

PERCEPTION IS INDUCTIVE

One of the amazing things about the amazing Sherlock Holmes was his inductive ability. He could take a bit of mud, a piece of cloth, and the temperature of the day, and then tell the incredulous inspector something like, "The murder was committed by a lame Scotsman working as a shepherd in the hills far to the north of London." And everyone would say, "Amazing!"

The ability to follow bits and pieces of evidence or information to a conclusion is an important human ability. The character Holmes was better at it than most of us, yet all human perception is partly a matter of *induction: the creating of a conclusion from bits of information.*[5] When you perceive something, you select part of it, interpret it in a particular way, and remember only part of it. From those fragments, you create a perception: an idea of what the thing is in general. You do not need to see the burned-out *J* in the sign to know what "Eat at oe's" means. You do not need an interpreter to understand the sign on the automobile that says "4 sail." From the bits and pieces that you perceive, you can inductively arrive at the meaning of the sign.

Perception of the concept of self and of intrapersonal conflict is based on partial information. You may have taken a few bad experiences, for example with high school phys. ed., your bad luck in golf, and the teasing you experienced in intramural football, to mean that you are no athlete. You may be aware that the abortion issue puts your values of freedom and right to life in conflict. On the basis of that one conflict, you may decide that the two values are always in total conflict. You may feel that you were misled in early schooling about politics. Consequently, you may feel cynical indeed about elections. One of the keys to understanding intrapersonal conflicts is to realize that the conflicts may be less extreme than you think. They may be the result of bits of information about yourself or your world leading inductively to inaccurate conclusions.

PERCEPTION IS CONTEXT-BOUND

The perception of symbols and people does not occur in isolation. Symbols and people are always understood in terms of some sort of context.[6] The phrase "red letter" may mean a variety of things depending upon the situation. It might refer to Superman's chest insignia, a mark symbolizing adultery, a failing grade on a paper, an important (red letter) day, or a colored alphabet figure. Things are always perceived in terms of a background, situation, or context. The *you* at a party cannot be the *you* at home, in class, or on the job. Even if you were to act the same in each of these situations, the *you* would still be different. In each context, you would probably see yourself differently: you as a social person, you as a son or daughter, you as a student, or you as an employee. Any conflict you might detect among these various *yous* might be more a matter of the context than of what you were *like*. Each person must exist in a variety of contexts and the perceptions of self will vary. Perception is context-bound.

PERCEPTION IS MOTIVATED

The preceding discussion does not mean that individuals are totally at the mercy of contexts in their perceptions. While contexts are important in perceptions, motivation is also important. People are prompted to see themselves and others by several factors. Among these factors are needs or desires, fears, background, and expectations.[7] If, for example, you have some sort of *need* to perceive yourself as a scholar, the chances are, you will. Even if you do not do well academically, you may see yourself as a victim of the school system or your instructors. You are a scholar, you tell yourself; you have just not been given an opportunity to prove what you can do. Similarly, if you *fear* that you are bigoted, you may take every small indication of stereotyping on your part as evidence that you are a religious, racial, or other kind of bigot. In terms of *background,* if you have been led to believe that your home state is particularly attractive, the odds are very good that you will perceive other states as less attractive. If you have been taught that making money is the most important aspect of life, the odds are good that you will perceive yourself as being above low paying jobs. Finally, *expectations* are important to perception. If you expect to be an incompetent athlete, you may well perceive yourself as incompetent, even if you succeed in several sports. If you expect to be athletic, the chances are good that you will perceive yourself as such. Perceptions are motivated.

One of the important factors involved in motivation and perception is popularly called *the self-fulfilling prophesy.*[8] Simply put, the idea is that certain expectations, needs, or fears can help create the situation that is needed, feared, or expected. There is no magic here. If I assume that I cannot sketch, I tend to avoid sketching. As a result, I probably cannot sketch. If, on the other hand, I feel a need to be able to sketch, I might take lessons, practice, and study. As a result, I might find myself able to sketch. Motivation—whether to be something or not, or to expect something or not—can provide the stimulus needed for us to fulfill what we want to be or to become what we fear we might become.

In terms of intrapersonal conflicts, you must understand the motivation behind your perceptions of yourself. Your perceptions perhaps have been affected more by your fears, yours needs, your background, or your expectations, than by anything else. Before you can hope to mediate your particular intrapersonal conflict, you should examine any motivational factors in your perceptions of the conflict. Examining motivations in perceptions is, ironically, a process of perception. Still, you can do more than worry about your intrapersonal conflicts. You can attempt to understand what motivates your perception of conflict.

PERCEPTION IS PERSONAL

For our definition of perception to be complete, a concluding point must be made. Your perceptions are personal.[9] Certainly, they are influenced by your background and the people in your life, but they are also created by you as an active perceiver. Your perceptions are products of selectivity. While that selectivity is explained partly by the influence of others, much of it is personal. Perception of self is inductive, and you are the person drawing the conclusion about who you are. Perception is context-bound, but still motivated by your personal desires, fears, and expectations. In sum, the conflicts among your selves, your information processing, your behaviors, and your values are products of your personal perception.

PERCEIVING AND INTRAPERSONAL CONFLICTS

Understanding perception allows you to use the process of perceiving as a strategy for mediation. Some of your intrapersonal problems can be mediated by a *re-perception* of the conflict. The following six ideas are crucial:

1. Since perception is selective, you can discover what parts of you and your problem you have paid attention to—and what parts you have ignored.
2. Since perception is inductive, you can put together new bits of information about yourself and your problems, and add that information to your understanding.
3. Since perception is context-bound, you can analyze the kinds of surroundings which may have influenced your perception.
4. Since perception is motivated, you can analyze the forces that have prompted your perception.
5. Since perception is personal, you can realize that your intrapersonal conflict is YOUR PERCEIVED CONFLICT.
6. Finally, since perception is active, you can create a better and more accurate perception of yourself and your conflicts.

In using these strategies, your first task is to put the conflict into words: What, exactly, is troublesome? Next, you can use what you know about perception to help you mediate the problem. Let me illustrate how these strategies of mediation can be used.

Case study one: the lawyer-to-be. Joan is a college student who is working on a prelaw degree and wants very much to go to law school. She is doing well academically, but is not happy with herself. She studies a great deal and is interested in her subjects. She is frustrated, however, because her grades are more important to her than the subjects themselves. Any grade lower than an A puts her farther away from her dream of the money and respect that she thinks the title "attorney" will give her. Surely, she says to herself, there is nothing wrong with wanting good grades. There is nothing wrong with the profession of law. Yet, she is still not happy with what she is doing.

One of the things Joan probably should do is to try to put her feelings into words. As she and I sit and talk, she finally explains that she is afraid that she is going into law for what she calls the wrong reasons. She wants money and a respectable job—and law just happens to be one way of getting them. At one point, she says, "I think I'm studying to be a lawyer just so I can have the kinds of things a lawyer has." Joan's perception of herself seems to be the problem.

Since perception is selective, I ask her what kinds of things make her think that she is studying law for the fringe benefits. "Well, I sometimes think about plush offices and secretarial staffs . . . and big fees." I listen for awhile, then ask, "Do you think that lawyers help people?" "Oh, sure," she answers, "I would like the chance to help people who are in trouble." "That doesn't sound like someone who is only out after the money," I respond. Then I continue, "What does that new realization do to the old perception of you as a money and status grabber?" She replies, "It doesn't make sense, does it?" She is beginning to see that *new information can inductively lead to new perceptions.* "Joan, what do your friends and family say about your law-school plans—you know the *context of the perception can affect the perception.*" She laughs, "I guess they always talk about all the money that I'll make—and how famous I may be. You see, no one in my family ever went to college." *Since perceptions are motivated,* I ask, "Have your parents always wanted you to 'have more than we did'? Could it be you feel guilty about doing something that may lead to your getting exactly what you've been encouraged to get?" She asks, "Do you mean that I might be too suspicious of my motives?" "That's exactly what I mean. Your *perceptions are personal;* they are yours—even though they are affected by other people and your environment. You said earlier that the thought of helping others excites you. That doesn't sound selfish to me and I suspect it doesn't seem selfish to most other people. *Perceptions are active.* We don't *have* them, we *make* them. And sometimes we need to re-create them in a more accurate fashion—what do you think?"

Case study two: deadlocks and wedlocks. Mark is the son of a fairly conservative, middle-class family in Pennsylvania. Mark and his friend Kate have discussed marriage, but neither one feels really ready to make what they consider such an important commitment. They have also discussed the possibility of cohabitation. Several of their friends are living together, and neither Mark nor Kate condemn those friends. Yet, Mark has been raised to believe that "nice people" do not simply move in together. If they choose cohabitation, Mark feels that his belief in marriage bonds and family life will be violated. If they reject cohabitation, Mark feels he will be old-fashioned and straightlaced. Mark is confronted by a conflict in values.

Mark must realize that his perceptions of both values (and choices) are indeed perceptions. He should begin mediation by trying to clearly express his feelings about the situation: should he feel old-fashioned or guilty? At this point, he feels both and thinks he must choose between the two. Mark should talk to himself about his problem.

Since perception is *selective,* what is it that leads him to believe that "nice people" do not cohabitate? What is it that makes him think that rejecting cohabitation for later marriage is simply old-fashioned? How have these bits of information led (*inductively*) to his feelings about those values? The *contexts of his perceptions* have undoubtedly affected his feelings: his conservative home environment made marriage seem the only right thing to do; his environment away from home and his new friends made cohabitation seem less wrong to him somehow. What he must learn is that his environment will continue to change, and he may need to modify his perceptions. He must understand that his perceptions are based on *motivations:* his desire to please his family, his desire to do what is right, his love for Kate—all these may pull him in different directions. He must decide which pull is stronger. He must decide what are (and should be) the more important motivations in his life. Finally, he must understand that his perceptions are *personal* and *active.* He is the one who has created these perceptions of love, of marriage, of the peer pressure from his friends. Because of that, he is the one who can re-create his perception of any one of them.

Mark may make a variety of decisions in this situation—and I would not suggest to him which one is right. What I would do is to encourage him to analyze this conflict in values. His analysis of his perceptions will at least help him to understand his intrapersonal conflict. At best, the analysis of his perceptions will help him mediate his conflict and the problem in his relationship with Kate. What he decides is important.

Case study three: you. This is a part of the book that I ask you to write. Think of a particular intrapersonal conflict you are experiencing. Does it have to do with perceptions of who you are? Does it have to do with values you have that seem to conflict? Does it have to do with conflicting bits of information? Does it have to do with decisions you must make? Whatever the problem is, you must first identify it.

You now know something about perceiving as an intrapersonal strategy for mediation. You know what questions you must ask yourself. Once you have asked yourself those questions about selection, induction, context, and motivation, then you can take advantage of the fact that perception is personal and active. You can mediate some of the conflicts in your life by creating a better, more accurate perception of yourself and your conflicts. You can begin to use one of the strategies for the mediation of intrapersonal conflicts.

EXERCISES

Fill in the blanks below before reading the rest of the exercise:

a) This is a perfectly _____ day!

b) The occupation I am studying for can best be described by the adjective _____.

c) I feel _____ about the idea of leaving school for the "real world" outside.

d) Actually, I would have to describe myself as a(n) _____ kind of person.

e) My closest friend in the world can be described best as _____.

When you supply adjectives or other descriptive phrases in the blanks above, you are stating a perception of the things or people mentioned. Your adjectives do not describe the things or people mentioned; instead, they describe how you *perceive* them.

For a–e above, answer each of the following questions:

1. How has selection affected your perception? (What have you exposed yourself to, what have you paid attention to, how have you interpreted the thing or person, what have you remembered or forgotten?)
2. How has induction affected your perception? (How have you put the perceived bits and pieces together to describe the perception?)
3. How has context affected your perception? (What is the rest of your world today like? What is important? Why?)
4. What factor(s) helped motivate your perception? (What are the needs, desires, or forces that "tinted" the perception?)
5. Now, do you understand that your perception is almost purely personal? (Use your answers to the previous four questions to help you.)
6. Are you convinced that the words you used to fill in the blanks are accurate—or would you like to re-create those perceptions, and change the descriptive words?
7. More generally, what does this exercise tell you about all the hundreds of times during the day that you perceive something?
8. What does the exercise tell you about those times that you *tell* someone else your perceptions?
9. What does it tell you about how intrapersonal conflicts can be the result of perception?
10. What does the exercise tell you about the possibility of using perception as a way to mediate some intrapersonal conflicts?

NOTES

[1] For an excellent discussion of passive vs. active views of perception, see David L. Swanson and Jesse G. Delia, *The Nature of Human Communication* (Chicago: Science Research Associates Inc., 1976).

[2] The following kinds of selective activities have become traditional ways of expressing how information is processed. Though this discussion relies on no particular source of information, an interesting treatment of the terms is found in John R. Wenburg and William W. Wilmot, *The Personal Communication Process* (New York: John Wiley & Sons, 1973), chap. 7.

[3] Scholars such as Marshall McLuhan, for example, argue that society is well past the point where symbols are in the environment; humans live now in a *symbolic environment*.

[4] At times, selective interpretation is called *selective perception*. As I use the term, *perception* is the general process that is made up of four sub-processes, one of which is selective interpretation.

[5] Induction is one of two traditional types of logical reasoning; the other is deduction, for which Holmes is also famous. For a treatment of both induction and deduction, see Lionel Ruby, *The Art of Making Sense: A Guide to Logical Thinking*, 2nd ed. (Philadelphia: Lippincott, 1968).

[6] The word *context* can be thought of as *situation*: the context forms a background for understanding the symbol.

[7] Several interesting perspectives on these issues are reprinted in the same text. See Kenneth K. Sereno and C. David Mortensen, *Foundations of Communication Theory* (New York: Harper & Row, 1970), chaps. in Part Three.

[8] See William W. Wilmot, *Dyadic Communication: A Transactional Perspective* (Reading, Ma.: Addison-Wesley, 1975), pp. 117–22.

[9] While the perceptions of other people influence your perceptions, the perception—ultimately—is your own.

5
LANGUAGE AND VERBAL SELF-ANALYSIS: AN INTRAPERSONAL STRATEGY

In 1970, four students were killed by National Guardsmen during a student-guardsman clash at Kent State University. The Guardsmen declared that the students were rioting; the students who survived claimed that they were merely demonstrating. Who was right—and why did it matter?

In 1976, Secretary of Agriculture Earl Butz was forced to resign from his post because of a controversy over comments he made about black Americans. His attackers said his comment reflected the kind of person he was. Did it—and why?

You are bringing a fellow classmate to meet your parents. On your way there, you caution your friend that your parents would not approve of obscenity. Your friend asks if you mean that there is something wrong with him or her and his or her language. What do you say?

In the first two situations, other people were in the midst of some sort of conflict. In the last situation, the conflict between you and your friend may not have been as bad as the conflict he or she begins having with him- or herself. How can such situations be handled?

One of the ways of mediating intrapersonal conflict is by understanding the role of verbal symbols in such conflicts. Symbols have been discussed before as things that mean something besides themselves. Now, the discussion can be more specific. Verbal symbols are oral or written words that relate to *ideas about things*. One of the classic ways of explaining that statement is to describe the relationships among *thoughts, words, and things.*[1] Visually, the relationship can be seen as the following:

Word———Thought———Thing

There is a direct connection between words and thoughts: when a word is spoken or written, some sort of thought will occur immediately. Similarly, there is a direct connection between thoughts and things: when a thing is observed, some thought about it will usually emerge. In contrast, *there is no direct connection between words and things.* Words as verbal symbols refer to ideas or thoughts about things, instead of to things directly.

Communication and language use are difficult partly because of this indirect connection between things and words. How is it that you use a word to describe a thing that both you and a friend see, and yet find that misunderstanding has occurred? One of the problems of language use is that any one word, even if it is meant to refer to a single thing, may produce any one of dozens of thoughts about the thing. Your friend Sally does not react to the word pony; she doesn't react to the thing that is a pony. Instead, she reacts to one of many possible thoughts about the pony or ponies in general as illustrated in the diagram.

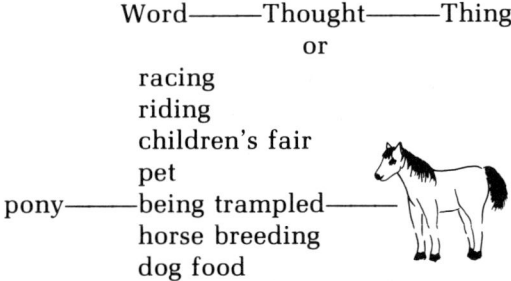

```
              Word———Thought———Thing
                        or
              racing
              riding
              children's fair
              pet
    pony———being trampled———
              horse breeding
              dog food
```

Words are (verbal) symbols because they refer to ideas or conceptions of things besides themselves.

To understand verbal symbols and how verbal self-analysis can aid the mediation of intrapersonal conflicts, six ideas should be examined: (1) language and labeling, (2) language as both arbitrary and rational, (3) language and perception, (4) language and abstraction, (5) language and stereotyping, and (6) verbal self-analysis and interpersonal conflict mediation.

LANGUAGE AND LABELING

One of the most important ideas about verbal symbols is that the use of language is a labeling process. The four-legged animal which eats oats, has a mane, and neighs is not a horse; that animal has simply been labeled a *horse.* A group of people who throw rocks and bottles and use noise and violence is not a rioting mob. It may be *labeled* a *mob* by some people, but by others it might be labeled a group of *patriots, rebels,* or *demonstrators.*[2] My daughter might label a dandelion a *flower,* and I correct her, saying that it is a *weed.* What I mean is that to me and other lawn owners, the dandelion is labeled a *weed.* Language is a matter of labeling or calling a thing by a particular verbal symbol.

The labeling process is crucial because of the relationship between words used in labeling and thoughts about those words. Society might excuse National Guardsmen who killed students during a riot; it might be less willing to excuse them for killing members of a demonstration. Even though the group of students might be the same *thing,* labeling with different words prompts different thoughts—and different actions are justified. Consider another example: your friend Tony admits he paid less income tax than he should have. If your friend labels his action *creative tax figuring* rather than *cheating* or *dishonesty,* he will expect a more sympathetic reaction. Labels—most people realize this at least subconsciously—affect what we think about the things we know about.

LANGUAGE AS ARBITRARY AND RATIONAL

Frequently, language is viewed as arbitrary. There is nothing particularly "pony-ish" about a pony that determined the label. Cows are called *cows* simply because they are called cows. When words are used for *no apparent reason* in labeling, language can be said to be *arbitrary.* Yet, the arbitrariness of language should not be considered as characteristic of all use of language. Labeling is often done for *very good reasons,* rather than for no reason at all; language is often *rational* instead of arbitrary. For example, the dictionary may tell us that we use *cow because of* the Middle English *cou*—and perhaps it has an even earlier root-meaning. Even contemporary words such as *income tax* have rational meanings: in this case a tax on income. There are good reasons for calling the lookout post at the top of a ship's mast a *crow's nest;* there are good reasons for calling the backlash in a fishing reel a *bird's nest;* there are good reasons for calling a growing savings account a *nest egg;* and there are good reasons for labeling a child's desire to leave home as a need to *leave the nest.* As language has developed and continues to develop, some labeling is rational rather than arbitrary. Some language use is based upon good reasons.

The reasons for labeling should not make you think that labeling is done automatically. In most instances, people have *choices* about what labels they will place on something. The bird's nest in the fishing line can also be called a maze of string; the nest egg can be called *a little cushion;* leaving the nest can be called *cutting the apron strings;* and birds other than crows build their nests high above the ground. Even though there are reasons for the labeling mentioned earlier, the labeling is still largely a matter of human choice. What do you call a group of rock-throwing, noisy people? Do you always call a cow that is black and white merely a *cow?*

LANGUAGE AND PERCEPTION

How you perceive something—the thoughts you have about the thing—is a crucial factor in language. How you perceive something, how you selectively interpret something, and how you inductively make sense of bits of information, are all related to the choice of a language label for the thing. Influences upon perception affect the labeling by verbal symbols. If your background involves childhood on a farm, the black and white cow will have a special name or label. If you were to have entered Washington, D.C., during the Vietnam War expecting to find a riot, the chances are good that you would have found something to label a riot. If you want very much to find that your university is a good one, the odds are that you will begin to label it as such. The concerns of perception, then, are related to the matter of verbal labeling.

LANGUAGE AND ABSTRACTION

Labeling occurs at different *levels of abstraction,*[3] with different degrees of concrete detail. Suppose I ask you what your favorite pastime is. One of the least concrete answers might be "Sports." I might ask further, "Do you mean all kinds of sports?" You might reply, "Well, football." "All kinds of football?" "Well, not professional football." "College football, then?" "Yes." "Interscholastic or intramural?" "Intramural." "Offense or defense?" "Defense." "What position?" "Linebacker." You have probably become irritated by my constant questions, but the series of answers illustrates various levels of abstraction in language. When you say you play linebacker, you are labeling what you do at a fairly *concrete* level of abstraction. When you say you play defense, you begin leaving out details, and label what you do with more abstract verbal symbols. "Intramural," "college," "football," and "sports," are all at continually higher levels of abstraction. When you say you like sports, you are telling the truth, but telling it at such a high level of abstraction that you give me little information. As the questioning continues, you add more and more information as you move to labeling at lower levels of abstraction. Verbal symbols, then, are not simply used; they are used at varying levels of abstraction.

The difficulty with varying levels of abstraction is that any one of several labels may be accurate symbols for the same thing at the same time. You, my hypothetical friend, enjoy sports, football, college football, intramurals, and defense, as well as playing linebacker. Being able to understand language means that you can understand something at various levels.[4] If conversation or expressions of thought occur at the highest levels of abstraction, the language may be vague and general. If it all occurs at low levels of abstraction, you might have trouble seeing how all of it relates. Effective use of language requires your use of various levels of abstraction. Effective use of language also requires that you understand the various levels of abstraction that someone else might use.

LANGUAGE AND STEREOTYPING

The understanding of language also demands that you consider verbal labelings *provisional: something for the time being;* something temporary until you find out more.[5] As you decide to label the thoughts you have about things, you use perception, reasons for labeling, and levels of abstraction. You ought to make sure that those labels do not deceive you into believing that there is a direct relationship between things and the labels you use for them. Labeling has the effect of placing something into a category.[6] You may label a rock-throwing crowd a *riot* because it fits into the category of events that you have labeled as such before. The crowd may be labeled a *demonstration* by someone else, because it fits into the category he or she has labeled as such in the past.

What communicators must realize is that the labeling of things can become *fixed* and *inflexible*. Fixed labeling at any abstraction level is *stereotyping*. You may think you know what politicians are like. Every political officeholder becomes labeled with the same verbal symbols. As a bumper sticker says, "Study the criminal mind. Take a congressman to lunch." Clearly, not every congressman is a criminal, but apparently the owner of the bumper sticker has stereotyped them all as such. Religious, ethnic, and racial groups are the most commonly stereotyped, but all of us stereotype or label all kinds and classes of things and people. We are not prepared to examine individual cases to see if our labeling is accurate because it is easier to ignore individual differences and to label whole groups. When the labeling is done without giving thought to changes—when it is done automatically and not provisionally—it becomes stereotyping. Stereotyping gets in the way of more accurate perception and language labeling.

VERBAL SELF-ANALYSIS AND INTRAPERSONAL CONFLICTS

Intrapersonal conflicts are the creations of perception. You are the person who perceives the conflicts, but now a new idea must be added. You are the person who uses verbal symbols to label your roles, behaviors, values, and the conflicts among them. One of the strategies that can aid the mediation of intrapersonal conflicts is a working knowledge of verbal self-analysis. Verbal self-analysis, based on our previous discussions, concerns two major areas: first, how you label yourself; and second, what your language use says about you. In using language or verbal self-analysis for mediation, remember the following points:

1. Don't confuse words and things; the *words* you use to describe yourself *are not you*.
2. Language and verbal symbols are no more than labels that you attach to yourself.

3. These labels may be either arbitrary or rational; make sure you have *reasons* for the labels you attach to yourself.
4. When you examine the language you use, you are simply creating a perception of what you say; make sure the perception is as accurate as possible.
5. The labels you use for yourself, and your language use generally, should be analyzed for abstraction; make sure you are using appropriate and flexible levels of abstraction.
6. Use your perceptual skills to avoid stereotyping either yourself or others.
7. The language you use, or the terms you use to describe yourself, can be changed. When you do change them, you may change a part of *who you are.*

Together these strategies can help you mediate some of your intrapersonal conflicts. Consider the following case studies:

Case study one: the clown. Ralph Smith was once the class clown. He threw paper airplanes, chewed gum, and made jokes in school. Now, Ralph is twenty-two years old and has his first job after college. Not much has changed except that he is older. He is now the one who jokes constantly with the secretaries. He is usually found near the water cooler or coffee machine, talking about the last football game or the first basketball game. Everyone likes Ralph, even though it is obvious that he does not work as hard as some of the other people. Ralph is now the office clown.

When he is laughing and telling the latest funny story, Ralph seems entirely happy. There are times, however, when he is not completely happy with himself. People are so used to hearing him tell jokes that he finds that everything he says is treated lightly, even when he's serious. One day, he confesses to his friend Bert that he is tired of always being the jokester. Bert is surprised:

Bert: What do you mean? Everyone thinks you're great!

Ralph: I know . . . a joke a minute. Some days get to be pretty long.

Bert: I don't understand you, Ralph. I know people who have real problems, but you aren't one of them.

Ralph: Bert, it's been like this all my life. I've always been the class cutup, and I guess maybe I always will be . . . Oh, well, things could be worse . . . You know, I heard a good one the other day. It seems there was this traveling saleswoman with very big feet. Well, she . . .

Instead of letting Ralph finish his story, let's look at his intrapersonal problem. Part of the reason why Ralph is unhappy is because of the label he attaches to himself. Since there is a rather direct relationship between words and thoughts, everyone must be concerned with the labels he or she attaches to him- or herself. Ralph is unhappy with the office clown label, yet he uses it to describe himself—as though it is his label once-and-for-all. In certain sorts of conflicts: EXAMINE WHAT LABEL YOU ATTACH TO YOURSELF.

Next, Ralph (and you) may wish to analyze whether the label is really accurate. Here again, language or verbal analysis can help you. What words does Ralph use? Are all of them joking and funny? You have just seen that Ralph can be serious and concerned, as well as unhappy. Few people hear the words of Ralph, the serious person. That is probably his fault. Ralph has not only labeled himself, he has stereotyped himself as the clown. He calls himself that and others call him that. More important, Ralph continues to ACT like the clown, even when he doesn't want to. There is no magic here. It is just that, once you attach a label to yourself, you may begin acting a part. You can begin to assume (wrongly) that there is a direct relationship between the label and you. We know, though, that such a direct relationship does not exist. If Ralph would begin to listen to his serious side and allow others to see him saying serious things more often, his problem might decrease. If he can change the clown label for himself and present his serious side as well, other people may change the labels they have for him. The process may be slow, but it can work. Once you examine the labels you have for yourself and find them inaccurate, you can begin to change them. This change is the use of language as a means of mediation for intrapersonal conflicts.

Case study two: the queen and the drone. Jane is a person who studies very hard. She is currently enrolled in college, where she is studying industrial management. Jane considers herself to be too busy studying on weekends for much socializing. She is proud of what she is accomplishing, but she is also lonely. Jane happens to share a dormitory room with Francine, who is one of the most popular girls in school. While Jane has always been told that she would make a fine businesswoman someday, Francine has always been told that she would make a terrific model. Jane's studies over the weekend are made easier because Francine is seldom around.

Jane is too busy studying to be social; Francine is too busy socializing to study. Francine is unhappy because her grades are very low, while Jane is unhappy because she feels very lonely. These very different people share a very similar problem: they are trapped by the labels they have given themselves and by the labels others attach to them. People assume that Francine the Queen Bee would never refuse an invitation—and she doesn't. People assume that Jane the Drone would never accept an invitation—and she doesn't. The behavior of both women seems automatic. They simply are what they are.

That, of course, is not accurate. Here again, the two steps of verbal self-analysis are important. First, both women should analyze the labels attached to them—and then see if those labels can or should be changed. If Jane could see herself as a whole person and not solely as a student, she might accept some of those invitations. If Francine could see herself as a whole person and not solely as a socialite, she might refuse some of those invitations. At this point, the women are acting out stereotypes that they and others have used to label them. If they can escape from the labels, they might discover themselves as real, not stereotyped individuals. When their behaviors change, it might not take too long for other people's labels to change as well. How we label ourselves and our problems can be a source of intrapersonal conflict. How we change those labels and examine our actual verbal language and behavior can be a method of mediation.

Case study three: you. This case study is about you. How do you label yourself? Do you consider yourself beautiful, selfish, ambitious, hostile, popular, or what? Now consider how much of your language and behavior is used to live up to those labels. Have you been fair to your self, or have you stereotyped your self? Is there a more accurate label for *who you are*? Have you discovered a way to use language as a strategy of mediation?

The case studies are designed to help you see verbal self-analysis in action. If some ideas are still unclear, you may wish to review specific parts of the chapter. If the comments were clear to you, you are beginning to see verbal self-analysis as a strategy of mediation.

EXERCISES

Complete the following sentences before reading the rest of the exercise. Use adjectives or descriptive phrases to fill in the blanks, but stress qualities instead of physical characteristics.

George Washington was _____.

Abraham Lincoln was _____.

Adolph Hitler was _____.

The teacher I remember most was _____.

My brother (or sister or cousin) is _____.

I am _____.

Now that you have attached labels to each of the persons above, tell how *each* of the individuals would react to the situations described below:

When approached by a sick dog, this person would _____.

After having made a mistake, this person would _____.

Upon finding a lost wallet, this person would _____.

If you approached this person with your personal problem, he or she would _____.

If you criticized this person, he or she would _____.

I suspect that your labels for the first three people are labels you have heard other people use. The other people are or were known to you directly: the descriptions, though, are probably still based upon labels others have used. More important, I suspect that your statements about what these people would do are always consistent with the labels you gave to them: You may have described Lincoln as honest ("honest Abe"), so when you decided what Abe would do, you actually decided what the HONEST PERSON would do. You were not reacting to the people, I suspect, as much as you were reacting to the labels you gave them.

You may have stereotyped some of these individuals as just part of a whole group of people. Here, something else might have happened: your label might not have been consistent with what you said they would do. In stereotyping or any case of labeling, another question can be asked. What happens when people don't live up to the labels?

More important, what do you do when you don't live up to the labels you have for yourself?

NOTES

[1] The discussion following, including the diagrams, owes much to C. K. Ogden and I. A. Richards, *The Meaning of Meaning* (New York: Harcourt, Brace & World, 1946), especially chap. 1.

[2] The idea of *labeling* is a complex topic, especially in studies of *general semantics*. For a helpful introduction to general semantics, see William H. Youngren, *Semantics, Linguistics, and Criticism* (New York: Random House, 1972).

[3] What "my" discussion with "you" illustrates is what is termed the *abstraction ladder*—a way of *going up* or *coming down* in levels of abstraction. For an excellent discussion see S. I. Hayakawa, *Language in Thought and Action*, 3rd ed. (New York: Harcourt Brace Jovanovich, 1972), pp. 153 ff.

[4] The inability to move from one level of abstraction to another is called *dead-level* abstraction and is a basic human problem. See Wendell Johnson, *People in Quandaries* (New York: Harper & Row, 1946), pp. 270 ff.

[5] In general semantics, the *intentional* person does not see beyond the label for the changes that might occur in something. The *extensional* person tends to take labels less seriously and to use objects and language in more creative and flexible ways.

[6] Part of the reason that changing labels is difficult is because labeling does place something into a category of similar things. A new label means that the thing is taken out of one category of things and put into another: a two-step process.

6
NONVERBAL SELF-ANALYSIS: AN INTRAPERSONAL STRATEGY

You are out late one night and you look in the mirror the next morning. "That's exactly how I *feel*, too." The expression on your face tells it all.

You sit alone in a restaurant. At a table in the far corner, two strangers are doing more talking than eating. The man is moving about in his chair and pointing a finger at his companion. He is speaking softly, but the man's face seems red and his eyebrows are furrowed. "He is really angry," you say to yourself.

It is Sam's first date with this certain other person. He is tired—and a little nervous. He showers and sprinkles lotion on his face after shaving. "I needed that," says Sam. He decides to wear the blue slacks and the turtleneck sweater that everyone always admires. He looks in the mirror, and then decides to wear the new shirt instead of the sweater. He returns to the mirror. "There. That's more like it."

Sometimes it is said that a picture is worth a thousand words. In the situations above, words or verbal symbols have not been as important as other kinds of symbols. In Chapter 5, we talked about verbal symbols. In this chapter, we will concern ourselves with symbols that are neither spoken nor written words. These are the nonverbal symbols. Nonverbal communication, or transactions involving nonverbal symbols, is an exciting area of study for professionals and nonprofessionals alike. That is one of the problems with nonverbal communication studies. When an area of study is comparatively new, it sometimes becomes the topic of popularized books and articles which may or may not be helpful to people. Books on body language and people-reading may be interesting, but they should be based on some understanding of nonverbal symbol use generally.

You can begin to understand nonverbal communication and self-analysis by exploring five areas of concern: (1) types of nonverbal symbols, (2) the meanings of nonverbal symbols, (3) the functions of nonverbal symbols, (4) commonly found meanings of nonverbal symbols, and (5) nonverbal self-analysis and intrapersonal conflicts.

TYPES OF NONVERBAL SYMBOLS

There are many types of nonverbal symbols. Basically, nonverbal communication refers to any communication which does not use *words* or verbal symbols. It is helpful, here, to understand the difference between *verbal* and *oral*. *Verbal* refers to words (spoken or written) or to a code such as Morse code. *Oral* means spoken aloud. Verbal and oral are frequently misinterpreted. When someone refers to a "verbal agreement," he or she probably means that the agreement is not in writing. Words used in communication, however, whether oral or written, are all *verbal* symbols. Verbal symbols can be written or oral. On the other hand, some *nonverbal* symbols *are* oral—that is, given aloud. The *ah, er,* and *um* that creep into most people's speech are oral, but they are not verbal because they are not words. In sum, then, any communication not involving words is nonverbal communication. This is why the types of nonverbal symbols are so numerous.

Over the years a number of fairly distinct classifications of nonverbal symbols have been developed, and recently some new labels have been attached to make their discussion easier.[1] *Kinesics* is the study of how bodily action can be used for communication. *Proxemics* is the study of the use of space or distance for communication. The study of touching behavior has been labeled *haptics* by some researchers. Eye contact and eye movements are crucial to human communication. The study of how eyes and eye movements can communicate is termed *oculesics*. *Objectics* is a term that is used at times to describe how people communicate by the use of such objects as wedding rings or smoking pipes. Time itself can be used to communicate certain messages, and the study of time can be termed *chronemics*. *Vocalics* is the study of how the voice can communicate certain messages. Environmental factors such as office furnishings or desk arrangements can be used for nonverbal communication. Finally, physical characteristics such as appearance and body build can communicate certain messages nonverbally. Indeed, the types of nonverbal symbols are numerous.

THE MEANINGS OF NONVERBAL SYMBOLS

Now that we have mentioned the wide range of nonverbal symbols, a very important question arises. What do they all mean? Unfortunately, the answer to the question is difficult. Over the past few years, the study of nonverbal communication has become popular. A magazine that features pictures of young ladies once ran an article on what various feminine "leg-crossings" *meant*. Popular books claim to teach people how to understand each other completely by knowing what various nonverbal symbols *mean*. The major problem with these sorts of discussions is that nonverbal symbols—like verbal symbols in language—do not *mean* anything. People *give meanings* to nonverbal symbols in much the same way that people give meanings to verbal symbols. Legs crossed in a particular position *may* mean an invitation to romance; they may also mean an uncomfortable chair, a leg cramp, or almost anything else. The meaning of nonverbal symbols is a matter of how they are interpreted.

Many of our previous discussions of perception and language are relevant here. Expectations, desires, and backgrounds all contribute to what nonverbal symbols mean. If a man is looking for romance, a particular pair of crossed legs may mean one thing to him. If he is a chair designer, they may mean something else. If he is a fashion expert, the same crossed legs may mean something else again.

To explain the idea with a different example, it may happen that on a certain afternoon you yawn. The yawn may simply be a reflection of your lack of sleep. Still, you may perceive it as a reflection of boredom or apathy. What, then, does it really mean? To you, and to others, the meaning that you give to the nonverbal symbol is most important. But the thought you have about the thing depends more on you and your perception than on anything else. Nonverbal symbols do not mean anything; people give them meanings.

Nonverbal and verbal symbols usually occur together. During a long distance phone conversation with my sister, she reported that my mother was in the same room and was laughing at her. It seems that while describing something to me over the phone, my sister was gesturing to explain it. Obviously, my sister knew that her gestures were impossible for me to see. That, however, did not matter. It was simply easier to use the hands to explain to me what she meant. The use of nonverbal symbols to aid verbal symbols is a perfectly natural human tendency. Try to give directions to someone without using your hands. Try to talk with no facial expression. Try to express the joy that you feel without moving your body or your hands, or without changing your facial expression. I suspect you cannot.

One researcher has estimated that during simultaneous verbal and nonverbal communication, roughly 65 percent of the meaning of the communication is created by nonverbal cues.[2] Research also indicates that when verbal and nonverbal cues seem to conflict, the nonverbal symbols will be the ones believed.[3] You may tend to not trust the salesperson with the shifty eyes even when he or she is saying pleasant things. All this indicates how important nonverbal messages are to communication. It does not indicate that verbal messages are unimportant. In virtually every situation in which you find yourself, verbal and nonverbal symbols will combine to create what is to you the meaning of the message.

THE FUNCTIONS OF NONVERBAL SYMBOLS

The ways that verbal and nonverbal symbols combine to help the creation of meaning relates to the *functions* that nonverbal symbols can perform. Nonverbal symbols can serve the functions of repeating, complementing, accenting, substituting for, or contradicting the verbal message.[4]

Sometimes, nonverbal symbols simply *repeat* the message of verbal symbols. Frequently, when you answer "no" to a simple question, you find yourself also shaking your head from side to side. The shaking may serve no other function than to repeat what you have said. At other times, the nonverbal symbol *complements* the verbal message by clarifying or explaining. Try to give directions to someone without pointing. Usually that is not easy; people rely on hand signals, head nods, and bodily movement as ways of complementing their direction giving. You probably find yourself doing the same thing when you indicate the height of a child, the smallness of the dent you put in the family car, or the largeness of a fish that got away. In other situations, nonverbal symbols may serve as a means of *accent*. To say that you are angry may not be enough; to accent your feelings, you pound the table. To say that you are sorry may not satisfy you; you accent your shame by looking downward. To tell someone you do not wish to see him or her again, you may accent your words by turning your head, turning your body, or walking away.

On still other occasions, nonverbal symbols can either *substitute* for or *contradict* the verbal message. A V with the hands may be used instead of the words *peace* or *victory*. A nod of the head may be used in place of *good morning* or *hello*. A shake of the head may be substituted for *no, no way,* or *nothing*. In each of these examples the verbal symbol is omitted and the nonverbal symbol substitutes for it. The nonverbal symbol serves as the focus of meaning creation. Nonverbal symbols may also become the focal point when the verbal and nonverbal symbols conflict with one another. A nonverbal symbol contradicts the verbal when a "hello" is accompanied by a grim, unexcited face. When words of love are accompanied by acts of thoughtlessness, contradicting messages occur. Contradiction between verbal and nonverbal symbols is crucial. When there is a contradicting relationship between the verbal and nonverbal, people tend to believe the meaning of the nonverbal symbol. We (think we) know that "the eyes never lie," that we "could tell by her face she didn't mean it," or that "he didn't sound like he was angry." Scattered research tends to support these commonsense opinions. When there is contradiction between the verbal and the nonverbal symbols, the nonverbal message seems generally most believable.

What you should note in this discussion of nonverbal functions is that most often, nonverbal symbols act in relation to verbal symbols. Understanding nonverbal symbols requires remembering also the discussions of language and perception. The meanings in communication are still in people who are transacting.

COMMONLY FOUND MEANINGS OF NONVERBAL SYMBOLS

There is a great deal of research and speculation on nonverbal communication that should be mentioned. Certain kinds of nonverbal cues seem to mean much the same thing to large groups of people. The meanings of nonverbal symbols are not really the meanings *of* the symbols. They are the meanings that a great many people *give to* these nonverbal symbols. Let us examine some of these research findings.

Kinesics

Much research has focused on the meanings that can be given to postures, head movements, body movements, and facial expressions. One researcher has estimated that the human body is capable of assuming about one thousand different *postures*.[5] As an observer, you might attach meaning to any of those positions. The most consistent research finding, though, is a simple one: postures that include leaning toward someone generally are seen as expressing warmth or positive feelings; leaning away seems to express a colder or more negative feeling.[6] The same general conclusion relates to head movements. Head nodding is seen in many cultures as a friendly gesture of acceptance or friendliness. A shaking of the head, and perhaps even a motionless head, seems to indicate less acceptance. What must be added about both those findings is that movements of the body or the head express only general feelings or impressions.[7] Other bodily activity, and verbal symbols as well, must be relied upon for more specific communication of feelings. You may well have found yourself in the position of shaking your head at the comment of a friend. If so, the chances are good that your friend understands your negative feeling generally, but asks, "What's the matter?" Head and body movements normally mean only general things.

Gestural behavior—arm and hand movement—is one way of making the meaning of bodily action more specific. Gestures can serve to clarify the meanings of people in several ways.[8] They can be used as *emblems*: gestures which have a more or less direct relationship to a specific verbal message. The OK with the fingers, the V for victory or peace, the motion across the throat to indicate death or execution, and the thumbs-up or down that decided the fates of gladiators are all examples of emblems. Gestures can also serve as *illustrators* which more or less demonstrate what is being said. The box was this high (hand out) by this wide (two hands parallel) by this long (two hands parallel again). The road goes off in this way (hands out in a direction, then a turn). Bodily action and particularly gestures can be *affect displays*: motions which intentionally or unintentionally express emotions. Fingernail biting, finger drumming, hand wringing, and toe tapping are examples. *Regulators* are nonverbal cues which can be interpreted as ways of controlling communication and interaction. You may motion a friend to slow down when he or she is talking excitedly, or to speed up if a story begins to drag on and on. You may stretch out your hand as an indication that you want your friend to feel free to go on. A final category of gestural and body movement is termed *adaptors*: segments of actual behavior which are used to communicate a desire, need, or message about that actual behavior. The clenched fist is an adaptor which has a fairly clear meaning in specific situations. In a scene of hostility, your clenched fist may express your eagerness for a fight; in another situation, it may seem to mean that you actually have someone by the throat—"where I want him." Lip movements, stroking, and leg movements may indicate your desire for romance. They are adaptors because they are a part of actual sexual rituals and activities.

In addition to these specific ways in which nonverbal symbols can be given meaning, researchers have studied the meanings attached to gestural activity in general. Scattered studies have produced some—but not consistent—evidence that such activity can indeed make a message more understandable.[9] In addition, there is evidence that gestural behavior helps listeners remember what you say.[10] There is evidence that higher levels of such activity may prompt others to consider you more aggressive—more interested in getting their approval.[11] What you do physically, then, can have an effect upon the meanings that people create about what you do.

Facial expression is a kind of nonverbal cue which depends upon *context* for meaning. Classic studies have been done of the same pictured facial expression set in situations which were tragic, upsetting, or joyful.[12] People tended to interpret the same pictured expression according to whichever feeling was indicated by the setting. While common sense tells us that a smile expresses warmth and positive feelings, that same expression may become a sneer, a leer, or a grimace, if the setting is changed.

Proxemics

The use of space and distance is a source of nonverbal meanings. People tend to *map out* their own personal space, and then to protect it.[13] In communication studies, it is traditional to point out that certain cultures specify different distances of personal space. The North American, who keeps his distance, will think the South American is pushy. The South American who enjoys getting close, will consider the North American to be aloof or cold. What must also be said is that within any culture different individuals respond to distance in different ways. Some people simply are accustomed to getting closer than others.

You may dislike elevators for a variety of reasons. One reason may be that the elevator forces you to be closer to strangers than you desire; so you either watch the fascinating lighted numbers of the floors or stare at the floor of the elevator. Either strategy seems to increase the distance *felt* between you and others, and the experience becomes more tolerable. Consider also the behavior related to staking out space at a table in the student union or at the library. When there are several chairs but only a person or two, people tend to place books, coats, purses, or umbrellas on either side of "their place." When another person arrives, he or she will probably sit in an empty chair as far away from others as possible; it is unlikely that the newcomer will sit next to someone else if another alternative is available. Your use of space can mean all sorts of things to other individuals. Stepping back and away from someone, or moving a chair forward or backward are among the kinds of behaviors included in the study of proxemics.

Haptics

Touching behavior is another sort of nonverbal symbol.[14] Touching in American culture is usually reserved for extremes of emotions. When a person is extremely angry, he or she may shove, slap, or strike someone else. When people are in love, they hold hands, wrap arms around one another, and caress each other. Between those extremes, people seem to interpret touching behavior in different ways. Some people are what can be termed *touchers*: a conversation is not complete without a friendly push on the shoulder, a slap on the (other's) knee, or a hand on the arm. Other people are what can be called *non-touchers*: a push, a slap, or a hand on the arm is considered either too aggressive or too intimate. Conversations between two touchers or two non-touchers is no problem; conversations between a toucher and non-toucher may create meanings about the other that each dislikes. The toucher considers the other aloof and cold, if not hostile. The non-toucher considers the other to be overly forward or overly aggressive. In all cases, touching is a fundamental means of nonverbal communication.

Oculesics

What (you think) the eyes tell you can be important in communication. Although there have been numerous studies of how and what the eyes communicate, two researchers have summarized these studies in a helpful way. Argyle and Dean say, for example, that there are four major factors that determine how much *eye contact* will exist in a communication transaction.[15] The first factor is the *role* of the communicator, since the person listening usually demonstrates more eye contact. The second is the nature of the *topic*. If the topic is impersonal or general, eye contact is easier. If the topic is personal, eye contact tends to decrease. The third factor involves the *sex* of the communicator. Women tend to engage in more eye contact than men. (An exception to this is in cultures where there are specific taboos against women establishing eye contact.) The fourth factor is the *relationship* between or among the communicators. If you are friends with another person, you will tend to establish more constant eye contact.

The question remains: What does eye contact or lack of it mean? We all "know" that we cannot trust someone who cannot "look us in the eye." We all "know" that it is more difficult to lie when you "look the person square in the eye." Those truisms have received some support through the years. Argyle and Dean, however, say more about what eye contact does and what it may mean.[16] One of the functions of eye contact is *information seeking:* when a person is talking and is attempting to remember partially forgotten information, he or she will tend to break eye contact, perhaps to avoid distraction. A second function of eye contact is to signal that it is time for the other person to speak; the channel is open to the other person. When you have finished what you are saying, your looking squarely at the other person probably will prompt him or her to say *something*—even if there is nothing to say. A third function of eye contact is that breaking it can serve to conceal, supporting the commonsense view that "the eyes cannot lie." People tend to look away when they are insecure, timid, or possibly lying. Finally, eye contact functions to establish and recognize social relationships. As you grow to like another person, one of the ways you tend to express this is through increasing eye contact. If you begin to dislike someone more, one of the ways you may express it is by failing to establish eye contact.

Objectics

Though not much objectics research has been done, the history of human beings is filled with a concern for objects—and how they relate to a person's identity. The personal items found in Tutankhamen's tomb revealed much about him and his culture. The cigarette case, the cigar holder, and the smoking pipe may all give clues as to the nature of a person. Meanings are attached to the executive's briefcase, the minister's Bible, and the physician's stethoscope. Badges, signs on desks, elevator shoes, false eyelashes, and jewelry are all objects which can function as nonverbal symbols.

Chronemics

Time may not be money to everyone, but the use of time may have more significance than money. The professor who structures his or her role so that there is no time for research may be trying to communicate a legitimate inability to do research to his or her chairperson and dean. The executive who keeps appointments exactly on time may be seen as being concerned, considerate, and efficient. The physician who schedules three appointments for the same time and then keeps most of the patients waiting may be seen as having no concern for anything but money. A city council meeting called at the last minute may be viewed as an attempt to keep citizens away from an open meeting. A decision-making conference called for 4:30 P.M. may be viewed as an effort to curb long or negative discussions by hungry and tired individuals. Time and its use, then, may be an important nonverbal symbol.

Vocalics

The voice is a tremendous source of nonverbal meanings. People make judgments on a variety of vocal factors, including vocal quality, vocal variety, and pauses. The research on vocal quality tends to provide consistent stereotypes about men and women, but they are stereotypes. Judgments of personality based on vocal cues seem to be inaccurate as often as they are accurate.[17] In terms of vocal *quality, breathiness* is an interesting variable.[18] Breathy men tend to be labeled as young and artistic, while breathy women are judged as feminine, more attractive, but personally shallow. Throatiness or gruffness in men tends to be viewed as a sign of maturity, realism, or sophistication; in women, throatiness may be seen to indicate less intelligence, more apathy, and a cloddish character. Nasality is consistently judged negatively in both men and women. Resonant and mellow voices create perceptions of energy, health, and pride in men; liveliness, pride, but lack of humor in women.

People generally tend to express preference for listening to voices with changes in *inflection:* they want pitch variety instead of monotones. Just as undesirable as the monotonous voice with no pitch change is the voice with a *pattern,* or *singsongy* characteristic. Changes in pitch, volume, and the rate of speed in speech can create more interesting communication. Lack of these can create unfavorable meanings in the communicator's listeners.

Pauses are another way in which meanings can be created nonverbally. The fewer and less obvious the pauses, the more the communicator is seen as extroverted and outgoing. Unfilled pauses—simple gaps in the conversation—seem to imply that the communicator is thinking. Filled pauses—*ahs, ers,* and *ums,* seem to create the feeling that the person is excited or nervous.[19] Filled pauses may also mean that the person is attempting to keep control of the conversation.[20] We have mentioned how people may look away to signal that they are not finished; that the channel is not open. One of the ways of assuring that no one jumps in while we finish expressing an idea is to fill the awkward space with an *er* or a *you know.* What does the pause mean? Well, that depends on the situation and the people.

Environmental factors

Another category of nonverbal symbols is termed *environmental factors.* The way you have decorated a dorm room or a bedroom may mean one thing to your parents; something else to your friends; and something else to me. The arrangement of my office, where the visitor's chair is next to mine instead of on the other side of the desk, may tell you something about me. The clutter on my desk may tell you something else. The sign that I am thinking of buying for my office—"Creative Minds Are Rarely Tidy"—might tell you something else about me. All of us live in various situations or environments; the things we do with these environments may allow others to create meanings about us.

Physical appearance

A final category of nonverbal symbols is *appearance*. Some of the factors of appearance are beyond your immediate control. Although you may gain or lose weight, you have a fairly consistent body build that may mean something to someone.[21] The muscular person may be perceived as athletic, dynamic, or impulsive; the frail individual may appear weak, intellectual, timid, or sensitive; the heavy person may appear to be jolly, unathletic, and sluggish. These judgments may be wrong as often as they are correct, but they are among the judgments that people are likely to make.

Clothing also contributes to your appearance, and here you have more immediate control. The one major research finding that is consistent is that *appropriateness* is the key to meaning creation.[22] Any time you are dressed in a way that someone considers inappropriate, impressions might be negative—whether you are dressed too well, not well enough, or simply inappropriately. That finding, however, is affected by how well acquainted you are with the other person. When you do not know the other person, his or her judgments are likely to be much more severe. Among friends, the factor of clothing appropriateness is generally less important.

NONVERBAL SELF-ANALYSIS AND INTRAPERSONAL CONFLICT

Your understanding of this discussion of nonverbal symbol use provides you with certain tools for intrapersonal mediation. One of the main ways you have of knowing who you are and what you are doing is by analyzing your own nonverbal communication. As I have attempted to stress, nonverbal symbols do not have meanings any more than verbal symbols do. People attach meanings to the nonverbal cues that they perceive. Much of what other people think of you is based on their interpretation of your nonverbal communication. Similarly, much of what you think of yourself and your problems is based on your analysis of your nonverbal communication. Your task is to use the discussion of nonverbal symbols to better understand yourself and your problems. As you analyze yourself and your conflicts, remember to:

1. Realize that your nonverbal communication can mean different things to

different people; don't begin thinking of nonverbal symbols in simplistic terms.
2. See if your nonverbal communication does what it should in relation to your language: make sure nonverbal symbols accent, complement, and so forth, the language appropriately. Avoid verbal and nonverbal messages that contradict.
3. Compare your meanings for your nonverbal communication with the meanings that are commonly given to such symbols.
4. Adjust your nonverbal symbols to help make you seem the person you want to be.

To help you learn to use nonverbal analysis as a means of mediating intrapersonal conflicts, consider the following case studies:

Case study one: this . . uh, you know, is a problem. Cindy McMahon has just finished a series of interviews for her first job. She has been an excellent student in public relations, and her recommendations from her professors have been strong. In addition, she has been active on the student newspaper staff and the college yearbook staff. Still, her interviews have not been very satisfying. She has decided to seek the help of a former instructor who has helped her in the past. Professor Doris Kleets and Cindy meet in the professor's office. Cindy explains that none of the interviewers have seemed very impressed with her, even though her credentials have initially interested them. Part of their subsequent conversation goes like this:

Cindy: Professor Kleets, I don't know what else to say. It's like, well, I . . . umm . . . you know, a thing like this is hard to . . well, you know, handle.
Prof.: Cindy, maybe you can explain in more detail what sorts of things they have said to you.
Cindy: Well, you know, it's like that . . uh, sorta . . . well, most of them have said that the . . . uh . . . job or whatever . . . kinda means that I would, you know, need to work with their . . . uh . . . clients or whatever. And, like wow, that's what I . . . uh . . . really sorta want to do, you know, as my job. So it's like I can't see, er . . . you know, what the problem is.
Prof.: Well, Cindy your academic record is excellent, so I don't think that's the problem. But, the interview is a special situation. These people want to see what YOU are like. They have a set of papers in front of them, but their clients will never see the record: they will see—and hear—YOU.
Cindy: Are you trying to say that there's something wrong with me?
Prof.: Not exactly, Cindy, but I have a good way of showing you what I mean. Let's continue talking, but let me tape record us—okay?
Cindy: Well, . . . I don't know . . . I will if it'll help.

At this point, the conversation continues along the same lines. After a few minutes, Professor Kleets plays back the recording to Cindy.

Cindy: Do I really sound like that, you know, I . . . uh . . . Wait a minute! I'm doing it again!

Prof.: Do you remember in the basic communication class when we talked about nonverbal communication? We discussed filled pauses—the "ers," "uhs," and other "garbage" phrases that people put into their speech.

Cindy: And that's . . . uh . . . what I'm doing, you know . . . Wait! I'm doing it again, right?

Prof.: I'm afraid you are. Nearly everyone will use those sorts of things sometimes. But they can become a problem when the habit of using them becomes a noticeable thing. The people who know you and like you may not even notice you doing it. But what about the interviewers? They hear you for the first time—just as their clients will. At a time when people are concerned that graduates can't read, write—and speak—well, the interviewers are going to be even more conscious of how you say what you say.

Cindy: I don't sound very pleasant—I never thought about it, you know, before . . . There! I did it again.

Prof.: Don't be too hard on yourself. You have certain habits, but now you are beginning to be conscious of them. That's the first step. You have needed to analyze your nonverbal communication. You know that people may attach meaning to how you speak. They may think you are withdrawn, or that you lack confidence, or that you simply are not pleasant for people to listen to. They may be right in this judgment or they may be wrong, but they can make that kind of judgment. But habits that are learned can be unlearned. After you become aware of bad nonverbal habits, you can begin to change them, so that you *sound* like the pleasant, confident person that I know you *are*.

You should remember, just as Cindy was learning, that nonverbal analysis can be a means of mediating the particular intrapersonal conflict between who you are (or sound like) and who you want to be.

Case study two: how to win friends. Phil is beginning to think that no one likes him. He seems to have no trouble meeting people—in fact, that is very easy for him. What is more difficult is to become more friendly with the people he meets. He has many acquaintances, but no close friends. Phil is so concerned about the problem that he has begun reading books on how to better influence people. In one particular new book, the author suggests that friendly handshakes and big smiles are keys to friendship. No problem here: he always has a big smile and a handshake or a pat on the back. At another point, the author suggests that eye contact is important and that getting close to someone may help that person feel liked and secure. Again, no problem here. In fact, Phil says to himself, I do those things more than anybody I know. As a matter of fact, I do all those things all the time . . .

Phil begins to remember some of the reactions to his "good" nonverbal behavior. HE is the one who always moves closer; HE is the one who always has the handshake, the pat on the back, or the touch on the elbow; HE is the one with the big smile and the loud "How are you?" Maybe, he thinks, I have gone too far.

And, indeed, Phil probably has. While people may attach favorable meanings to handshakes and so forth, the loud "hello" and the touching and the closeness and the rest may seem exaggerated. If those nonverbal behaviors are felt to be inappropriate, the behavior may be considered aggressive and pushy.

Phil's nonverbal mannerisms may explain part of his inability to establish close friendships. Once he realizes this, he can begin to make his nonverbal symbols work for him, instead of against him. That is, he can begin to use nonverbal self-analysis as a means of mediating intrapersonal conflicts. He will not have to question his ability to win friends—and as he helps his own image of himself, he will help his relationships with others.

Case study three: you. Just as the people in the other cases confronted their own problems, you can confront yours. Take time to analyze your own nonverbal communication. Are there meanings that you attach to your own symbol use which are uncomfortable for you? You know something about nonverbal symbols, so use that information to develop your skills in nonverbal self-analysis. Analyze yourself, evaluate your nonverbal symbol use, and modify aspects of your own nonverbal communication.

There are no magical cures for intrapersonal conflicts. Yet, nonverbal self-analysis can help you with some of your problems. If the case studies made sense to you, it is because you are learning to think of nonverbal analysis as a strategy for mediation.

EXERCISES

Assume that you are a casting director for a television production. You have several bit parts for which you must find actors and actresses. Each character has only one or two lines, but the audience must "believe" the actors. For each of the roles below, describe what YOU would look for in personal appearance, vocal qualities, and mannerisms.

1. the "hanging judge"
2. the cowboy
3. the saloon keeper
4. the mayor
5. the dance hall girl

Research done by Joseph Turow indicates that the casting of bit parts is a matter of stereotyping the nonverbal aspects of the characters. The mayor, for example, must *look, sound,* and *act* like a mayor even though he or she may have few lines. The nonverbal communication of the characters is vital.

Analyze the appearance, the vocal qualities, and the mannerisms you have specified for the bit parts. How have your descriptions differed or been the same as the rest of the class?

Now, discuss how easy it was to conjure up the stereotyped characters. Do you see how important nonverbal communication is in our perceptions of others? Do you see how easy it is to stereotype the nonverbal symbols of others?

Now, explain the problem of your own nonverbal communication. Do you ignore or pay attention to your use of nonverbal symbols? Do you see that nonverbal symbol use can be changed—and that intrapersonal conflicts can be mediated?

NOTES

[1] Some of the labels here, including *chronemics, oculesics, haptics,* and *objectics* are borrowed from James C. McCroskey, *Introduction to Rhetorical Communication,* 2nd ed. (Englewood Cliffs, N.J.: Prentice-Hall, 1972), chap. 6. The other labels have developed over years of research by various scholars.

[2] The estimate is made by R. L. Birdwhistell. For a discussion, see Mark L. Knapp, *Nonverbal Communication in Human Interaction* (New York: Holt, Rinehart and Winston, 1972), p. 12.

[3] The scattered research here simply supports the commonsense belief which we shall discuss more in the next section.

[4] The following division of functions is based mainly on Paul Ekman and W. V. Friesen, "The Repertoire of Nonverbal Behavior: Categories, Origins, Usage, and Coding," *Semiotica* 1 (1969), 49–98.

[5] Gordon Hewes, "The Anthropology of Posture," *Scientific American,* 196 (1957), 123–32.

[6] See A. Mehrabian, "Significance of Posture and Positions in the Communication of Attitude and Status Relationships," *Psychology Bulletin,* 71 (1969), 359–72; and M. Reece and R. Whitman, "Expressive Movements, Warmth, and Verbal Reinforcement," *Journal of Abnormal and Social Psychology,* 64 (1962), 234–36.

[7] Paul Ekman, "Differential Communication of Affect by Head and Body Cues," *Journal of Personality and Social Psychology,* 2 (1965), 726–35.

[8] Ekman and Friesen, "Repertoire of Nonverbal Behavior," 49–98. Further clarification of those categories is found in Knapp, *Nonverbal Communication,* pp. 5–6.

[9] G. L. Thomas, "Effect of Oral Style of Intelligibility of Speech," *Speech Monographs,* 23 (March 1956), 46–54; P. W. Gauger, "The Effect of Gesture and Presence or Absence of the Speaker on the Listening Comprehension of Eleventh and Twelfth Grade High School Pupils," doctoral dissertation, University of Wisconsin, 1951, abstract in *Speech Monographs,* 19 (June 1952), 116–17; and W. T. Heron and E. W. Ziebarth, "A Preliminary Experimental Comparison of Radio and Classroom Lectures," *Speech Monographs,* 13 (March 1946), 54–57.

[10] Ray Ehrensberger, "An Experimental Study of the Relative Effectiveness of Certain Forms of Emphasis in Public Speaking," *Speech Monographs,* 12 (1945), 94–111.

[11] H. Rosenfeld, "Instrumental Affiliative Functions of Facial and Gestural Expressions," *Journal of Personality and Social Psychology,* 4 (1966), 65–72.

[12] See, for example, N. L. Munn, "The Effect of the Knowledge of the Situation upon Judgment of Emotion from Facial Expressions," *Journal of Abnormal and Social Psychology,* 35 (1940), 324–38.

[13] A "protection of territory" is another way of phrasing the same concept.

[14] An interesting discussion is found in McCroskey, *Rhetorical Communication,* pp. 116–18.

[15] Mark L. Knapp, "The Field of Nonverbal Communication," *On Speech Communication,* ed. Charles J. Stewart (New York: Holt, Rinehart and Winston, 1972), p. 70.

[16] Ibid.

[17] Knapp, "Field of Nonverbal Communication," p. 71.

[18] David Addington, "The Relationship of Selected Vocal Characteristics to Personality Perception," *Speech Monographs,* 35 (Nov. 1968), 491–503.

[19] Frieda Goldman-Eisler, "A Comparative Study of Two Hesitation Phenomena," *Language and Speech,* 4 (January–March 1961), 18–26.

[20] H. Maclay and C. E. Osgood, "Hesitation Phenomena in Spontaneous English Speech," *Word*, 15 (1959), 19.

[21] Abner M. Eisenberg and Ralph R. Smith, Jr., *Nonverbal Communication* (Indianapolis: Bobbs-Merrill, 1971), p. 105.

[22] R. Hoult, "Experimental Measurement of Clothing as a Factor in Some Social Ratings of Selected American Men," *American Sociological Review*, 19 (1954), 324–28.

7
INTRAPERSONAL DECISIONING

Decision making is a topic that has been discussed before. As an individual, you are called upon to make decisions about information acquisition, behavior, and value formation. In another sense, the whole notion of self-concept is based on making decisions. Only you create the ideas about you that we call the self-concept. You create the self-concept by decisions just as you make decisions about value or behavioral conflict. To understand that general process of decisioning or making decisions, you must understand something about *argumentation*.

THE NATURE OF ARGUMENTATION

For years, argumentation has been related to the idea of debate. Argumentation and debate occur in debating societies, interscholastic debating circuits, law courts, and political assemblies. Argumentation, however, is something that affects your life every day. As I shall use the term, *argumentation involves presenting and examining claims and reasons*.[1] To understand how you are involved in argumentation every day, I will discuss some major elements of argumentation.

In many ways the most important element in argumentation is the *claim: any statement which you present but which is questioned*.[2] You may say, "I am not athletic," and feel that your statement is absolutely true. Actually, of course, I or anyone else might *challenge* or question how true that statement is. In conflicts involving values, you may say, "My belief in the value of national security is in conflict with my belief in the value of international brotherhood." That again, is something that can be challenged by someone. These statements about your *self* and your values should be considered as claims. They should be treated as something you are prepared to believe, but something that may be questioned.

When you treat statements about yourself and your problems as claims, you can avoid thinking about your perceptions as being *right* or *wrong*. In human activity, claims are not so much right or wrong as they are *strongly supported* or *weakly supported*. You do not ask, "Is it true that I am wishy-washy?" Instead, you ask something like, "Do I have enough reason to believe that I am wishy-washy?" You begin to use a process that is best illustrated by the statue of *blind justice*.[3] In law, juries are supposed to weigh the evidence for two basic verdicts: guilty or not guilty. They look at all the information which supports or *weighs for* the guilty verdict. Then, they are supposed to look at the weight of information for the verdict of not guilty. They balance the two decisions and choose one rather than the other. In making decisions about yourself and your problems, you can use the same process. Treat each statement about your selves and your conflicts as claims. Then, weigh the support for the statement and the support against the statement. The process is not one in which you make the "right" decision. It is one in which you try to make the decision—and choose the claim—that has the best support. The result is not that you prove the statement about yourself, but rather, that you begin to believe the statement.

To believe a claim, though, means that you should have something to go on or some reason to believe as you do. *Evidence* is a second important argumentative term that is really *anything that supports a claim*. To present the claim that you are unathletic, you might offer as evidence that you failed to make the college basketball team, that you are not very tall, or that you have been told that you are unathletic. Such things may support the claim about your lack of athletic ability, but they do not prove the claim. Evidence, as we shall discuss later, may be a variety of things and do a variety of things; it does not, however, *prove* anything. Argumentation involves human judgments about things that are important; it does not deal with absolute facts or truth. I might present evidence against your claim. I might point out that you are good at badminton, golf, or bowling. These might not show that you are a super athlete, but they might give me reason to reject your claim.

To further argue your claim, I might ask, "What does height, or ability in basketball, or what someone says have to do with your athletic ability?" In essence, I ask you for a *warrant: the connection between the evidence and the claim*. It might seem obvious to you that athletic ability and ability in basketball are the same thing. I disagree. I say that your evidence might support a claim that you lack ability in basketball—but certainly not the claim that you are unathletic. I reject your warrant, saying that there is no connection between basketball ability specifically and athletic ability generally.

On the basis of this hypothetical discussion, I must point out that, in making a claim, you must be careful to use *qualifiers: words or numbers which express how confident you are in your claim.* Since no claim is ever absolutely true, we use such qualifiers as *probably, possibly, sometimes,* or *maybe.* Or we may express ourselves as being 80 percent certain of something or other. The qualifier is not a way of copping out; instead, it is a way of being honest about how sure we are of a claim.

Another way of making a claim more realistic is by using a *reservation: a word or phrase that shows there are some exceptions to a claim we wish to make.* Earlier, you might have said, "Except for badminton, bowling, and golf, I am unathletic." Or, using a different reservation, you might have said, "Unless we count such things as badminton, bowling, and golf, I am unathletic." Your using a reservation would have helped me to understand what you were trying to say. In addition, it would have helped you understand what it was you were trying to say.

DECISIONS, ARGUMENTATION, AND INTRAPERSONAL CONFLICTS

Making intrapersonal decisions can be easier if you apply strategies of argumentation. Keep the following procedures in mind.

First, express your conflict or problem as a statement. You may want to even put the statement in writing. Writing the statement can have the effect of forcing you to be highly specific about what you need to mediate. Your statement may look something like one of these:

1. I am much less industrious than I would like.
2. I am afraid I am too pushy with other people.
3. I don't know whether I should cut class on Friday or not.
4. I don't know how the theory of evolution affects my religious belief that God created man and woman, not apes who turned into man and woman.
5. I don't know which is more important: the right to life or the personal freedom to be allowed to die.

The task of writing the statement may be difficult. Yet, the benefits to be gained from the task are worth the trouble. You may find that, once you state the conflict, the problem does not seem so severe. If that is the case, the process of telling yourself specifically what the problem is may end the conflict. You have become the receiver of your own message and that, by itself, has mediated your problem. It is likely, however, that the conflict may still exist.

Second, label the kind of problem that confronts you. Statement number one is a conflict between the perceived self and the desired self. Number two is a conflict between the perceived self and the feared self. Number three refers to a decision about behavior; four relates to a decision about information processing; and five refers to a decision about conflicting values. Once you understand what sort of conflict you face, you will have some idea how difficult it might be. Conflicting values may be more difficult to mediate, simply because values are such basic views about the world. Certain kinds of behavior, such as cutting class, probably are not nearly as difficult because they are not as basic as values. You will find that the more information you have about the decision, the better you are able to try to mediate it.

Third, consider your statement to be a claim, instead of a fact or a truth. Make sure that you realize that your statement is your perception of something about you. Whatever your perception is, it is something that can be challenged. It is something that can be inaccurate. Do not be convinced, once-and-for-all, that you are pushy, lazy, or in danger of having to give up your religion.

Fourth, examine the evidence that supports your claim. What are those bits and pieces of information that make you believe the claim? What have you done? What have you said—or heard? What have you read? How have you inductively put those pieces of evidence together to form the perception? Have you selectively perceived something incorrectly? Have you forgotten some important things about you or the problem? Are you paying attention to only negative things? Finally, how strong do you think all these indications are? Do you really think that there is enough evidence to support the claim?

Fifth, examine the evidence that does not support the claim. You have already examined why you think there is some kind of conflict. Now, examine all the evidence against the claim that you have a conflict. For example, are there some parts of the theory of evolution that support your religious beliefs? Is there any way that your values of life and freedom may not conflict? Are there indications that you are industrious at times? Are there reasons why you definitely should go to class?

Sixth, ask yourself whether the evidence for and against the claim really relates to the claim. Look for a warrant. You recall that you hated a summer job you had once, but does that mean you are not industrious? You heard a minister argue that evolution and the Bible conflicted, but does that mean that they do? You know that you want to enjoy some time off from school, but does that mean that you have to cut class? You ought to have faith in the evidence only when you can explain to yourself how it relates to the claim. Any evidence that does not support or weigh against the claim should be disregarded.

Seventh, after looking at the claim and the evidence, ask yourself how sure you are about the original claim. Phrase a qualifier: "*Perhaps*, I am not industrious enough;" "*Maybe some* of my religious views ought to be changed because of information about evolution." Consider reservations: "*Unless I will have trouble making up the work*, I can cut class." If you do this, you will have some idea whether there are important exceptions to the claim. In short, you will know something about how sure you are of the claim.

Finally, weigh the evidence for and against the claim. Which is better supported: "I am industrious," or, "I am not industrious enough"? "I must change my religious views," "I should keep my views," or, "I should modify my views"? "I should cut class," or, "I should go to class"? "I am more committed to freedom than to the right to life," or, "I am more committed to the right to life than to freedom," or, "There really is no important conflict"?

The final decision is still yours. The whole process of making decisions about yourself and your conflicts is still intrapersonal. *You* still have to make the decisions. But the decisions may be important ones, and you should examine them with care. Knowledge of argumentation cannot solve all your intrapersonal problems. It can, however, provide a strategy for making decisions about intrapersonal conflicts.

To see even more clearly how such a process can be used as a means of mediation, examine the following case studies.

Case study one: green or black? John has just completed a class in basic communication. He has become more interested in the study of communication, so he plans to enroll in a more advanced class. He can enroll in the class taught by either of two professors, Dr. Green or Dr. Black. They both teach the same class, but Professor Green has the reputation of being "harder." They (whoever "they" are) say that Green demands more work, and grades more harshly. John is not afraid of work, but he wants no lower grade than is necessary. His decision must be made soon since registration time is approaching.

"What shall I do?" he asks himself. Then he remembers something about intrapersonal decisioning that he learned in the basic communication course. "Okay," he says, "let's see if any of this works."

"I've got two choices: I can enroll for Green *or* I can enroll for Black. Now that I've stated the problem, I am supposed to identify the kind of problem it is. That's easy. It's a behavioral conflict. Now, where is that book? . . . Okay, now, I treat each choice as a claim. All right. What is the evidence for enrolling in Green's class and what is the evidence against it? Oh, I see, 'I should enroll in Green's class' because I hear he is a good teacher and because he forces you to learn. Now, 'I should enroll in Black's class' because I hear he doesn't assign a lot of work, and because he grades easier."

"What next? See if the evidence really relates to the claim: is there a warrant or connection? I guess there is, since each of the reasons or evidence relates to what happens if I take the class. What about qualifiers and reservations? How about these: I probably should enroll in Green's class, unless I am concerned about higher grades ... That doesn't sound bad ... and, I should enroll in Black's class, unless I am concerned about really learning ... that makes it tougher. I am concerned about higher grades, but I'm also concerned about learning."

"Let's balance the evidence for and against the claim—that's easy because what supports Green is evidence against taking Black ... and the other way around. I guess it's really up to me about which is stronger: the need to learn from a better teacher at the risk of the lower grade, or the need for a chance at a better grade and less work at the risk of learning less ... uhm ... well, I guess I will just have to ... ."

Let us leave the case study at that point. I am far more interested in what you would do than what John would do. Remember that even if you follow the strategy closely, as John did, the decision lies with you.

Case study two: negatives and affirmative action. Ellen is quite excited about her first after-college job offer. She hurries to tell her roommate, Peg. Peg completely destroys Ellen's day by asking a simple question, "Did they have to offer the job to a woman?"

Ellen's reaction is one of hurt and anger. "I'm as good as any man I know. What makes you think I was offered the job because of affirmative action?" Her friend replies, "Hey, I'm sorry. I didn't mean anything by it. I was just asking. Listen, I'll see you later. I have to go to econ."

When Peg leaves, Ellen is much less happy than when she had entered the room. The job is a good one, but (she tells herself), "Peg thinks I may have gotten the job just because I am a woman. I might expect some chauvinistic male to ask that, but not another woman."

What Ellen faces is a conflict about information. She has been told that she is just what the company wants—but what does that mean, that she is a woman? She tries to fit this new idea into the rest of her thinking about the job offer. It doesn't fit with the rest of what she knows. She could become discouraged and bitter as a result of the conflict, but instead she tries to reason it out.

"Let's see, I was the most qualified person that they interviewed—that's what they said. I was hired, they said, because I had the right courses in school, because I had a good academic record, because I had had experience in a summer job that was related to this position—and because I can work well with people. Sounds like strong evidence to me: I was the best person for the job. Now, what is the evidence that I wasn't the best person for the job—that I was just a woman? Well, there isn't any that I know about—just Peg's question about affirmative action, and she doesn't even know if the man-woman ratio is out of balance. That's not evidence about this particular job or company at all! No, I'll show my credentials to anyone. I simply was the best person for the job—I feel certain of it; I don't have any reservations about saying that at all. Peg can believe anything that she wants to, but I'm going to be great in that job."

In leaving Ellen and her mediated problem, you may want to consider her process of making the decision about the information. Was anything left out, or ignored? Would you have come to the same conclusion if you had been Ellen? Why or why not?

Case study three: you. All of us face decisions about conflicts of values, self-concept, behavior, and information at one time or another. If you are currently experiencing such a conflict, use the steps suggested to learn the process of decisioning for mediating intrapersonal communication. As you approach your personal decisions using the suggested steps, this decisioning strategy can become second nature to you. You will begin to add it to your collection of communication tools.

EXERCISES

1. The following situations relate to choices you may have to make—if you have not already made them at some point. For each situation, state the conflict, identify what kind it is, and treat the statement as a claim. Look for evidence for and against the claim, look for warrants, qualifiers, and reservations. Then, weigh the evidence for and against the claim. The decision you make may be a better one because of the process.

   a) **Jack:** Hey, Alex, I found us a ride to Miami for the break, but it leaves in the middle of exam week.

   Alex: The good news and the bad news all in the same breath. You know I have finals up until the last day—I can't just cut out.

   Jack: Ah, you can talk to the profs. They'll let you take the exams early. This may be our last chance at transportation. C'mon, what do you say?

   Alex: Even if they would, they wouldn't do it because of a ride to Miami. Besides, I would have to cram all my studying into three days and I probably wouldn't do as well.

   Jack: Lie to them. Tell them your grandmother is sick. C'mon you'll do all right with the exams.

   Alex: ... well ... I don't know what to say ...

   b) **Harry:** Come and see my apartment.

   Joyce: I've about had it with you. I have never seen such an aggressive person. I just met you. You are the most boorish and forward person I ever saw—or I ever hope to see!

   Harry: All I did was ask if you wanted to see my apartment. No one's ever called me those names before—exactly. Maybe once ... no, twice. Well, it doesn't matter what you think. *I* don't think I'm like that. I think ...

   c) In 1978, some researchers made news in such media as the *New York Times* and "NBC News" by claiming that millions of Americans were "battered husbands"— men who are beaten by their wives. Some weeks after the release of the report, some among the same mass media were reporting that the research has had some serious problems: NBC's "Today" program, for instance, reported that the estimate of "millions of men" was based upon a study of only fifty-seven or so families. In addition, included in the men considered to be battered, were men who had been pushed, shoved, or hit "once or more" by their wives. The American people who saw or heard the initial reports and the later ones were faced with a problem of processing information. Which report, if either, was to be believed? What did you decide, or what would you have decided? What process could you use to help you?

2. All the discussion about intrapersonal decisions may still seem less than important to you. If that is the case, keep a diary or log of one day's activities. As you become aware of the dozens of intrapersonal decisions you must make, identify the types of conflicts, then consider how strategies of decisioning might help you every day.

NOTES

[1] This conception of argumentation is one developed by Richard E. Crable, *Argumentation as Communication: Reasoning with Receivers* (Columbus, Oh.: Charles E. Merrill, 1976), chap. 1.

[2] The major terms discussed here (*claims, evidence, warrants, qualifiers,* and *reservations*) are described more fully in Crable, *Argumentation as Communication,* chaps. 3 and 5. Those descriptions are based upon conversations with Professor Stephen Toulmin, of the University of Chicago's Committee on Social Thought, and his book *The Uses of Argument* (Cambridge, England: Cambridge Univ. Press, 1969), especially chap. 3.

[3] The discussion here is based upon material in Richard E. Crable, "Models of Argumentation and Judicial Judgment," *Journal of the American Forensic Association,* 12 (Winter 1976), 113–20.

PART 3

INTRODUCTION

Part 3 is a study of *interpersonal* conflicts and strategies. In Chapter 8, the focus is upon conflicts and communication between you and one other person. You will spend much of a typical day transacting with other people. These transactions can be fraught with all sorts of problems. You may experience differences in perceptions and problems in the relationship you have with another person. These problems can be termed *interpersonal conflicts*, the topic for Chapter 8.

In an interpersonal situation, you and the other person are affected by each other. In addition, each of you is affected by yet other people and other events, many of which are out of your immediate control. The interpersonal situation is complex partly because the two people are communicating with themselves as well as with each other. Consider Figure 3.1.

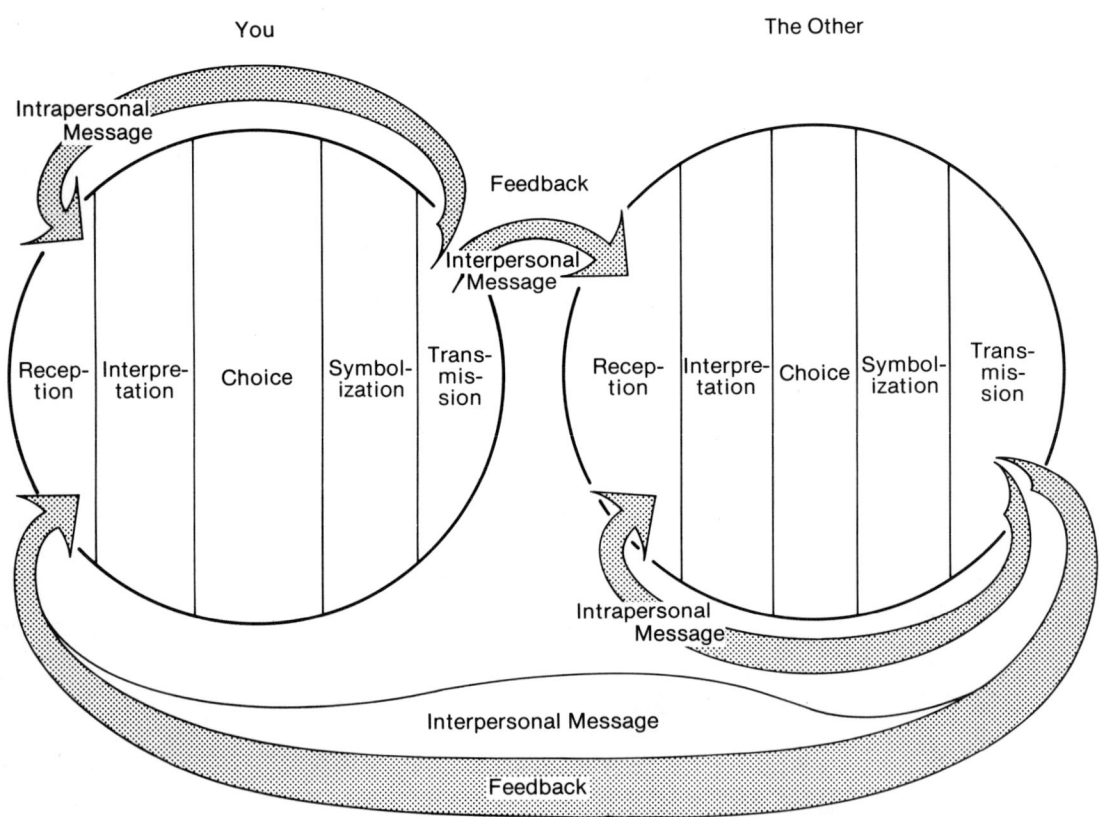

Fig.3.1 The Interpersonal Setting

Sometimes interpersonal conflicts can be mediated by some of the same strategies that we discussed in Chapters 4 through 7. "Applying What You Know in New Ways," following Chapter 8, will show the relevance of these strategies. Chapters 9, 10, and 11 will introduce other strategies of interpersonal mediation; listening, feedback, and interviewing.

Part 3 (Chapters 8 through 11) is designed to increase your understanding of interpersonal conflicts and how they may be mediated through communication strategies.

8
INTERPERSONAL CONFLICTS AS PROBLEMS

You and your friend Cathy are returning from a class in which you have taken an examination. At one point, Cathy shows you a "crib sheet" which she used during the exam. You stop and look at her. She says, "C'mon, don't look at me like that. I bet half the people there had one." "Well, I didn't . . . and I'm not very happy about you using one," you say. You continue the walk in silence.

An announcement has just been made at the company in which you work. It seems that Jack Parkins has just been named supervisor of your area. You and Jack have been working side by side for two years and he has become a good friend. Now, all of a sudden, he is your boss. Soon after you read the announcement, Jack approaches your desk. You congratulate him on the promotion and tell him how happy you are for him. But you feel that something has changed. You're not sure you can explain it even to yourself, much less to Jack.

Sandy and Dennis have been married for seven years and their one child is now enrolled in school. Sandy worked before she married Dennis, but since their marriage has been a housewife. Now, Sandy wants to get her former job back. Dennis, who has become accustomed to being the family breadwinner, objects. Dennis is disappointed in Sandy and Sandy is angry with Dennis.

These situations illustrate strained relations of very different kinds between two people. The conflicts, as well as the situations themselves, are related to interpersonal communication.

Interpersonal communication, as I shall use the term, refers to two people engaged in communication.[1] The addition of a second person does not mean that we cease to engage in intrapersonal communication. Rather, interpersonal communication means that we must be concerned with three sorts of communication at the same time. Person One is engaged in *intra*personal communication. So is Person Two. Yet, at the same time, each is communicating with the other. Intrapersonal conflicts and strategies are not things you can forget. You have to add to them the special concerns of two people communicating together.

This chapter is devoted to a discussion of four topics: conflicting perceptions of the other, conflicts in roles, conflicts in relationships, and conflicts in ethics. Your understanding of those topics will bring you closer to understanding interpersonal conflicts as problems.

CONFLICTING PERCEPTIONS OF THE OTHER

Just as you have perceptions of the "selves" who make you what you are, you have perceptions of any other single person. Sometimes the perceptions you have of the other person are not very important. The impressions you have of the clerk in the drugstore or the student down the hall may not be of much concern. At other times, the perceptions you have of the other person can be crucial. Your impressions of a co-worker, a family member, a lover, an instructor, or a roommate can affect some important part of your life. Parts of your life are *defined* by your transactions with such people.[2] Part of who *you* are depends upon who you think *they* are. Conflicts of perception that relate to these important others can be problems in at least two ways.

First, *interpersonal conflict can arise when your perceptions of another person's selves are in conflict.* In this way, your *intra*personal conflict can lead to *inter*personal conflict with the other. In any interpersonal situation, you might believe that you know the other person as he or she actually is: his or her *actual self.* Yet, your perceptions of the other person are simply perceptions. What you actually know is a *perceived other.* You perceive that important other person as not just a collection of chemical elements or physical dimensions, but as perhaps a creature of love, of selfishness, of intelligence, or of kindness. In addition, you probably have some goal for the other person. You probably have a perception of the *desired other.* You may wish that this other person were more loving, more aggressive, or more forgiving. Then, too, you may have a perception of the *feared other:* something that you do not wish the other person to become, or something you fear he or she is becoming. You may be afraid that your friend is becoming too cynical or too idealistic. You may be afraid that your boss is becoming too much of a "yes-person" for the company. Finally, you may have an impression of what this other person thinks you think of him or her: *perception of the other's perception.* You may sense that the other person thinks you are too critical of him or her. You may sense that the other person thinks you are jealous of him or her and his or her accomplishments.

Perceptions of the other do not have to be in conflict. You may feel that your cousin Tina is almost exactly the kind of person you wish her to be. At least, you may feel that she is not the kind of person you feared she might be. You may be satisfied that she knows accurately what you think of her. In situations like these—and they are frequent, I suspect—there may be no interpersonal conflict.

Unfortunately, though, you will find that conflicts between your perception and the self-perception of another do occur. Your fiancé becomes more like the person you feared he might become. You find that the boss you desired him or her to be is not the boss that you perceive. You may discover that the other person is misinterpreting your reactions to him or her. Any of these situations can lead to serious interpersonal conflict. At first, you may simply be disappointed in the other person. Your husband is more like the person your mother warned he would be than who *you* were sure he would be. Your instructor does not measure up to the ideal you had in your mind. In themselves, these are *intra*personal conflicts you experience, but in an important sense they can become *inter*personal conflicts. Over sometimes a very short period of time, your disappointment can lead to unhappiness. The unhappiness can lead to resentment. Resentment can lead to hostility, and hostility can lead to broken marriages, ended friendships, new roommates, or the need to look for a new job. Conflicts in your perceptions of the other's selves, then, can become serious interpersonal problems.

Perceptions can be related to interpersonal conflict in a second way. This second kind of conflict involves *the difference between how you perceive the person and how he or she perceives him- or herself.* In an earlier chapter, we noted that people create self-perceptions of their behavior, their values, their knowledge or grasp of information. They also create impressions of their *social selves*: their qualities of friendliness, trustworthiness, and popularity—just to mention a few. At the same time, you create perceptions of these same qualities or characteristics: you develop perceptions of your friend's behavior, your boss's values, or your employee's grasp of information. You create impressions about this other person's friendliness, trustworthiness, and popularity. The self-perceptions of these other important people may be compatible with your perceptions of them. If so, no problem exists. No interpersonal conflict results.

Yet your perceptions of anyone else's personal characteristics will not always be compatible with his or her self-perceptions. Surely you know someone who doesn't "know it all," even though he or she might think so. Certainly you have distrusted someone who felt that he or she was entirely trustworthy. If you are like most people, you probably have perceived that the boss is not nearly as friendly as he or she thinks. At other times, an instructor may use an obscene word. You may be shocked even though the instructor fails to see anything wrong with his or her behavior. You may have found that a close and seemingly open-minded friend is—like most of us—bigoted about something or other. These are times when others' self-perceptions come into conflict with your perceptions of them. These are times when perceptions can come into conflict in ways that are disturbing.

Perceptions of others, then, can become the source of interpersonal conflicts. The conflicts can be between the selves that you perceive in others. They can also be between others' self-perceptions and your perceptions of them. Whichever the case, you probably experience such conflicts in your interpersonal communication.

CONFLICTS OVER ROLES

While some interpersonal conflict occurs because of perception, other conflict occurs in relation to *interpersonal roles:* the *parts* that you and another play in your interpersonal situation. A role is always played in relation to someone else's role. The role of employee makes no sense without the role of employer. Wife makes no sense without husband, and *vice versa.* Teacher-student, friend-friend, lover-lover, parent-child, and counselor-client are all roles that make sense because of each other. The roles indicate a set of expectations or duties. The teacher is supposed to perform certain duties in relation to the student; the student role requires certain behaviors. Friends share certain expectations such as being sympathetic and keeping secrets or confidences.

Some of the expectations in role playing have to do with the *quality* of the role enactment: husbands are supposed to be faithful, employers are supposed to be fair, and teachers are supposed to be knowledgeable. A second set of expectations has to do with the formal or *organizational* nature of the role enactment: husbands and/or wives are expected to make money for the family; employers are supposed to pay their employees; and teachers are expected to be in charge of their classes. When both the qualitative and organizational expectations of roles are met, a feeling of compatibility may exist. When either qualitative or organizational expectations are not met, conflict can arise. Let us examine each situation.

At times, interpersonal roles are played well, in qualitative terms. Sometimes, however, interpersonal roles are not played well. At times, expectations are not met. The faithful husband who has an unfaithful wife can experience severe conflict. The friend who betrays a confidence should expect an angry response from the person who trusted him or her. The child who disobeys the order of a parent should expect a talking-to—or perhaps more. If you fail to read assignments and to submit papers, you should expect some kind of unfavorable response from the instructor. Not playing the interpersonal role well can lead to unfavorable reactions from the other person. The other person may be hurt, disappointed, crushed, insulted, unhappy, or angry. Whatever the reaction, the failure to fulfill interpersonal roles and expectations may mean a change in the relationship. The instructor may become more demanding. The husband may become constantly suspicious. Even the friend may become something less than a friend. These reactions to role failure might lead to even greater failures in role fulfillment. The student may become less enthusiastic, which might make the instructor more strict, which might make the student less enthusiastic, and so forth. The wife might become resentful and less faithful, which might result in further suspicion and the end of the marriage. The friend who betrayed the confidence might react to the angry reaction with his or her own angry reaction, and the friendship might end.

Nothing actually makes these increasingly serious reactions happen. More positive reactions can occur when expectations and roles are not fulfilled. The faithful husband and his unfaithful wife may set up new expectations which do not include being faithful. The student who has failed to complete assignments may suddenly be spurred toward better scholarship. The betraying friend may be extremely sorry and apologize, which may deepen the friendship. When you or the other person do not meet qualitative role expectations, compatibility is still possible.

I am convinced, though, that most role-playing failures can result in serious interpersonal problems. Most people seem to be more secure knowing what their roles are and what the roles of others are. There is comfort in being able to assume that expectations will almost always be fulfilled. When qualitative expectations are not met, we can experience interpersonal conflict.

In addition to having a qualitative dimension, *most interpersonal roles have an organizational dimension.* The organizational nature of the role refers, not to expectations about what someone should *be,* but to expectations of what he or she should *do.* As an individual in a modern society, you will be called upon to perform well in *organizational* terms. Role enactment, then, is partly organizational, or based upon the part you play in the organization.

The employee-employer relationship is in large part a matter of the organized nature of the roles. What would your role be as an engineer in a corporation, as an accountant in a company, or as a physician in a medical building? Jobs create certain expectations about what you are supposed to do for the organization. What (in *your* perception) is the boss supposed to do to help you with your tasks? What (in the *boss's* perception) is supposed to be done to help you? What is your responsibility in helping others in the organization? What are their perceptions of your task? If these perceptions of organizational roles are compatible, the situation is comfortable for everyone. Each person understands the expectations of the job and (presumably) tries to meet them. Not all situations are that compatible. Frequently, your perception of your own or someone else's role—the organizational dimension—conflicts with another person's perceptions. Who is supposed to do what? can become a major organizational problem. The problem is not totally a conflict of job roles. It is more a problem of perceived roles and expectations.

In a more intimate relationship such as marriage, conflicts of our perceptions of roles have become popular topics. The roles of husband and wife create different sorts of expectations for different perceivers. A wife can be perceived as a full partner, a housekeeper, cook and bottle-washer, a lover, a breadwinner, a child-rearer, and a variety of other things. A husband can be perceived as a full partner, a breadwinner, a housekeeper, a child-rearer, a lover, a cook and bottle-washer, and a variety of other things. The husband and wife roles can be defined in very different ways.

It is entirely possible for husband and wife to agree on each other's roles. The husband can be the breadwinner and the wife can be the maintainer of the home environment. The result can be a compatible situation. In addition, the wife can be the breadwinner and the husband can be the maintainer of the home. The result still can be compatibility. Or, the roles can be shared and a compatible situation can exist: In the Crable house, I am as likely to clean up the kitchen or bake cookies as Ann is to paint a room or help with a writing project. The point is that agreed-upon roles—whatever they are—are a source of marital compatibility.

Problems arise when perceptions of roles conflict and expectations are not met. The husband can reject his wife's desire to begin a career, and accuse her of neglecting her home commitments. The wife can reject the husband who wishes to become the homemaker and house maintainer. The husband who wishes his wife would begin a career may feel that his wife is not contributing to the family income. The wife may become angry with a husband who is "married" to his job. She may feel that he is failing to meet his family commitments. Many other situations are possible, but the point should be clear: The marriage can be seen as a small but important organization with certain roles and expectations. When the organizational roles of the members come into conflict, severe interpersonal problems occur.

Not all organizational roles remain the same over time. The parent-child relationship can be used as an example of how roles and expectations change through the years. If you recall how you have changed in relation to your parents, you can begin to understand the family as a dynamic organization. As a baby, of course, you were almost totally in the control of one or more parents or guardians.[3] In every aspect of your life, you played the role of subordinate. Your clothes, meals, playtimes, and sleep patterns were decided for you. As you grew older, you probably were allowed more and more freedom. Finally (after what may have seemed an eternity) you consider yourself an equal. You earn money, you choose your clothes and your friends, and you may have begun to live by yourself. Your role in the parent-child relationship has changed greatly. As you reach adulthood and middle age, you may suddenly realize that your role has changed even more significantly. You may now find yourself giving help, comfort, and advice to the same person or people who once gave help, comfort, and advice to you. Even later, you may find that your role has changed again. As your parents become more elderly, they may become entirely dependent upon your love and care. Your roles may become the exact opposites of what they were when you were a baby.

If the people involved understand these dramatic but slowly developing role changes, then the relationship between parent and child may remain compatible. Complete compatibility during the parent-child role changes, however, cannot be guaranteed. Preteens may be perceived by their parents as babies. Teenagers may still be perceived as children. Grown children may still be perceived as teenage dependents. The perceptions of both parents and children are important here. If a teenager wishes to be treated as a child and the parent wishes the same thing, no obvious conflict results.[4] Conflict can result if the parent wishes the child to grow up too quickly. Conflict can also occur if the teenager wishes to grow up more quickly than the parent thinks is wise. The factor that may lead to conflict is not whether the child *is* mature, but whether both parties *perceive* the same level of maturity.

The way you perceive your parents' role is also important. At forty years of age most people are not bordering on senility—even though the teenager might not agree. Most people of retirement age are mentally alert and capable. If the teenager perceives the parent to be incompetent and the parent does also, conflict does not necessarily occur; but, if perceptions of competence differ, conflict is likely. As perceptions of roles change, so do perceptions of expectations. When those roles and expectations somehow clash, interpersonal problems are likely to develop.

The employee-employer, husband-wife, and parent-child situations are not the only ones in which the organizational dimension of roles can come into conflict. Still, these examples should provide some understanding of such conflicts in roles. When perceptions of roles and expectations do not match, the situation may become one of interpersonal conflict. Role expectations—in either qualitative or organizational terms—can be a source of interpersonal problems.

CONFLICTS OVER RELATIONSHIPS

Not all interpersonal conflicts arise over problems caused by role expectations. Some conflicts have to do more with relationships: factors that describe the *kind of interaction* between people. We can begin to understand conflicts over relationships by learning how factors such as liking, distance, similarity, dominance, and climate affect interpersonal relationships.

Conflicts over liking and distance

The relationship between you and another person can be described in a variety of ways. Several years ago, Professor Wayne Brockriede summarized several factors that can be used to describe relationships. Among them are *liking* and *distance*.[5] How much you and someone else *like* one another is a way of defining your relationship. Sometimes liking is also referred to as *interpersonal attraction*.[6] Whichever term is used, the concerns are the same. Do you like another person? How strong is the liking or disliking? In other words, how intense is the attraction that one of you feels for another? When someone asks about your relationship with (say) John, you might say, "Well, we like one another very much—very much."

Another way of describing relationships is by the perception of *distance* between people. How close do you feel to another? Closeness, as Brockriede says, may be either interpersonally or socially defined.[7] The Romeo-Juliet relationship was one of interpersonal, not social, closeness since the lovers were of different social groups. Two multimillionaires might be socially close, but interpersonally distant. They may both belong to a particular social group, but not be close interpersonally.

Sometimes liking and distance do not correspond. In general, you probably feel *closer* to someone you *like*. That, however, is not always the case. You may actually *love* another person, but feel that he or she is socially "out of your class." You may be forced to share a *close social* relationship with someone you do *not like*. When you are describing the relationship you have with another, the factors of liking and distance may be interrelated.

Often, liking and distance do not conflict. If you and another person agree about the liking or distance that exists between you, the situation can be highly compatible. You may both agree that the relationship you have is best. You may both be satisfied with how much you like or dislike one another. Both of you may be satisfied with the social and interpersonal distance between you. But this kind of compatibility does not always occur. Surely, you have liked someone far more than he or she has liked you. Surely, you have wanted to get closer, either socially or interpersonally, to another person. Certainly, at one time or another, you have felt that you would rather have more social distance between you and the other. You may even have loved someone, but felt that they were too far "above" or "below" you socially. These situations are the kinds that lead to severe interpersonal conflicts. The problem is to mediate the conflicts in liking and distance.

Conflicts and similarity

Another way of describing interpersonal relationships introduces two other terms: *homophily*, which means interpersonal similarity, and *heterophily*, which means interpersonal differences.[8] No two people are completely different, or *heterophilous*. If you did not have some similarity with all other people, communication would be impossible. You would have no language, ideas, or actions that other people could understand. If, on the other hand, you were completely similar to another person, communication would be unnecessary. There would be nothing to communicate about. Each of you would already know everything that the other thought, felt, knew, and did.[9] In realistic situations, your relationships with other people can be labeled somewhere between complete heterophily and homophily.

When you interact with another person, the question is not, Are you similar or dissimilar? but rather, How similar and dissimilar are you? The question of *dissimilarity* is partly a matter of *observable* factors. An Iranian is likely to be different in important ways from his or her Swiss friend; a member of the Roman Catholic faith is likely to be somehow different from a member of the United Methodist church; a person of sixty-eight is obviously different in some ways from a person of thirty years of age; a male differs from a female in certain biological ways; and a Republican may well be different in some respects from a Democrat. In the same way, the question of *similarity* is partly a matter of *observable* factors. Two eastern businesspeople are likely to have more things in common than either would have with a small town druggist from the Midwest. These stereotypes, of course, should not be considered as facts; they are simply tendencies that we label as seeming to exist.

What is more important than the similarities or differences themselves is what happens because of them. Research suggests that you tend to communicate more with the people who are more nearly like you.[10] You may find yourself searching for a fraternity or a sorority of people like you. You may find that you move from one place of worship to another in search of those who share your religious biases. You may switch roommates, change friends, or form new romantic relationships in efforts to be near people like you. You should also expect to find that your communication with these similar people will be easier and more effective. Communication, as I mentioned earlier, deals with the re-creation of meaning; the more similar you are to another, the easier this re-creation of similar meaning should be. Finally, this more effective communication can lead to even more interpersonal similarity. The result of all this is a self-perpetuating circle: high levels of similarity can lead to better communication which can lead to more shared meanings and more similarity which can lead to better communication—and so on.

Sometimes, *perceptions* of similarities and differences are more important than *observable* factors. You may perceive that you are much more similar to someone else than you really are. You may feel dissimilar even to someone who was born in the same town, raised in the same neighborhood, and educated in the same schools. Once you go away to school or enter college, you may feel that you become more unlike your childhood friends. The people you felt were so similar to you are now perceived as dissimilar in important ways. The process can also work in reverse. You may have felt that you were different from someone at some earlier time. All of a sudden, the two of you begin to experience and share the same kinds of things. The person you once perceived as dissimilar may now be perceived as being very much like you.

Perceptions of similarity become more complicated when we consider both of the two people. If you and another person perceive yourselves as similar to one another, no problem exists. You can expect easier communication and probably increased similarity. But people do not always agree on perceptions of similarity. You may feel that you are very similar to another who may feel the opposite. Or, a friend may assume that the two of you are very much like one another, and you may not agree. The point is that perceptions of similarity can be as important as similarity in an observable sense. Just as interpersonal dissimilarity can lead to interpersonal conflict, *perceptions* of dissimilarity can be a source of interpersonal conflict. At times, you may want to change perceptions of interpersonal similarities and differences. In either case, your need is for mediation.

Conflicts and dominance

Another important way of defining relationships is by noting who is dominant, or *in charge*.[11] Dominance seems to be a natural factor in animal behavior. Animals such as deer will fight one another to determine who is leader. Certain animals will be dominant—and certain others will be *submissive:* they understand that they are within the control of the dominant animal. Chickens have an even more interesting sense of dominance and submission. When a flock is being formed, members will physically attack one another to determine who is dominant over whom. When the dominance issue has been established, it will be reinforced by dominant members pecking the heads of any chicken below them in "the pecking order." Later, reinforcement is conducted by a pecking *motion* by the dominant chicken, and a lowering or tilting of the head by the submissive one. In numerous groups of animals, dominance is an important way of defining relationships. People seem to be no exception.

Humans are concerned with the dominance-submission problem in various ways. In business organizations, the concern may be phrased in terms of budgets. It is a truism (which is probably not always accurate) that power is determined by the amount of money controlled. In marriages, the issue may be expressed in phrases such as, who "wears the pants" in the family. This expression is related to a concern for the role of head of the house. What seems to be the case is that people can become extremely concerned with "who is in charge."

In certain relationships that you experience, you may be dominant and the other person submissive. In others, you may be submissive and the other may be dominant. When the roles of dominance and submission are comfortable for each of the two people, the relationship is said to be *complementary:* the roles fit well with one another. The traditional student-instructor relationship is complementary. The student is comfortable with the position of being submissive, and the instructor is comfortable with the dominant position. No conflict exists in the relationship. Conflicts can occur, however, when one person or the other decides not to play the traditional role. The instructor who considers him- or herself as just a facilitator may create conflict if students want someone to be in charge. The student who decides that he or she is a complete equal to the instructor may create conflict if the instructor is not prepared for equality. The reversal of any established dominance-submission relationship can lead to interpersonal problems.

Sometimes, individuals simply *share* dominance. You and a friend or loved one can decide that there will be no truly dominant individual. This is called a symmetrical relationship. A symmetrical relationship can be comfortable and compatible, but it also can mean a continual fight for dominance. In national terms, the sharing of overlapping powers between congress and the president means that they will continually fight for power. In interpersonal terms, the sharing of dominance by two co-workers may easily lead to a battle for power. The kind of relationship which probably prompts less conflict than a symmetrical relationship is a *parallel* relationship. In parallel relationships, the dominant role shifts as situations or problems change. When your roommate and you are faced with a problem involving finances, you may be the dominant force in the solution. When the problem concerns dating, your roommate may have the solutions. With a shifting of dominance such as this, your interpersonal conflicts may be few.

In short, a complementary relationship means that one person is dominant and one is submissive; a symmetrical relationship means that there is an equality of dominance; and a parallel relationship means that there is a shifting of dominance in different situations. If you are comfortable with the relationship you have with another, no conflict may arise—no matter what sort of relationship it is.

The complementary relationship may not always be comfortable. You may find that you wish to have more of a parallel relationship with a parent: you would shift control in particular situations. You may decide that you really want to be the submissive member in a relationship where you are now an equal. You may feel that you want to be dominant in a situation where you are the submissive member. You may find a symmetrical relationship uncomfortable: you are tired of constantly competing for dominance. Whatever your relationship is with a second person, you probably perceive both good and bad features in it. When the conflict concerns how you feel about the dominance-submission issue, you may feel the need for interpersonal mediation.

Conflicts and climate

Factors such as power, liking, distance, similarity, and dominance can be used to describe your relationship with another person. Another factor is at least as important: interpersonal *climate*. Specifically, I am referring to how supportive or defensive your relationship is with another. Do you feel that a particular friend is "on your side"? Do you feel that he or she accepts you as you are and likes you despite your problems? If the answers are "yes," your relationship probably is supportive. Or, do you sense that he or she "gets in a cheap shot" whenever possible? Do you feel that he or she is overly critical of you and what you do? If the answers are "yes," your relationship probably is defensive. Jack Gibb has identified six sorts of behaviors that can lead to your feeling of *defensiveness*.[12]

Defensiveness can develop if your friend constantly tends to *evaluate:* to judge or to find fault with something. Everyone evaluates other people and their actions, but evaluation can become a habit. A problem can develop if your friend feels that he or she must judge your clothes, your social life, the way you talk, your academic major, your toothpaste, and your other friends. Instead of feeling your friend will be supportive of what you do, you may begin to dread his or her reaction. You *know* something will be wrong with whatever you have said or done. The result is defensiveness: you *get ready* for his or her next comment.

Two other factors leading to defensiveness are termed *superiority* and *control*. If your friend constantly feels that he or she is somehow above you, you may begin resenting this feeling of superiority. In addition, the person who feels superior may always take control: he or she will tell you what to do, when to do it, and how to do it. After all, the other person feels superior; for him or her to take control is a natural step. Your natural reaction to such behavior is defensiveness. The other does not (you feel) know it all, so why does he or she try to take control?

Two other factors that can create defensiveness are *certainty* and *strategy*. Some people, I am sure you know, feel that their opinion is always right—no matter what the topic is. Being near someone like that can prompt you to feel defensive: can't *you* be right at least sometimes? In addition, a person who is certain that he or she is correct (and wishes to take control) may have a *ready-made* plan for everything. He or she may discuss the problem you have, but the discussion is really unnecessary. The other person already has a plan or *strategy* worked out. He or she may even have a plan to get you to accept the strategy. You, on the other hand, probably prefer others to be *tentative* rather than certain in their opinions. In addition, you probably want them to be *spontaneous* in talking about your problems. You probably do not feel you need the friend's arguments for a strategy that he or she has already worked out.

A final factor that can create defensiveness is *neutrality*. If you were ever to appear as a defendant in court, you would want a neutral—unbiased—person as a judge. In sports you want neutral or impartial referees. In interpersonal relationships, however, you probably do not want neutrality. You want a friend who can *empathize* with you: someone who is biased *toward* you and your interests. People tend to establish relationships with people who understand and sympathize. Your friend's effort to be neutral and unbiased toward you is not what you need in a moment of crisis. You need someone on your side. The friend who is not can make you feel defensive. Your friend's attitude of neutrality might be enough to create interpersonal conflict. Neither you nor any single friend could behave in all these negative ways, but any one of these behaviors can lead to a defensive climate and interpersonal conflict.

One other point should be made which emphasizes the idea that conflict is a matter of perception. Extremes of behavior—even if you intend them to be supportive—can lead to defensiveness. Gibb's point is that constant evaluation, for example, can make the other person defensive. It also may be true that the friend who *never* gives you evaluative comments can create defensiveness.

When you want evaluative feedback, you may depend upon a friend to give it to you. His or her failure to provide the feedback you ask for can create conflict. We also discussed how strategy is seen by Gibb as less preferable than spontaneity. Yet, there are times when a friend can help by guiding you in a direction he or she has already planned: sometimes the best help can come from a prepared strategy. In short, you can avoid the behaviors that Gibb says create defensiveness, and still create conflict. Interpersonal climates of defensiveness or supportiveness are matters of perception. In the same way, conflicts in climates are matters of perception. Like all communication-related problems, easy and absolute solutions usually are not possible. Sometimes, even your attempt to avoid conflicts in climates can create conflicts in climates. Sometimes, the mediation of relationship problems is especially difficult.

CONFLICTS IN ETHICS

The final sort of interpersonal conflicts that we will discuss here are problems involving *ethics*: questions of what someone should or should not do. Ethics is a subject that seems only to concern human beings. When human beings kill lower animals or other human beings, they are always subject to the charge that what they do is unethical, if not illegal. True, it may be decided that they are not at fault because they kill in self-defense or as an unstable person. Yet, their action is always subject to question.[13] If the same killing were to be done by a stampeding horse, a rabid dog, or a frenzied chicken, no ethical charge would be made.

Humans are the animals which have superior intellect. Unlike lower animals, they always have *choices* of action. Animals are moved by physical drives, physical situations, or physiological problems such as disease. Lower animals do not *choose* to act; they *are moved* to do things by instinct or other factors. You and I are the only sort of animal that is held *responsible* for its behavior. Wild horses, dogs, and chickens may be killed for what they do, but they are never blamed for what they do. They are never held responsible. Humans are always subject to blame, even if they are sometimes not found responsible for unethical and illegal activity.

A major factor in human action is that people can be held responsible for anything they do. The reason for this is that human action is always subject to *interpretation*. A leaf falling from a tree has very limited interpretations; a bite from a rabid dog has probably only one interpretation. But what about humans? What, for example, about the soldier who runs from the battlefield? He could be fleeing in panic; he could be running for reinforcements; he could be trying to draw the gunfire of the enemy; he could be trying to circle around; he could be. . . . The problem of interpretation is obvious. What about the friend who betrays a confidence? Does he or she do it for the sake of gossip, to get help for you, to get information, or what? Is it the right thing to do? Is it ethical?

The question is difficult. In some senses, the betrayal is perhaps ethical: the friend is trying to help. In some senses, it is unethical: the friend is betraying a secret that he or she promised to keep. Whether the betrayal is ethical or not is a matter of what *you* mean by *ethical*. My belief is that there is no such thing as an ethical or an unethical act; there are only acts judged as ethical and unethical by some standard or yardstick for measuring ethics.[14] Interpersonal conflicts over ethics, it seems to me, arise from two sources: first, different ethical standards; and second, different applications of an ethical standard. Let us look at each as a source of interpersonal conflict.

Conflicts and ethical standards

Centuries of study in philosophy and ethics have created numerous ideas about what ethical behavior is. Instead of discussing these ideas in terms of philosophy, let us look at them in terms of how they may affect the perceptions you have of a friend. Think about a situation in which a friend did indeed betray a confidence. He or she told a mutual friend some intimate detail about you that was not "for publication." How *might* you evaluate the ethics of your friend?

You might first of all use an *abstract and absolute* standard of ethics that says that there are certain things that are simply wrong[15]—such as betraying a secret. If you used this abstract and absolute standard, you had to evaluate your friend's ethics unfavorably. He or she did violate the absolute standard against lying by telling a secret after promising not to. Second, though, you might use a standard known as *hedonism*: the right thing to do is the thing which gives pleasure to the individual.[16] Using this standard, you assumed that betraying the secret gave your friend some sort of pleasure. By that standard, he or she was blameless. A third possible standard is known as the *categorical imperative*: the right thing is the thing that you would wish that everyone did.[17] Is betraying a secret to a mutual friend something you would want everyone to do? If not, you probably judged your friend unfavorably. A fourth possible standard involves all sorts of *relative* things.[18] In *relation* to that particular *situation* (the existence of a mutual friend), was the act ethical? In *relation* to this point in *history*, was the act ethical? Does everyone do it? In *relation* to our *cultural norms*, was the act ethical? Has our culture always allowed the betrayal of secrets? You could have used the situation, the time in history, or the culture as yardsticks for the measurement of your friend's ethics by this relative standard. Finally, you can use *gamesmanship* as a way of judging the ethics of a friend.[19] Gamesmanship means that an action has certain rules that people are responsible for knowing. The cynic in you may believe that buying a used car is risky—regardless of what the dealer says. You know (or should know) that any used car is a used car; it is not as good as the day it was built. If you believe that it is, you are ignoring the rules of the game. In the same way, you know (or should know) that telling your secret was risky—regardless of the pledge of your friend. When you tell a secret, the gamesmanship standard suggests, you ought to expect that there is a good chance that the secret will be repeated. Have *you* never betrayed a secret? If *you* have betrayed one, how can you now blame a friend for doing the same thing? Those are the rules of the game, says the person using gamesmanship as an ethical standard.

Some of these standards will seem right to you and some will seem highly questionable. That is the nature of ethical standards. The point is that the ethical decisions that you make during the course of a day probably are based upon one or several of these standards. Interpersonal communication involves a second person, and that person also must make ethical decisions. A major source of interpersonal conflict is that you and this second person may find yourselves using very different ethical standards. You (guided by the absolute standard that one does not lie or betray a secret) asked that the secret be kept. Your friend (guided by the gamesmanship standard that the game of secret-telling involves secret-sharing) pledged secrecy. The secret was told and you were angry. Your friend, you said, was unethical. But that is not necessarily the case. Your friend may well have been ethical as judged by his or her standard, but unethical as judged by your standard. He or she was neither ethical nor unethical, but *both* when judged by both standards. That realization might not have helped you. You might have remained angry and perhaps come to dislike your friend. Conflicts over which ethical standards are being used are a major source of interpersonal conflict.

Conflicts and the application of ethical standards

The situation is only slightly better when the two of you are using the same ethical standard. Even the same ethical standard can be applied to a situation in different ways. In terms of the secret betrayal, both you and your friend may use the same abstract and absolute standard of ethics: lies should not be told and secrets should not be betrayed. Yet, your friend may be affected by another abstract and absolute standard: friends should be helped whenever possible. For your friend, those two instances of the same kind of standard may conflict. He or she can help you by getting advice from a mutual friend, but that means betraying your secret. He or she can keep the secret and not get help for someone he or she cares for—you. What should your friend do? Either action makes his or her conduct somehow unethical—even by supposedly absolute standards. The way the friend applies his or her standard, even if it is the same kind of standard that you use, may cause conflict. The application of standards of ethics can be a second major source of interpersonal conflict.

I hope that you have been struck by how complex an ethical problem can become. It is far too easy to say, "My friend was unethical." Such a statement only tells about part of the situation. Anything you or someone else does can be judged as ethical or unethical by the other person. The questions become: first, What ethical standard are you using? and, second, How has that standard been applied? Answering those questions may not solve the problems you have with someone else. But they do allow you to understand better the problem before you; they do help you identify the specific problem which needs mediation.

CHAPTER SUMMARY

When we discuss interpersonal problems, we do not forget about intrapersonal problems. We simply have to consider them both at the same time—just as you have to do every day of your life. We discussed how problems of perceiving the other person can be related to questions of your perception of their *selves*. In addition, when another person's self-perceptions are not compatible with your perception of them, the result may be interpersonal conflict. Our second main concern was conflicts in roles. Human situations mean that people play different interpersonal roles. Roles, in either qualitative or organizational terms, can be entirely compatible to you and others. They can also lead to interpersonal conflict. Relationships is a third area that can prompt interpersonal conflict. When your relationship with another is not like you wish it to be, you may want to mediate the situation. The problem in the relationship might be related to liking, distance, similarity or dissimilarity, dominance or submission, or interpersonal climates. Whatever the problem, you may perceive that it is severe enough to make you want to mediate it. Finally, we discussed ethics as a source of interpersonal conflict. Conflicts may arise over standards that are being used—or the application of those standards. In either case, the matter of ethics is a complex, but important, source of interpersonal conflict.

As I have said earlier, communication is not a miracle cure for all types and kinds of interpersonal problems. There are, however, certain communication strategies which can alleviate some of those problems; there are some skills and strategies which can help you mediate your interpersonal conflicts. Following this chapter is the first of several special features called "Applying What You Know in New Ways." You can use that section of the book to learn how to apply the strategies learned in Part 2 to the interpersonal situation. Chapters 9 through 11 discuss new strategies for mediating interpersonal conflict.

NOTES

[1] The term *interpersonal* is used in different ways by different writers. I am using the term as a synonym for *dyadic*, or two-person communication. Some writers use *interpersonal* to mean a fairly intimate and personal *kind* of communication—in contrast to communication that is impersonal, formal, and so forth.

[2] See Robert Monaghan, "Self-Concept: Through the Communication Looking Glass,"

Fundamentals of Communication, ed. Richard E. Crable and Richard O. Forsythe, with Steven L. Vibbert (Columbus, Oh.: Collegiate, 1977), pp. 53–58.

[3] Because of divorce, death, separation, adoption, and so forth, the number of people in the "parent" role, of course, will vary.

[4] The phrase "no obvious conflict" is used because even mutually satisfactory role-playing can lead to conflict years in the future.

[5] Wayne E. Brockriede, "Dimensions of the Concept of Rhetoric," *Quarterly Journal of Speech,* 54 (Feb. 1968), 2–4.

[6] See for example, James C. McCroskey, Carl E. Larson, and Mark L. Knapp, *An Introduction to Interpersonal Communication* (Englewood Cliffs, N.J.: Prentice-Hall, 1971), chap. 3.

[7] Brockriede, "Dimensions," 3–4.

[8] I will avoid the labels *homophilous* and *heterophilous* and use the commonsense terms *similarity* and *dissimilarity.*

[9] The idea that communication depends upon both similarity and dissimilarity is a major theme developed in Kenneth Burke, *A Rhetoric of Motives,* 2nd ed. (Berkeley: Univ. of California Press, 1969).

[10] For a more detailed description of the concepts here, see Michael Burgoon, Judee K. Heston, and James McCroskey, *Small Group Communication: A Functional Approach* (New York: Holt, Rinehart and Winston, 1974), chap. 7.

[11] See for example, Paul Watzlawick, Janet Helmick Beavin, and Don D. Jackson, *The Pragmatics of Human Communication* (New York: Norton, 1967). The terms used in this section *(complementary, symmetrical,* and *parallel)* are from the same source.

[12] Jack R. Gibb, "Defensive Communication," *Journal of Communication,* 11 (1961), 141–48.

[13] This perspective on ethics is based on various writings of Kenneth Burke; the ideas are developed in Richard E. Crable, "Ethical Codes, Accountability, and Argumentation," *Quarterly Journal of Speech,* (64) Feb. 1978, 23–32.

[14] The idea of standards is developed in Richard E. Crable, *Argumentation as Communication: Reasoning with Receivers* (Columbus, Oh.: Charles E. Merrill, 1976), chap. 8.

[15] The *codes* of the great religions are traditional sources of these standards (for example, the Ten Commandments). This standard and others mentioned here are explained more fully in Steven L. Vibbert, "A Descriptive Analysis of Ethical Justification," unpublished master's thesis, Purdue University, 1977, chap. 1.

[16] See Hunter Mead, *Types and Problems of Philosophy,* 3rd ed. (New York: Holt, Rinehart and Winston, 1959), pp. 274–83.

[17] See Neal Klausner and Paul Kuntz, *Philosophy: The Study of Alternative Beliefs* (New York: Macmillan, 1961), pp. 613–20.

[18] These *relativistic* standards are important, but less identifiable with particular philosophical systems.

[19] I was first made aware of the potential importance of this standard in a lecture by Wallace C. Fotheringham, Professor Emeritus, The Ohio State University, in 1970.

APPLYING WHAT YOU KNOW IN NEW WAYS
(How to Apply Intrapersonal Strategies in Interpersonal Situations)

Communication strategies and skills can usually be applied in a variety of situations. Chapters 4, 5, 6, and 7 discussed strategies for *intra*personal mediation. Those strategies are also useful in *inter*personal situations.

Perceiving as an interpersonal strategy

To mediate interpersonal conflicts, you must understand the role of perception in the interpersonal situation. We have discussed the process of perception earlier. In applying strategies of perception in the interpersonal situation remember the following.

1. The perception you have of the other person and your relationship is, in fact, a perception.
2. Analyze what "parts" of the other or the relationship you have paid most attention to (perception is selective).
3. Analyze how you have put the parts of the perception together (perception is inductive).
4. Examine the context or contexts of the perception and the effect of it or them (perception is context-bound).
5. Analyze what may have motivated the perception (perception is motivated).
6. Understand your perception as a personal one; you have created it.
7. Adjust the perception you have of the other or the relationship if you find the earlier perception is unjustified (perception is active).

Use these strategies in the following case studies:

Case study a.   John came home from work. He walked in, patted John Jr. on the head, and smiled. "Just like his old man." he thought. John looked through the mail he had brought in with him. In the midst of the regular bills and junk mail, John found a letter saying he would be audited by the Internal Revenue Service. John, Jr. came over to his father to ask for a drink of water. John exploded, "Get your own drink! Can't you ever do anything for yourself? I swear, I've never seen anything like it. You're just like your mother."

If you had been there, how could you have helped John with his perception of his son?

Interpersonal conflicts as problems

Case study b. You consider yourself a decent sort of person—the kind who makes a mother proud. In one of your classes, your instructor, Mr. B., occasionally makes sly and suggestive remarks as he lectures. Whenever you have to talk individually with him, all you can think of are his sexual allusions and innuendos. The relationship is becoming very difficult for you. How might strategies related to perception help your situation?

Verbal analysis as an interpersonal strategy

Earlier we discussed strategies of verbal self-analysis. Those same strategies can be applied in the interpersonal situation if you:

1. Don't confuse the words you use to describe a person with the person him- or herself.
2. Remember that words are simply labels.
3. Decide whether you have good reasons for the labels.
4. Remember that the language a person uses does not prove what kind of person he or she is.
5. Analyze the abstraction level of any language that seems to be a problem.
6. Use perceptual skills to avoid stereotyping, or to discourage stereotyping in others.
7. Remember that language use is behavior; it can be adjusted.

Study the following cases to learn more about verbal analysis in the interpersonal situation:

Case study c. Mary and Fred have been having a disagreement. At one point, Fred says, "I don't think you should take such a strong stand on something you are ignorant about."

Mary: Now I'm ignorant, huh?
Fred: I didn't mean you were ignorant. I just . . .
Mary: Well, that's what you said.
Fred: You just don't know anything . . .
Mary: Now, I don't know anything. Good. I'm not ignorant; I just don't know anything.
Fred: Listen . . . oh, what's the use?

How might either Fred or Mary (or both) benefit from a verbal analysis of their conflict?

Case study d. Reread case study B about the instructor's language. How might a verbal analysis by either you or the instructor help mediate the situation?

Nonverbal analysis as an interpersonal strategy

In applying nonverbal analysis to the interpersonal situation, you can:

1. Remember that nonverbal symbols can mean different things to different people.
2. Isolate the nonverbal cues that seem troublesome.
3. Determine the meanings you attach to the nonverbal cues of the other person.
4. Try to discover the meanings that the other person attaches to any of your nonverbal cues that seem troublesome.
5. Compare those meanings to commonly interpreted meanings of such nonverbal cues.
6. Adjust nonverbal cues that are troublesome, or suggest changes in the nonverbal cues of the other person.

Examine the following cases to see if nonverbal analysis might help mediate the interpersonal conflict:

Case study e. You are about to take a female friend you have been dating home to meet your parents. Through your letters, your parents know something about Lisa. You have told them she is pretty, kind, and personable. She is a good student and works evenings at a local restaurant. As Lisa opens the door of her apartment, she says she is ready to meet "the folks." You don't know what to say. She is dressed in a tight, low-cut, red dress—obviously braless. You tell her that you cannot take her to your parents' home dressed like that—and you have a fight with her.

How could both you and Lisa have benefited from using nonverbal analysis to mediate the situation?

Case study f. Select one of television's situation comedies and watch it one evening. Notice how characters match the verbal messages of the scripts with certain nonverbal characteristics. Note how comedy effects are sometimes created when the characters make their verbal and nonverbal messages contradict one another.

Now, think about Morris. Morris is the guy with the smoothest line in town. He explains that his success with the opposite sex is because he knows how to talk to girls. What you may discover is that Morris' compliments and "sweet nothings" are accompanied by a sarcastic smirk. Perhaps all of us have behaved like Morris at one time or another. How can the study of nonverbal analysis help Morris—and the rest of us?

Argumentation and decisioning as interpersonal strategies

Strategies of argumentation may also help you mediate interpersonal conflicts. In Chapter 8 conflict over roles and expectations was discussed. What happens when a wife says, "You have got to quit living for your company! You have to give some of your time to your family." And a husband replies, "My time! You're the one who's married to her job!" At least two very different things can happen.

First, the situation can become nothing more than a *quarrel*. A quarrel, unlike argumentation, stresses little more than claims: "You're married to your job." "No. You are." "Hah! You don't spend any time with the kids." "Me? You don't spend as much time as I do." In a quarrel, two people are more concerned about shouting claims than they are about providing *evidence*. Note how easy it is to "argue" without having any evidence for either claim. That is not argumentation, as far as I am concerned; that is quarreling.[1] The second basic distinction between argumentation and quarreling is that neither party is willing to lose, or to give in. They each believe that the situation is *I win-you lose*. Each wants to win, regardless of how it is accomplished. The result is that, in quarreling, there is little hope for any progress. Claims will be thrown back and forth, but nothing will be settled.

The situation of interpersonal conflict does not have to end in quarreling, yelling, and shouting. The situation could become the setting for argumentation. In order to use argumentative/decisioning strategies for mediation in the interpersonal situation, you can:

1. Have each person phrase the conflict in words (for example, "You spend too much money." "I don't spend too much money.")
2. Treat each statement as a claim (a challenged statement that needs support or evidence).
3. Examine the evidence for each claim. How much evidence is there? How strong is it?
4. See if there are exceptions to the claim and phrase them as reservations.
5. Consider how confident each person is about his or her individual claim and create a qualifier.
6. Restate the claim (with reservations and qualifiers).
7. "Weigh" the evidence; see which claim is better supported.
8. Try to agree on which claim is better supported—or at least state where the new disagreement lies.
9. If necessary, begin the process again, using sides of the new disagreement as claims to be examined.

This may seem to you to be an elaborate process, but that is one of the reasons it can work. When you and the other person try to settle your conflict together through strategies of argumentation, you are less likely simply to quarrel. You and the other person become concerned, not with who wins, but with which claim really has the best support. You both begin to realize that the process is one that you can both win. You both win to the extent that you make a joint agreement on the strength of the claim. You make a joint decision which strengthens rather than weakens the relationship. You take upon yourselves the roles of mediators and you make a decision.

The strategy discussed is somewhat idealistic. Both people must agree that their relationship is important. Both must agree that the goal is to mediate the conflict—not prove that one or the other is wrong. Not everyone is capable of making those kinds of agreements, but *your* constant efforts to examine evidence for claims can help both of you avoid a quarrel. *Your* use of argumentative strategies of problem solving can aid your attempts at interpersonal mediation.

As practice in using argumentation for mediation of interpersonal conflict, consider the following cases.

Case study g.   A student and an instructor have been discussing the student's grade on a recent essay test. After about five minutes, the following exchange occurs:

Student: I still don't understand the grade.

Teacher: Well, I have told you how I graded the essays. Now, your essays simply were not as strong as I would have liked.

Student: I thought they were pretty good.

Teacher: Well, I guess I don't agree with you.

Student: What was wrong with them? I deserved a better grade than that.

Teacher: They were not nearly as good as some of the other essays.

Student: But I saw some of my friends' papers and mine was . . .

At this point you probably have the feeling that the situation is going nowhere, except toward becoming a quarrel. What is it that makes it appear to be a quarrel? How might the use of strategies of argumentation have helped one or both of them make the situation better?

Case study h.

Thelma: It's going to be a nice day today—the weather forecaster says so.

Joyce: Well, it may be a nice day—but I know that by looking at the sky, not listening to the weather forecast. Those things are never right.

Thelma: I swear, you'll argue about anything. It *is* going to be a nice day, and I'm going shopping. I was going to ask you to go along, but now I'm not so sure I want to.

Joyce: All I said was . . .

Thelma: I heard you. Look, I'll see you later.

There are times and places for argumentation, and this may not have been one of these times. Thelma considered the weather forecast as evidence, but Joyce reacted to that (rather than the "nice day") as a claim. Neither one seemed to understand what the other was saying. How might both have been helped by argumentation before the casual remark became a major issue?

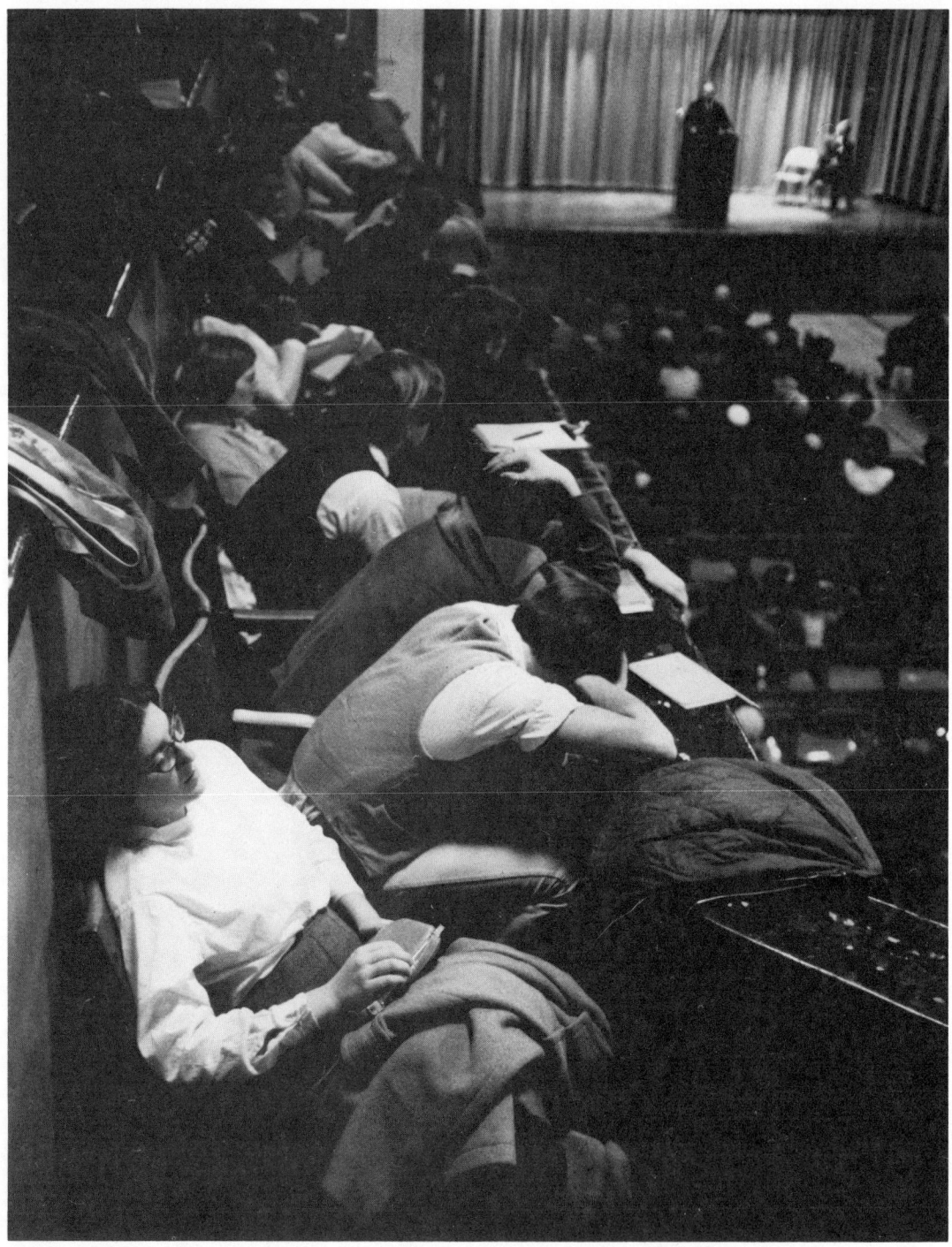

9
LISTENING AS AN INTERPERSONAL STRATEGY

Ralph is a teenage high school student. He is relaxing in his room with a blaring stereo, his friend Larry, and the latest edition of *Playboy* magazine. His mother enters the room and asks him to go to the corner store and get milk and bread. He says he will and continues reading. In loud tones, his mother asks him again to go to the store. No response. She shouts, "Turn that record off and listen to me! Are you deaf?"

You have been up late studying for a sociology final. The next morning, you sit in a management class and the instructor sounds very far away. You try to pay attention, but your mind keeps moving toward the sociology examination. Suddenly you hear your name. The instructor has just asked you a question about theory Y, but what was the exact question?

You go to your academic counselor. You are trying to find out if the classes you are taking seem the best for your occupational goals. The counselor is friendly and competent, and assures you that you are an intelligent, personable person and that you will have no trouble getting a job. You thank him or her and return to your apartment where you had been reading about the high rate of unemployment. You are not satisfied with the earlier discussion.

Most of us think we listen well. Research, however, suggests that few of us truly listen thoroughly and effectively. In the situations above, listening problems could lead to serious interpersonal problems.

I suspect that you already know the importance of listening in communication. Actually, you probably spend far more time during an average day listening than you do speaking.[1] You listen to messages from a variety of other people. You have been listening to messages all your life, but there are still some factors which should be discussed.

First, listening is a special sort of communication activity. Listening does not simply mean the ability to hear. The parent who screams, "You are not listening to me!" illustrates the point. When the children do not obey, the problem is probably not one of hearing. I once knew a father who constantly yelled at his three children. The children could obviously hear him, but they were not listening—and, it seemed to me, the more he screamed the less they listened. Increased volume will not improve listening, unless it is used to gain attention.

Hearing and listening are two very different things. The hearing process really involves primarily *reception*. That is why you can be near someone without knowing what he or she has just said. That is why you can be listening but not even know you are: "Did you hear that commercial?" "No, what did it say?" "It said that that car gets thirty-five miles to a gallon . . ." "Oh yeah, I guess I did hear that." Listening, on the other hand, involves the processes of reception, interpretation, and perhaps choice.[2] As you hear, you receive stimuli; but as you listen, you attach meaning to the stimuli and perhaps make some sort of choice. The child who continues to misbehave probably has received the voice as a stimulus. He or she either has not attached any significance to the words, has attached some undesired meaning, or has decided to disobey.

Listening problems can be a source of many interpersonal problems. Part of the reason you may have a conflicting relationship with another person is that you are not really listening. You may be misperceiving a friend's verbal messages. You may be listening, but only to certain things that are being said. There are several relationships between listening problems and interpersonal conflicts that should be discussed.[3]

LISTENING/INTERPERSONAL PROBLEMS

First, you simply may be *physically unable* to listen well. One of the reasons you may experience conflict with an instructor is that the two of you only interact during an early morning class. At eight o'clock in the morning, you may be hungry, tired, and sleepy. Those are not conditions that improve your listening, or your perception of the other person. You may see your roommate most often in the morning when you are rushing to class and when you are tired at the end of the day. The only other times when you interact may be when you are trying to study late into the evening. Again, those conditions will not help your interaction. You may interact with an employer only after classes, when both he or she and you are tired. Being physically unable to pay attention can be a source of communication *interference*. Specifically, it can result in listening and interpersonal problems.

A second listening problem is being *emotionally unable* to listen. When you are angry, upset, or frustrated, you will find it difficult to concentrate on the person before you. Instead of carefully attaching meaning to what is being said, you may be thinking primarily of your own feelings. Emotional, as well as physical, factors can make you a poor listener.

A third listening difficulty can be explained as *lack of interest*. A wife may not really be concerned about a husband's success in tennis, or his problems at work. A husband may not be interested in his wife's job accomplishments. A student may not be interested in the instructor's research. An instructor may not be interested in the student's campus activities. Some people can fake listening. When I was a student, on more than one occasion I had difficulty being interested in class, so I would pretend. I would furrow my eyebrows, nod appropriately, and jot things down: even if only x's and o's. The problem, of course, is that usually listening is not faked well. When the speaker feels that you are hearing but not listening, problems can occur. The other person may take your lack of interest in what is being discussed as lack of interest in him or her. That response can lead the other to perceive that you feel yourself superior. He or she might perceive that you dislike or feel interpersonally distant from him or her.

Even when you are interested in the subject, you may experience a fourth problem: *not being able to follow the conversation*. If your friend is scientifically oriented and you are not, you may get lost in the conversation. Your friend may be more religious than you, and you may have difficulty following the discussion. If a friend uses vocabulary that is unknown to you for any reason, you may lose track of what is being said. Any of these problems can be serious. They may cause you to miss the point or to misperceive your friend, and problems in perception can lead to interpersonal conflicts.

At times, people not only follow the conversation, but get ahead of it. *Going ahead of the conversation* is a fifth kind of listening problem. If Jane and you are very close, you may think you know what she will say before she says it. You might even help her by finishing sentences for her, or helping her select the right word. This kind of situation results from a constructive goal: you want to help and sympathize with your friend. The results are not always positive. You may fill in the wrong word or sentence ending. You may speed ahead by planning a response to what you think she is going to say. You may actually not be correct. She may be saying something else, which you miss because you are way ahead of her. One result is that you are not really listening to Jane; you are listening to you. Secondly, you may create interpersonal conflicts. You may misperceive her, and she may feel you are uninterested in listening to what she has to say.

A sixth listening problem is *being distracted* for some reason. Listening takes a great amount of concentration, yet you may find yourself looking at the clothes or makeup of the other person. You may find yourself being distracted by the sights or sounds around you: noise or interference in the channel. You may become hung up on a certain word or idea that is voiced by the friend. An obscene phrase or a mistake in grammar can become the focus of your attention. In any of these situations, listening suffers. Any of these situations can lead to misunderstandings and conflicts.

A final listening problem involves a listener *becoming quarrelsome* with the other person. We have already seen how almost any statement can be questioned or challenged. Almost anything can be a claim. The listener has the ability to question (verbally or nonverbally) *everything* that is said. If you as listener do challenge many of the things being said, your listening accuracy will decrease. You can spend so much time thinking about what is wrong with what has just been said that you miss what is about to be said. There is a place in interpersonal relationships for argumentation, but the constant and silent challenge of virtually everything is quarreling, not argumentation. Your constant challenging of the other person will have little chance for progress. Also, being quarrelsome verbally or nonverbally as you listen can create misunderstanding and conflict.

Listening problems are numerous and serious. They are not related to *hearing* as much as they are to the problems just discussed that affect how you attach meaning. You are not likely to listen well if you are physically or emotionally unable to listen, if you are disinterested or distracted, if you are quarrelsome, or if you are falling behind or going ahead of the conversation. Those are serious listening problems which can lead to serious interpersonal conflict.

STRATEGIES FOR LISTENING

Once you know how listening and interpersonal problems may be related, the major question remains: How should a person listen? The question is more difficult than it seems. There is no *right* way to listen. In different situations, you may need to listen in different ways. Listening should be done with a purpose in mind.[4] David W. Johnson has identified five general purposes or intentions in listening: listening to understand, to probe, to interpret, to support, and to evaluate.[5] To these we should add at least one more: listening to alter behavior or create change of some sort. Let us look at how each of these can become a strategy for interpersonal mediation.

The process of using listening as a strategy of mediation really involves three steps. *First, you should define the problem you are attacking.* Is it a problem with a relationship? If so, what elements of the relationship are you trying to mediate? Dominance? Similarity? Power? Distance? Is the problem one of your perceptions of the other person? In what way is the perception uncomfortable? What needs to be done, do you think? Is the problem one of conflicting interpretations—his or her self-concept and your concept of him or her? *Second, you must select the goal for your listening. Third, you must respond as a listener in ways that will help you achieve your goal of mediation.* We can use some of the problems named in step one as a way of explaining steps two and three.

Your problem may be that you and the other person have conflicting role expectations. Your fiancé has decided that he would like to be the houseperson. You might have no objection to that, but you are not aware of his reasons for wanting to do so. You probably should adopt a strategy of listening *to understand*. Before conflicts develop, you want to arrive at a mutually compatible decision on the future marital situation. You should use your knowledge of listening problems to avoid them: get physically and emotionally ready to listen. Avoid being quarrelsome with what he has to say and resist distractions. Follow what he has to say; do not get ahead of his thinking or fall behind. In addition, allow yourself to freely express your interest in hearing him. Your eye contact, your head movements, and your facial expressions can say a variety of things. At the extremes, nonverbal cues can say either "I love you and I want to understand," or "I love you, but this is all rather silly." Listening to understand involves more than choosing a goal (the second step). It also involves the third step of responding in ways that will let him know that your goal is to understand.

A different kind of problem occurs when a friend has done something that you find inexcusable. The friend does not seem to want to talk about it. Conflict may be avoided by your efforts *to probe*. Probing is the use of listening to discover hidden or unknown information. Probing your friend for information that will help you mediate the conflict can be difficult. Your probing listening response, however, can help you achieve your goal. An interested head nod may help your friend to discuss a difficult topic. A concerned facial expression—instead of a wandering glance—may help. You may want your friend to "Go on, I'm beginning to see." You may want to ask a pertinent question aimed at getting more information. If you concentrate on that kind of response and avoid the listening problems we've discussed, you have a better chance of getting more information from your friend. Your goal of probing may be related to a different listening goal: *to interpret.* If you felt that a friend's behavior was inexcusable, your reaction may have been that you did not understand it. You may need to reinterpret or re-create a perception about the person. Successful probing while you listen can lead to a more accurate perception. Probing and reinterpreting can avoid some kinds of interpersonal conflicts.

Another sort of problem can arise when you think that your roommate Pete, for example, feels much too submissive toward you. If that is the case, you may want to listen to him with a desire *to support* him. At times when the two of you are talking about something that you are considered the expert on, you can try to listen well as a way of bolstering him. Recall the discussion of defensive and supportive climates, and try not to be too certain of yourself. Do not assume that you have the problem already solved. Be empathetic. Approach the problem as a problem for the two of you; do not be "in control." Listening well to Pete in this situation is partly a matter of avoiding those general listening problems. Listening well here also means listening supportively. Your efforts to support your roommate may mean that, gradually, he feels less submissive to you. Conflict may be avoided when the dominance relationship becomes more what you want it to be.

At other times, your listening goal may be *to evaluate.* You may not be sure of how you feel about a friend of the opposite sex. Is he or she really the sort of person that you might wish to marry someday? Is your relationship with the other really what you think it should be? You may need to evaluate or reevaluate the person or the relationship. That does not mean that you become quarrelsome as you listen. It does not mean that you become so distracted with the problem before you that you fail to listen. What listening to evaluate may mean is that you use the strategies of argumentation for evaluation. What sort of person or relationship concerns you? What evidence do you have that this is the person or relationship for you? What evidence is there that you are not satisfied? There is no reason why you cannot listen and evaluate at the same time, but there may be a problem if you try to do so. The person who is listening to evaluate probably will respond as an evaluator—not as a supportive or probing person. You may find that you ask more pointed questions; that your facial expression is more serious than at other times. The point is that listening to evaluate is a kind of listening strategy. Like all other communication strategies, you should be aware that you are doing it as you do it. If you find you are evaluating as you listen, make sure that evaluation, and not support or understanding, is how you have *chosen* to mediate your conflict.

Finally, we come to another and even more difficult strategy for listening: listening *to alter* perceptions or relationships. You already may have engaged in perceiving, and verbal and nonverbal analysis of the other person. You may find that the only way to mediate the conflict is by helping the other person to change. That may be a difficult task, yet common sense tells us that we should try to do it in various situations. As you listen, a frown or cringe can show displeasure. A well-phrased question may make that person aware of a problem for the first time. Breaking eye contact or turning away at a crucial time may communicate how displeased you are with the conversation. All these listening responses may only make the other person more defensive. They may create even more problems. On the other hand, they may prompt your friend to reevaluate something he or she has said or done; they may prompt your friend to see him- or herself in a new light. The result of all this may be a change in the friend—you hope in the direction that is necessary for your relationship. When relationships are strong but conflicting in some way, people can and do change. Strategies of mediation are never surefire, but by listening well and listening to alter the relationship, certain conflicts can be mediated.

What we have seen in this chapter is that listening can be a communication strategy of mediation. Listening is more complicated than hearing, and problems of listening can be complex. We discussed several basic listening problems. Awareness of listening problems can help you to avoid them more effectively, and thus become a better listener. There are several types of listening goals. In the interpersonal situation, you do not just listen, you listen with some

Listening as an interpersonal strategy

purpose in mind. We discussed the strategies of listening to understand, to probe, to interpret, to support, to evaluate, and to alter perceptions and relationships. To effect these strategies, you must make certain that your listening responses are consistent with your goals. For example, choosing a *supportive* goal, but listening *evaluatively* may do more damage than good. Effective listening can be an important strategy for interpersonal mediation.

To use listening effectively as a strategy for mediating interpersonal conflicts, you can:

1. Try to discover the nature of the listening problem. Being physically or emotionally unable to listen may mean that you or someone else *cannot* listen well at a particular time; being distracted or getting ahead of the conversation may mean that you or another *will not* listen well.
2. Try to overcome the listening problem. If exhaustion is the problem, you may want to put off the conversation until another time if you can. If being quarrelsome is the problem, you may need to hold yourself back or suggest that the other person do the same.
3. Discover the sort of listening response that seems appropriate or desirable.
4. Keep that response firmly in mind as a guide to *what* and *how* you say and do what you do.

To sharpen your skills in listening, analyze the following case studies.

Case study one: I don't know why you say hello.

Ken: Hey, what's happening?

George: Not much. How are you? I haven't seen you in a long time.

Ken: No, it's been awhile. How have you been?

George: Well, I . . .

Ken: You know I was just thinking about you. I was in a physics class and I said to myself, "Ole George ought to be here to help me." I know how you get into electricity and all that . . .

George: You know, I changed majors. I am . . .

Ken: Remember back in high school? I guess you will always be better in science than I am. Yeah . . .

George: I'm in English now . . .

Ken: Well, I've got to run. It was good getting a chance to talk for a minute.

In this case study, notice how each person begins with the same sort of "How-are-you-I-am-fine-what-have-you-been-doing" conversation. Frequently you find that you do not even realize you have asked a question such as, How are you? Such phrases are simply greetings. If you find that hard to believe, go into detail about how you are the next time someone asks you. He or she probably will be surprised that you are answering the question as if it were a question. Ken's problem goes beyond that: He fails to listen to anything that George is trying to say. His problem may be that he is disinterested or that he is so distracted by past events that he fails to notice George at all.

Ken needed to stop and actually allow himself to listen to George. Ken was in his own little world and needed to step outside it long enough to listen to George.

Even if he had, however, Ken would have faced a different problem: How should he have listened to George? George seemed to want to tell Ken about the change in major, and perhaps the direction of his career. Was George seeking an understanding response, a supporting response, or what? We—as well as Ken—will never know. Ken needed to improve his listening skills in two ways: first, to avoid common listening problems; and second, to use listening responses as a strategy of interpersonal mediation.

Case study two: the frustration of getting ahead.

Wife: Honey, did you read about that code of ethics that congress is adopting?
Husband: Well, I've read some things about them needing a code of ethics.
Wife: I read where the . . . uh . . .
Husband: President?
Wife: No, the . . . leader of the . . .
Husband: Senate?
Wife: No, the House. He was going to . . .
Husband: Yeah, I bet he was going to fight it all the way, right?
Wife: No, he was the one who supported it most. He said . . .
Husband: That it wouldn't pass though, I bet.
Wife: No, he said . . . . oh, never mind.

The husband obviously is not listening to his wife, but the problem can be phrased in more specific terms. What specifically seems to be his problem? Is there some way in which the wife might have helped her husband?

Case study three: you asked for it.

Joan: You know, I just broke up with Harry, and now I'm not sure I did the right thing. What do you think?
Jan: Well, you know I think Harry and you were just perfect for one another.
Joan: I think I did the right thing, but I had to have someone to talk to.
Jan: Well, I think you broke up with him pretty quickly. You know you have a tendency to do things on impulse—you remember that coat you bought last fall? Harry was a nice guy . . .
Joan: Well, I really have to leave. Thanks for listening to me.

Jan was obviously listening to Joan's words, but not her feelings. Joan seemed to want and need a supportive response, and Jan became evaluative. Surely, I do not suggest that Jan should have lied about her feelings. Yet, she could have phrased her responses to include some sort of reinforcement. How might Jan have phrased her comments so that they were both honest and more like what Joan needed?

These case studies call upon you to see how listening can be used as a strategy for mediation. If the comments were clear to you, you understand one of several ways of coping with interpersonal conflicts.

NOTES

[1] See the interesting study in Larry Samovar, Robert D. Brooks, and Richard E. Porter, "A Survey of Adult Communication Activities," *The Journal of Communication*, 19 (1969), pp. 301–307.

[2] Even when there is no choice about behavior, listening probably will involve choices about whether to believe or process the information.

[3] Some of the following listening problems have the traditional labels used in communication studies. My goals here are to discuss other problems and to introduce new labels such as *getting ahead,* and more importantly, to relate them to interpersonal conflicts.

[4] An excellent discussion of listening with an emphasis upon purpose is A. Craig Baird, Franklin H. Knower, and Samuel L. Becker, *General Speech Communication,* 4th ed. (New York: McGraw-Hill, 1971), chap. 7.

[5] See David W. Johnson, *Reaching Out: Interpersonal Effectiveness and Self-Actualization* (Englewood Cliffs, N.J.: Prentice-Hall, 1972), chap. 7.

10
FEEDBACK AS AN INTERPERSONAL STRATEGY

You've been shopping all day and in this particular shop, you find a suit that is just what you've been looking for. The salesperson says, "It's you!" and you buy it. Later, your friend Susan sees the suit and you ask her what she thinks. "Yeah, it's you all right," she laughs. You ask her what she means.

A third-grader named Tommy asks you what you think of a picture he has made. You look at the lines, circles, and colors. "You might have tried something too hard," you say. "You shouldn't have tried to do so much all in the same picture. You know, you always try to do things that are well beyond your ability." Tommy tears up the picture.

"Well, here's the pie I promised you," says your sister. "What do you think?" You take that long-awaited first bite. The crust is a little chewy, but not as chewy as the peaches in the pie. You try to finish the bite as best you can. "Just like Mom makes," you gulp. She replies, "If you don't like it, why did you ask me to bake it?"

You have asked for a meeting with the boss. You know that salary decisions are approaching soon, and you want to know how you're doing. The boss enters, and twenty minutes later you are sorry you've asked for the meeting. Maybe it was better not knowing what he or she thinks.

All these situations have to do with potential interpersonal conflicts. All of them could be helped by certain strategies of mediation.

Listening to another person, as we have just seen, requires activity on the part of the receiver. To listen, you must attach meaning to the messages of the other person. In addition, you respond in some way. The listening responses you give to a friend are more than verbal and nonverbal cues; they are also feedback. Earlier we said that feedback is the response that someone makes to a message presented by a source. Now, feedback can be defined more specifically. *Feedback is the set of responses to a message which allows communicators both to assess the effect and to improve the quality of messages.* Two things are important here. First, feedback is the way communicators assess whether meanings are being re-created accurately. Second, feedback allows communicators to change symbols to improve the meaning re-creation.

Listening responses that you use for such purposes as probing or evaluating may be simple. You may nod or shake your head. You may smile or frown. At times, good listening and these brief responses are all you need for mediation. At other times, mediation may require the use of more detailed feedback. This chapter is devoted to helping you understand (1) the mediating functions of feedback, (2) specific ways to give feedback, and (3) how to avoid *feedback games.*

FEEDBACK AND MEDIATION

Feedback can be used in a variety of ways and for several different purposes. You might use feedback *to check (or confirm) your understanding of verbal and nonverbal messages.* Verbal and nonverbal symbols, as you know, have no meanings in themselves. People give meanings to them, or re-create messages that they think are similar to what a source *meant.* When you use feedback to discover if you are re-creating messages accurately, in essence you say, "This is what I think you mean. Is it?" If, for example, your conflict with Anne is that you feel defensive, you might say, "What I see you doing is taking control. Is that what you are trying to do?" If your problem is that your perception of Anne conflicts with her perception of herself, you may say, "I think you are seeing yourself as an expert on student government, then, right?" The conflict may be mediated by your giving of that kind of feedback. Anne has the opportunity to say, "No, I'm sorry. I wasn't trying to take control;" or "Yes, I was trying to take control, but I shouldn't have been." If your friend does not make that kind of response to your feedback, you may need to try another method of mediation. If she does say something like that, the conflict you perceived may be mediated immediately—simply because you cared enough about the interpersonal relationship to check your understanding.

A second way that feedback can help mediate conflicts is by allowing you as a receiver *to check your reaction with the reactions of others.* You might say to Jack, "I get angry with you when you try to seem so superior—am I the only one who responds that way?" A similar and more subtle approach would be to ask a third person, "I get angry with Jack when I feel he's trying to be superior. Am I just sensitive, or do you ever feel that way?" In either situation, the goal is the same. You are attempting to mediate the conflict by finding out if your feeling or perception is one you ought to change. Finding out that Jack affects several people the same way gives you some new information. You can either accept Jack in his as-is condition or try to change his behavior. At worst, using feedback to check your perceptions against others' may erase some of your guilt feelings about those perceptions. At best, checking reactions may mediate your conflict altogether. You may be able to perceive your friend in a new, more satisfying way.

You will find that you can benefit as much from receiving as from giving feedback. Receiving feedback can mediate some problems by allowing you *to check the understanding of your own verbal and nonverbal messages.* Your conflict may be that you and another person are more distant than you would like. The problem may be that you seem unable to increase the *liking* between you and someone else. In this situation, you may want to ask for feedback. You might say, "I love you. Do you know that?" You might say, "I've been trying to make our working relationship here at the office go more smoothly—have I been more cooperative?" Sometimes you will receive feedback without asking for it. If you do, you can begin immediately to check the meanings you are re-creating in another person. Sometimes you will need feedback that is not volunteered. Your relationship with the other person may depend upon whether he or she understands what you are trying to do. Compatibility in your relationship may depend upon your asking for feedback. You can use the feedback you request to see how your meanings are being re-created.

The feedback you ask for will not always be favorable or positive. Sometimes the friend may say, "Actually, I have thought you were being more distant." The friend may say, "I didn't notice any difference in you at all." When that kind of feedback is given, you can use it in a fourth way: *to plan a change in your communication.* You can use the feedback to see how you should modify your verbal or nonverbal messages. You may have been trying so hard to be likable that you were perceived as insincere. You may have been trying so hard not to be dominant that the other person feels you are too submissive. Your own verbal and nonverbal self-analysis is not always enough for you to know how you are communicating. Sometimes you must rely upon feedback from others to change your communication and to mediate interpersonal conflicts. Sometimes that feedback will be given freely; at other times, you will need to ask for it.

Feedback can serve another and more general purpose in mediation: *to stimulate interaction.* You may feel that the relationship you have with another has not progressed as far as you would like. You decide that you need more interpersonal contact; you want to begin playing a more intimate role with the other person. The feedback process can help you. *Giving* feedback involves taking a risk, since you never know completely how it will be received. *Asking* for feedback involves the same kind of risk. You never know absolutely whether the feedback will be favorable or negative, but the person who takes the risk of giving or asking for feedback may begin to establish a better relationship with the other person. If feedback is given well—and received well by the other person—trust between the two people seems to increase. As the two people begin to trust one another, risks become less and more feedback can be given freely.[1] More constructive feedback can generate more trust. The result is an increasingly open and closer relationship that may solve your problem of interpersonal distance. Feedback, then, can increase interaction. The increased interaction may be the key to mediating certain types of conflicts.

SPECIFIC STRATEGIES OF FEEDBACK

The *trust-risk* cycle just described, as well as the other ways that feedback can be used for mediation, is based upon the assumption that you know how to give constructive feedback. Feedback can either help or hinder your attempts at mediation. To help you understand how to use feedback constructively, let us examine what happens or can happen when feedback is given. Graphic illustrations may help you.

First, any interpersonal relationship begins with two people; each person has a self-perception or self-concept. When you and another person begin to interact, there is an immediate effect. A *perception of the other* is created—something that is at first very sketchy. Figure 10.2 represents the initial interaction. As the two of you continue to interact, the concepts begin to *overlap*. Your self-perceptions are affected by your perceptions of the other; your perceptions of the other are affected by your self-perceptions. Figure 10.3 represents the developing relationship.

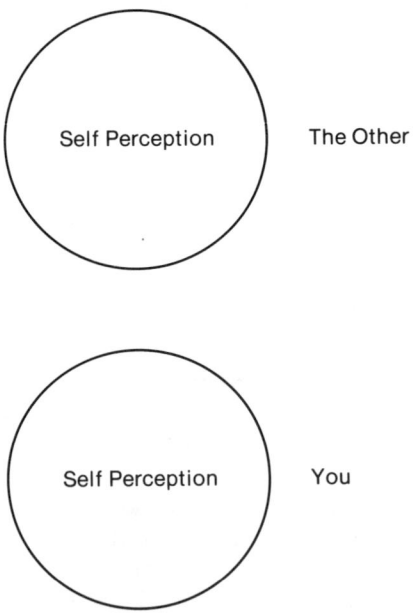

Fig. 10.1 Before interaction

Feedback as an interpersonal strategy

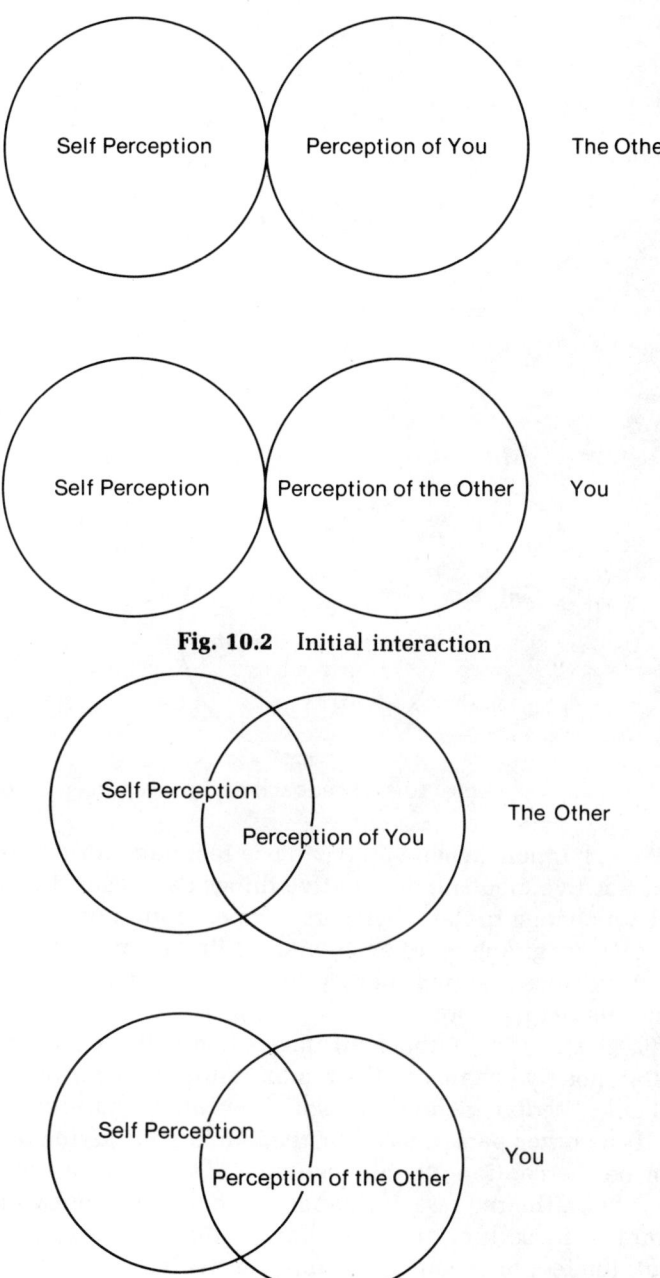

Fig. 10.2 Initial interaction

Fig. 10.3 Continuing interaction

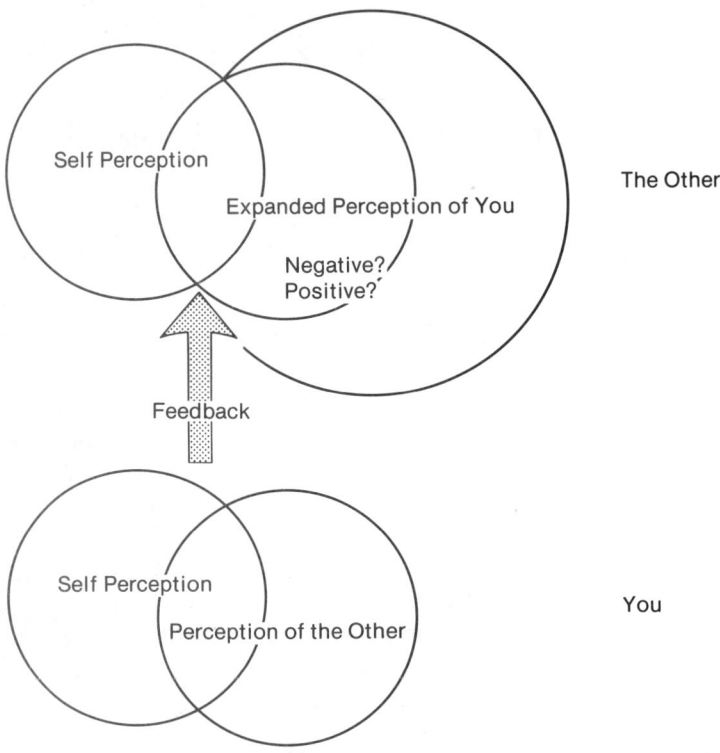

Fig. 10.4 Feedback and perceptions of you

What happens when you try to use feedback for mediation? Unfortunately, either positive, neutral, or negative things can occur. Probably the initial effect will be a change in the other person's perception of you. After all, you are taking a risk by giving feedback—and adding to how the other person perceives you. Will these added perceptions be positive or negative? Figure 10.4 represents the question.

Three specific feedback strategies can better ensure that the feedback will result in positive changes.[2] First, make sure that your friend is willing to receive feedback. *Feedback should be solicited* rather than forced upon the other person. If the other person asks for feedback, your giving of it probably will help his or her perception of you. Feedback is also appropriate when you *sense*, but do not hear, the request. If the person really does not want the feedback, your attempt to force him or her to hear it may make your conflict worse. To be useful, the feedback generally must be freely accepted and, you hope, sought.[3] Unwanted feedback can actually create conflicts.

A second strategy of giving feedback is to make sure that the *feedback is well timed.* Timing your feedback requires you to be sensitive to the other person. Do not give feedback at a time when you feel the other person is too emotionally or physically drained to use it. Do not wait for six months and give feedback at a time when it cannot possibly be used. Do not use a single event as a launching pad for a sermon about what someone "always does." One thing a person with a specific problem does not want to hear is a history of his or her past failures. Choose the time for giving the feedback carefully. Give it at a time when it will likely be both acceptable and useful. If you do not time the feedback well, it can be worse than useless; it can harm a relationship that already may be in conflict.

Third, make sure that your *feedback is descriptive of how you feel*. Feedback is simply your response to something. It is, or should be, your personal reaction. Do not tell your friend, "You are just too aggressive and dominant." You have no way of knowing whether that is really the case or not. All you know is what *you* feel. Try saying something such as, "You know, I felt that you were too aggressive at the meeting last night." Remember, in most cases you are not *evaluating* the person as a judge would do.[4] Instead, you are simply describing how you feel. Similarly, do not *prescribe* to a friend what he or she ought to do.[5] You probably are not the world's greatest authority on whatever the problem is. Do not try to play the role of doctor. Don't say in effect, "Be less aggressive, cut down on the dominance, and call me in the morning." Avoid evaluation and prescription in giving feedback. All that evaluation and prescription probably will create is a feeling of defensiveness—and a negative perception of you.

If you concentrate on feedback that is welcome or solicited, well timed, and descriptive, you have a better chance of making a positive gain in how the other person perceives you. We have not yet discussed how feedback can alter the other person's perceptions of him- or herself. How can feedback be used to affect self-perceptions? If you use certain strategies of giving feedback, some positive change might occur. If you fail to use these strategies, the result may be no change in the other's self-perception, even though the person may have formed no negative perceptions of you. The question, then, is whether no change or a positive change in self-perception will occur.[6] Figure 10.5 represents the problem.

A fourth feedback strategy is to make sure that *feedback is specific, rather than general*. You might not antagonize your friend Georgina by telling her, "I felt your behavior was too 'superior.' " On the other hand, she probably will not gain anything from the general nature of your feedback. She cannot change her superior behavior. Be more specific. Did she use a haughty laugh or did she say something condescending? Did she try to take control? What did she do that made you feel as you do? Even if she has a positive new perception of you, *general* statements about superiority are not likely to affect her. In giving feedback, be as specific as you can about how you feel. If Georgina knows about specific things, she has a better chance of taking action—and of altering her self-perception. General comments will be useless to her.

A fifth feedback strategy aimed at helping develop the self-concept is to make sure that the *feedback is practical, instead of beyond the control of the person*. Telling a friend that you feel he or she is dominant because of his or her

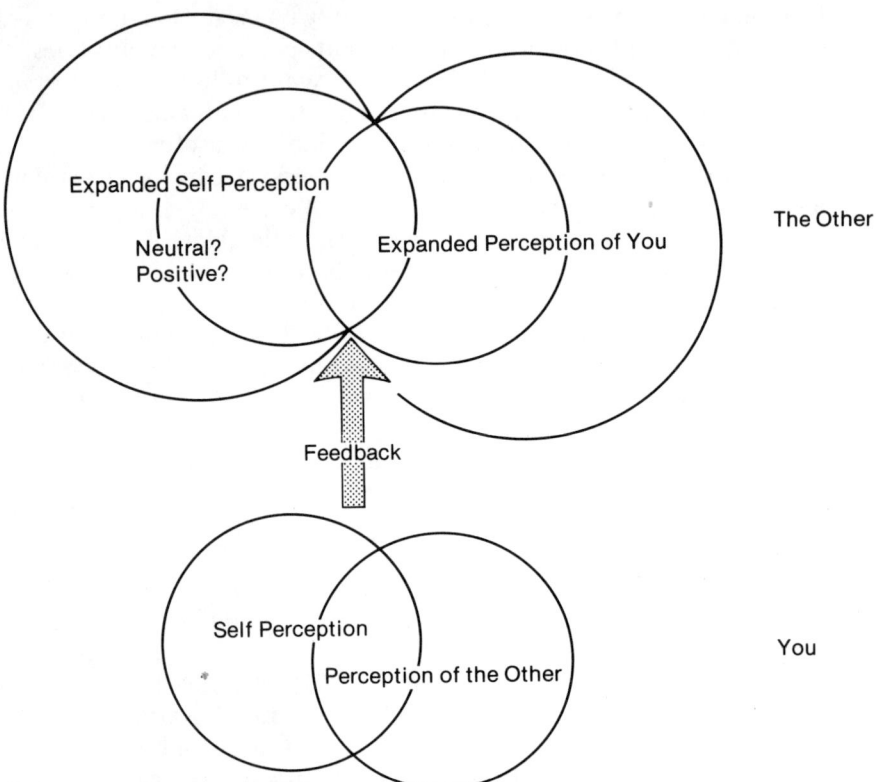

Fig. 10.5 Feedback and self-perceptions

height does not help a great deal. The friend cannot become shorter. Telling a friend that you feel too submissive because of his or her high intelligence is not practical. People can change their language use, their nonverbal behavior, their voice volume, and so forth. To give successful feedback, you must concentrate upon practical things: the things that a person can control and change. If you do not, the feedback probably will be a waste of time and effort for both of you, and there is little hope for positive changes in the other's self-perception.

Using the five strategies of feedback can help you mediate conflicts by affecting two sets of perceptions: self-perceptions and perceptions of the other. Feedback can also be used to improve the overall relationship. *Feedback should be mutual.* It is unlikely that only one person will give feedback, but it can happen. Employees may receive feedback, but feel that they cannot give it to an employer. Children get feedback all the time, but a parent may not be anxious to receive it. Better relationships can be developed if both people give and receive feedback. Figure 10.6 illustrates the point. As discussed earlier in this chapter, giving feedback involves a risk—a risk that an employer or a parent may not want to take. If the risk is taken and IF THE FEEDBACK IS GIVEN WELL ACCORDING TO THE GUIDELINES just given, then a trust-risk

Feedback as an interpersonal strategy 133

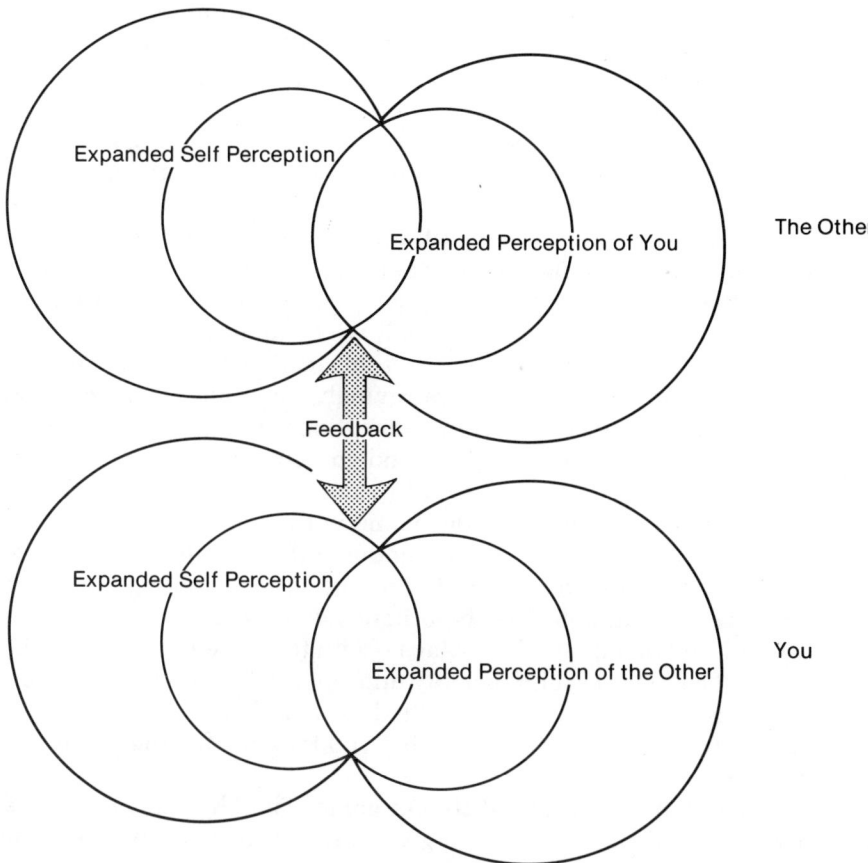

Fig. 10.6 Feedback and relationships

cycle can develop. The result is that feedback can be a continual source of growth, development, and interpersonal mediation. Feedback is an important communication tool for mediation.

FEEDBACK GAMES

One of the good things about feedback is how useful it can be in interpersonal mediation. One of the bad things about it is that knowing the strategies is not the same thing as using the strategies constructively. Feedback can become an interpersonal *game* that people play. Let us look at a few roles in the *feedback game*.[7]

Sometimes, people openly ask for feedback. Sometimes the reason for asking is questionable. The Trapper is the person who uses the request for feedback as bait—and you may become the Prey. The Trapper asks for feedback and sits back to wait. When you give it to him or her, the trap is sprung. "Aha!"

says the Trapper, "Now I see what you really think of me!" Or, "Well, that is exactly what I was thinking of *you*!" Or, "Well, we'll see about that!" Whatever the exact response, the invitation to feedback can be a trap, and you can be the unknowing "trapee."

The Mind Reader presents a different kind of game plan. The Mind Reader asks for feedback, but intends to show that he or she has already thought of it. No feedback is new to this person, who has previously been aware of what you now suggest, and has a response ready. The Mind Reader may say, "Yes, I thought about that, but you see . . . ." or, "Well, yes, I used to think that that was a problem, but . . . ." He or she knows all and considers all—but does not change. After all, why should he or she, given that . . . .

The Gamester plays a different feedback game. The Gamester may smile, ask for feedback, nod approvingly—and not even hear it. He or she will not argue or quarrel with your perceptions. The Gamester's only goal is to get the game of feedback over with, and go home. He or she cannot be affected by the feedback—partly because it has not really been heard. The Gamester has merely smiled and played your game with you.

Sometimes, feedback has another effect on the game player. The Flirt may openly ask for feedback, but not be serious about getting any. The suggestion box, for example, can be a handy tool. It is a convenient means of feedback placed in a convenient place—with the hope that no one will supply feedback. The Flirt is psychologically unprepared for any feedback, even though he or she asks for it. If it is given, the Flirt may become angry, hostile, indignant, or tearstained. Your problem is that you took the flirting seriously, and the Flirt did not.

The Flatterer plays a different game. The Flatterer not only asks for feedback, but is thrilled when you give it. He or she verbally and nonverbally suggests that you have been kind, insightful, and tremendously helpful. That sort of response to your feedback can be very reassuring—until you find that the Flatterer has not taken a word of what you said seriously. Being hypocritical can become a way of life for the Flatterer, who proclaims that feedback is good generally, and yours is the best. Unfortunately, none of it affects either the Flatterer's perception of you or of him- or herself.

Finally (though I am sure there are others) you may discover the Expert. The Expert resents feedback, even though he or she asks for it. After all, the Expert has had the beginning communication course; what can you tell him or her that is new? Or, the Expert has had Psychology 101, and would already know if he or she were doing anything to hurt a relationship. The Expert has an inflated opinion of him- or herself and his or her knowledge. For your feedback to have an effect, it would have to break through this shield of knowledge, and that may be impossible.

My point in describing these game players is not to argue that feedback is always ineffective, but simply that asking for feedback or accepting feedback is not the same as taking it seriously. When you have interpersonal problems that you feel can be mediated by feedback, use it. Give it well and receive it

USING FEEDBACK FOR MEDIATION

In this chapter, we have examined the nature of feedback, specific strategies of feedback, and feedback games that people play. The feedback response is more complicated than a simple listening response. Feedback, as we discussed it here, involves your use of verbal and nonverbal skills in giving a highly specific and perhaps detailed reaction. That sort of activity involves risk and must be done well. By using constructive strategies of feedback and avoiding feedback games, you may find feedback extremely useful in mediating interpersonal problems. In using feedback, remember to:

1. Make sure that the feedback is asked for, or at least welcome.
2. Time your feedback carefully; give it when it will do the most good.
3. Describe *your* feelings and reactions instead of evaluating or prescribing.
4. Be as specific in your comments as possible.
5. Focus on things that can be changed or modified.
6. Be ready to accept feedback in return.
7. ABOVE ALL, AVOID FEEDBACK GAMES.

To help you learn to apply these strategies of giving feedback, consider the following case studies.

Case study one: the proposal. You have been working on a proposal for handling sales receipts differently. Jack, your supervisor, has just listened to the idea. You ask him what he thinks.

Jack: Well, it's a nice try, but no one will buy it. It can't work—and probably wouldn't be desirable if it did work. Beginners...

You: Well, you have had more experience than I have, but...

Jack: You're right, and I can tell you something else. It takes a lotta years in this business to get the hang of it....

That may be the last proposal you ever discuss with Jack. Jack's feedback was weak from a number of standpoints. First, he set himself up as the ultimate authority—and assumed that everyone else would agree with him. In terms of timing, he might have helped by being sensitive to the difference in your levels of experience. "Beginners," as he calls them, may be more sensitive to unfavorable feedback at that point in their careers. Moreover, his comments were not very specific; he didn't discuss any individual problems with the plan. In addition, he may have been playing a feedback game. What do you think?

Case study two: that first interview. It is your first job interview and you are really interested in a position described. As Ms. Banes, the interviewer, finishes the meeting, she asks if you have any questions.

You timidly ask if she thought the interview went well and how you seem to fit with the position. "You did just fine," she says.

As you leave, you are happy. Then you ask yourself, "What did that really mean?"

In that situation, the "just fine" comment may or may not have meant that you were suitable for the position. That sort of feedback is not specific and could, perhaps, be said of most of the interviewees. On the other hand, you may have been playing a feedback game: Did you really want feedback—or did you just want reinforcement? How might you have asked for more feedback?

If you have understood the comments in these case studies, you probably are beginning to see how to use feedback as a strategy for interpersonal mediation.

EXERCISES

In learning to give constructive feedback, you probably should begin to work with situations that pose little risk to either you or the person receiving the feedback. Consequently, the exercises that follow get more and more difficult.

1. Everyone in class should draw a picture of a tree, or some other such object. Trade pictures and ask for feedback from each other. Analyze the kind of feedback you get (it may help to have the feedback written on the same page as the picture). Were feedback strategies used constructively?
2. Pair up with another member of your class (or work with a friend outside of class). Have each person present feedback about the way the other is dressed. Make note of and analyze the comments given.
3. Pair up with yet another member of the class. Have each person present feedback about the other's participation in class. AT THIS POINT, IF NOT BEFORE, YOU MAY DETECT SOME FEEDBACK GAMES BEING PLAYED. If there are, what are they? If you detect such games, what does this tell you about how people respond to the risk of giving and receiving feedback?
4. Finally, you are ready to work with feedback outside the classroom. For the next several days, keep track of some of the more important times you are asked for feedback—or of times you ask for feedback. How did you or the other person respond? Analyze how well you have begun to use feedback for interpersonal mediation.

NOTES

[1] For an interesting discussion of *trust* see Gerald M. Goldhaber, *Organizational Communication* (Dubuque: Ia.: William C. Brown, 1974), pp. 78–80.

[2] The material in this section is based upon certain ideas in Howard W. Polsky, "Notes on Personal Feedback in Sensitivity Training," *Sociological Inquiry,* 41 (Spring 1971), 175–82.

[3] There are exceptions, of course. You may find that the feedback that you are unwilling to hear eventually makes sense to you.

[4] Evaluation may be asked for at times, but when evaluation becomes a habit, feedback may be worse than useless. See the earlier discussion of supportive and defensive climates.

[5] Being *prescriptive* with feedback may make another person think that you think you have all the answers. The result can be defensiveness.

[6] It is possible but unlikely for *well-given* feedback to create negative impressions of the person giving it.

[7] This method of looking at human games of various types is consistent with how Eric Berne sees human behavior generally, although these game players are not based upon his analysis. See Eric Berne, *Games People Play* (New York: Grove Press, 1967).

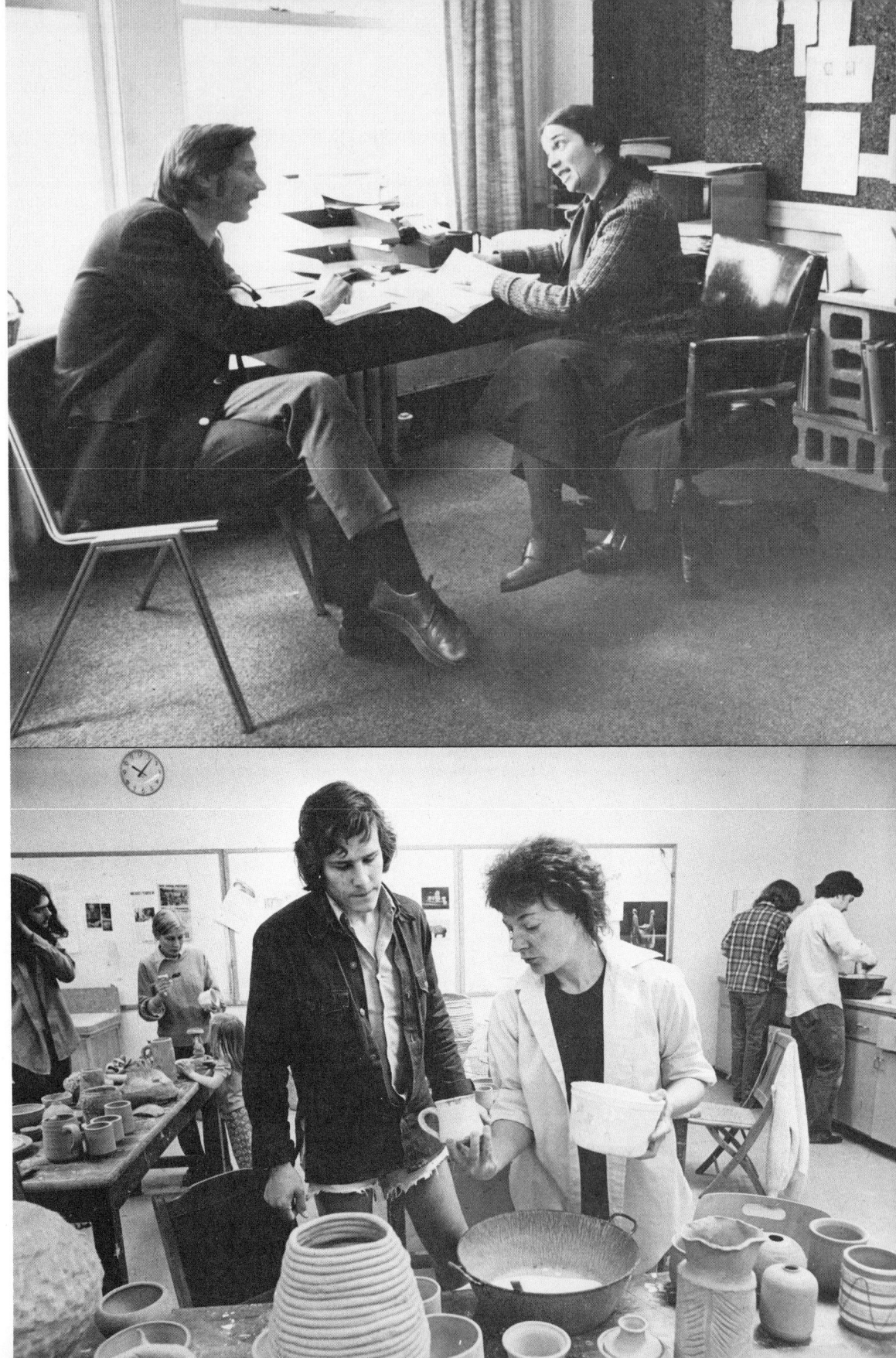

11
INTERVIEWING AS AN INTERPERSONAL STRATEGY

As a part of your work responsibilities, you have been assigned to give some thought to better training procedures in your department. Part of the problem has been that your department works closely with another department in the company. Any training program must help the interaction between the two departments. You have sent memos to the supervisor of the other department, but he or she has seemed to be uncooperative, and has not sent the information you asked for. This has slowed progress in your project.

Finally, you set up a meeting with him or her as a way of gaining cooperation and getting information. Now that you have the meeting scheduled, what are you going to do when it takes place?

The situation is not unusual. Some interpersonal conflicts develop over time, and a time finally comes when the two people have to meet in order to settle their differences. In such situations, listening and feedback skills and strategies are important. Still, there are some problems in these situations which require more than those strategies. You may need to use strategies that have to do with *interviewing*.

Sometimes interviews are planned and arranged, such as the one just mentioned, but sometimes an interview just begins to occur. For example, you may have passed a friend on the street by accident. After exchanging greetings, you remember that you need to ask him or her about an assignment for a class you missed. At that point, you begin conducting an informal interview.

The interview is sometimes viewed as a particular kind of communication *situation.* Here, we will look at it as a *process.* To explain the interview process as a general strategy of mediation, this chapter will (1) explain the nature of interviewing, (2) explain interviewing goals for mediation, (3) explain questions as tools for mediation, and (4) explain some general approaches to the interview process.

THE NATURE OF INTERVIEWING

Interviewing is a *process of communication between two parties who are usually in close proximity, who use questions extensively, who both speak and listen from time to time, and at least one of whom has at least one purpose.*[1] Five ideas are important here. First, interviewing involves two *parties.* Each party is a *side*: employers/employees, teachers/students, clients/counselor. The sides or parties in interviewing may each have more than one person. In this chapter we will focus upon two parties of one person each; that is, a total of two people. Second, interviewing usually places you and another person close to one another. At times, interviews do take place by telephone, but usually they occur in a face-to-face situation. Third, questions form a significant part of the communication. Questions become a major way of knowing if an interview is in progress. Fourth, each person both speaks and listens from time to time. The person who requests the interview is usually called the *interviewer.* That person usually asks more questions, but the other person—the *interviewee*—usually asks questions as well. Regardless of who asks more questions, the point is that each takes turns speaking and listening. The fifth characteristic of interviewing is that either one and usually both of the people have one or several specific purposes. This emphasis upon goals or purposes is what makes interviewing different from casual conversation. Interviewing involves two people, usually in close proximity, an emphasis upon questions and turn taking, and specific purposes.

GOALS OF MEDIATION IN THE INTERVIEW

Interviews are usually labeled by the nature of the goal in the situation. Such labels are usually fairly self-explanatory.[2]

The *employment* interview, for example, occurs when two parties are trying to solve their individual problems. An employer needs an employee, and a potential employee is interested in a job. At one time or another, nearly everyone will need to know how to participate in or conduct an employment interview. Such interviews may be very formal or very informal, or somewhere in between. Regardless, the employment interview is important. *Informative* interviews take place when people ask for and give information, opinions, and beliefs. The Gallup Poll and other organizations use informative interviewing. News programs frequently use an informative interviewing process to "get the news." The *persuasive* interview is used when people want to change attitudes, values, or behaviors—when they want to persuade. The door-to-door salesperson and the door-to-door evangelist are examples of persuasive interviewers. The *evaluational* or appraisal interview frequently is used when supervisors have to make salary and promotion decisions about subordinates. The goal here is to judge the merits of work and people. The *reprimand* and the *complaint* interview often may be mirror images of one another. In the reprimand interview, a subordinate may be "called on the carpet" and unfavorably criticized. In the complaint interview, the subordinate may criticize unfavorably the actions of a supervisor. The *counseling* interview usually involves a professional of some sort and a client. Physicians, clerics, psychologists, social workers, and psychiatrists are among the people who engage in counseling interviewing. *Problem-solving* interviews are just that: two people come together for the purpose of solving a mutual problem.

You should know four things about these types of interviews. First, the *interview types are based upon the primary (not exclusive) goal* of the transaction. The persuasive interview may also include the goal of counseling. The evaluational interview may also involve problem solving. The counseling interview may also involve information getting and giving. People in the employment interview may have the one goal or several. It is simply convenient to use one label for an interview, even though several things may be accomplished. Second, you should understand that *each of the goals is related to a need for mediation*. The persuasive interview is used when one person feels he or she should (or has to) persuade someone of something. The counseling interview is used for mediating specific psychological, social, or spiritual problems. Interviews may have different specific goals, but they all have the same general goal: mediation.

Third, let me reiterate that *these interviews may be either formal or informal*. Most of your interviewing, I suspect, will be informal. You probably will not sell automobiles for a living, but you will need to engage in persuasive interviewing. You may want to change a friend's language habits or a parent's perception of you. Similarly, you probably will not work for a polling organization, but you will need to be able to conduct informal informational interviews. As an engineer, you may need information from your research and development supervisor. As a nurse, you may need information from an attending physician. As a movie lover, you may need information about an upcoming film. In the same way, you may use counseling interviewing informally to help someone you love. You may use a reprimand interview to "lay out" your inconsiderate friend. You may use a problem-solving interview when you and your spouse work on your income tax returns. You may use a complaint interview when you return damaged merchandise to a department store. Interviews are not something only for professional newspeople and pollsters. They are used by everyone everyday—including you. Whenever you and another person get together and use questions to achieve some individual or mutual goal, you are engaged in interviewing.

A fourth thing you should understand about these interview types is that you can *create interview situations to mediate your specific conflict.* You can turn a casual conversation into an interview. You probably have been talking with a friend when a problem occurred to you. In the midst of the conversation, you may have said, "While we're on the subject, I've been wanting to ask how you felt the party went last night." Or, you may have said, "Since you are here, I want to ask you if I have appeared as cranky lately as I think I have." Every day you face situations where you have interpersonal problems of some sort. In the instances just described, the casual conversation has been turned into an informal interview. Sometimes interviews are *formal,* and *scheduled* to take place at some particular time. Most of the time, I suspect, your interviews will be *informal.* You begin these unscheduled activities when the situation is right. You already use interviewing activities to mediate your problems.

QUESTIONS AS TOOLS FOR MEDIATION

Since everyone interviews other people, the major question is not, *Do* you use questions to achieve your goals? but, *How well* do you use questions in achieving your goals? Questions in the interview situation should be thought of as tools. Whether beginning the *formal* or the *informal* interview, you should not just start asking questions. Your first thought should be about the problem or conflict you are trying to mediate. Do you need to get information or opinions about something? Do you need to give feedback to someone else? Do you feel you need to persuade someone? Do you need to give or to get counseling or advice about something? Are you interested in correcting someone's behavior through a reprimand interview? Do you wish to complain about something? In short, your first thought should be about the conflict that needs mediation.

Once you know what you want to accomplish, you should think about the questions you need to use to reach your goal. There are several important types of questions. Each type can be used for a specific purpose, so each type is a special tool.

One way of describing questions is by noting whether they are *open or closed questions.* Open questions present all sorts of possible answers to the question. If you say, "What do you think of the football team?", "How do you feel?", or, "What did you think about last night's class?" you are asking open questions. They should be used when you want to give the other person a wide variety of possible answers. Closed questions, on the other hand, are useful in limiting the number of possible answers. If you say, "What place in the league do you think the football team will be in at the end of the season?" you are asking a closed question. Other examples include, "Do you feel better today than yesterday?" and "Did you think last night's class was better than last week's?" Closed questions can be useful when you are trying to get specific information.

You should realize that many questions are somewhere between being open and being closed. Notice how the following four questions begin getting more closed: What do you think of the football team?; How good do you think the players are?; How successful do you think they will be?; What place do you think they will be in the league? You should decide upon the kinds of questions you will ask by deciding how much specific information you want. If you want a *free response* or *any* kind of answer, an open question will work for you. If you want a specific bit of information, an extremely closed question will serve as a better tool. If you want a yes or no answer—an extreme form of closed question since there are only two possible answers[3]—use an appropriate question. You cannot use an open question and expect a closed answer.

Besides being open or closed, questions can be *neutral, leading,* or *loaded.*[4] Neutral questions are ones you may use when you want an unbiased answer. What should we do about what happened last night? is an example of a neutral question. In asking it, you do not indicate that any special answer is correct or desired. Sometimes, though, you may want to indicate the answer you are seeking. I think you should apologize for your behavior last night, don't you? is an example of a leading question. Leading questions can be useful to you when you want to make it difficult for the other person to disagree. There is a great difference between What should be done . . . ? and You should apologize, right? You may wish to make the question even more difficult for the person answering. If so, you may use a loaded question: a leading question that has a strong emotional flavoring. I think you should apologize for your crass, thoughtless behavior last night, don't you? is an example. The loaded question biases the answer even more than the leading question. After all, a person *must* apologize for crass, thoughtless behavior, don't you think? Loaded questions and leading questions (*my* last question was leading) can be used when you want to indicate the appropriate answer, but be careful. Leading and loaded questions may create defensiveness.

A final category of question is *primary/secondary questions*. Primary questions are the questions you ask first about any one topic. If you do not get the kind or amount of information you want, you may want to use a secondary question—any question that follows up the primary question. In the interview, you will ask a primary question and then follow it up with as many secondary questions as you need. When you are satisfied, you may ask another primary question about a different topic. Then, you may use as many follow-up questions to this second primary question as you need.

Primary questions can be any of the types we have discussed. The primary question can be open, closed, or somewhere in between. It might be neutral, leading, or loaded. Secondary questions also can be any of the types discussed. In addition, secondary questions can be of special types[5] (some of which are not questions at all!). Some special types of secondary questions are defined here:

a simple probe: any kind of secondary question
a confrontive probe: one that may create an intense response (Most doctors are only interested in money. What do you think?)

a reflective probe:	asks for a consideration of something, without confrontation (Some people say doctors are only interested in money. Do you agree or not?)
a mirror question:	restates an answer in the form of a question (So, you think doctors are only interested in money?)
a filled pause:	an *Um?* or *Huh?* that is your response
a nonvocal response:	a quizzical look, a frown, or smile

Any of the secondary questions—or the nonquestion symbols—listed can be used for probing, for following up a primary question. As your interview progresses, you are the one who must decide if you are accomplishing your goal. When you have succeeded in doing what you feel you needed to do, the interview may be over; but if your problem or conflict is still troublesome, you may use any number of primary or secondary questions to achieve your goal. Just as you can create an interview, you may well have the power to say when it is finished.[6]

You should know some of the relationships among these three major categories of questions: (1) open/closed, (2) neutral/leading, (3) primary/secondary. Any single question you use may be primary, closed, *and* leading, or, it might be open, neutral, *and* secondary. The categories are discussed so that you will know how certain questions can be used. Once you understand the nature of different types of questions, you are better able to use them as tools. Knowing about questions as tools is important in your use of interviewing for mediation.

GENERAL STRATEGIES OF INTERVIEWING

Textbooks on interviewing can provide a wealth of information about how to begin and end the interview. Such texts can tell you something about various question *sequences,* and *schedules* of questions for formal interviews. My concern here is not primarily the formal interview. If your future or present job requires you to be a professional interviewer, you will need specialized knowledge. Our concern here is with some general strategies of interviewing. They can help you in your role in engineering, agriculture, law, accounting, management, nursing—or whatever your role in life is or will be. In addition, interviewing strategies can be used in mediating the everyday interpersonal conflicts that we all experience.

To review what we have discussed, the basic strategies for interviewing are to:

Decide what your goal in mediation is.
Decide if interviewing can accomplish your mediation.
Decide what kinds of questions will most likely accomplish what you need to do.

Besides these basic strategies, there are four factors that will increase your chances of being successful in the interview.

First, you can *be sure that your timing is appropriate.* If possible, choose a time when the person can attend to the ideas to be discussed. Be aware that tiredness, emotional stress, distractions, and preoccupations will not help your effort.

Second, *be aware of how important verbal and nonverbal cues are.* You may need to introduce your purpose in getting together. You will need to be aware of your verbal and nonverbal behavior. How are you being interpreted? What is the feedback from the other person? What do his or her verbal and nonverbal responses tell you as the interview progresses? In addition, you will need to think about how to end the interview. How will you know when it is ended? What will you say and do when you are satisfied that you have mediated the situation? What will you say or do if you begin to feel that mediation cannot be accomplished? Before the interview begins—even if it is informal—think about your verbal and nonverbal behavior.

Third, *be aware that the other person may have his or her own mediational goals.* If the interview has been called by the other person, be sure you understand the goal of the interview. Are you there to be reprimanded, to help with a problem, to supply information, to be persuaded, or what? If you are not sure of the reason for the interview, remember that interviewees are usually allowed to ask questions. In many of the interview situations you face, both of you may have goals of mediation. Be sure that you are aware of what the other person's goals may be.

Finally, *be sure to listen during the interview.* That advice sounds all too obvious, but it is important. If there is one mistake that is made most frequently during an interview, it may well be the failure to listen well. To use probes or secondary questions means that interviewers first must listen to an answer, and then ask another question. As an interviewer, you cannot afford to be thinking of the next question during an answer. Conversely, as an interviewee, you cannot afford to be thinking of your last answer as a new question is asked. The questions may not be related. An interviewee who falls behind the conversation is just as bad as the interviewer who gets ahead by thinking of the next question. Interviewing requires you to listen and think at the same time—a skill that can only be learned through practice.

Practice is important to every part of the interview process. You now have the tools to use interviewing for interpersonal mediation. You know what interviewing is and what it can do. You know how different questions can serve as tools for various purposes. You know something of the general strategies for using interviews for interpersonal problems. You may find that interviewing is one of your most helpful methods of mediating interpersonal conflicts. Just remember to:

1. Define or identify your conflict or situation.
2. Decide the goal of your mediation.

3. See if interviewing of some sort can help. Can the conflict be mediated by face-to-face contact and constructive questions?
4. Determine the kinds of questions you want to have answered, or the kinds of questions you want to answer.
5. Pay attention to timing.
6. Use other strategies (listening, feedback, and so forth) well to help the progress of the interview.
7. Try to anticipate the goals of the other person in the interview.
8. Give thought to how to begin the interview.
9. Consider how you will know when the goal is accomplished, so that you can end the interview or allow it to end.
10. Adjust your interview techniques if the situation or the other person is not as you expected.

As a help in learning how to apply these strategies of interviewing, consider the following case studies:

Case study one: the assignment.

Kate: Hey, I'm glad I ran into you. I need to get that assignment for biology class from you. You were there, weren't you?
Teresa: Yeah. It really wasn't much. We are supposed to explain what we found in the frog we worked on.
Kate: Yuch! I found more than I wanted. Was that it?
Teresa: Yeah. Well, I've got to be going.

Later, what Kate found out was that the "explanation" was to be a written report on the dissection. Teresa had not given Kate any inaccurate information; she just had not given her enough. Teresa should have known the importance of telling Kate all the details. On the other hand, Kate should have asked more carefully for the information. She could have probed the idea of the explanation. She could have asked, "What kind of explanation?" or, "You mean we are just going to discuss it in class?" If either person had looked at the situation as an informative interview, the situation might have had a happier ending.

Case study two: do you have any questions? Jill is interviewing for a job in an electronics firm. At one point, the interviewer asks, "Well, do you have any questions?" Jill thinks for a moment and asks, "What are the promotion policies of the company?"

Mr. Black: Good question. The company is always ready to promote people who do their jobs well.
Jill: I see. Are there fringe benefits to the job—like health insurance?

Let's interrupt the interview. Jill has just missed the opportunity to perhaps improve her chances of getting the job. She could have probed more into the company's policies on promotion. If she had shown real interest in the demands of the company and its goals for employees, the interview might have become more interesting. She would have shown herself to be a careful, concerned, and systematic person. As it turned out, she accepted a very general answer to an important question. She had asked a good question, but probably like several other interviewees that day, she failed to really interest the interviewer in her thinking about the job.

Case study three: "yep."

Frank: I've been bothered lately. I'm not sure our relationship is what it used to be.
Edna: What do you mean?
Frank: Would you put the book down and listen?
Edna: Yep.
Frank: Do you think our relationship is what it was once?
Edna: Yep.
Frank: Do you really?
Edna: Yep.
Frank: Would you put down the book?
Edna: Nope.

The situation here may not be as exaggerated as it seems at first. Frank, of course, got little information from Edna. Her preoccupation with the book was one problem, but Frank's interviewing skills were another. Whether Frank knew it or not, he had begun to function as an interviewer in a problem-solving situation. His problem in questioning was one of failing to ask more open-ended questions, probes, and the like. Can you suggest questions that might have worked more effectively?

In all three of the cases, strategies of interviewing might have helped the mediation of a situation. Interviewing, like listening and feedback, can be important in the interpersonal situation.

EXERCISES

1. Interview a member of your class to discover something of the interests and background of this other person. Don't be satisfied with statements such as I am from Ohio. Concentrate on probing for more specific information: Where in Ohio? What size city? or Where in the country? Find out if the place of residence has had any special influence upon the person's attitudes, activities, or occupational goals.

    Then reverse the process, and be interviewed by the other person. Again, the emphasis should be upon probing for specific information.

    Note the effects of the situation upon the interview: this is a classroom; this is a class exercise; there are other people in the room, and so forth. Explain how these factors affected the interviews.

2. Interview another person in class, but this time emphasize the kind of questions asked. It may be interesting to have the other person play a role: the overly-talkative interviewee, the closed-mouth interviewee, the hostile interviewee, and so forth. Varying the kind of interviewee you have (or are) can present a challenge to getting the information you want.
3. Plan and execute an interview with a person outside class. Possible assignments might include interviewing:

   a school administrator

   a city official

   a local contractor

   a prominent attorney
4. Consider a current interpersonal conflict you have with someone—or a conflict you have had recently. Apply the strategies discussed to this situation. How might you approach (or how should you have approached) the situation using interview strategies?

NOTES

[1] This conception of interviewing is based upon that in Robert S. Goyer, W. Charles Redding, and John Rickey, *Interviewing Principles and Techniques: A Project* (Dubuque, Ia.: William C. Brown, 1968), p. 6.

[2] An excellent discussion of these various types of interviews is found in Charles J. Stewart and William B. Cash, *Interviewing: Principles and Practices* (Dubuque, Ia.: William C. Brown, 1974), pp. 14–18.

[3] The extreme closed question—with only two possible answers—is often called a *bipolar* question.

[4] Sometimes leading and loaded questions are called *directed* questions since they indicate the desired or appropriate response.

[5] A more detailed explanation of probes and their use is in Gary M. Richetto and Joseph P. Zima, *Fundamentals of Interviewing* (Chicago: Science Research Associates, Inc., 1976), pp. 16–19.

[6] Formal interviews, of course, may be more structured and less easy to end.

PART 4

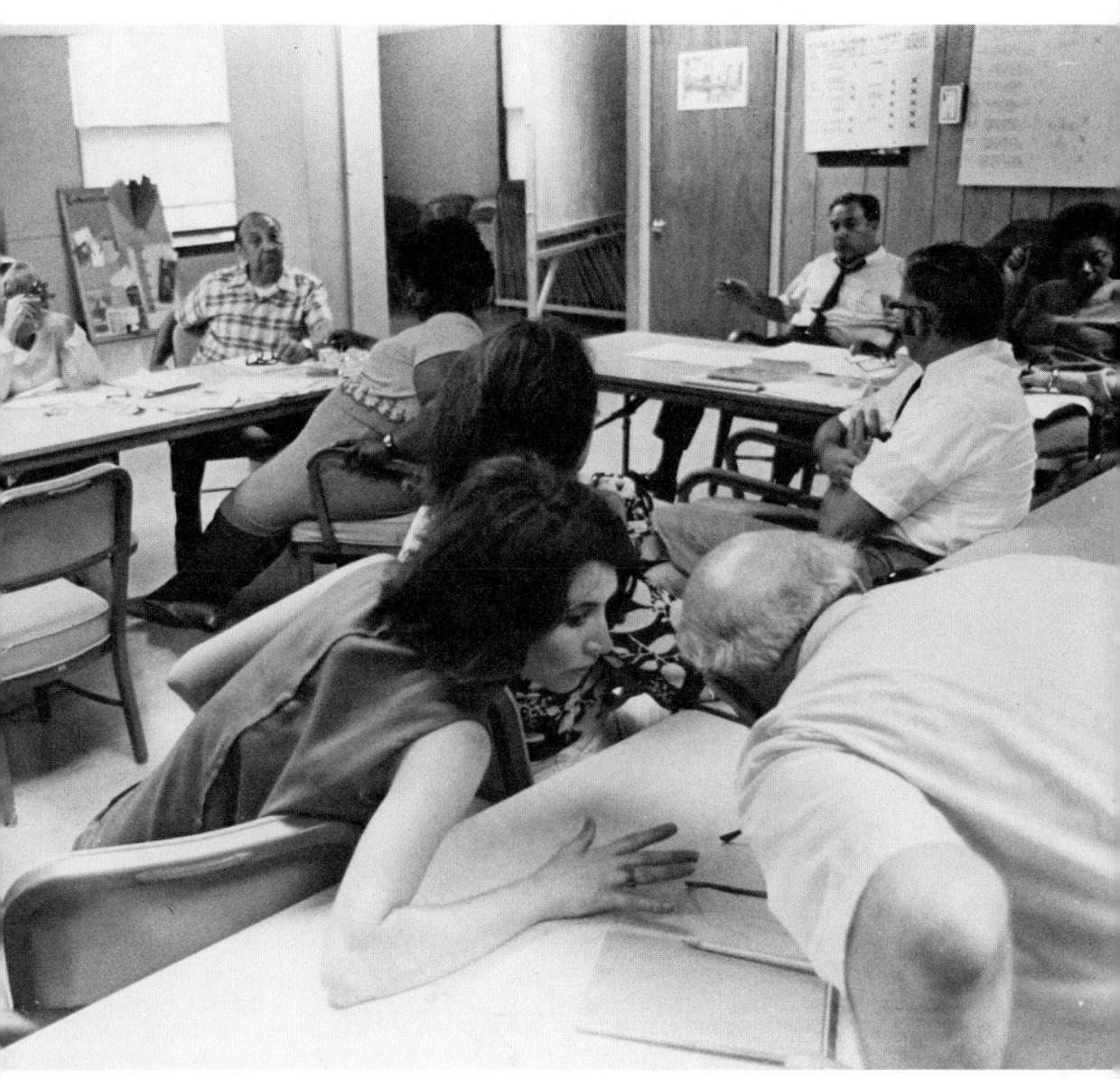

INTRODUCTION

The focus of this part of the text is on *group conflicts and strategies*. During your lifetime, you will probably participate as a member of one or more groups. Some collections of people have no common goal: they are not groups, but *aggregates*. Groups share a common purpose. As a group member, you may experience conflicts of different kinds and it will be useful to know about strategies of mediation for those conflicts.

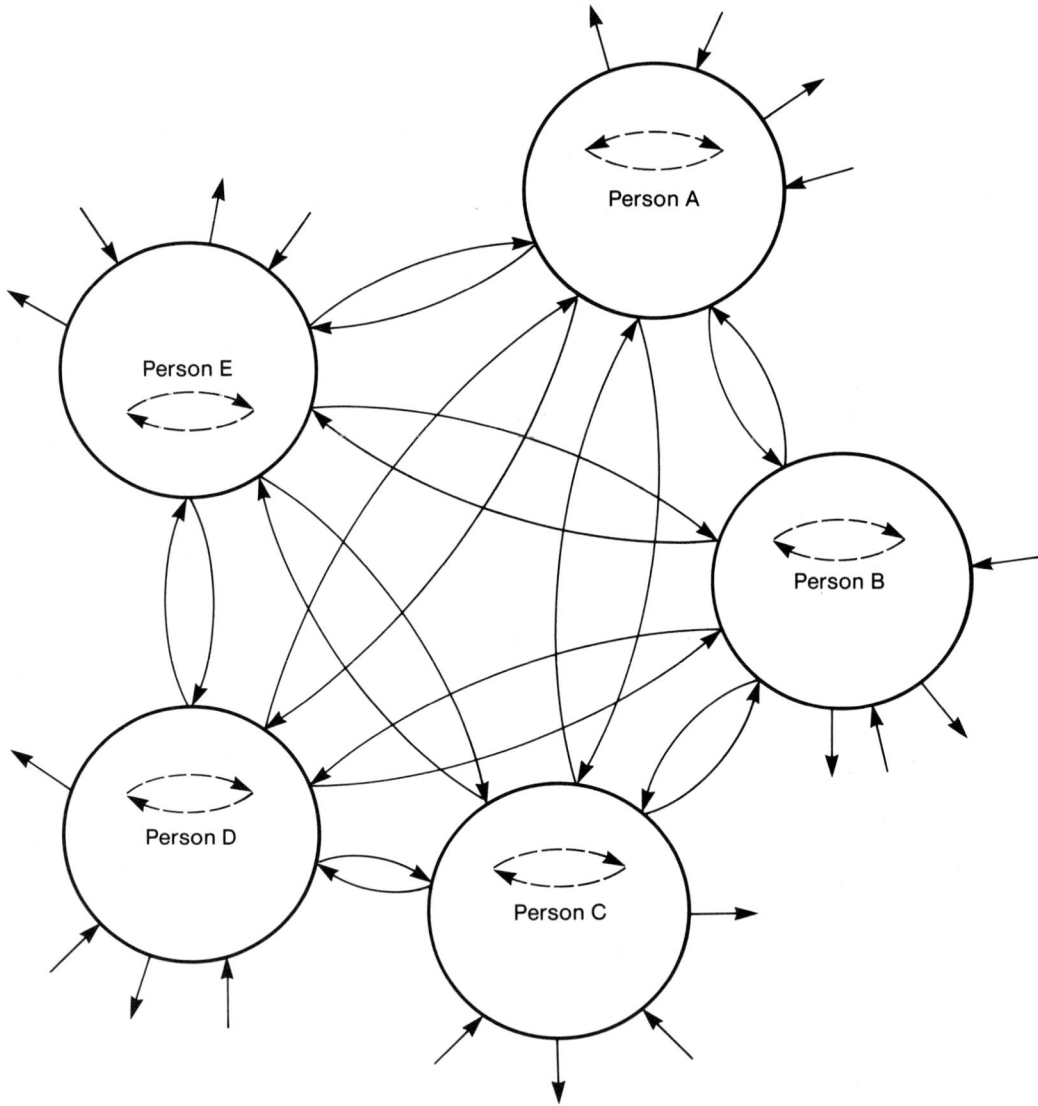

Fig. 1 The small group setting

In the Fig. 1, the arrows refer to the idea that transactions aimed at recreating meaning can occur among all the people involved at one time. Within that group activity, *interpersonal* problems and strategies of mediation cannot be ignored: Person A, for example, can engage in interpersonal communication with any one of the other members. At the same time that interpersonal and group transactions are occurring, note that each person can be communicating *intrapersonally* (see the broken arrows). Finally, as all these other transactions are occurring, each person (and the group) is part of an ongoing system: group members influence and are influenced by people and things *outside* the group (see the straight arrows outside group.)

Group conflicts can be of several types, as Chapter 12 will explain. Sometimes these conflicts can be mediated by strategies you have learned in earlier discussions. The section entitled "Applying What You Know in New Ways" which follows Chapter 12 will help you to see the application of earlier strategies to the group situation. Chapters 13, 14, and 15 will describe several other strategies of mediation for group conflicts.

12
SMALL GROUP CONFLICTS AS PROBLEMS

Small group communication can be extremely complicated. When you become a member of a group involved in some activity, you continue to communicate *intra*personally—and so does each of the other people. You communicate *inter*personally with a number of separate individuals—and so does each of the other people. In an important sense, though, something else happens as well. You begin to communicate with more than one person at the same time: the several people around you become an *audience* of people. Meanings for language and nonverbal symbols become much more varied. Messages sometimes become more numerous. The network of channels becomes more complex. In short, the group situation is a complicated setting for communication.

To understand how group communication conflicts can become problems, you must understand at least five problem areas: group membership conflicts; people-task balancing conflicts; conflicts in climate; decision-making problems; and problems of dysfunctional roles. Those are the five topics that will concern us most. Before those problems can be fully understood, you should know something about group communication generally. The nature of small group communication is our first topic.

THE NATURE OF SMALL GROUP COMMUNICATION

There are numerous ways of defining small group communication. For our purposes, small group communication will be *communication among three or more perhaps equally active parties who are usually in close proximity and who share a common goal or purpose.*[1] Four things are important in the definition. First, a small group is made up of three or more parties. (The interview, on the other hand, may have several people, but they somehow represent only two parties, or sides: interviewees/interviewers.) Each member of the small group may represent a different party, side, or position—represented by one or more people. In a small group, you should expect to find at least three such parties. Second, all the parties have the capacity to transact. They all, perhaps not equally, take turns talking, listening, asking questions, and so forth. Third, the parties are usually, but not always, in close proximity. Sometimes group communication is carried on with a conference telephone call. Sometimes group communication can occur through the mail; but these are the unusual instances. Usually the group members will be positioned so closely together that nonverbal cues are extremely important. Finally, members of a small group share a common goal or purpose. (In the interview situation, each party may have a particular purpose, and there is no reason to expect that the purposes are the same.) In the small group, however, the purpose will be shared or else the group is merely a *gathering of people*.

As an individual in contemporary society, you experience many gatherings of people. Your family, your club, your classes, and your Greek organization are examples. Are these *small groups* as I use the term or are they merely crowds of people? That depends upon the situation. If your family is sitting in the living room with some members reading and some talking, that is probably not a small group. When your family *gets together* to decide about arrangements for Aunt Minnie's surprise party, then it is a small group: a purpose or goal is shared by these fairly equally transacting, face-to-face parties of three or more people. Similarly, if club members are chatting before a meeting, they probably would not be considered a small group. If the same people gather to comfort—in various ways—a member whose father has just died, a small group is in action. If your class meets as a unit for the purpose of sharing information, it can be termed a small group. Yet, if the class is only a gathering of people with different goals and levels of interest, it does not serve as a small group. The major characteristic of the small group is the common or shared purpose.

Since the shared purpose is so basic to understanding small groups, you should understand that you probably are or will be a member of different types of groups. Traditionally, the kind of group is determined by the common goal of the group. One type of group, the *problem-solving group*, is illustrated by the family making a decision. Problem-solving groups may be the most familiar type. Sometimes such groups are called *committees*. In business and government, they may be called *task forces*. In medicine or the military, they may be called a *team*. Whatever their specific title, people frequently get together for the purpose of making a decision about a problem.

Sometimes people form a small group for the purpose of *finding or sharing information*. The class which is meeting for the purpose of mutual learning is an example. Governmental agencies sometimes create a fact-finding group.

Research in the social sciences is frequently done by teams of people who share the goal of discovering information. In your future job, you may find yourself a member of a task force which must discover information about new markets or an accounting procedure. Information and knowledge are being discovered and created at rapid speed. The chances are good that eventually you will find yourself engaged in an information-finding or sharing group.

Another type of group is represented by the earlier example of the club which meets for the purpose of comforting a member. *Counseling or therapeutic groups* include orientation meetings, sensitivity groups, and special groups such as Alcoholics Anonymous and Parents Anonymous. The goal here is to have people help other people. Mutual support and understanding are often the key ingredients in such groups. Even when there is a leader such as a psychologist, a psychiatrist, or a specialist in rehabilitation, the emphasis is upon people who share a common goal.

Though the three types of groups mentioned have become traditional categories of small groups, you should realize that there are others. Groups frequently have shared goals which are not exclusively one of the three mentioned. *Study and growth* meetings sponsored by churches, clubs, and so forth, are neither exactly problem-solving nor information-sharing groups. The common goal of these groups may be to help one another persuade one another toward higher understanding. *Search committees* in education, government, and business may have the task of discovering information *and* solving a problem. These committees may present their views about people who should be hired or about which plant site should be chosen. Even *parties* (social occasions) of various sorts or in honor of someone or something may serve the functions of small groups. *Social clubs* themselves may be seen as groups whose goal is enjoyment. To understand a group, you should know its *specific shared purposes*. The general categories of information finding and sharing, problem solving, and counseling or therapeutic groups do not describe well all the groups you may experience.

An understanding of the nature and the kinds of small groups prepares you to understand certain conflicts that can exist in them. Later in this chapter we shall examine people-task balancing problems, conflicts in climates, and decision-making problems. Our first topic, however, is group participation conflicts.

GROUP PARTICIPATION CONFLICTS

Some of the problems that you will confront in a small group relate to *participation* conflicts. Even though you and the group share a goal, the group consists of different people. As a group member, some of your problems will arise simply because of who you are. To explain that, we shall analyze the group in terms of intra/interpersonal conflicts, problems involving status, representation problems, and group membership conflicts.

Intra/interpersonal problems in the small group

This chapter was introduced by noting that intrapersonal communication and interpersonal communication are part of the small group setting. During the small group experience, you and others communicate intrapersonally as well as with other single individuals. Intrapersonal and interpersonal *communication*, then, have to be added to the special concerns of the small group. Similarly, intrapersonal and interpersonal *conflicts* cannot be forgotten, but simply have to be added to the special conflicts that arise in the group setting.

Any of the conflicts we previously discussed as intrapersonal or interpersonal may be problems in the small group. As you sit amid other people who have a common goal, you may experience conflicts in self-concept. You may experience problems related to value conflicts or information-processing conflicts. You certainly will find the need for intrapersonal decision making. You also may discover interpersonal conflicts between you and any one (or several) of the other group members. You may not find power, liking, or distance relationships to be comfortable for you. You may feel the need to mediate factors of dominance, similarity or dissimilarity, and so forth. Even if you do not experience these problems (which is unlikely), another member may. It is helpful to be aware of intra/interpersonal conflicts that occur during the small group experience.

My goal here is not to backtrack to review material already covered, but to look at group problems realistically. Some group problems are not *group* problems at all. They may be the intra/interpersonal problems of individuals which happen to manifest themselves during the small group experience. When they do exist, the need is for the mediation of conflicts that are not necessarily group conflicts.

Problems involving status

A dictionary would define *status* as a *condition, position,* or *standing.* Those terms are nearly as difficult to define as the word *status* itself. Yet, we all know someone who enjoys high status. In contemporary society, a member of the medical profession typically enjoys a high social position—so do politicians and entertainers. In some respects, status is related to the idea of *power* that we discussed earlier. People can get power from any of the sources discussed earlier—and status may come with the power. In another sense, power and status are far from the same thing. Hitler may have had power, but most of us would deny him a lofty status. A minister may have little (earthly) power, but he or she may enjoy wide respect. For whatever reason, people clearly vary in the nature and amount of their status.

Status becomes especially important in everyday small groups. Most groups will have members with varying amounts of status. You may be working with the rest of your family to solve a problem. Yet, you may not have the same status as your mother or father—and either one of them may enjoy higher status than the other. In a club project committee, you may be club president. Your status may be higher than that of an elected member. In an occupational setting, a task group may well have members of different status. A search committee for a new plant site may have a vice-president, a first-line supervisor, and several higher-level supervisors. It would be a mistake to assume that the joint project was being conducted by members of equal status. In any situation, the status of the group members may vary considerably.

A variance in status does not mean that conflicts will occur automatically. If (as a person of lower status) you are comfortable with the different levels of status, no problem arises. That is especially true, I suspect, if the members of higher status do not use their status to dominate or manipulate the group. But compatibility cannot be assured. You may resent the difference in status—and feel unable to affect the group process. One of the members with higher status may begin to play a superior role. It may even be that you wish to be submissive in the situation, but the member of higher status does not fulfill his or her position. There are all sorts of ways in which the concept of status can become a hindrance to the group effort, and to your personal desires.

Problems of representation

Among the things that can become problems in the group situation is the idea of *representation*. In politics, a member of congress is elected to represent the views of several tens or hundreds of thousands of people. Your responsibility in the small group setting may be to represent other people; you may be called upon to "speak for" others. In business, a task force may be composed of someone from engineering, someone from marketing, someone from research and development, and someone from sales. Each person may have the responsibility of representing a whole group of people in the organization. In government, a blue-ribbon committee may attack a problem. The members may represent various groups within society: the elderly, the black community, the young, management, labor, and so forth. In a hospital staff meeting, members may represent physicians, nurses, the technical staff, the personnel department, the administrators, and the service facilities. When you find yourself in a small group setting, do not be surprised if you are called upon to represent the views of others.

Representation presents some possible group membership problems. For one thing, almost nobody can represent accurately the views of another person—much less those of several or many other people. Representatives are not usually *delegates*. Delegates are people who have been told how to vote or to speak on a particular problem: *delegates* to a national political convention are usually told how they must vote on the first ballot. *Representatives*, on the other hand, usually have no direct guidance as to how to vote or what to say.

They are called upon to represent fairly the views of the people whom they represent. At times, exact guidance will be almost nonexistent.

Your membership in a small group may create conflict for you in several ways. First, you may perceive your role to be that of delegate, but others may think of you as a representative. You get little guidance, and guidance may be exactly what you seek. Second, you may perceive yourself to be a representative, but others may view you as a delegate. You get all sorts of advice about how to perform your duties, but you want none of it. Finally, you may confront a situation where your views and the views of those you represent come into conflict. If you do and say what your engineering department wants, you might not represent your own views. On the other hand, if you represent your own views, you might not be representing the views of the engineering department. Any of the situations just discussed can be a source of conflict. You may need to mediate a problem created by your membership as a representative.

Conflicting memberships

Another problem with group participation can arise because you are seldom a member of only one group. You may be the student representative on a campus-wide committee. Whose views do you represent as you attack a common problem or goal? Certainly, you should represent students. You may also be a devout member of the Jewish faith. You may be living in off-campus housing. You may be a management major. You may be a political liberal. You may be a student who has an automobile. You may be married. What views will you represent? In some situations, the question is no problem at all. The views of all these different groups may be compatible, but that probably will not always be the case. The views and interests of any of these groups may conflict with those of any of the others. As a student, you want a pedestrian campus; as a student with an automobile, you may want no change. As a management major, you may want a program expanded; as a student generally you want no increase in university or college fees. The decisions that you are called upon to make may be difficult. They may be difficult in part because of the conflicts in your group memberships.

We have discussed conflicts arising from group participation. Some of those problems are intra/interpersonal in nature. Some arise from problems of status or representation. Some are created by the various large groups of which you are a member. These are not the only sources of small group conflict. Other sources of conflict can be problems of balancing people and tasks.

PEOPLE-TASK BALANCING PROBLEMS

Some of the problems faced in groups arise from the nature of groups themselves. Groups are made up of people who have a common goal—but who are still individuals. Problems may be based upon the conflict between task and interpersonal needs, between personal and group goals, or between leadership and membership responsibilities. Let us examine each.

Task and interpersonal conflicts

In any group situation, you will be concerned about accomplishing a task. The task may be to solve a problem, to share or discover information, or to reach any other shared goal. If the group is to succeed, you must be concerned about reaching the group goal. The group, however, is made up of individual people. People are not machines who work exclusively with information and reach a solution. If a group is to succeed, you as a member must be concerned about the interpersonal quality of the group. Members must be able to work together to accomplish the shared task. Your concern for the group task and the people of the group must be *balanced*. Your group can fail if people get along well, but fail to reach the group goal. The group which completes a task by destroying interpersonal relationships among members may be just as much a failure as the group which fails at the task.

In some situations, balancing the people and the task may be no problem. Sometimes the work of the group will progress smoothly, with good interpersonal relationships among members. On other occasions, you will not find such a pleasant situation. Group members may disagree with one another on many issues. You may be faced with what seems to be a "no win" problem. Do you strive to accomplish the task? Do you strive to mediate the differences among group members? Or, do you attempt to accomplish both, knowing that you may accomplish neither? The conflict between task accomplishment and interpersonal relationships can become a severe problem. Your need for mediation may become serious.

Personal and group goal conflicts

Another source of group problems is the possible conflict between personal and group goals. In defining group settings, the idea of a shared goal was stressed. Groups must have a common goal, or they are nothing but unguided gatherings of people. In reality, though, individuals will have personal goals as well. In research in small group communication, these personal goals are often called *hidden agendas:* personal tasks that a group member pursues which may conflict with the group task.[2] You may sense that a certain group member is more interested in a personal goal than the group goal. You may feel that someone has his or her own ax to grind. In group terms, you suspect that this person has a hidden agenda which conflicts with the plans of the group as a whole.

Personal goals do not have to be in conflict with the group goal. Personal and group goals may be entirely compatible. They may also be in direct conflict. When you perceive that a group member is much more concerned with pursuing his or her individual goals, you probably will experience conflict. What do you do? Realistically, you cannot expect a person to reject all his or her personal beliefs for the good of the group. Yet for the group to succeed, something must be done. You need some means of mediating the conflict between personal and group goals.

Leadership and membership conflicts

A third and final source of people-task balancing conflicts is the problem of leadership and membership. A group obviously needs members in order to exist as a group, yet a group with no guidance is likely to flounder and fail. Who will direct the group when it faces a seemingly impossible problem? Who will provide support and guidance when they are needed? Who can be relied upon for fairness and impartiality? These and other questions are the concerns of leadership. Some groups have formal leaders.[3] A committee will have a chairperson. A board of directors will have a chairperson-of-the-board. A medical team will have a head physician. A military company will have a commander. Other groups which are less structured may have no formal leader. Still, the tasks of guidance and leadership must be performed by someone.

The problem of leadership may create a number of conflicts. What happens when you are the formal leader, but you would rather be simply a member? What happens when someone else is leader, but does not want to—or cannot—fulfill the responsibilities? What happens when a competent leader suddenly can help your group no longer? What happens when you or another member begin to challenge the formal leader for power? If no member has been named the formal leader, how is leadership decided? How should it be decided? These are a few of the basic questions that can come into focus. Each one of them—and countless others—can create conflicts within you, within any other member, or within the group as a whole. When these questions become problems, your success and the group's may depend upon finding answers. Your success may depend upon mediating the conflicts involved in balancing membership and leadership in the group.

Groups, then, are best defined by the existence of a common task. What you must also remember about groups is that they are composed of people. Sometimes personal goals will conflict with the group goal. Sometimes the completion of a task will conflict with the quality of the interpersonal relationships, and sometimes the matter of leadership can be a source of conflict. In sum, some group problems are conflicts involving the need to balance tasks and people.

PROBLEMS IN CLIMATE

As we discussed earlier in relation to interpersonal relationships, *climate* is a concern in communication. Climates can be described as supportive, defensive, or something between those extremes. Characteristically, groups develop their own climates. In the group setting, a climate of defensiveness can lead to extreme conflict. Group members may begin to disagree on everything. They may come to dislike one another *personally*. They may not be able to agree upon an acceptable *procedure* for completing the task. They may begin to engage in extensive quarreling about *content, information, or issues*. Some of these disagreements might occur regardless of the climate. Yet, a defensive climate is likely to create conflict from matters that normally would be no problem. In traditional group terms, the climate becomes characterized by *conflict,* a term which you know much about by now. Behaviors which create extreme defensiveness are sources of group conflict.

Surprisingly, even behaviors that generally create supportive climates can create equally serious problems. Extreme support within the group can lead to *conformity* or even *groupthink:*[4] a going along with whatever is said or done. As discussed in Chapter 1, extreme levels of conformity do not help any group. A climate of conformity can make everyone's ideas "just fine"—no matter how poor they may actually be. Such a climate may speed the progress of the group and make all group members feel extremely comfortable, but a question arises. Are speed and a comfortable feeling more important than the task being done well? For you and others in the group, a climate of conformity may be just as undesirable as a climate of conflict. The result of extreme conformity, ironically, may be conflict at the intrapersonal or interpersonal levels.

Closely related to the concerns for conflict and conformity is the question of *risk taking*. Risk taking is the willingness of members to share an idea; to "send up a trial balloon."[5] In climates of conformity, members may be reluctant to share an idea: they may not want to "rock the boat." Perhaps more often, conformists may be more than willing to take the risk of presenting a new idea. After all, in a climate of extreme conformity, it may be that anything goes. In climates of conflict, a complex situation also arises. Members may take too many risks. They may not care what happens. On the other hand, they may avoid taking risks. After all, they reason, the idea will be immediately rejected. The problem with risk taking is simply stated: How do you as a group make sure that people feel free to take risks that may reasonably help the group? The group does not need reckless and foolish ideas that are presented with an "I don't care" attitude. It also does not need a situation in which good ideas are missed because no one will take a risk.

The question of responsible risk can be a source of group conflict. Group members must be confident that their views can be presented and heard fairly. Groups must know that the risk taking is for the benefit of the group. How is risk to be handled in a climate of conformity? How should it be treated in a climate of conflict? Does the climate need to be modified before risk taking can be controlled and managed for the good of the group? These are some of the questions about climate that can serve as the base for group conflicts.

PROBLEMS OF GROUP DECISION MAKING

We discussed decision making at the *intrapersonal* level. Our discussion became more complex with regard to *interpersonal* conflicts, because in the interpersonal setting, decision making has to be done with one other person. The situation must take into account not only your perceptions of evidence, appropriate qualifiers and reservations, warrants, and the nature of the claim before you, but also the perceptions of one other person.

Now, you find yourself in a group of several or many people. You will find at least two serious sources of general conflict. First, you must deal with the views and judgments of several or many people. The strength of evidence, the worth of warrants, the appropriateness of reservations and qualifiers are all somewhat individual matters.[6] Your task as a group member will include all the problems that arise from these different interpretations. How do you reconcile various interpretations of a claim? How do you decide upon appropriate qualifiers and reservations? In short, a major problem is how you make a group decision about anything: procedures, information, problems, methods of counseling, and so forth.

The group decision-making process presents a second major type of problem: the need for *consensus*. Consensus is not just a unanimous vote; groups may be merely able to arrive at a decision they can all live with. We call this mutually satisfactory decision a *consensus*. In some cases, group consensus will not be required. The Supreme Court, for example, does not have to have all its members agree upon one decision. Justices can issue a minority report stating how some members differed with the majority. Congressional committees have the same privilege. In situations such as those, decision making may be fairly simple. All the material, evidence, and views are heard and read, and people decide for themselves. The majority prevails. Frequently, though, a majority decision is not enough. At times, group members may have to make a jointly satisfactory decision. They must reach a consensus.

Reaching a consensus may be easy, difficult, or somewhere in between. If the group is characterized by conformity, group members may simply go along with the first suggestion mentioned. If the group is characterized by conflict generally, consensus may be difficult or impossible to obtain. Even if the group is well balanced between conformity and conflict, people may feel so strongly about the matter that consensus is difficult. The difficulty of reaching consensus will vary with the nature of the group, the members of the group, and the goal of the group.

Reaching consensus does not guarantee that conflict will be avoided. If your group's consensus is reached because no one is willing to risk disagreement, you still may experience conflict. You may know you should not have gone along when you did. In other situations, *you* may be satisfied with the decision, but one or several other people remain dissatisfied. Arriving at a consensus may avoid group conflict, but intrapersonal or interpersonal conflict can arise if there is personal dissatisfaction. The point is simply that the consensus must be a true consensus, and not merely a false statement of agreement.

In discussing group decision-making problems, we have focused upon two major areas. First, conflicts arise from having several or many people participate in any kind of decision-making situation. Second, the unique task of compromise arises, since most groups are supposed to arrive at a consensus of opinion or a consensual decision.

PROBLEMS OF DYSFUNCTIONAL ROLES

Research indicates that consensual decisions about most problems are superior to individual decisions.[7] Consensus demands that each member must analyze information and ideas clearly. All the members contribute somehow to the common goal. On the other hand, each member has the power to hinder the success of the group. Each member can stop the group from arriving at consensus.

Specifically, each member may play a number of *dysfunctional roles* in the group. Patton and Giffin have provided an interesting and useful set of categories for the kinds of behaviors which can interfere with the progress of the group.[8] Not every group you experience will contain someone playing each of these dysfunctional roles, yet as you experience more and more groups, you will find your knowledge of these roles to be useful.

First, Patton and Giffin identify the Dominator. The Dominator attempts to control the direction or the procedures of the group. There can be no "fairly equal transaction" in the small group if one member tries to dominate completely. Dominant behaviors might include any of the defensiveness-creating activities we discussed in "Conflicts and Climate" in Chapter 8: strategy, control, evaluation, and so forth. By creating a defensive climate, the Dominator actually may prompt other members to react defensively. The only time that the Dominator might not cause extreme conflict is if every other member is comfortable with a submissive role. With a group of several or many people, the chances of all but one wishing to be submissive probably is slight. Dominators, then, can be extremely destructive to the thoughtful, sound progress of a group toward consensus.

Closely related to the Dominator role is that of the Fighter. The Fighter, more than anything else, is interested in what we have called quarreling. No one else's information is quite good enough. No one else's suggestion for a solution is sound enough. The Fighter is explicit about how he or she feels. Insults, laughter, and condescension are potential tools of the Fighter. Rather than wishing to take control, he or she simply wishes to disagree and to be disagreeable. The Fighter may not have a plan in mind for the group, but will know a bad plan when he or she hears one. The Fighter hears many "bad" plans, information, and ideas—"bad" seems to be the way he or she selectively perceives everything.

A third dysfunctional role is that of the Fixer, who has only one fixed approach or solution to all problems. Groups usually depend upon the possibility of consensus, but the Fixer is so closed minded that agreement is almost impossible. Fixers are set or fixed in their ways, and can destroy many of the creative and original ideas of the group generally. Creativity and originality call for new approaches, and the Fixer wants none of that. In essence, the Fixer may be less concerned about the progress of the group than he or she is about doing something "the way we've always done it."

The Attention Seeker may be even more destructive to the progress of the group. At least the Fixer is predictable. The Attention Seeker is not. He or she may use humor, irrelevant stories, criticism, or ongoing comments about the progress of the group. The Attention Seeker will be less interested in the group's goal than in the group's acknowledgment that he or she is around. Whatever will get and hold attention is worth doing. The Attention Seeker feels that he or she, rather than the group, is what is important.

The Attention Seeker may play another dysfunctional role: that of the Projector. The Projector is a person who feels self-conscious or guilty about his or her attitudes or actions. To get over this guilt, the Projector may blame others for the same attitudes and actions he or she dislikes in him- or herself. The feelings are projected onto someone else and then that person is criticized for those feelings. The Projector's actions and words may seem to be nothing more than attention-getting strategies, but beneath it all he or she may be covering up feelings about him- or herself.

The dysfunctional roles discussed so far have to do with people who take active, but destructive, steps. The Withdrawer is unlike these. The Withdrawer attempts to get away from the group. He or she may wish only that the group would get finished so he or she can go home. The Withdrawer may daydream or doze during meetings. He or she even may physically leave the group. These activities may occur all or part of the time. Sometimes, the Withdrawer will only turn away from sensitive issues or delicate problems. Whatever the case, instead of dominating or controlling the group, the Withdrawer attempts to leave the group either physically or mentally.

Two final roles should be discussed: those of the Depender and the Isolator. They are alike in that they relate to how members react to authority. They differ because they react in opposite ways. The Depender will be the first person to rely upon someone—anyone—for guidance, direction, and control. The Isolator, in contrast, is the first to reject any and all attempts to guide, direct, and control. Group success usually depends upon fairly equal transactions, but it also depends upon some degree of leadership. The Depender is unwilling to play any guiding role; the Isolator is unwilling for anyone to show leadership. In their separate ways, they both can hurt the progress of the group.

These categories of dysfunctional roles should be looked at realistically. One person can play several of these roles at the same time. You might play any one of these roles at some time. In groups you experience, you may find people to be generally cooperative. There will be exceptions. At a particular point in a discussion, a usually cooperative person may begin playing one of these dysfunctional roles. One person playing one of these roles at a crucial time may be destructive to the group: the enactment of one of these roles can create severe conflict in the group.

CHAPTER SUMMARY

We discussed how groups must be understood in the context of intrapersonal and interpersonal communication. When groups are meeting, several or many individuals are communicating intrapersonally. At the same time, several or many pairs of individuals are being influenced by their interpersonal relationships. These activities are occurring as the group develops problems that are fairly unique to groups. We began with a study of the nature of groups, identifying four basic characteristics: three or more parties, fairly equal transactions, close proximity, and a common goal or purpose. We discussed major purposes of groups, but also the ways in which certain groups do not fit well into the basic categories. In determining the nature of the group, its specific goal is most important.

Next, we turned our attention to group problems that arise from conflicts of participation. We discussed the questions of interpersonal relationships, status, representation, and conflicting memberships. People and task balancing was a second area of group problems. Here, the conflicts between task accomplishments and interpersonal relationships were described. Here also, we discussed conflicts between personal and group goals, and conflicts between membership and leadership. A third area of group conflicts involved problems in climate. The major factors of conformity, group conflict, and risk taking were discussed—both individually and in terms of their interaction. Fourth, we explored decision-making problems. We focused upon two major ideas: conflicts involved in any sort of decision making by several individuals; and conflicts involving the unique demand for consensus. Finally, we examined the various sorts of dysfunctional roles that members may play in a group. The group's progress can be hurt—or halted completely—if even one member is playing the role of Dominator, Fixer, and so forth. The group must be constantly aware that dysfunctional roles can lead to group conflicts.

Nothing ensures that these group conflicts will arise. On the other hand, nothing can guarantee that they will not occur. Your activities in groups have been many, and they probably will increase as you continue or begin a career. Group problems cannot be ignored because group activities may be important. More effective communication cannot mediate all the possible problems that you will encounter, but there are certain communication strategies that can be used to mediate some of the conflicts. The chapters remaining in Part 4 are devoted to explaining and illustrating these various communication strategies for the mediation of small group problems.

NOTES

[1] Note the similarity between this definition and the definition of interviewing on page 138.
[2] This potential conflict between personal and group goals will be discussed more fully in Chapter 13 on *gaming strategies*.
[3] Formal leaders may either be appointed or elected.

[4] See Irving L. Janis, *Victims of Groupthink* (Boston: Houghton Mifflin, 1973).

[5] For a discussion, see Vincent DiSalvo with Craig Monroe and Benjamin Morse, *Business and Professional Communication: Basic Skills and Principles* (Columbus, Oh.: Charles E. Merrill, 1977), pp. 193–95.

[6] It should also be pointed out that most judgments are socially learned or group-related. See Richard E. Crable, *Argumentation as Communication: Reasoning with Receivers* (Columbus, Oh.: Charles E. Merrill, 1976), pp. 191–93.

[7] See, for example, Harold H. Kelley and John W. Thibout, "Theoretical Analysis of Individual and Group Decisions," *Small Group Communication: A Reader,* ed. Robert Cathcart and Larry A. Samovar (Dubuque, Ia.: Wm. C. Brown, 1970), pp. 149–59.

[8] The material here is based upon Bobby R. Patton and Kim Giffin, *Problem-Solving Group Interaction* (New York: Harper & Row, 1973), pp. 40–41. Their discussion is based upon other, earlier sources.

APPLYING WHAT YOU KNOW IN NEW WAYS
(How to Apply Earlier Strategies in the Small Group Setting)

The strategy of perceiving in a group

In a sense, you already know several group communication strategies for mediation. You know something about *perception*. In the small group setting, you must realize that your perceptions of status, conflict, conformity, and leadership are just that: perceptions. They are active creations, based upon selective information processing, induction, and so forth. Some of the group problems you encounter may not be group problems at all. They may be problems in your (or someone else's) perception. If so, your analysis of these perceptions and the creation of new perceptions about the group or group members may be used as strategies for mediation. Remember to:

1. Understand that your perceptions of the group and any conflicts are, in fact, perceptions. What is your perception of the conflict?
2. Analyze the selectivity of your perception. (What have you ignored or paid particular attention to?)
3. Analyze how you have inductively pieced together the perception.
4. Examine the context of the perception.
5. Analyze the motivations for your perception.
6. Realize that your perception has been actively created by the factors above.
7. Adjust your perception if you now find it unjustified.

Use these strategies in the following case study:

Case study a. The group is involved in selecting a guest for class. This is the second day of discussion and various local people have been considered. The following exchange occurs:

Rita: Well, at least we have it narrowed down to two people. I guess that's progress.

Tim: Yeah, but we can't seem to agree on which person to ask.

Hazel: One of the factors is that we don't know which one might be able to speak to the class—we oughta consider that.

Rita: We could just set up a priority, and ask the first. If that one can't make it, we could ask the other. I don't mind doing it—the asking, I mean.

Hazel: This isn't getting us anywhere. We still have to decide which one we want most.

Rita: Well, it was just an idea. What do you think of me asking both?

Tom: It's all right with me; both of them are okay.

Hazel: You mean we ought to go on a first come, first serve basis? That's stupid.

Rita: What do you think, Tom?

Tom: I don't care what we do as long as we do something. But I'm not stupid.

Rita: Then, we all agree. I'll just ask each one and the one who can come is who we'll have.

Hazel, in particular, left the group feeling that she was an unimportant member. What accounted for her perception? Examine the context of the group and its assignment. Did this affect her perception? Do you think Hazel's perception was justified, or should she modify it? How could the situation have been handled differently by Rita to help the situation—or did she do all she could?

The strategy of verbal analysis in a group

In using verbal analysis in the group setting, you should:

1. Remember that words are (either arbitrary or rational) labels.
2. Decide whether labels are used for good reasons.
3. Remember that labels mean different things to different people.
4. Analyze the abstraction level of the language.
5. Use perceptual skills to avoid stereotyping.
6. Adjust language behavior (or suggest such adjustment in others) if the language has become a barrier to group progress.

Use these strategies to learn more about verbal analysis in the group.

Case study b. Review the situation in case study A. This time, pay particular attention to Hazel's use of the word *stupid*. Note Tom's reaction to it. Do you think Hazel's choice of words hurt her influence with the group? Do you think she was really calling the group *members* stupid? Why might Tom have reacted as he did? Did you have less sympathy for Hazel after she used the word? What might this tell you about the need for Hazel to use verbal analysis in the group?

The strategy of nonverbal analysis in a group

Nonverbal analysis can be used as a strategy for mediation in a group if you:

1. Remember that nonverbal cues may be interpreted in different ways.
2. Isolate the nonverbal cues that seem troublesome.
3. Try to discover the meanings attached to the nonverbal cues.
4. Compare those meanings to common meanings for such symbols.
5. Try to adjust (or suggest the adjusting) of troublesome nonverbal symbols.

Use these strategies to respond to the following questions:

Case study c. Look at the first study again. What sorts of nonverbal symbols do you suppose accompanied the verbal comments? Usually, the verbal and the nonverbal symbols are somehow related. If Hazel had the feeling that she was an unimportant member of the group, how might Rita's nonverbal communication have helped that perception? How do you suppose Hazel expressed the verbal symbol *stupid*? Given the reaction of Tom, might Hazel's nonverbal communication have made the comment more biting? Finally, concerning Tom: What did his long silence and later "I don't care" comment indicate about his attitude toward the group? How do you suppose that attitude was expressed nonverbally?

Decisioning and argumentation in a group

To help you use argumentation and decisioning in the group setting, you can:

1. Phrase the conflict as a statement or statements.
2. Treat each statement as a claim, phrased with reservations and qualifiers.
3. Examine each claim for evidence and the strength of the connection (warrant) between the evidence and the claims.
4. Weigh the evidence.
5. Try to agree on which claim is better supported.

Use these strategies in the following case discussion.

Case study d. Examine case study situation A for a final time. Amidst all the other problems, the group failed to decide between the two speakers. If you had been a member of the group, how could you have suggested a better method of deciding which speaker to invite?

Strategies of listening in the group situation

To effectively use listening strategies in the group situation, you can:

1. Try to discover the nature of the listening problems. (Is it that people cannot or will not listen?)
2. Try to overcome the listening problem.
3. Discover the nature of the listening response that seems appropriate or desirable.
4. Keep that desired response in mind as you respond.

You can use these strategies in the following case study:

Case study e. You are a member of a task force within your company. The job of the group is to suggest better methods of using the company newsletter. In the task group are you (as a fairly new employee), the personnel director, the editor of the newsletter, a supervisor from the advertising department, and the senior vice-president of the company.

Senior V-P: Well, let's get going. The problem we have is simply that the newsletter does not seem to be the chief vehicle for company news—rumor is the news carrier.

Editor: I'm not sure we have evidence for that. I think most people do read the newsletter. I hear them talk about it . . .

Senior V-P: Look, we're not here to crucify anyone.

Personnel Dir.: No, we're simply interested in whether the newsletter can serve its purpose better.

Supervisor: And, we've got to be honest; the letter is perceived as company policy, not news. The news they get is from the rumor mill. The letter doesn't do it.

Editor: C'mon. Nothing is going to be helped by exaggeration . . .

Supervisor: I know what you're going to say. You think that it's just a matter of "beefing it up a bit." But I don't agree. We need a whole new format.

Senior V-P: What do you think?

You: Well, I . . uh . . . I've only been here a short time. I've really enjoyed the newsletter . . .

Editor: There, see?

You: But, there is a well-developed rumor mill . . .

Supervisor: There, see what I told you?

Senior V-P: We don't seem to be going anywhere except in circles. Jones, just what are your goals for the newsletter? What do you want it to do?

Editor: There are a number of things . . . .

This situation can be analyzed from the standpoint of strategies of perception, verbal and nonverbal analysis, and argumentation and decisioning. What do those approaches to the case tell you? Our particular concern here, though, is for strategies of *listening:* The editor seemed preoccupied with self-defense. What kind of listening problem is that? What did you think of the way the editor was cut off in the middle of sentences? How do you describe that as a listening problem? You were called upon to provide a listening response. What kind of response do you think was asked for? What kind was given? How did the response given contribute to the perception of "going around in circles?"

Strategies of feedback in a group

Strategies of feedback can be useful in mediating group conflicts if you:

1. Make sure that the feedback is solicited, or at least welcome.
2. Describe your feelings, instead of evaluating or prescribing for others.
3. Make your feedback specific.
4. Focus upon things that can be changed.
5. Prepare to accept feedback in return.
6. Avoid feedback games.

The following questions can guide your learning of feedback strategies in the group situation:

Small group conflicts as problems

Case study f. Review the situation in case study E. The supervisor gave the editor feedback about the newsletter. The feedback, however, was weak from several standpoints. What are they? How could the feedback have been improved if certain strategies had been followed? What might the better feedback have sounded like? How might it have helped the conflict in the situation?

Interviewing strategies in a group

Interviewing, which is normally thought of in the interpersonal setting, can be useful in the group setting. You can learn to:

1. Identify a goal of mediation which seems related to interviewing.
2. Determine the important questions to be answered—or asked.
3. Pay attention to timing, nonverbal communication, and so forth.
4. Consider the goals of any particular person within the group.
5. Consider how the interview should begin and how you will know when the goal is reached.
6. Adjust the techniques according to the situation and interviewee.

In learning to use interviewing within a group, consider the following case.

Case study g. Look one more time at the situation in case study E. Toward the end of the exchange, the vice-president begins a special kind of transaction with the editor: What kind of interview is it? Why do you think it was necessary or desirable? What sort of question was used first in the interview? Does it appear that the interview will be directed or nondirected? Which should it be? Why?

In case studies F and G, I purposely called your attention back to case study E because as you develop skills in using communication strategies, you will find it important to apply perhaps several strategies to the same situation. Mediation may be accomplished by any one or several different strategies.

13
CONSENSUS AND WIN-WIN GAMING AS GROUP STRATEGIES

Some small group settings you experience are fairly unimportant: You and five others try to determine what sort of pizza should be ordered. Other group settings are crucial: Which of three multimillion-dollar plant sites should be purchased? Whether the group process is crucial or unimportant, you can benefit from understanding as much about the process as possible. One of the ways of understanding a group process better is to see what kind of *game* it is. Any group involves several or many people and a common goal. The question here is how the group members *relate* to one another in the decision-making process.

VARIOUS TYPES OF GAMES

Group processes can be described as either *win-lose, lose-lose,* or *win-win* games.[1] These descriptions refer to how group members relate to one another. In a win-lose game, the only way for certain members to win is to have other members lose. In the lose-lose game, each member loses something—maybe everything. In a win-win situation, each member wins. To illustrate how these various games are played in complex situations, let us see how they might be played in a simple situation.

A group of people has to make a decision. They have a bull, a cow, and enough grain to feed one animal for four years. One party wishes to retain an inventory of grain, one wishes to keep the cow, and one wishes to keep the bull.

173

If the decision is viewed as a win-lose game, then group members will fight one another to make sure "their" animal or feed will be kept. The decision becomes, Shall we sell the cow or the bull?—or what? If the decision is viewed as a lose-lose game, group members will attempt to figure out how each side can give in. They know that to reach a decision each side must lose something. The decision becomes, Shall we sell the grain, the bull, and the cow so that no side wins? On the other hand, the decision may be viewed as a win-win situation. Each group member tries to discover if there is some way for everyone to get what they want. The decision becomes, How shall we keep the grain, the bull, and the cow?

In this particular situation, the win-win attitude could be the best answer. The decision might be to feed the grain to both the cow and the bull. During that time, the cow could be bred to the bull. Before the grain was totally eaten, a calf could be bred, weaned, and sold. The proceeds from the sale could be used to buy enough grain to feed both the cow and the bull for an extended period of time and a reserve supply. During that time, more breeding could be accomplished and other calves could be sold. The result would be that all sides could win.

The bull and cow situation is simplistic, but it can be used as a model for more complex group situations. In any group setting, a number of decisions must be faced. The problem for the group is the *gaming attitude* of the group members. Will they perceive the situation as a win-lose situation, a lose-lose situation, or a win-win situation? Let us examine another, more complex situation.

In one small midwestern college town, parking for automobiles was a major issue. In order for merchants to have enough convenient parking for their customers, much of the available street parking was reserved for "thirty minutes only": enough time for shoppers, but hardly enough for students or faculty members. Merchants still complained that they needed more restricted parking in their commercial area.

The campus was nearly surrounded by the commercial area and students and faculty members had their own problems. Students wanted a pedestrian campus after a number of recent accidents involving faculty automobiles and student pedestrians. Faculty members complained that they already had enough problems in parking: all that was available to them was the campus area with its two parking lots and street parking.

Representatives of the three parties—merchants, students, and faculty—created a task force to study the problems. A lose-lose attitude would have been created if everything remained the same: no one would be happy. A win-lose attitude would have existed if one of the parties (or two) could have found a solution, even if it created more problems for the remaining party or parties. A win-win approach would mean that each party should be satisfied.

The actual solution was to build a parking tower upon the ground previously occupied by one of the faculty parking lots. The tower was built partly by a grant from a private foundation concerned with urban development, and partly by a fee charged for the public's use of it. The campus itself became pedestrian, the faculty had expanded parking facilities, and the merchants had increased areas of restricted parking.

How a group finally arrives at a decision will depend much upon their attitude. The word *attitude* is used here because some group members may not realize that they are playing a game at all. They simply want to have their ideas accepted. Others in the group may be taking a lose-lose attitude without knowing it. They simply assume that to reach consensus, everyone must lose a little. Even one group member may be enough to create a win-lose or lose-lose game in the small group. If members are free to choose, a win-win attitude seems best.[2]

The win-lose situation may involve sets of personal goals which seem to conflict. When one member or several members have their way, others cannot have their way. The win-lose situation may also exist where one set of personal goals conflicts with the group goal. If the group goal is to be reached, personal goals may not be met—and vice versa. In either case, the creation of a win-lose situation may be unhealthy for the group's interaction. The same can be said for the lose-lose situation. Personal goals as well as the group goal may be unattained. After all, in the lose-lose situation, members expect everyone to lose somewhat for the benefit of agreement. Even in this compromise situation—with everyone giving in a little, the group may suffer. The result may be that no one is entirely happy with the decision. The *group* goal, in fact, may be unfulfilled in the effort to keep everyone *personally* happy.

The win-lose and lose-lose situations are both specific problems involved in balancing people and tasks as discussed earlier. The balancing problem can be important, partly because of the displeasure of one or more of the group members. It is important also because virtually anyone in the group may engage in the kind of behaviors that signal a win-lose or lose-lose situation. The person who decides that his or her solution is the only one possible may provide a signal for battle lines and sides to be chosen for a win-lose game. The person who contends immediately that everyone must compromise may provide a signal that a lose-lose situation exists. By verbal and nonverbal means, the group can be turned toward either a win-lose or lose-lose attitude.

THE WIN-WIN STRATEGY

Fortunately, even one member of a group—you, for instance—can be sufficient to create a win-win attitude. You or any other member may have the power to turn the group's attention from win-lose or lose-lose attitudes. This does not mean that you attempt personally to control the direction of the group: that would be an *I win-you lose* situation. Instead, it means that someone must be responsible for suggesting some basic assumptions or ground rules for the group. If the group can accept these assumptions and act upon them, the win-win attitude can be the result. The strategy of win-win gaming can be based upon the following four ideas.[3]

First, the group must have a "we versus task" attitude instead of a "we-they" attitude. Any group that begins to interact will be made up of individuals with different biases, beliefs, and ideas. As we saw earlier, these individuals may also represent certain groups of people; they may belong to various other groups in addition to this one. The temptation may be strong for group members to argue for their side or their group or their belief. That means that these groups, beliefs, or sides can be seen as being *against* other sides, beliefs, or groups whom they do not represent. In short, the creation of a *we-they* attitude is entirely possible. One of the results may be a win-lose attitude. Another result may be a lose-lose attitude, where no one expects to win completely. Focusing upon the task or goal as truly a group problem can help the situation. You, as a group member, can suggest that despite group differences, the group should be united against the common problem or task. The target is not other group members, but the problem at hand.

Second, the group should identify who this "we" is. The *we* who are against the problem probably will not be only the members of the group. Whom do the members represent? How many different positions are being represented? Are there conflicts among the people whom the members represent? Identifying who makes up the *we* will provide an idea of how many people are being affected by the group decision. Identifying all those people and groups may also provide ideas about what sort of help is available to the group members. Clarifying who is being represented in the group may provide a means for mutual understanding in the group.

Third, it must be made clear to the group that the solution must take everyone's views into consideration and be acceptable to everyone. The phrase *be acceptable* is important. No one in a group should expect to win on every point. On the other hand, no one should have to expect to lose dramatically. *Consensus* is not the same thing as *compromise*—although they are sometimes viewed as synonymous. Compromise means that everyone loses a little so that the task can be accomplished. The result may be that no one is satisfied. Consensus means that a group finds a method by which virtually everyone agrees with the solution or the completion of the task. The parking situation was a clear example of the search for a consensus. In that situation, everyone won. The solution required seeking an alternative that was acceptable to everyone. That solution was different from how each side wanted the problem handled, yet it took note of everyone's personal goals and the goal of the group. The solution was more creative than the original solutions proposed by the various parties, but that is why it worked. The solution meant that each side pulled away from its original position long enough so that other solutions could be examined. When other solutions were examined, one was found that left everyone contented. In that sense, everyone won.

Problems, of course, vary in their difficulty, but most problems have several or many solutions. If members approach the group saying, "I will argue for my position," the result can be total conflict. If they can approach the task saying, "This is my position; let me hear yours and we'll try to make sure that we all win," the result may be the mediation of the group problem. A win-win situation can exist, even in more complex situations. To put this third concept into action, a final idea is important to the win-win strategy.

Fourth, the group must understand that open and honest communication is crucial. Personal and group goals cannot be merged in a final solution if personal goals are unknown. The hidden agenda is traditionally discussed as a destructive force in a group, not because it is a goal, but because it is hidden, or secret. The group cannot deal with hidden goals openly. Comments will be made and behaviors observed which make no sense to the group as a whole, because the group is unaware of what an individual is trying to accomplish. The win-win strategy requires that everyone in the group understand all the personal goals of members. Only then can these goals be integrated into the final group decision. Hidden agendas and secret goals may contribute to group conflict. Sincere and open communication about personal goals among supportive individuals is a main ingredient in win-win gaming.

QUALITY VERSUS ACCEPTANCE

Concentrating upon these four ideas is a way of creating a win-win strategy. Yet, groups and tasks do differ, and sometimes a balance must be struck between how good a decision is and how well it satisfies the group members. Norman Maier has argued that a group decision can be viewed as the product of *acceptance* multiplied by *quality*.[4] Sometimes, a group will have to be more concerned with the quality of a solution than with how satisfying the solution is to all members. At other times, the group's total acceptance of the solution is more important than the nature of the solution. Maier's argument means that the group should know the relative importance of agreement and the quality of the solution.

There are four basic situations that might confront a group: (1) The quality of the decision may be very important, while acceptance may not be; (2) acceptance may be highly important, while the quality of the decision may not be; (3) both may be of high concern; and (4) neither may be of extreme concern. These four are the basic situations. Obviously, there can be other situations: both quality and acceptance, for instance, may be of *fairly high* concern; or one or the other may be *a bit more* important. A decision of high quality and a fairly high level of acceptance may be just as good as a decision of fairly high quality and a high level of acceptance. Their *products* (quality times acceptance) would be basically the same. Let me illustrate.

As a group, your task may be to appoint one of the group as a representative to a larger group. Assuming you are all of fairly equal ability, the choice (quality of decision) is not nearly so important as the fact that everyone agree to the choice (acceptance). If, on the other hand, you are not all equally prepared to speak for the group, then quality may be more important than acceptance by everyone. In another situation, the group members might be of unequal ability, but the support of the whole group is essential. In that case, both the quality and the acceptance of the decision are extremely important. Finally, each member may differ in ability, but the job of representative is not very important. Moreover, the group's support may not be necessary. In this last situation, neither quality nor acceptance may be terribly important.

Usually, the decisions are not so clear-cut. Let us say your group is charged with the task of suggesting ways to save energy in a classroom building. The best, most effective ways are very unpopular: closing faculty offices during restricted times, lower heating levels, and so forth. You find that you can get fairly good acceptance of less effective measures—or you can get very little acceptance of very effective measures. The choice may be difficult, because the *products* of the decisions may equal the same energy savings—or it may be easy, since it does not seem to matter. In either case, the solution is less clear-cut and the situation more complex.

What makes the quality/acceptance problem even more complex is that their relative importance may be related to the kind of leadership the group must have. There is some indication—and reason to believe—that when the concern for quality is high, the group may benefit from more direction. When the concern is for acceptance, the group may benefit from a more completely free atmosphere.[5]

In trying to create a win-win strategy, you should analyze the group and the task with care. Clearly, you want everyone to win as you push toward a consensus, but the group must decide the relative importance of quality and acceptance. Gauging the relative importance of quality and acceptance is merely a part of the total strategy of win-win gaming. Once the win-win strategy has begun, the overall result may be mediation of the group's main problems.

In order to use win-win gaming effectively for mediation, you can:

1. Adopt a win-win attitude, which means you:
2. Adopt a *we versus the task* approach, and
3. Identify who the *we* are, and
4. Take everyone's views into consideration, and finally
5. Insist upon open and honest communication.
6. Then, determine the relative importance of quality and acceptance.

In order to practice win-win gaming strategies, consider the following case studies.

Case study one: the appointments. Mr. Horn needed to go to an important business meeting and his wife had committed them to a dinner engagement for the same evening. She could make apologies for him at the dinner, but she did not want to miss it herself. To complicate the situation, their teenage son, Harry, wanted to use their one and only automobile to go to a movie with friends. Mr. Horn resented all the other plans that were made (as he put it) without his consultation. Mr. Horn left the house and drove off, telling his wife and son to cancel their plans.

In this situation, a win-lose attitude was present. Mr. Horn was unwilling to even consider the fact that all their plans might have been coordinated. Instead, he won and let the other members of his family lose. A win-win attitude might have helped. Was there some way, for example, that the son could have driven his father and mother to their respective appointments—and then gone to the movie? We shall never know that, since Mr. Horn was unwilling even to discuss such creative possibilities.

Case study two. The group has been trying to choose a new novel to study in class, and has narrowed the selection down to three. Of the five people in the group, one is really opposed to Novel A. Two people would rather have that one than Novel B, but they do not feel strongly about the decision. The fourth person strongly favors B and the other person favors Novel C, but would accept Novel A willingly. What should they do?

The situation could be mediated in several ways, but two ways strike me as perhaps best. First, they should decide if the quality or the acceptance of the decision is more important. One of them is really opposed to Novel A; only one person favors B (although two more would accept it); and only one has expressed a preference for C. For a class project, acceptance may be more important than which decision they make. They probably should determine which novel has the least total rejection and choose that one.

There is, however, a second path open to them: They could begin the search for a novel which would be more generally acceptable. That would take more time—perhaps more than they have—but it is possible. In most group decisions, there will be the possibility of reconsidering solutions that have not been seriously thought of before.

In these two cases, strategies of consensus and win-win gaming could be useful in the mediation of group conflict.

EXERCISES

1. One of the best ways to discover the difficulties of arriving at a group solution to a problem is to work with something that is important to you. With the permission of your instructor, form groups of five or six people in class. Take upon yourselves the responsibility of creating a way for using peer grading on a class assignment. *Peer grading* means that all or some part of your grade will be decided by other members of the class. You may find that making a decision about something that really affects you is the best way to learn about consensus and win-win gaming.

2. This is your task: In groups of five or six people, create an exercise that can be used to teach win-win gaming to a class of high school students. Every member should assume that he or she will have some responsibility for helping conduct the exercise, so acceptance as well as quality is important. *Note:* To make the situation more interesting, after each of your groups has made a decision, have the groups in your class compare their exercises. See if the class as a whole can reach consensus about the best single exercise for the high school class.
3. Review your activities during the past few days. Try to remember any recent times when you have been a part of a group concerned with a group decision. Think of the nature of the winning attitudes in the group. What were the relative concerns for quality and acceptance? Did the group even consider these factors? What kind of decision was made? As you rethink the decision, were you satisfied (and are you now satisfied) with the group process and the group decision?

NOTES

[1] The names of these games become clearer with the personal pronouns attached: *I win-you lose, I lose-you lose,* and *I win-you win.*

[2] Here, I refer to situations where members are *delegates*—or have at least been given strict instructions on what positions to take.

[3] The ideas are based largely on those in Alan C. Filley, *Interpersonal Conflict Resolution* (Glenview, Il.: Scott, Foresman, 1975), pp. 25–30.

[4] N. R. Maier, *Problem-Solving Discussion and Conferences: Leadership Methods and Skills* (New York: McGraw-Hill, 1963).

[5] Though research needs to be done, the view is supported by some of the conclusions in Alan C. Filley and R. J. House, *Managerial Process and Organizational Behavior* (Glenview, Il.: Scott, Foresman, 1969), chap. 7.

14
DECISION-MAKING PROCESSES AS GROUP STRATEGIES

The Yellowbud, Ohio, village council is meeting to discuss recent energy shortages and the need for village-wide conservation. Members of the council have collected as much information as possible about energy supplies and energy consumption. The information includes state government figures, information from the regional energy suppliers, and the results of local public polls. Now what do they do?

Recently, your company has been hurt by cost overruns on several of its major projects. The estimates have always seemed accurate—until the project was well underway. Then, costs began to spiral and the company began suffering unacceptable losses. How does your group begin the attack upon the problem?

Your club has sponsored a Halloween carnival for charity for a number of years. Lately, attendance and earnings have been down. Something needs to be done to revitalize the carnival. What should be done?

The three different situations involve groups with tasks that are rather different. The first group has been called upon to examine and evaluate information; the second is confronted with a problem that demands a new procedure or solution; and the third group faces a problem that requires a creative, original solution. In a particular group, you may confront the need for skills related to one, two, or all of those situations. Moreover, to solve any group problem, argumentation may be a valuable skill.

This chapter, then, focuses upon four types of group strategies: information analysis, problem solving, creativity, and argumentation within the group. All of these processes involve decision making and all of these decision-making strategies can be useful to you for the mediation of group problems.

INFORMATION ANALYSIS

In some groups you experience, your task may be to gather and to analyze information. If that is the task of your group, you will find that information analysis is more complex than it might seem. Conflicts can arise over the kind of information necessary, the sources of information, the quantity of information, and the quality of the information. Someone in the group or the group as a whole must be able to analyze the information. The following ideas can be helpful to you.

First, consider the kind of information that the group needs. If the problem has to do with, say, energy, some information might be irrelevant. If your concern is for ways of conserving energy, information on the history of energy production probably will be irrelevant. Similarly, information about recent energy exploration, advances in new sources of energy, or current marketing techniques probably can be ignored. Your group's concern should be to focus upon the kind of information that you need.

Second, consider the various sources of information that might be helpful. Information must usually be sought out, so the second consideration might be the potential sources of information. You might ask the following questions:

A. How much do I as an individual already know about the issue or task? (One of the reasons you may find yourself on a task force or committee is that you already have some knowledge or experience.)

B. How much do others in the group know about the issue or task? (One of the truly great advantages of groups is that they allow several or many people to pool or share ideas and insights.)

C. What are the sources of outside information about the task or issue? (Sometimes the outside sources may be other people within the company or organization; sometimes those sources may be government studies, scholarly publications, newspaper accounts, trade journals, and so forth.)

D. What are the sources of information that list sources of information? (Indexes, reference works, bibliographies, footnotes in books, and so forth usually do not contain much information about an issue. They can be extremely useful, though, to identify sources of information.)

E. Which of the above sources of information can be tapped in the amount of time that the group has? (The group should not waste valuable time on sources of information that are impossible to obtain before a deadline.)

A second step in information analysis, then, is to discover all the potential sources of information.

Decision-making processes as group strategies 185

Third, as a group member involved in information analysis, *consider the quantity of information* your group has gathered. A great deal of information may be obtained from a small number of sources. On the other hand, a great many sources of information may provide very little information. Because there may be no direct relationship between the number of sources of information and the quantity of information, you might wish to ask the following questions:

A. How much information does the group need to complete its assignment? (The amount may vary widely depending upon the nature of the task and the time allowed for completion.)
B. Does the group now have enough information? If not, how do you know? If it has enough, how do you know that? (Most topics or issues that are important may have been discussed or examined by thousands of people and in thousands of printed sources. It is unlikely that a group will have *all* the information. The question is whether the group has *enough* to complete its task.)
C. Is the information drawn from a number of different sources or just a few? (One book, for example, may provide dozens of ideas and bits of information. Yet, the one book is only one source of opinion or information—and one source or just a few may not be enough for the group task.)
D. Does this quantity of information come from sources with a variety of viewpoints, or just one? (Even if the sources are numerous, they may all represent the same position on the issues. At some point, the group must ask whether there is an adequate quantity and variety of viewpoints being represented by the information.)

By asking these questions, you may be able to guide your group's assessment of the quantity of information.

In group tasks as well as individual tasks, quantity is not the same thing as quality. A group may have much information, but the information may not be of high quality. *Fourth*, then, *consider the quality of the information*. Some questions that may help you judge the quality of the information your group gathers include the following:

A. How reliable or credible is the information—and what does the group mean by *reliable* and *credible*? (In general, *reliability* means that your group can *depend upon the accuracy or truth* of the information. *Credibility*, as we have seen, refers to how believable something is to the group. In any particular group task, the exact definitions of reliable and credible may differ. Your group must decide what reliable and credible mean, and then whether the information has these qualities. Your group may need to take into account whether sources of information are biased or prejudiced, for example.)
B. How recent is the information? (Many topics and subjects change quickly as more and more information is discovered. On certain topics, a one-year-old

report may be recent enough; on certain other topics, a one-year-old report may be hopelessly out of date. The group must decide whether the information is recent enough for its purposes.)

C. How relevant is the information? (Sometimes information that seems good may not even relate to the task at hand. In analyzing one city's problems, another city's problems may or may not be relevant. The relevance might depend upon the similarities between the cities in size, geographic location, population, industrialization, and so forth.)

D. How accurate is the group's interpretation of the information? (The gathering of information involves those processes of reception, interpretation, choice, and symbolization. Has the group or have members of the group accurately recreated the meanings of the information? Do members agree upon the interpretation of the information? Does the original source agree with the group's interpretation of the information? Your consideration of these may give you insight into the accuracy of the group's interpretation.)

E. Is the information consistent with what the group already believes about the task or topic? (When the group discovers information consistent with what it already believes, conflicts over information may be minimized. A different situation occurs when the group's earlier beliefs conflict with the new information. At least three things may happen: (1) the group may decide to ignore the new information; (2) the group may decide to reject its earlier beliefs; or (3) the group may combine its earlier beliefs with the new information so that each is *modified* and both are acceptable.)

F. Are the bits of new information consistent with one another? (If the group has been careful to obtain information from a variety of sources, that variety can be a check for accuracy. Consistent information from a variety of sources is one indication that the information is reliable. If the bits of information are inconsistent with one another, then the group must reexamine each bit of information. Some of the information may simply be rejected—or more information may be sought. Whatever the result, checking the consistency of the information can be a check upon the quality of the information.)

Information gathering, then, may be a more complex task than the group anticipates. At the very least, information gathering means information analysis. Information analysis involves a concern for kinds, sources, quantities, and qualities of information. Information analysis can be an effective strategy for the mediation of conflict that involves gathering and evaluating information.

DEWEY'S STEPS TO REFLECTIVE THINKING

Some group tasks, however, involve a more direct emphasis upon the solution of problems. The term *emphasis* is important here. Nearly every solution of a problem will involve the gathering of information, so nearly every problem-solving group will also be an information-gathering group. The difference lies in the end product. The information-gathering group is finished with its task when it gathers all the necessary and relevant information. *The problem-solving group is not finished with its task until the information is used to solve a problem.*

To make the group mediation of problems easier, several methods of problem solution have been proven effective. This section will include a discussion of one of these: Dewey's Steps to Reflective Thinking, also called the Reflective-Thinking Model.

Years ago, John Dewey proposed several steps which could be used by individuals wishing to solve problems.[1] The steps have been shown to be valuable in group problem solving.

First, your group should *become aware of the problem.* Some groups are established because a problem is already known to exist. Some groups, though, already exist and begin to search for problems that should be solved. This second situation is not as unusual as it might seem. The March of Dimes, for example, was once an organization that funded research and projects related to polio. With polio virtually eliminated, the group sought other problems that needed solution. One result is the "Mother's March Against Birth Defects." Similarly, the American group that funded research and projects related to tuberculosis became the American Lung Association. With TB virtually eliminated, the group has turned its attention toward such problems as air pollution and smoking, both of which also affect the lungs. In corporations and medical organizations, standing committees or boards may exist. Their task may be to solve whatever problems arise. Before solution can begin, however, the group must take that first step and become aware of the problem.

Second, your group should *define the problem* that you now recognize. What is the nature of the problem? What are its boundaries? How can it be defined? Neither a group nor an individual can attack a problem effectively without knowing what the problem is. Still, this may be one of the more difficult steps in the process. In teaching small group communication, I have seen students flawlessly describe the importance of this step on an exam—and then ignore it when they were working in a small group problem-solving situation. The temptation in groups seems to be to move immediately to the discussion of possible *solutions.* That temptation is one of the main reasons why the various steps in reflective thinking are important. If your group follows Dewey's steps it should come to a more systematic, intelligent solution. Following the steps in order is not crucial, but somewhere early in the discussion the definition of the problem should be explored. Your group's definition of the problem can be helped if you consider the following points:

1. Phrase the problem as a short, concrete statement, and write it. You might write, "How can library material be made more available to students?"

Avoid such generalities as, "What can be done about the library?" or "What can be done about library material?"
2. Ask other members to do the same.
3. Compare interpretations of the problem.
4. Discuss what you find in the comparison: Do you agree on the definition of the problem? Is something like, "How can library material be made more available to students?" still too general? Maybe you are concerned with books, but not periodicals—or with part-time students, but not full-time students.
5. Once you think you agree on the nature and definition of the problem, you may want to write it again individually—as a check.
6. Finally, as you discuss the problem, don't speak about it as *the problem;* instead, use the exact definition.

These procedures can help in your definition of the problem.

Third, the group should *analyze the problem.* This is the stage of the group process of problem solving where information gathering and analysis are important. What are the *facts:* the beliefs that are well supported and shared by nearly everyone who has expertise in the area? What *assumptions*—unstated but accepted beliefs—relate to the problem? How serious is the problem? How long has the problem continued? Who is affected by the problem? How are they affected? Who is not affected by the problem? Why? What are the major aspects of the problem? How are they related? These are among the specific questions that the group may wish to answer at this point in their process. The exact questions, of course, will depend upon the nature of the problem and the group. In analyzing the problem, the group must gather and analyze all the information that may aid the understanding of the problem. At this point also, then, the strategies of information analysis are especially helpful. Good information is essential to your group's solution of the problem.

Fourth, the group should *establish standards or criteria for the solution* of the problem. Standards or criteria are nothing more than yardsticks for measuring or gauging the final solution. Does the solution need to be economical? Does it need to involve no change in company personnel? Does it need to be a long-term or short-term solution? Does it need to be a solution that works immediately, or can it take effect slowly? Does the solution need to solve the whole problem, or may several solutions be presented to solve different parts of the problem? At times, the group will be *given* the standards that are important. At other times the group may have to establish its own standards. At still other times, the group may be given certain standards, but have to create others of its own. In any case, your and the group's attention to standards for a solution are important.

Fifth, the group should *suggest possible solutions* to the problem. What might work? What has worked in similar situations? What do other people say will work in this situation? Are there solutions that have almost worked in the past that could be revised and improved? At this stage in the process, the group should worry about only one thing: the creation of as many ideas as possible. Suggestions should be as freely given and as freely accepted as possible. Judgments of the solutions should be withheld until all possible solutions have been suggested. Research has suggested that the more ideas, the better. You and your group should take this into consideration when solutions are suggested.

Only after all possible solutions have been presented should the group enter the sixth phase of the process: Sixth, the group should *compare solutions with criteria or standards—and select the best solution*. Each of the suggested solutions should be judged according to the standards for solution. Some of the solutions may fail to meet any of the standards. Several may meet two or three of the standards. One or two may meet nearly all the standards that are being used. The group task is to use the standards and select the solution that all members can agree meets most or all of the standards. The task may be difficult. Some members may disagree that one solution is clearly superior. At the point where only two or three solutions are being considered, the group may have to create other standards of judgment. Which advantages does one have over the other(s)? Are the advantages important or not? Do the advantages relate to important *new* standards for evaluation? The group may need to gather additional information—or reanalyze the problem. These are not steps backward when the number of solutions has been narrowed to two or three. Instead, these steps are ways of carefully and deliberately arriving at the *best* solution from a group of several *good* solutions.

The seventh and final step in the process is the group's *testing or implementation of the solution*. Some group solutions can be tested before they are put into effect. If testing is possible, the solution might be used in some sections of a business, with some employees, or at some stated times. Frequently, however, testing is not possible. Because of factors such as time and money, the group solution must be put into effect immediately. When that is the situation, the group may be responsible for both implementing and evaluating the solution. Ongoing evaluation and modification may take the place of initial testing. They may serve the same functions.

Attention to these steps can help your group keep its efforts aimed at the problem. You should not think, however, that these phases in the decision-making process are *rules*. A group might create the criteria for a good solution prior to suggesting solutions. A group might need to go back and redefine the problem on the basis of the analysis of the problem. Dewey's Steps to Reflective Thinking should serve as a guide for the group. The group should use the steps creatively to make sure that the problem and the solution are considered carefully.

CREATIVITY AND DECISION MAKING

Some of the conflicts experienced in groups may call for more creativity than information analysis or problem solving. Even when groups are expected to be creative, the same arguments may be repeated. The same expressions of frustration may be heard. Even a group that tries to follow Dewey's reflective-thinking model may become frustrated. The steps may be followed as though they were rules. At such times, you may help your group by focusing upon strategies of *creativity*. This section will present two of these strategies, including *brain-storming* and *synectics*.

Brainstorming

Brainstorming is the process of generating as many ideas about a given topic or problem as possible. One of the advantages of group activity is that each member added to the group should add additional ideas to the group's thinking. The group may want information about how to define the problem or how to analyze it. The group problem may be to suggest various standards or criteria or to suggest possible solutions. In any of those phases of decision making, brainstorming may be of help.

Brainstorming is based upon several basic assumptions.[2] First, *the more ideas* about definitions, standards, or solutions that are generated, *the better* for the group. In a sense, an increase in the *quantity* of ideas leads to an increase in the *quality* of ideas. There is no magic here. As more and more ideas are developed, the group can be more selective about those that they will use. A focus upon a large quantity of ideas may also encourage someone to throw out a "shaky idea" which turns out to be one of the best. To encourage these trial ideas, a second assumption of brainstorming is that *no initial evaluation should be made of any idea*. This is one of the main benefits of brainstorming. If a group suffers from low levels of risk taking, the rule against initial evaluation may encourage people to take the risk of presenting an idea. Even if the idea is only partially developed or half thought out, it may be valuable to the group. If members know that evaluation of all ideas will only occur after all ideas are presented, they may respond to the more supportive climate.

A third assumption of brainstorming is that *hitchhiking on an idea is desirable*. An idea from one member may spark a related idea in another member. Those related or hitchhiking ideas should be presented. The result of hitchhiking should be that members transact freely—without the threat of initial evaluation. Their goal becomes the creation of as many ideas as possible. They get their ideas both from themselves and from the ideas of other group members. The result may be a more creative and thoughtful definition, analysis, set of standards, and final solution.

If your group becomes bogged down in the decision-making process and progress seems to stop, you may wish to encourage a strategy of brainstorming. The free-flowing ideas of all group members may be the key to the progress you desire.

Synectics

Synectics is a method of creative problem-solving developed and publicized primarily by William J. J. Gordon.[3] The whole synectic approach is too complicated and complex for all of it to be described here. Yet, there are some basic ideas which you may find helpful to your group activity.

One of the basic approaches to creativity that Gordon discusses has to do with *the strange* and *the familiar*.[4] Sometimes groups have difficulty finding information or solving a problem because the task before them is strange and new. They have never faced the situation before—perhaps no one has faced the situation before. At other times, the task involves difficulty because the group problem is too familiar. The group may have lived with the situation for months or years. They simply may be so close to the problem that they have difficulty even realizing what it is. In some respects, the problem can be expressed in the cliché: They can't see the forest for the trees. Two of the basic problems facing groups involve opposite situations. In one situation, the problem is too strange to be solved; in the other, the problem is too familiar to be solved.

One of the basic strategies of synectics is to reverse those situations. The group must begin to either *make the strange familiar* or the *make the familiar strange*. If the group is too close to the problem, the members should attempt to relate the problem to some other, less familiar problem. Sometimes, insights may be gained simply by *seeing the problem in a new—and strange—way*. A group dealing with charge accounts might begin thinking of charges as personal loans. The group which had been so close to the problem may now see it in a more objective way. The reverse is also true. If the group finds the problem too strange, members may want to try to relate it to a different and more familiar situation. A group concerned with a company's morale might begin to see the business as an enlarged family unit. If so, then more familiar solutions may be applied. The result is that the group sees the problem in a new, more familiar way—and can solve it more easily.

The strategy of making the familiar strange and the strange familiar works on the basis of *metaphor:* a comparison between two things without the use of *like* or *as*. The problem "becomes" a different one—either a more familiar or a stranger one. To make the use of metaphor more clear, Gordon identifies four different sorts of metaphors which have been useful to group problem-solvers: personal, direct, symbolic, and fantasy.[5] When you attempt to see the problem in a new way, these terms may be guides for you and your group. Let us examine each of these by assuming that your group task is to create a better means of using general reference material in a library.

To solve this problem, you might use a *personal metaphor. You personally* become the library whose task it is to dispense information. How do you do it? What keeps you busiest? What is easiest for you? Would you need additional ears, eyes, or arms to complete your task? What sorts of things get in your way? When do you have the most difficulty? Who gives you the most difficult problems? Answers to those questions may give the group keys as to what should be done with general reference material.

A *direct metaphor* involves seeing the problem as something that is directly comparable. The reference section involves basic problems of classification, shelving, indexing, and so forth. How can improvements made in these general activities benefit the current situation? How have shelving methods been improved elsewhere? How can they be applied here? How has classification been improved elsewhere? How can those methods be helpful here? In using a direct metaphor, the group looks for situations and processes that are literally similar to the problem they face. By looking at related situations, members may find related solutions.

A *symbolic metaphor* is a comparison the group makes between the task or problem at hand and something that is like it *in principle*. A symbolic metaphor for the reference section of the library might be the neighborhood supermarket. In some ways, the same principles or problems apply to each. Material must be easily available; there must be adequate shelf space; people should be able to find what they need largely without help; shelves must be restocked when material or products are removed; and so forth. On the basis of those similarities, how can supermarket solutions be applied to library problems? What changes would be needed since the metaphor is symbolic rather than direct?

The final sort of metaphor is the *fantasy metaphor*. Here, the group begins to think of comparisons that may or may not really exist in the real world. The fantasy metaphor is not limited to what is possible at present. The group might see the library reference section as a centralized computer with individualized terminals all around the library. Reference material would all be programmed and students would be trained to get information automatically and immediately from the central computer. The computerized reference material would not need assistants, reshelving, shelf space, or duplicate copies. Perhaps some feasible ideas will come from this fantasy solution. Can the use of microfilm and microfiche be expanded? Can certain areas become individualized information-gathering centers somehow? The trip to fantasyland and back may be a source of creative and worthwhile group ideas.

The entire synectic approach cannot be discussed here, but the familiar/ strange and metaphor approaches may be useful sources of group creativity. What you must remember is that the task of most groups is not simply to come to agreement. Usually the task will require the presentation of a sound solution or collection of information. Such tasks can be completed best in an atmosphere of creative activity. Your use of what you know about brainstorming and synectics may be valuable to your group's decision-making efforts.

ARGUMENTATION AND GROUP DECISION-MAKING

Even with a win-win strategy, a decision-making method, and creativity, your group process probably will involve argumentation. Information may conflict, standards may be in disagreement, and solutions may be the subject of conflict. In such situations, your knowledge of argumentation may be valuable to your group.

Decision-making processes as group strategies

	Economical	Easy to Do	Popular	Quickest-Working
Solution 1		✓		✓
Solution 2	✓	✓		
Solution 3			✓	
Solution 4	✓		✓	

Fig. 14.1 Solutions judged by standards

In gathering and analyzing information, for example, no bit of information should be considered *evidence: a completely and immediately acceptable statement*. Everything that the group discovers should be thought of as a *claim: something that is or should be challenged*. If each bit of information is considered as a claim, then each bit of information should also be considered in terms of the evidence for it. What makes the group think that the information should be accepted? What is the evidence for it—expressions of belief? objects? reports of occurrences? Then you can determine *the relationship between this evidence and the information*—ask for *a warrant*. Does this evidence really relate to the acceptance of the information? How? What makes you think so? How confident are members of the group about the information as a claim? What should be the qualifier: the statement of your confidence in the claim? Do you have *reservations: situations where you would deny the claim?*

If the group follows this argumentative approach to information gathering, the information should be presented with more confidence. The method can even be used for comparing conflicting information. Which information is better supported by the evidence available? Which needs less qualification and fewer reservations? Argumentation can be the deciding factor in the information analysis discussed earlier in this chapter.

Argumentation can be just as helpful in problem-solving tasks. When the group is forming a definition of the problem, ask which of several definitions seems better supported. When the analysis of the problem is discussed, find out which information about the problem is most acceptable. Do this by using the procedure just described. When the group is suggesting standards of judgment or criteria, evaluate them in terms of how well supported each is. Argumentation can help you and the group in the beginning phases of the group task.

Argumentation may be most helpful, however, at the time the group is comparing standards or criteria with suggested solutions. Each solution and standard should be phrased as a claim: "Solution number one is economical. Solution number two is economical. Solution number three is . . ." Now examine the evidence for each of these claims. Which claim has the best support? Which claim needs less qualification and fewer reservations? Now, phrase each of the solutions with a second (and so on) standard: "Solution number one is easiest to implement. Solution number two is easiest to implement. Solution number three is . . ." Examine the evidence, warrants, qualifiers, and reservations for each claim. Which solution appears to be best in terms of this second, or third, or fourth standard?

In group problem-solving, it frequently may be the case that one solution may be best in terms of several standards, while another might be best in terms of other standards. If this is so, the group may want to reexamine the standards themselves. State the problem as a series of claims: "Standard number one is most important. Standard number two is most important," and so forth. What is the evidence for each claim? From that examination, your group should be able to decide upon the most important standards. Then the solution which is best in terms of these important standards can be selected. A variation of this strategy of argumentation is to decide upon the relative importance of the standards as they are suggested. Making those decisions early may simplify the process. When the group knows which standards are most important, it can judge the quality of the solutions earlier. Either approach to decision making almost certainly will involve argumentation. Your knowledge of how to deal with the argumentative situation may help your group mediate certain problems of decision making.

With this discussion of argumentation in the small group setting, we conclude our examination of group decision-making strategies. Conflict in a group may arise regardless of whether the group is primarily concerned with information analysis, problem solving, or creativity. Indeed, any one group might take advantage of all of those strategies to complete its task. Argumentation, as we have seen here, is a strategy which can be applied to the various sorts of group decision-making tasks. Separately or in combination, these strategies can be

	Most Impor.	2nd Most	3rd Most	4th Most	and so on
Person 1	Economical	Easy to Do	Quickest	Popular	
Person 2	Economical	Quickest	Popular	Easy to Do	
Person 3	Popular	Easy to Do	Quickest	Economical	
Person 4	Quickest	Economical	Popular	Easy to Do	
Person 5	Easy to Do	Economical	Popular	Quickest	
Person 6	Economical	Easy to Do	Popular	Quickest	

Fig. 14.2 Standards rank-ordered (Note that this rank-ordering of the standards for judgment can be done either before or after the standards are applied to the solution.)

Decision-making processes as group strategies

useful for the mediation of conflicts in the small group setting. Specifically, you can:

1. Determine the nature of the group task (information analysis, problem solution, creativity production).
2. Follow the steps of information analysis if that is the task:
   A. Determine the kind of information you need.
   B. Determine the sources of potential information.
   C. Examine the quantity of the information.
   D. Examine the quality of the information.
3. Follow the steps in Dewey's reflective-thinking model if problem solving is the task:
   A. Become aware of the problem.
   B. Define the problem.
   C. Analyze the problem.
   D. Establish standards for the solution.
   E. Suggest possible solutions for the problem.
   F. Select the best solution by comparing solutions with standards.
   G. Implement and/or test the solution.
4. Follow the suggestions for creativity if that is the emphasis of the task:
   A. Brainstorming: emphasize quantity of ideas, no initial evaluation, and hitchhiking.
   B. Synectics.
      (1) make the familiar strange and the strange familiar.
      (2) use any or all of the four types of metaphors.
5. Decide if the task requires the use of two or all three of the mentioned sets of strategies. (For example, does the problem solution require a great deal of creativity and/or information analysis?)
6. Use your knowledge of argumentation to:
   A. Test information quality.
   B. Test how well standards match solutions.
   C. Test how important various standards are.

To synthesize your learning of these strategies, consider the following case studies:

Case study one: how much is too much? The group was assigned a class project for the small group unit, and they decided to investigate the differences in gasoline prices in their city.

Joann: Well, I'll tell you what I did. I called up all the gas stations I found listed in the telephone book—and asked their prices for regular gas. I found out that the same brand of gasoline doesn't vary by any more than one cent per gallon.

Jack: Are you kidding? I know two Gasso stations whose prices are five cents different. How do you explain that?

Larry: Jack's right. I always go to the station across town because I save a bundle.

Joann: Well, all I know is what they told me. Both of them said . . . .

Larry: *Both* of them? There are at least four that I know about. Are you sure you know what you're talking about?

Margie: Leave her alone. This is not a personal battle—it's a group project. Let's get on with it.

John: Good idea. Now I went around to the stations in my neighborhood, and the ones on the way to campus. I found a varying price of four cents. . . . That means to me that someone is making a lot of money.

Larry: Wait a minute. Did those prices include different companies? I can see where a price difference might be because of different company costs. I'm concerned about different prices by the same oil company distributors. It seems to me . . . .

Let's interrupt the group at that point. They seem to be having some problems processing their information. First, it does not seem that they have agreed upon the kind of information they want: the prices charged by different companies, by the same companies, or what? Then, too, it is obvious that Joann only talked with (for example) two of the four stations pumping one kind of gas. Larry was concerned about whether those two (of four) were enough, but his attempt to analyze the information came across as a personal attack. Are there other problems *you* see?

For one thing, the group did not use argumentation systematically. They could have begun their search for information and understanding by phrasing claims: There is (or is not) a significant difference between stations involved with the same company; or There is (or is not) a significant difference among stations pumping all kinds of gasoline. Phrasing the claims would have given them guidance in their research—at least they would have known what stations to compare. Their figures on prices could then have supported or failed to support one of the claims. In addition, they could have established standards for *significance:* does that mean two cents, four cents, or what? Two cents is significant, for example, could have been approached as a claim. In essence, applying strategies of argumentation could have helped the group mediate their problems.

Case study two: the class project. The group's assignment is to discover a small group communication project which can be graded by the instructor—but which does not call for role playing. Here is part of the interaction:

Mary: I think we ought to just pick a topic and discuss it. How in the world are we going to think up a new way of conducting this class?

Harriet: Well, that is the assignment. We can at least give it a go.

Ward: We could do something in public—kind of a group discussion that is really a debate—and we could invite the instructor.

Mary: Now how are we going to do that . . . walk up to someone and say, "Hey, could we borrow your auditorium?"

Ward: It was just a thought.

George: We could pretend that we were businesspeople who . . .

Mary: No, we can't role play.

Harriet: We could plan a party—and be graded on our plans.

Mary: No. Plan a party? This is a serious. . . . C'mon, you guys need to think of something. . . . Well?

The group has stopped for a moment, so let's look at what has happened. Among other things, the group is not systematically trying to solve the problem. They have ignored such things as agreeing on the nature of the problem and analyzing it, and have jumped right into the solution stage. Certainly, the members are frustrated, but unless someone can help them become more systematic they may well remain that way.

Even if we overlook the jump into the solution stage, that stage itself was not handled well, especially by Mary. For this particular task, the group needed to be creative. Mary was always ready to evaluate and reject the offered solutions. No wonder that, as the group finished the exchange, Mary was the only one talking. Beginning a brainstorming session or using the synectics approach might have been a key to this stage of the task—assuming that they finally defined and analyzed the problem.

In these two cases, strategies of decision making might have helped the groups mediate their problems and conflicts.

EXERCISES

1. My wife and I had a problem with our automatic washer: the water would not drain out of the clothes after the wash cycle. We called the nationally-advertised store where we had purchased the machine and a repairman arrived the next day. He entered the basement, looked at the machine, and said that the drain hose that went into the drain was "crimped." He said I could fix it with a coat hanger. We found a coat hanger, but he took it out of my hands and tied the hose so that the water would drain out. He made out a bill for $22.00 and left. My wife and I discovered that $12.75 of it was for the "service call"—and the rest was for labor! I called the service manager and told him that virtually no labor was involved. He said that the service fee only paid for the man's trip. I asked him why it was called a "service call" if no service was involved. He said the work was guaranteed. I asked him how often they guarantee coat hangers. He stated that the repairman would have to be paid for his labor—and I asked what labor. . . . The resulting dilemma was this: the store manager wanted a satisfied customer; the service manager did not want to "absorb" the money I wouldn't pay; the repairman wanted the charge paid; and I didn't want to pay for a service charge plus a $9.25 coat hanger which was mine to begin with. With or without playing roles, try to arrange a good decision for the problem.

2. I am supervisor of a basic communication course which enrolls about 5,000 students per year. The course uses standardized testing, so three times a semester, about 2,550 students take exams in an auditorium in the evening. With that large an enrollment, and with forty-five graduate students who teach the course under my supervision, I

feel that evening "mass testing" is the best answer. The forty-five instructors do not want to help make up dozens of different tests. (Since classes meet at every hour during a six-day week, even dozens wouldn't be enough to keep test information from "floating around.") Students do not like evening exams, but earlier hours are hard to schedule because of dinner times in dorms, and so forth. Either by playing roles (represent teachers, scheduling people, and students) or by simply discussing the problem, see if you can find a better solution to the ongoing conflict.

NOTES

[1] The steps in the reflective-thinking model are based upon ideas in John Dewey, *How We Think* (Lexington, Ma.: D. C. Heath, 1933).

[2] Though *brainstorming* has become a traditionally recognized method, the treatment here is based on ideas in Alex F. Osborn, *Applied Imagination: Principles and Procedures of Creative Problem-Solving*, 3rd rev. ed. (New York: Charles Scribner's Sons, 1963), chap. 13.

[3] William J. J. Gordon, *Synectics: The Development of Creative Capacity*, 2nd ed. (New York: Collier Books, 1968).

[4] *Ibid.*, pp. 35–37.

[5] *Ibid.*, pp. 37–53.

15
ROLE ENACTMENTS AS GROUP STRATEGIES

While group tasks may vary, the problem of balancing people is always present. Every group must confront the conflict between the concern for the task and the concern for people. Without people, groups obviously could not exist. Without relatively satisfied people, groups could not long operate. Yet, a group of satisfied people does not ensure that a task will be completed. To help you learn to balance the concerns of tasks and people, you should know something about role playing in groups. By that, I do not mean that people in groups should *act out parts*.[1] Instead, I mean that groups need and expect certain kinds of services from their members.[2] When these services or functions are performed, we can speak of them as *group roles*.

Group roles arise in various ways. Your role might be to provide a particular sort of information. At other times, your role might be one that others in the group simply expect you to play; other members have come to depend upon you to do certain things, and your role has become a matter of expectations. At still other times, a role is simply something you or others just happen to perform for a brief time. During the course of a group project, you may perform various roles that we shall discuss. Finally, conscious role enactments can become communication strategies. As you observe the group, it may become obvious that a certain action needs to be taken. You may consciously perform that service as a strategy for helping the group. In sum, roles are not insincere playacting. They are the kinds of things you can do in a group to help mediate the problems of balancing people and tasks in the situation.

There are at least four different kinds of roles which can be used to help the group complete its task: task roles, maintenance roles, organizational roles, and leadership roles. This chapter is devoted to explaining how each type can be used for the mediation of group problems.

TASK ROLES

Patton and Giffin have isolated a number of *task* roles that can be played by members of a group.[3] Each of these relates to services that can be performed to help the group reach its goal.

The role of *initiator,* for example, is one which focuses upon new ideas for the group. The group may have difficulty getting started. In most groups, some of the first meeting may be devoted to small talk, to comments about the task, and so forth. The group may need someone to get it started on the task. One of the disadvantages of the small group decision-making process is that it usually involves more time than individual decision-making. Time will be spent by the group on unimportant details, and you wish to play the initiator by getting things started as soon as possible. The initiator role can also be helpful when the group reaches a dead end or a stalemate. In situations like that, an initiator can encourage the group to go in new directions or to explore new information.

The roles of *information/opinion giver and seeker* are closely related. They mean just what you might think. At certain points in the activity of the group, the group may need to hear opinions and information. The new insights may be either simply personal opinions or expert opinions. When the group needs information and opinions, you should be ready to provide anything that you have to give. Similarly, groups may need information and opinion seekers. Certain members of the group may have important opinions and expert information, but they may be reluctant to share them. In that situation, the group may need someone to ask these people for their insights. Your service to a group may be to ask others for the information and opinions they have. Both seeking and giving information and opinions can help the group complete its task.

Sometimes the greatest group need is for clarification of what has been said or presented. The *clarifying* role is one that you may be able to play even if you do not have a great deal of information yourself. If the information is highly technical, you may be able to provide a *translation* into more common terms. If a member has been vague about a point, you may be able to elaborate or explain what you think he or she meant. In either case, the group's steady progress toward its goal may depend upon someone's ability to clarify ideas.

In some ways, the *coordinator* plays a role similar to that of the clarifier. The group may need someone to *synthesize* all the different points of view. During long hours of discussion, it is not unusual for a group to begin rehashing the same ideas—or to begin talking in circles. At such a time, you may be able to collect all the different points of view and to coordinate ideas. If this is done toward the end of a discussion, the coordinator may become what Giffin and

Patton call the *consensus tester*. This task role involves coordinating all the various points of view to see if everyone agrees with a particular idea. Sometimes group members may not see that several of the group may be saying the same thing. There may be agreement without the group realizing it. Instead of wasting time, you may play the role of consensus tester to see if the group is really in agreement. If consensus has been reached on a standard or a definition of the problem, the group can move on to other areas of the problem.

A final task role is that of the *evaluator*. At some points in the group process (particularly brainstorming) evaluation should be avoided. Yet, at some point the group will need to evaluate information and ideas. Sometimes group members may be so sensitive of the feelings of others that evaluation is difficult, but it must take place at some time. Evaluation that involves ridicule or sarcasm can be destructive. If the evaluation centers upon ideas and information—instead of on group members—the evaluator can perform a valuable service for the group.

So far, we have discussed only roles having to do with the completion of the task. People and task balancing, however, requires that you know something about maintenance roles as well as task roles.

MAINTENANCE ROLES

Maintenance roles have to do with the human relations part of group interaction. Completion of a task is important, but it can be done best when members are sensitive to personal needs. Giffin and Patton have identified several of these maintenance roles.[4]

The *gatekeeper* is played by someone who makes sure that all members participate to the best possible extent. Some groups are dominated by the person who has seen, heard, and knows it all. People like this may take a superior role to all others in the group—whether they are superior or not. At such times, someone else may need to "close the gate" on their talk. A question such as, Well, what do some of the rest of you think, now that we've heard from Gale? may be the key. At other times, the problem may be someone's reluctance to speak at all. When that is the problem, you may need to try to "open the gate" and provide a channel of communication. A statement such as, Well, Hank, I think you know something about this, may be helpful. The gatekeeper knows that for the group to maintain its good rapport, people should feel free to contribute. The gatekeeper knows also that one or two members should not be allowed to dominate the group. Interpersonal relations may be the problem facing the group. If so, the gatekeeper can be of service.

The problem of the group may not be a matter of who is using the channels of communication. Members may simply feel timid about voicing an opinion or idea. You may be able to perform the role of *encourager* in that type of situation. The encourager's role involves sincere nods, smiles, and encouraging comments. Once members find that at least someone will respect their opinions and listen to them, risk taking may be easier. In groups, constant evaluation and criticism can be contagious. Encouragement can also be contagious, and you can use it to mediate or avoid some group conflicts.

Another role that can be played to reduce interpersonal conflict is described as that of the *harmonizer*. The harmonizer attempts to settle the differences between members before they become quarrels. The harmonizer role can be played in relation to ideas. Are these ideas so very different? Are there points of agreement? The harmonizer role may also relate to personalities. The harmonizer may "break into" what seems to be a conflict over personalities. As harmonizer, you may remind the members that no interpersonal conflict should get so serious that it interferes with the task. Whatever the specific activity, the harmonizer can act as peacemaker for the group and its conflicts.

A final maintenance role that might be performed is that of *tension reliever*. Some group problems can be so important that members become totally involved. Some discussions become so heated and serious that conflict seems likely to develop. A humorous comment may be necessary to regain the group's awareness that people, as well as tasks, are involved. The smile or laughter that results may be a welcome break for the group. After the moment of relaxation, members may be better able to get back to the problem.

The maintenance roles (gatekeeper, encourager, harmonizer, and tension reliever) are strategies that you can use to help the group. They are not simply nice things to do, nor are they ways of avoiding the task at hand. Too much tension relief, for example, can completely sidetrack the group. Too much playing of the role of harmonizer may blur important distinctions between ideas. Some disagreement and conflict are natural parts of group activity. The maintenance roles are primary strategies for helping the group reach its goal, not separate parts of the group process. Wise use of these role strategies can aid the mediation of group conflicts.

ORGANIZATIONAL ROLES

Task roles and maintenance roles are personal roles that people can play in groups. To be realistic, I must add that many of the roles people play in groups are *organizational* roles: behaviors prescribed for or expected of members in a group. As we saw in Chapter 12, group members frequently—and maybe usually—are members of several groups at one time. In any group you experience, members may be participating as representatives or delegates of another group or of the organization of which your group is a part. So, while maintenance and task roles are *intra-group* roles, organizational roles are more *inter-group* roles.[5] One of your group members, for example, may be representing the interests of the engineering department; another, the marketing department; and so on. As they play various task or maintenance roles, they will be performing organizational roles by representing the interests of people outside the group.

If the organizational roles are played so that they interfere with either task or maintenance roles, the result may be conflict.[6] Other members may perceive the organizational role player as being only interested in representing his or her other group. In that sense, the conflict can be either interpersonal or group in nature. Organizational roles can be played so that outside group interests are represented while the progress of the current group continues. The group depends for its progress upon the good climate that maintenance roles can provide and upon the sense of accomplishment which task roles can help provide. The group also needs the support and guidance which perhaps the organizational role player can provide. Surely, in most situations it makes no sense for the group to arrive at a decision that is rejected by all the other groups that are affected. Small group communication, like communication generally, occurs amid a whole system of other people, events, and groups. The group member who knows that he or she must perform well *organizationally,* as well as in terms of task and maintenance behaviors, is a vital element in a successful small group transaction.

LEADERSHIP ROLES

So far we have examined task, maintenance, and organizational roles. An even more familiar concept in small group communication is *leadership,* a term that is important for its own sake and for how it shows the relationships among the other kinds of role activity. In everyday terms, the *leader* may be viewed as the person who primarily guides or directs the group. Group leadership has been a subject of thousands of discussions, research projects, and speculations. In the past, efforts have been made to determine the nature of leadership *traits.*[7] What is it, after all, that makes a leader a leader? What qualities must a person have to perform as leader? Research into these questions has been extensive, but not satisfying. Traits of leadership can be identified, but they seem to vary from situation to situation.

Leadership, as we shall discuss it here, has to do with *doing what needs to be done.* The leader in any group is the person who serves the function that the group needs to have served. The information giver might be leader—but the harmonizer or the clarifier may also serve. A group does not progress because someone habitually performs the same role. The group progresses because someone performs the role that needs to be performed at the time it needs to be done. The question, What makes a leader? should be replaced with the question, What does a leader do? The answer to the first question will vary from situation to situation. The answer to the second question is that the leader does whatever is necessary for the progress of the group.

That idea of leadership introduces several important points. For one thing, groups may have an *appointed leader,* but this person may or may not function as a leader. The chairperson of a committee may be less important to the group than most of the rest of the individual members. People who become recognized as leaders as the group interacts are called *emergent leaders*.[8] A second idea about leadership is that the leadership role may be passed from one person to another and back again. Instead of there being *a* leader of the group, there may be several—at various times. Third, it is important to note that leaders become leaders in various ways. They may be elected or appointed, they may emerge, or they may have leadership passed to them temporarily. To function as leaders, their most important characteristic must be the ability to do well what needs doing in the group. This may involve performing one or a number of the task and maintenance roles at various times. Above all, leadership strategy involves constant attention to what the group needs.

Though little can be said positively about what specifically *makes* a leader, something can be said about different kinds of leadership. Leadership is basically the relationship between leader and members. This relationship can be described in general terms.[9] The *authoritarian* leader, for example, is a person who has tight control over the members of the group. He or she may decide procedures, evaluate information, and so forth—mostly by him- or herself. At the other extreme, the *laissez-faire* leader may exercise virtually no control over anything. He or she may be reluctant to provide personal opinions or to make any evaluation. Somewhere between those extremes is the *democratic* leader. The democratic leader will ask for information and opinions, and share evaluational tasks. He or she will invite as much group participation as possible, but may still keep and use the prerogative of making an important decision. The *diplomatic* leader is a subtle manipulator. He or she may use power or position in sensitive ways to guide the group in a particular direction.

In a democratic society, it might seem that the democratic style of leadership should work best. The situation is not so simple. First, different groups may require different sorts of leadership. If the group has never had anything but an authoritarian leader, for example, the change to laissez-faire leadership may hinder the group's progress. Second, some people are incapable of using a certain leadership style. You may feel comfortable as a democratic leader, but feel you could never function as diplomatic leader, even if the group needed it. Third, problems of time may affect the situation. Laissez-faire leadership and, to a lesser extent, democratic leadership may require more time than the group has. Authoritarian or diplomatic leadership may be the only effective leadership styles if time is important. Fourth, the nature of the group task may affect the situation. If the group must achieve maximum acceptance, the authoritarian style might be out of the question. Maximum acceptance may require either a democratic style or a laissez-faire style of leadership. Finally, leadership styles are most relevant to situations where there is an appointed or elected leader. In groups where the actual leadership shifts from one person to another, style of leadership that occurs in the group might not be very important.

In essence, leadership is important to the group. As an appointed or even an elected leader, you should examine carefully yourself, your group, the time you have, and the task—and then determine the style of leadership that is most helpful. These factors should be examined even in less structured situations. Your goal is to perform whatever service the group needs for its own sake and for its progress.

In essence, leadership can be seen as a role, but the enactment of it is related to the enactment of other roles: task, maintenance, or organizational.[10] Your efforts to enact these various types of roles may cast you—at least momentarily—in the role of leader. Leadership, then, is important both for what it is and for how it emerges as the other roles are played.

To use role playing in a group as a strategy of mediation, you will need to be able to analyze and adjust the roles you play.[11] To accomplish those tasks, you can:

1. Analyze conflict as you perceive it in the group.
2. Decide if the conflict involves group interaction, task progress, or intergroup problems of representation.
3. Enact maintenance roles, task roles, or organizational roles (respectively) for the conflicts above.
4. (In that enactment) serve the function of leadership needed.

To help you begin to use these strategies, you can work through the following case studies:

Case study one: who cares? (part one). The group has been given the responsibility of creating suggestions for an internship program in communication. In general, the idea is that students will begin to work in various jobs that involve their particular knowledge of, and skills in communication. It is hoped that some of the part-time employees will become full-time employees at graduation. Here is a part of their discussion:

Janet: Well, how do we start?
Tom: I don't care; I just want to get it over with.
Margie: C'mon, that's not the right attitude. This kind of internship might help all of us in some ways. Even if we don't get an internship, we'll be helped when the business community around here knows we can do something besides study.
Janet: Roy, what do you think?
Roy: Well, I guess we could gather information about the kinds of programs other people have set up . . . .
Tom: Listen, I don't want to spend all my life on this. Let's just think up an idea and get out of here.
Margie: You're no help at all.
Roy: You know, I think that there is a program like what we're talking about in . . . .
Tom: Will you stop with that?
Margie: Tom, if you don't want to help stay out of the way. Now, I thought what we might do is . . . .

At this point the discussion is not making much progress. There are several things which might have helped the group. For one thing, the group needed a harmonizer: the exchanges between Margie and Tom were not helping the progress of the group, but no one did anything about it. Tom's attitude might also have been helped by someone playing the maintenance role of encourager. Tom did not feel very committed to the group—and Margie's chiding may have made the situation worse. In terms of task roles, Roy was trying to play the role of initiator. While that role was needed, no one seemed to pay any attention to him—even after Janet played gatekeeper and asked for his opinion. There are some other problems; look at case study two.

Case study two: who cares? (part two).

Tom: Look, Margie, if you really want to help, let's forget the whole thing. I'm a sociology major, and we already have an internship program. Anything in communication would just overlap.

Janet: That's not true; but even if it was true, that doesn't affect the assignment we have. Let's get on with it . . . .

Roy: Well, I was thinking . . . .

Margie: As I said before, the first thing . . . .

These other comments are interesting additions to the case because we find out some things about Tom's motivation. In the terms that we have used, his organizational role as a sociology major hurts his ability to work through problems with this group. The group needed someone to point out the conflict and help him to see the need for balancing his roles. Finally, leadership was a problem. Margie seemed to want to play an authoritarian leader and take control. Roy kept trying to play the task role of initiator, and thereby serve as leader. The leadership need, however, seemed to be for a peacemaker: a person who could balance the task and organizational roles by paying attention to maintenance roles.

What should be obvious from the cases studied is that the concerns for task, maintenance, organizational, and leadership roles can be used in combination for the mediation of group problems. Your ability to use and understand those strategies can help when "your conflict" involves the transactions in a small group.

EXERCISES

1. The class should be divided into groups and each group should select a topic for problem solving: Should the spring break be extended? or Should more classes be held during evening hours? for example. In the group, students should attempt to play particular *dysfunctional* roles (see Chapter 12). One or two students in the group should be prepared to play a task and/or maintenance role. Begin the discussion and see what happens.
2. Use the same topic chosen above, but this time do not assign either task or

maintenance roles. Instead, assign the group members to *represent* various groups who might be involved in the discussion. (For the topics suggested in exercise 1, the groups might be full-time students, part-time students, parents, faculty, and administrators.) Each person should *concentrate* on the organizational role assigned and note the progress of the group—if any.

Then, the members should represent those same groups, but de-emphasize their organizational roles. Note the changes that occur in the group members' behavior.

3. Use the same topic or select a different one. This time, emphasize leadership style. Students should try to assert leadership in varying ways according to the style assigned. Do they emphasize one or another kind of role behavior (task, maintenance, or organizational)? If you discover a difference in emphasis, try to explain it.

NOTES

[1] This is not to say that people do not play individual and private *parts* in a group. For a discussion, see Eric Berne, *The Structure and Dynamics of Organizations and Groups* (Philadelphia: Lippincott, 1963).

[2] See Ronald Applbaum, *Fundamentals of Group Discussion* (Chicago: Science Research Associates, Inc., 1976).

[3] The discussion of these roles is a slight modification of that found in Bobby R. Patton and Kim Giffin, *Problem-solving Group Interaction* (New York: Harper & Row, 1973), p. 39. See also, Kenneth D. Benne and Paul Sheats, "Functional Roles of Group Members," *Journal of Social Sciences,* 4 (Spring 1948), 41–49.

[4] Patton and Giffin, *Problem-solving,* pp. 39–40.

[5] See James W. Julian and Franklyn A. Perry, "Cooperation Contrasted with Intra-Group and Inter-Group Competition," reprinted in *Small Group Communication: A Reader,* ed. Robert S. Cathcart and Larry A. Samovar (Dubuque, Ia.: Wm. C. Brown, 1970), pp. 82–91.

[6] See D. Roy, "Efficiency and 'The Fix': Informal Intergroup Relations in a Piecework Machine Shop," *Sociology: The Progress of a Decade,* ed. S. M. Lipset and N. J. Smelser (Englewood Cliffs, N.J.: Prentice-Hall, 1961), pp. 378–90.

[7] One of the better studies in leadership *traits* is J. C. Geier, "A Trait Approach to the Study of Leadership in Small Groups," *Journal of Communication,* 7 (1967), 316–23.

[8] One of the early classic studies that examined appointed and emerging leadership is L. Carter, et. al., "The Behavior of Leaders and Other Group Members," *Journal of Abnormal and Social Psychology,* 46 (1950), 589–95.

[9] A more detailed discussion of these leadership styles of relationships is found in Michael Burgoon, Judee K. Heston, and James McCroskey, *Small Group Communication: A Functional Approach* (New York: Holt, Rinehart and Winston, 1974), pp. 150–54.

[10] For an interesting treatment of the interaction of role-playing strategies, see Robert F. Bales, "Task Roles and Social Roles in Problem Solving Groups," *Readings in Social Psychology,* ed. E. E. Maccoby, T. M. Newcomb, and F. L. Hartley, 3rd ed. (New York: Holt, Rinehart and Winston, 1958), pp. 196–213.

[11] For a method of formally and systematically analyzing group role-playing interaction, see Robert F. Bales, *Interaction Process Analysis: A Method for the Study of Small Groups* (Reading, Ma.: Addison-Wesley, 1950).

PART 5

INTRODUCTION

Part 5 is a study of *one-to-many* conflicts and strategies. Normally, the person communicating to many other people is doing so in the context of some sort of organization. Even in one-to-many communication, intrapersonal, interpersonal, and group communication skills are important. Organizations are composed of people, and intrapersonal, interpersonal, and group communication occurs within all organizations.

One-to-many communication occurs basically in three ways. First, you may be involved in *serial communication:* communication *through* the organization. Messages may flow up, down, or across the organization—and in other ways we shall discuss. The wide arrows in Fig. 1 illustrate the major path of messages in serial communication. Second, some one-to-many communication occurs as you or someone else within the organization communicates *to* the organization. In Fig. 2, Person A is communicating to the organization; the shaded paths indicate the path of the major messages, even though all sorts of other messages are being sent and received.

Notice that messages in Figs. 1 and 2 occur mainly *within* the organization (see the squiggly line). Often, however, messages will be communicated *for* the organization to the outside public. We call such communication *public speaking*. Figure 3 shows the major paths of messages.

The one-to-many setting poses some of the same conflicts discussed earlier—and some new ones. Chapter 16 describes one-to-many problems as conflicts. Chapters 17 through 20 describe certain strategies for the mediation of conflicts in the one-to-many setting.

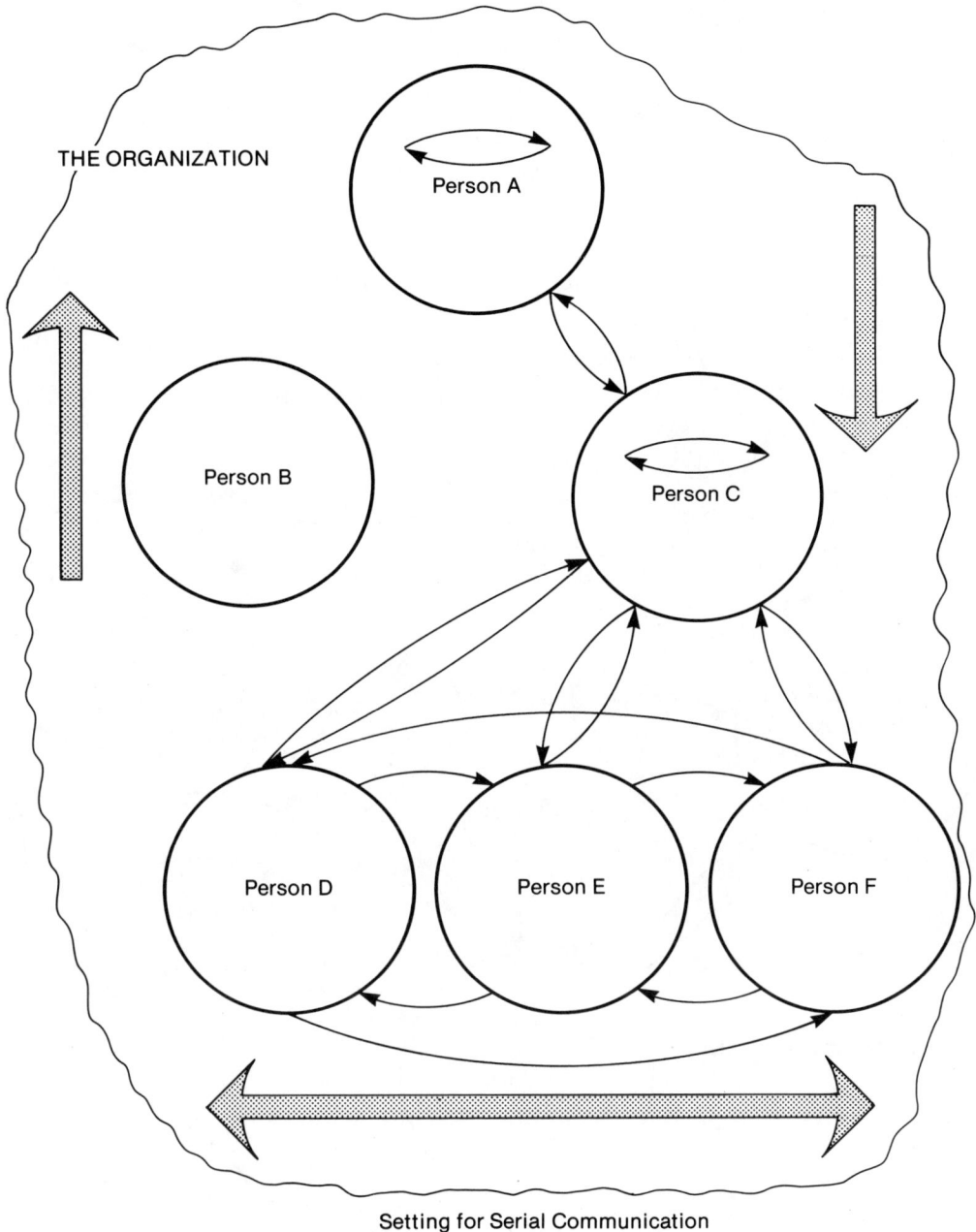

Fig. 1 Communicating *through* the organization

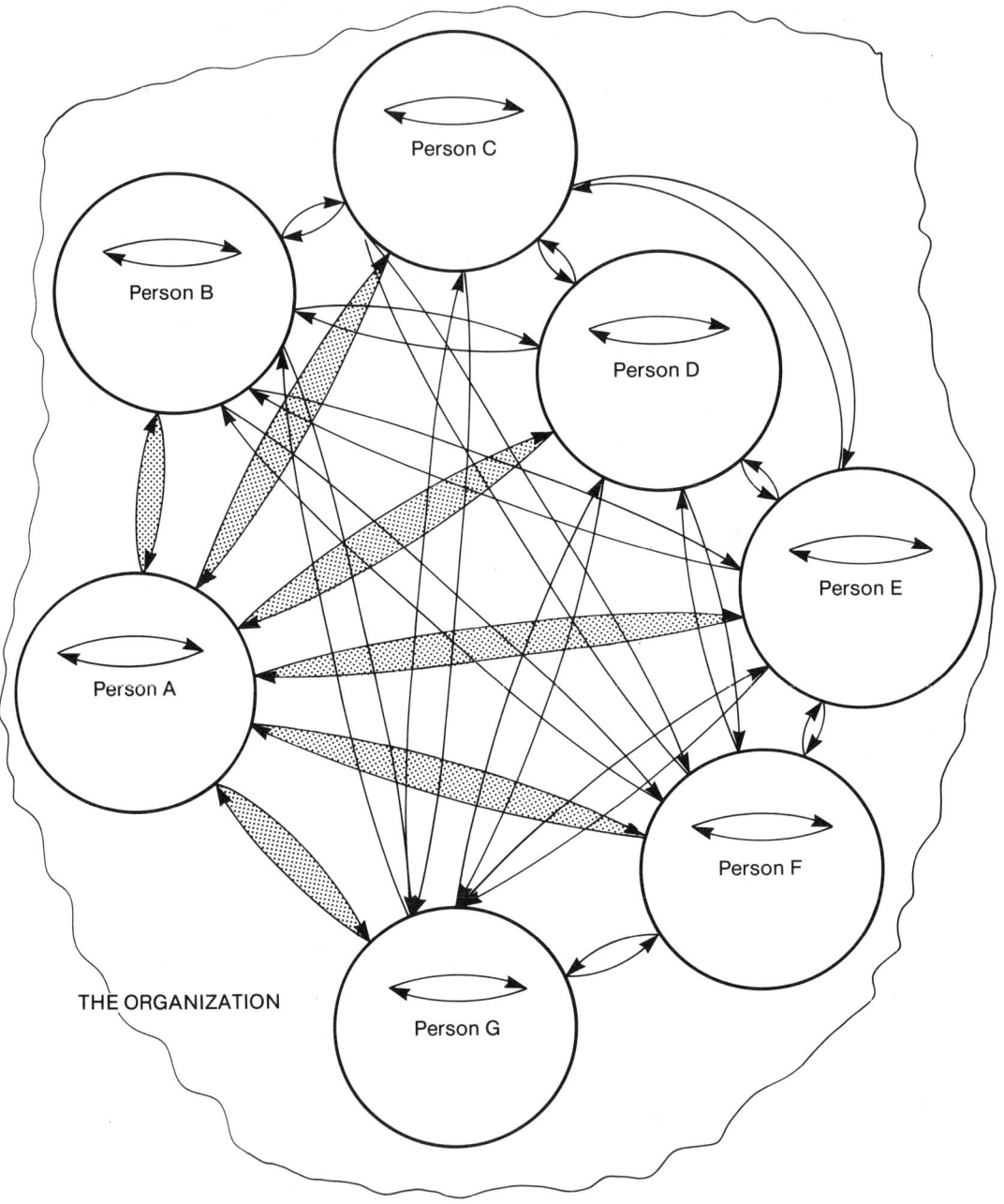

The Presentational Setting

Fig. 2 Communicating *to* the organization

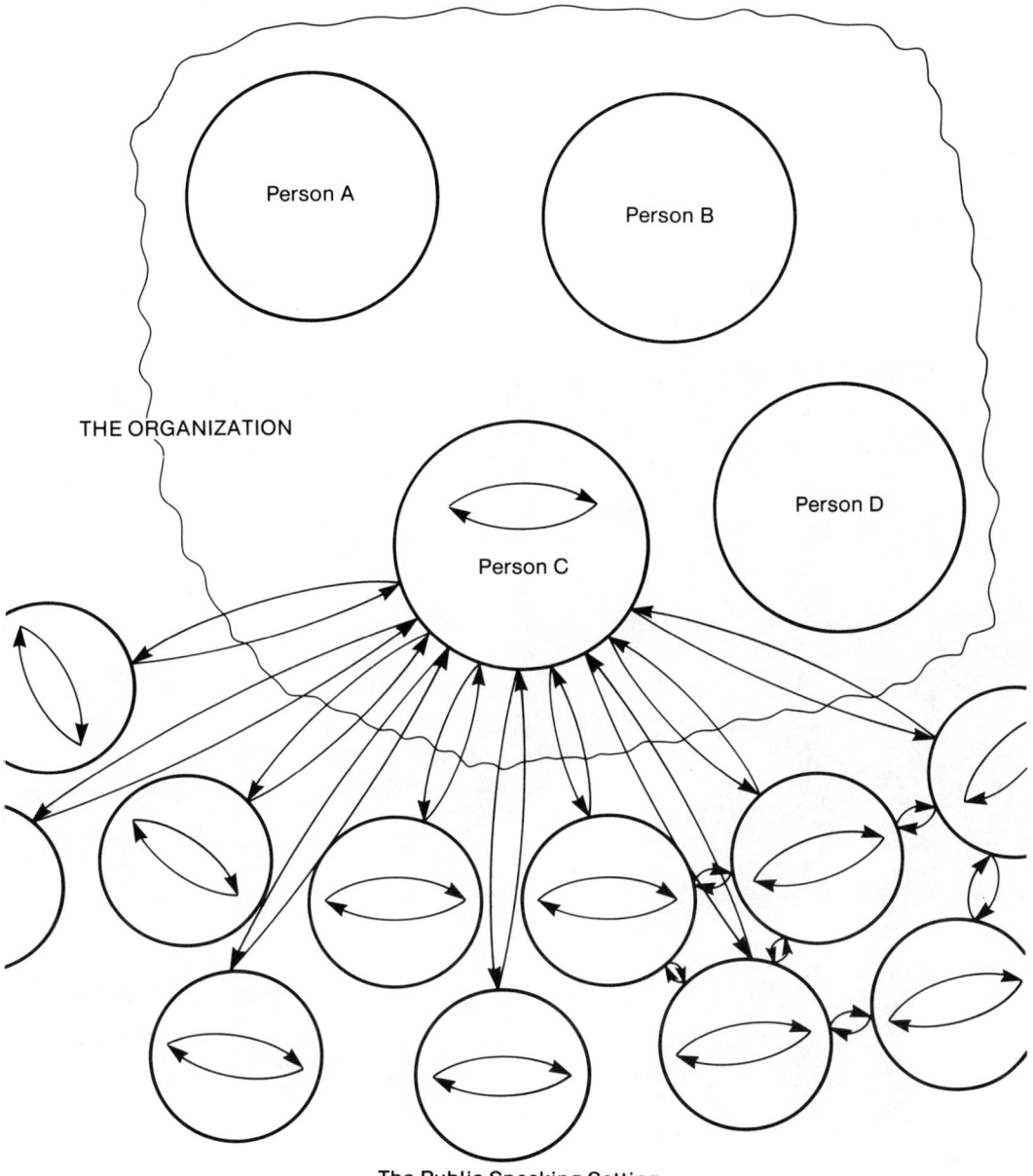

The Public Speaking Setting

Fig. 3 Communicating *for* the organization

16
ONE-TO-MANY COMMUNICATION CONFLICTS AS PROBLEMS

The chief executive officer of a Pennsylvania manufacturing firm becomes aware of waste in his organization: the fiscal year report indicates an overly large expenditure for raw material at the same time that large quantities of the material have been discarded as scrap. He sends a memo about the problem to his vice-president in charge of production. The vice-president underscores the need for better use of material in a memo to her managers. In the memo, the managers are instructed to pass the concern on to first-line supervisors. In three day's time, every employee is aware of the need for better use of scrap material.

In a conference room, a mid-level manager is presenting the results of a year's research into accounting procedures in the business. Attending the meeting are the officers of the company and several representatives from accounting. The session may last for two hours.

The setting is the local PTA meeting. Parents and teachers have gathered this particular evening to hear a vice-president of a local company discuss his firm's involvement in the educational life of the community. The speech will last perhaps half an hour—after which punch and cookies will be served.

These three situations share an important similarity. In each case, the major communicator involved experienced a conflict of some sort. In the first situation, the company president discovered information which the rest of the company needed to know. The president's problem? How to communicate the information. In the second situation, the manager had had the responsibility to research a problem and to suggest a solution. The manager's problem was to find a solution and to get the company to accept it. In the third situation, the vice-president had been asked to speak to the gathering about his company. The vice-president's problem was the need to represent the company fully and favorably.

All the situations involve the need to overcome a problem by communicating with a large number of other people perhaps (but not necessarily) simultaneously.[1] For lack of a better term, we shall call that kind of communication transaction *one-to-many* communication. We shall deal with problems involved in *serial communication* (such as the president's); *presentational speaking* (such as the manager's); and *public speaking* (such as the vice-president's). Notice that all these types of situations have to do with organizations. Serial communication has to do with the problems of speaking *through* an organization. Presentational speaking concerns speaking *to* the organization or its representatives. Public speaking has to do normally with speaking *for* organizations: politicians represent their supporters or their parties, ministers represent their denominations and congregations, and so forth. All these types of one-to-many situations present their participants with a kind of conflict: the need to have other people know or accept what it is they know or accept. All of these conflicts are related to the nature of organizations.

This chapter, then, deals with two main topics: first, the context of one-to-many problems, where we will examine the nature of organizations; and second, problems in the one-to-many situation, where we will examine problems of speaking through, to, and for the organization. First, then, let us understand the context for one-to-many problems.

THE CONTEXT OF ONE-TO-MANY COMMUNICATION CONFLICTS

Organizations are not clusters of buildings, inventories, and desks. *Organizations are systems of people.* Organizations, in fact, can exist without buildings, inventories, and desks. They cannot exist without people. Your understanding of organizations depends upon your understanding of how people become *organized.*[2] This section will examine three ideas: first, the organization of organizations; second, the individual in the organization; and third, the organization as part of a system.

The organization of organizations

In 1977, a major oil company used television commercials to explain how the company began. Said the company, "We got together to do it better." Regardless of whether that company "does it better," the idea of "getting together" is important to the discussion here. Organizations do not simply exist; they are created. People, in fact, do get together and form organizations.

One-to-many communication conflicts as problems

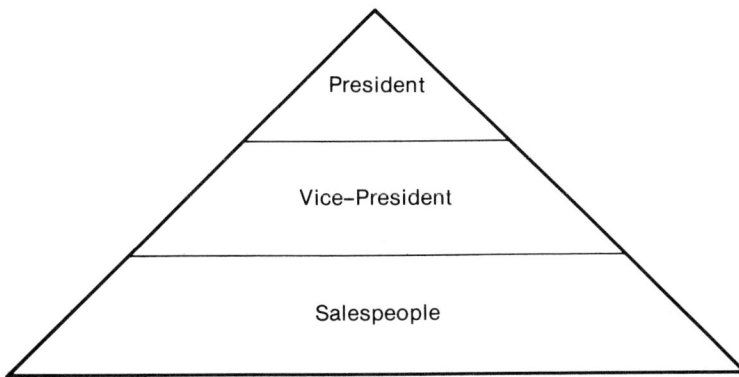

Fig. 16.1 Scalar division in a small firm

William Scott, an organization analyst, has identified several basic variables or aspects in the organization of organizations. They include: division of labor, structure, span-of-control,[3] and (we shall add) action in the organization.

Organizations make sense partly because they allow people to specialize. Not everyone has to do everything in the organization. There is a *division of labor*. Henry Ford's use of the assembly line for producing automobiles was a revolution in manufacturing. With the assembly line, came the division of labor. Each worker made small parts of the whole, then the parts were assembled by other workers who did nothing else except assemble. The theory was that the products could be made better, more cheaply, and more quickly by the division of labor technique.

In an organization, division of labor may be thought of in two different ways, including first a *scalar* division using the titles of people or a hierarchy of tasks. For example, in a small realty company just beginning business, there

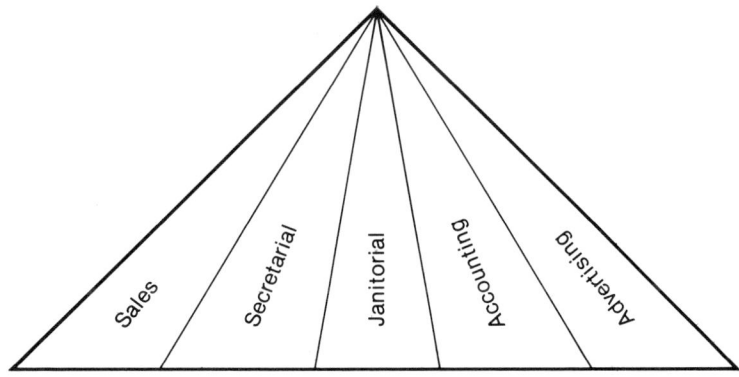

Fig. 16.2 Functional division in a small firm

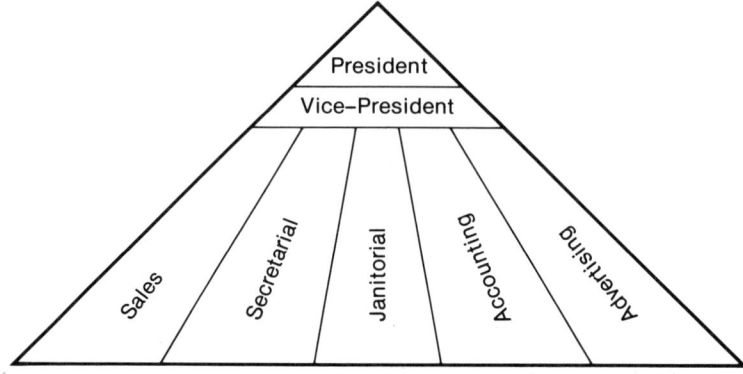

Fig. 16.3 Change in firm with additional employees

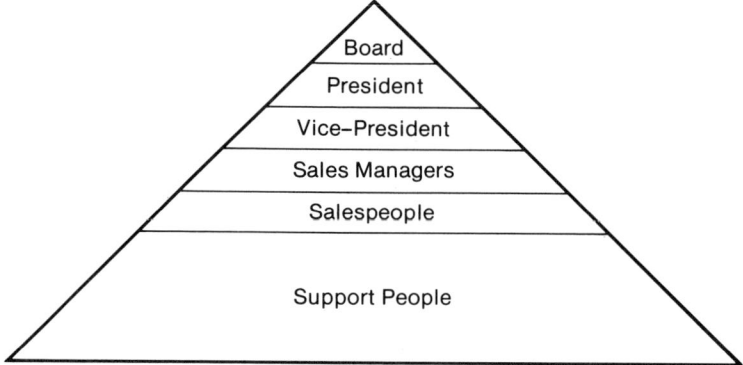

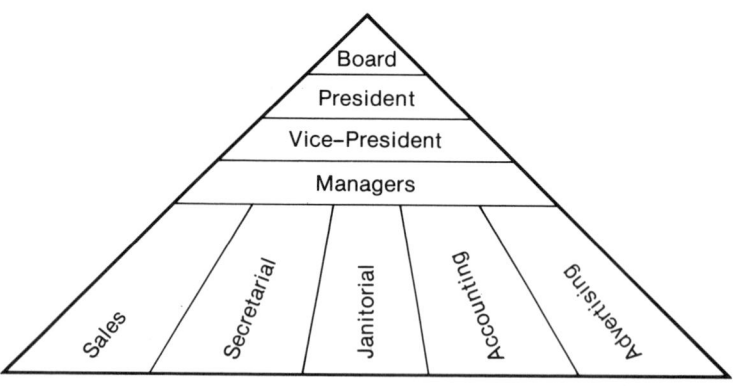

Fig. 16.4 (a) Changes in scalar division; (b) changes in functional division.

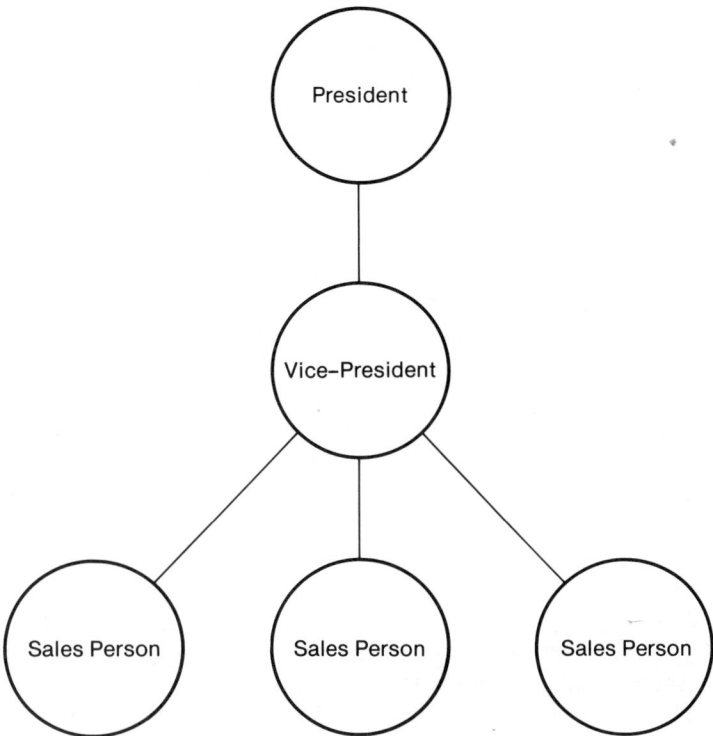

Fig. 16.5 A relatively flat organization

may be only five people working: the president, the vice-president, and three salespeople. The scalar division of the organization might look like Fig. 16.1. The second way of seeing the division of labor is to look at it *functionally*. In the small organization, *every* member may be responsible for *all* the organization's efforts. If so, the functional division of labor may look like Fig. 16.2. As the company grows, the scalar division may remain unchanged, but the functional division may change considerably. The vice-president and president may do mostly administrative work. Figure 16.3 shows how the various tasks may be performed with the addition of several new employees. As the company expands, it may employ a secretarial staff, a janitorial service, an advertising person, and (perhaps) a board of directors. Figure 16.4 shows what the company might look like as it continues to grow. Note how both the scalar and functional divisions of labor have changed.

One of the important variables in organizations, then, is how the organization is organized.

Another factor discussed by Scott and others is the *structure* of the organization. All organizations that may affect you can be described as *tall*, *flat*, or somewhere between. Whether an organization is tall or flat depends upon the number of *levels* in the organization. Figure 16.5 represents a flat organization, while Figure 16.6 represents a tall organization. In the example I used earlier about the realty company, the growth of the organization caused the company to move from a very flat organization to a fairly tall organization. More levels in the hierarchy were added and the company simply became *taller*. Organizations do not always become taller when they experience growth. At times, a company may begin to feel that it is *too tall:* it has too many levels, too many vice-presidents, too many supervisors, and so forth. If so, the company may begin to reorganize itself so that there are fewer levels. That is, as the company grows, it may decide to become *flatter*. This process of becoming flatter, rather than taller, may be less frequent than the reverse, but it may occur in your organization. Structure, like the division of labor, is an important organizational variable.

Related to the idea of structure is the important third variable of *span-of-control*. Span-of-control refers to the number of people in an organization who report to a particular person. A president, for example, may have several vice-presidents who are direct subordinates to him or her. These vice-presidents may each have several managers who report directly to them. Each of the managers may have several supervisors who report directly. Finally, each individual employee may have one of these supervisors as an organizational superior. The span-of-control of each of the levels (except the employees themselves) may be four or five.

There are no actual rules about how the span-of-control operates. In organizations which are labeled *centralized,* presidents and vice-presidents may have many, many people report to them. Among other things, this reporting means that these top officials have much direct power over many people. In a *decentralized* organization, the highest officials of the organization may have few people reporting to them. Among other things, that means that the supervisory power will be distributed at the various levels of the organization. Some corporate executives like the idea of centralized control; others like to delegate their authority to lower levels. Some organizations demand centralized control; others may thrive best with decentralization. Again, there are no actual rules about what your organization may think is the best span-of-control.

A final aspect of the organization of organizations has to do with *action in the organization.*[4] Organizations, generally, can be described as being *closed, open,* or somewhere in between. The closed organization is characterized by tight organization and control. Tasks are assigned, performance is expected to be good, and policies are expected to be followed. In the closed organization, employees are not expected to take an active role in improving or running the organization. In contrast, the open organization is characterized by the more active role employees play in improving the organization. Feedback may be constantly sought by the top officials of the company. The open company is receptive to information and ideas from outside. Rules and procedures might not be considered as important as the progress of the organization. Probably no

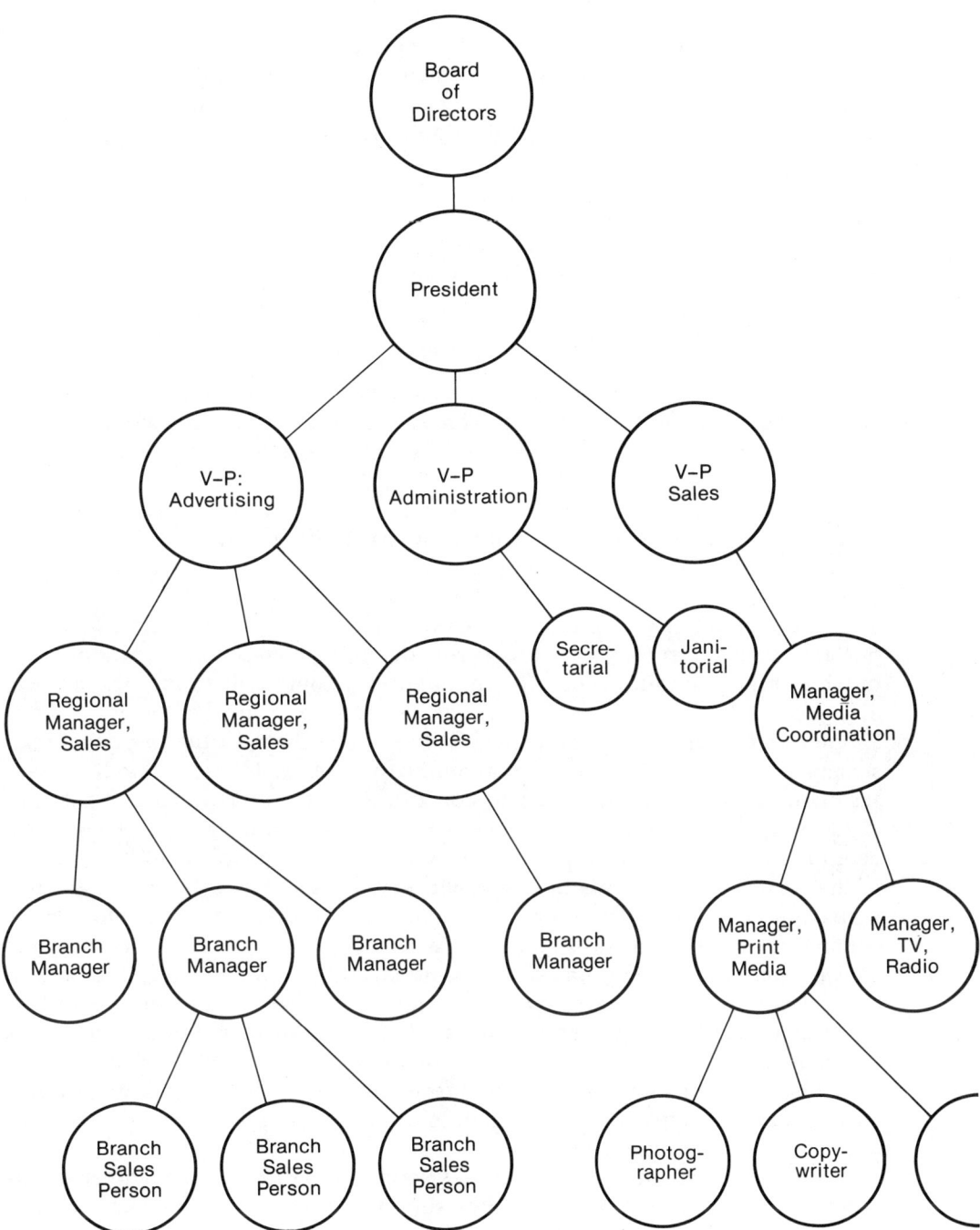

Fig. 16.6 A relatively tall organization

organization is either completely open or closed. Organizations might be more open during certain, less hectic times of the year; they might be more closed concerning a particular topic or problem. Whatever the situation, the kind of action that occurs within the organization is a major part of how organizations are organized.[5]

Some of the basic concerns about organizations relate to how they are organized. In this section, we have discussed division of labor, structure, span-of-control, and the action within the organization. We can now turn our attention to a study of the individual's role within the organization.

The individual in the organization

If we are to see organizations as systems of people, we should examine the role of individuals in the organization. This section will discuss formal and informal roles in the organization—from a different perspective from that which we have used before.[6]

Formal organizational roles are the result of who you are in the organization. Are you in an entry-level position—a typist, a clerk, or a salesperson? Are you a supervisor of entry-level employees? Are you a manager, an executive, or a board member? The role you play in the organization may decide things like salary, the possibility of promotion, or the amount of responsibility. More important for our purposes, the formal role determines who talks to whom—and in what order the talk occurs. Really important communication does not usually occur between a top-level manager and a member of the custodial force. People tend to conduct business with those *near* them in the organizational structure. This sort of formal communication—based upon formal roles—results in three traditional kinds of communication patterns or networks.

First, people communicate *downward* in the organization. Everyone, except for entry-level employees, has someone or several people below him or her in the structure. Presidents talk with vice-presidents, who talk with high-level managers, who talk with middle-level managers, and so forth. Second, people communicate *upward* in the organization. Everyone, except perhaps the chairperson-of-the-board, has someone or several people above him or her in the organization. Entry-level employees talk with their supervisors, who talk with their managers, and so forth. Third, *horizontal* communication occurs when people talk with others on the same organizational level. A supervisor from one area talks with a supervisor from another area. Upward, downward, and horizontal networks or channels carry most or all of the formal communication in the organization.

These networks help explain what your role will be as a member of the organization. In part, your role will be subordinate to those who communicate to you. Your role will be superior to those who communicate upward to you. Finally, of course, your role generally will be equal or similar to those who communicate across the same level to you. These roles decide what some of your communication will be. You may have to evaluate those people below you. You may be responsible for salary suggestions, promotions, or disciplinary action. You may be evaluated by those above you. You may be evaluated and supervised by a particular superior. You may have to talk with that person about promotion and salary questions. Finally, you may serve on committees or task forces with those who are on your same level. Each of these networks, then, has something to do with your individual role in an organization.

Though formal roles are important, they may be no more important to you than your *informal* roles. Informal roles may depend more upon who you are than upon the nature of your formal role. With formal roles, your power may come from your supervisory position. With informal roles, power may come from your *credibility* more than from anything else.

Credibility has been assigned a number of different labels, including *ethical force, ethos, personal power,* or *charisma.* Whatever the label, the term is difficult to define. Credibility means that you have some sort of influence upon situations and other people. Your credibility may be related to a number of more specific factors which should be discussed.[7]

The most obvious factor is simply *power.* You may have an informal influence over people simply because they feel you have some power. The power may come from knowing someone important to the organization. You may be the son or daughter of someone important. The power may come from your superior knowledge. The power that some secretaries are said to have comes because they have accumulated knowledge of procedures and information over the years that no one else has. The power may come from *seniority:* even though you are doing the same job as someone else, you may be the one who has been on the job longest. Whatever its source, power in the organization can lead to the creation of a powerful informal role.

Credibility and informal power may also come from high levels of *trustworthiness* or *goodwill.* Each of these is a somewhat different source of credibility. First, you may have great informal power within the organization because of your loyalty or general trustworthiness. In every organization, there are people who are considered dependable. Whatever happens, these people do their job—and then some. They can be trusted with difficult tasks and they can keep material confidential. Goodwill is more specific than trustworthiness. Goodwill means that the individual is trying to do the best thing for the organization and the people in it. Though trustworthiness and goodwill seem to relate closely, they are different factors. A person who is generally *not* completely trustworthy may display goodwill at a particular time. The person who *is* generally trustworthy may not always exhibit goodwill. There may arise a situation in which some personal gain is more important than the good of the organization. A promotion—even if the employee knows he or she is unqualified—may become more important than anything else. In that situation, the employee may lack goodwill even though he or she is generally trustworthy. Trustworthiness and goodwill are both important. The person who is perceived favorably with regard to both factors is a person who may enjoy informal-role power.

Dynamism is another factor that may explain credibility. Executives frequently compliment a particular employee as a "real go-getter." The person who is active, aggressive (in a positive sense), and enthusiastic may enjoy more credibility than his or her formal role would suggest. Companies frequently hire employees with the desire for them to move up quickly. The person who acts as if he or she can accept more and more responsibility may become a powerful person in the organization. Dynamism may be the key to an important informal role.

Similarity has been seen as another factor of credibility. When two individuals are somehow alike, they may have some influence upon one another. The vice-president who started as a mail clerk may be influenced by a promising new mail clerk—and vice versa. Dissimilarity, however, may result in lower levels of power. The person who doesn't fit in may not enjoy an important informal role even if he or she has an important formal role.

A final factor is *competence*. The truly gifted person may be a powerful person in the organization. Supervisors may come to depend upon a subordinate who simply knows a great deal. The vice-president who seems more competent and knowledgeable than the other vice-presidents may be a more powerful figure than they are. True competence can lead to an important informal role.

These factors of credibility are interesting for their own sakes. They may also be reasons why you play the organizational roles you play: they affect the relationship between you and the rest of the organization. In another sense, credibility (because of whatever factor) may prompt some interesting variations on the three main sorts of communication networks in organizations (downward, upward, and horizontal). Most organizations develop a whole system of *informal* communication, commonly known as the *grapevine*. The term *grapevine* is well chosen because this system may be a complex and tangled mass of channels of information. One person learns something which is transmitted to whomever is convenient—or whomever is a friend. This second person tells someone or several other persons, and so on. One result is a maze of communication channels. Another result is the creation of the "rumor mill"—which may or may not grind out accurate communication.

Another and less dramatic result of informal roles generated by credibility is what is known as *diagonal* communication networks. Instead of communicating upward, downward, or horizontally, a person may communicate *down and across*. A vice-president who has more faith in someone else's subordinate than in his or her own may communicate with that person. An employee may talk with someone else's supervisor (*up and across*) if that person is viewed as somehow more credible. Diagonal communication is neither good nor bad, but it does exist and you should know about it.

A third result of informal roles and different levels of credibility is *skip-level* communication. For one reason or another, a person may ignore his or her vice-presidents and speak directly with upper-level supervisors. An entry-level employee may ignore his or her supervisor and speak directly with the president of the organization. This skip-level communication may occur directly because of informal roles. The person who ignores levels may have a better personal relationship with a higher-up. The president may feel that his or her vice-presidents are not as trustworthy as one of "the old hands." In short, any of the factors of credibility and informal power may explain why communication has not followed formal channels.

Many of the things that are important to you as an individual in an organization are related to your role in it. We have discussed both formal and informal roles. These are important by themselves, but they are more important in their influence upon the nature of one-to-many communication in the organization.

Organizations and systems

We have discussed the organization of organizations and the individual's role within the organization. We will now think about organizations as parts of larger systems.[8] I mentioned before that organizations should be thought of as systems of people, instead of buildings and inventories. Generally, organizations will function well if the people in them are functioning and communicating well. One of the exceptions to this idea is when the organization does not perform well in its environment.

The *environment* of an organization is made up of at least three basic units; off-duty employees, all other people who come into contact with the organization, and all the other organizations which may transact with the organization. Let us look at how each unit becomes a part of the dynamic system than affects the organization.

First, the organization must deal with its off-duty employees. The normal working day may span something like eight hours—and usually more for executives and professional people. During that time, the individual's activity may be fairly well controlled. What the person says and does *officially* is a concern of the organization. Yet the organization must also be aware that you as an individual spend most of your time away from the organization. How satisfied you are with your work may determine what sorts of things you say about the company after hours. Dissatisfied employees who "talk over the back fence" may do more damage than an expensive public relations campaign can ever correct. When companies are officially telling the public how concerned they are about the community, they may be believed. When off-duty employees tell a different story, the companies' credibility may suffer. One unit of the whole system of the organization, then, is the employees—after hours.

A second major unit of the organizational system is that group of all other people who may affect the organization. These people include customers or clients, stockholders, civic leaders, and the families of employees. These are people who directly or indirectly can affect the health and success of the organization. Business leaders in the early 1970s sometimes found it difficult to gain support from citizens: the companies were accused of not caring about such issues as pollution. At about the same time, some of these same organizations found it difficult to hire young people: some of them did not want to work for companies which made chemicals or materiel for waging war. In the same way, companies generally find it difficult to succeed in public relations campaigns if families of employees spread rumors that are unfavorable. No organization can isolate itself from the people around it who must provide some measure of support.

The same is true with a third unit of the system, all other organizations which interact with the first organization. Organizations which affect other organizations include local, state and federal governments; tax agencies; regulatory agencies; union groups or associations; professional societies such as the American Association of University Professors and the American Bar Association; charity organizations; local or national civic groups; and other organizations which simply do business with the organization. Any of these other organizations can affect how an organization functions—or does not function.

Organizations, then, must be thought of in terms of a system in which they play a part. All sorts of people and other organizations are important factors in that system. To understand organizations, you must understand what occurs within them. To understand them fully you must understand what happens in the environment that is the organization's system.

In this section, the goal has been to explain certain variables in the one-to-many communication situation. We have discussed the organization of organizations, the individual's role in the organization, and finally, the organization and its system. Knowledge of these variables and factors is preparation for the other major topic in this chapter: one-to-many conflicts as problems.

PROBLEMS IN THE ONE-TO-MANY SETTING

The variables just discussed can be used to describe some potential problems that may arise in the one-to-many situation. You can use those variables to explain *your* problems when you as a single person try to communicate with many people in the organization. The problems you may encounter may include three different types: problems of communicating *through* the organization, problems of communicating *to* the organization, and problems of communicating *for* the organization. The rest of the chapter is a discussion of those three kinds of problems.

Problems of communicating *through* the organization

Some of the problems you will face in communicating in the one-to-many situation have to do with how messages *flow* through the organization. Some conflicts in communication involve what we called the organization of organizations. The division of labor, the organizational structure, and the spans-of-control may all lead to problems. A division of labor, for example, can only succeed if the people who do different things can coordinate their activity. In scalar terms, the highest executives must be somewhat aware of the problems of entry-level employees. The reverse is also true. The lowest-level employee must be at least somewhat aware of the goals and policies of the organization's executives. In functional terms, the people who do various tasks should know how each sort of activity relates to the organization as a whole. Coordinating a possibly large number of activities can be difficult. Entry-level employees frequently complain that they have no knowledge of organizational goals. Executives frequently feel that they do not know all of what goes on at lower levels.

One of the ways of improving the communication among the various levels is to keep the organization as flat as possible. The fewer the levels, the assumption is, the easier it is to have everyone communicate with everyone else. Yet, the flat organization—the centralized organization—may have problems of its own. The span-of-control that any one executive can exercise is limited. That means, for example, that a supervisor who has thirty people reporting to him or her cannot do an adequate job of supervision. The employee whose supervisor has thirty other subordinates must compete with all the others for time, attention, and guidance. So, factors in the organization of organizations can lead to basic conflicts: to divide labor means to lose some efficient communication; to improve communication the organization may try to keep a flat structure; to keep a flat structure, the spans-of-control may become out of control; to have spans-of-control means that communication may be difficult. The factors in the organization of organizations may become a circle of conflicts. The company—and you as a member of the company—may need some way of mediating the conflicts among these organizational factors. Your problem may be, How can we coordinate the efforts of this organization?

Formal and informal roles that individuals play in the organization can make the communication problem even worse. Some coordination must be done through formal roles and formal channels; upward, downward, and horizontally. But individuals are individuals and that means that some coordination will be done informally. What happens when messages flow diagonally or in a skip-level manner? Should these informal networks be discouraged, improved, or encouraged? Problems of coordination may be especially severe in some cases. Messages that flow through informal channels, for example, may conflict with the messages of formal channels. If that occurs, which will be believed? What should be done about the situation—if anything? In essence, formal and informal roles may conflict. Formal and informal networks may carry conflicting messages. The conflicts may lead to serious organizational problems. Your need—and the organization's need—may be for some method of mediation.

A final set of problems relating to the message flow involves the organization and its system. Sometimes the organization may not know how the forces in its environment are reacting to it. Are off-duty employees supporting or undermining the organization? How much support or hostility is being shown by clients, civic leaders, and other people in the system? What are the relationships between the organization and the other organizations around it? Are there unknown conflicts that seem to exist? If so, how can they be identified? Are there known conflicts? If so, how can they be treated? The organization does not exist in a vacuum. It exists in a dynamic system of other people and organizations. When that system presents its own share of conflicts, the organization's need may be for mediation. As a member of that organization, your goal may be to help mediate that conflict. In doing so, you face your own conflict about how to do it.

Problems of communicating *to* the organization

Sometimes, your personal conflict may be more direct. Your role in any organization presents you with certain responsibilities. In any supervisory (or higher) position, your responsibilities may include the creation of *proposals* for the organization to consider. You may be in engineering, marketing, management generally, sales, medicine, publishing, law, government, technology, architecture—or almost anything else. Still, as you reach supervisory positions or higher levels, you may be responsible for *making a presentation.*

Presentations are extremely common tasks in organizations. They involve a number of fairly set assumptions.[9] First, you as a representative of a larger group (a department or an area, for example) will have the *responsibility to research a particular problem.* The problem may involve a new accounting procedure, a new book for publication, an advanced computer system, a new client's account—or a thousand other things. To research the problem, you will have access to some or much help from the organization. The help may include released time to work on the project, extra staff, organizational money, computer time, and any of the files of the organization. This help is not provided for information gathering alone: The second assumption is that you will have *responsibility for developing a proposal* about what should be done about the problem. On the basis of perhaps months of research, your task will be to present arguments for the acceptance of whatever seems to be the best solution to the problem.

A third assumption is that you will have the *responsibility for presenting this idea to a small group of active decision makers.* The presentation is not a *public* speech. Rather, it will be given before the executive board, the board of directors, or a specially chosen task force. These are people who will decide whether to accept or reject the proposal you present. These are also people who will take their task very seriously. They may be supportive or they may be skeptical, but they usually will be active. They may ask questions, they may ask for a better explanation, they may challenge the evidence you use, and they may quarrel with you. In this sense, the presentation is not only not a *public* speech; it is not even a *speech* as you might think of it. The presentation is a tremendously dynamic situation that looks something like a small group problem-solving situation. In some ways, it is.

A final assumption of the presentational situation is that the *presentation may be important to your career*. The presentation in the real world is not like the classroom speech where you are graded and nothing more. The person who spends organizational time, staff, and money over a period of perhaps months is responsible for the outcome of the presentation. A well-accomplished task may be a career boost. A poorly conceived and presented proposal may have the opposite effect. The specific situation will vary, of course, but one thing is certain: The presentation that you make to the dozen or so people sitting around you may be more important than any public speech you may ever present. What is more important is that the presentational speech—unlike the public speech—is a common occurrence in our contemporary world.

You may experience serious conflicts related to the problem of speaking *to* the organization. You may not want the task at all. On the other hand, the task simply may be part of your responsibility. You may have to do it, even though you experience conflict. At the point when you decide to undertake the project another set of conflicts may arise. How do you present a proposal to this group of decision makers—most of whom are at formally higher levels than you are? How do you conduct the research? What do you do with material once you have gathered it? How do you create the proposal? How do you "sell" the proposal once you have created it? How do you know what the group is looking for and what they will "buy?" How do you put together the presentation? How do you interact with this *active* group of decision makers? In short, the presentational speaking situation can create serious conflicts. Your need may be for a set of strategies of mediation.

Problems of speaking *for* the organization

The tasks of communicating *through* the organization and *to* the organization are fairly—perhaps very—common. At times, your task may be to speak *for* the organization. You may be called upon to represent the organization in some ways to a public outside the organization. This task, for the purposes of the text, is *public speaking*. Public speaking differs from presentational speaking in a variety of ways. First, the audience probably will be much less familiar to you than the audience of the presentation. In fact, the public speaker may not know personally a single member of the audience. Second, the public speech, unlike the presentation, does not always involve persuasion about a proposal. The goal of the public speech may be to provide information, to explain the organization's functions, or to describe organizational plans. In addition, the public speech may be primarily a way of building rapport or goodwill between the organization and the audience. The public speech may even be based upon a more subtle goal: the humorous speech given to the Kiwanis or Rotary Club may be an indirect public relations effort by the organization. Most organizations virtually require their executives to become active members of civic groups and clubs. When those executives make even entertaining speeches, they are "representing" the goodwill of the organization.

A third distinction between the presentation and the public speech is that the public speech audience does not usually make decisions. It is usually a group of people that the organization simply finds important. The audience may be a civic group, attendees at a graduation ceremony, or any one of dozens of other groups. The listeners usually do not make decisions based upon the speech.

Finally, audiences of the public speech differ from audiences of presentations in the extent of their activity. Usually, public audiences do not interrupt with questions, challenges, or arguments. The public speech audience is the traditional audience. The people listen, they respond (mostly nonverbally or verbally to someone next to them), and they allow the speaker to remain in tight control. The small group atmosphere of the presentation is not usually present at the public speech.

There are, of course, some similarities between the two types of speaking. Speakers in both situations usually must prepare beforehand. Both speakers must know how to structure a message that can be understood. Both speakers must be able to communicate before some sort of audience. Both speakers must conquer any anxiety they have about speaking. In short, many of the skills of presentational speaking are valuable in the public speaking situation.

Still, the public speech may bring special conflicts of its own. How will you find out something about this audience—most of which may be strangers? How will you select what you want to say? What guidance should you get from the organization you represent? How long and complex should the speech be? What will you want to accomplish? How will you know if you are accomplishing it? The public speaking situation has some problems that are fairly unique to it. In facing the situation, you may need specific communication skills and information for the mediation of those conflicts.

CHAPTER SUMMARY

Most people with college credit or degrees will find themselves needing to communicate in a one-to-many situation. The majority of those situations will relate somehow to the organizations we are involved in. Few people represent only themselves when they communicate in the one-to-many situation.

This chapter looked first at variables in the organization. In studying the organization of organizations, we examined the ideas of division of labor, organizational structure, span-of-control, and the action of the organization as closed or open. In studying the role of the individual in organizations, we looked at both formal and informal roles—and the various kinds of communication networks that are caused by these roles. Finally, in this section, we discussed how the organization is part of a large environment of people and other organizations.

The discussion of organizational variables set the stage for the discussion of one-to-many problems in the second major section of the chapter. Here, we discussed the problems of communicating *through* the organization. The factors of division of labor, organizational structure, and span-of-control were seen as related to the problems of communication. How can the organization coordinate its efforts when messages are being sent upward, downward, and horizontally? What are the effects of messages flowing diagonally or in a skip-level manner? Then, the discussion turned to the problems of communicating *to* the organization. The nature of presentational speaking and its problems were examined. Finally, we examined the problems of speaking *for* the organization. The nature of public speaking was explained, and public speaking was differentiated from presentational speaking. The unique problems of the public speech were introduced.

The chapter, then, dealt with the conflicts in the one-to-many situation as problems. The communication strategies that can aid the mediation of those conflicts can be important to you. Chapters 17 through 20 describe some of those strategies. The strategies you learned earlier can also help you with conflicts in the one-to-many situation. The section following this chapter is designed to show how such strategies can be applied.

NOTES

[1] More specifically, the messages may be communicated at *almost* the same time. Frequently, as we shall see later in the chapter, messages flow *serially*, through several or many levels in the organization or community. This process actually will not occur simultaneously.

[2] For a text which emphasizes beautifully the dynamics of organizations, see Wendell L. French and Cecil H. Bell, Jr., *Organizational Development* (Englewood Cliffs, N.J.: Prentice-Hall, 1973).

[3] For a complete discussion, see William G. Scott, *Organizational Theory* (Homewood, Il.: Irwin, 1967).

[4] The idea of the *open* organization is related to the *social systems* theory of management. For an excellent discussion, see Edgar Huse and James Bowditch, *Behavior in Organizations* (Reading, Ma.: Addison-Wesley, 1973), especially chap. 13.

[5] For a detailed treatment of action in the organization, see Robert Mockler, *Management Decision Making and Action in Behavioral Situations* (Austin, Tx.: Austin Press, 1973).

[6] Although these terms and ideas have become traditionally accepted in organizational communication, a more detailed treatment of some of these concepts appears in Gerald M. Goldhaber, *Organizational Communication* (Dubuque, Ia.: Wm. C. Brown, 1974), especially chap. 1. A more thorough treatment is Ralph Stogdill, "Dimensions of Organization Theory," *Organizational Design and Research*, Part One, ed. James D. Thompson (Pittsburgh: Univ. of Pittsburgh Press, 1971), chap. 1.

[7] Although this discussion is not based upon it, an interesting and more detailed treatment is found in Roderick P. Hart, Gustav W. Friedrich, and William D. Brooks, "The Speaker as Resource," *Public Communication* (New York: Harper & Row, 1975).

[8] See Carol J. Elbing, "The Value Issue of Business," *Behavioral Decisions in Organizations*, ed. Alver O. Elbing (Glenview, Il.: Scott, Foresman, 1970), especially pp. 785–89.

[9] An excellent brief treatment of presentational speaking is Steven L. Vibbert, "Presentational Speaking as Communication Skill," *Fundamentals of Communication*, ed. Richard E. Crable and Richard O. Forsythe with Steven L. Vibbert (Columbus, Oh.: Collegiate, 1976), pp. 284–87. A more detailed discussion is in William S. Howell and Ernest G. Bormann, *Presentational Speaking for Business and the Professions* (New York: Harper & Row, 1971).

APPLYING WHAT YOU KNOW IN NEW WAYS

(How to Apply Earlier Strategies in the One-to-Many Situation)

Before we begin to discuss special strategies for mediation (Chapters 17 through 20) you should realize that you already know certain strategies that can be used for the mediation of some conflicts in the one-to-many situation. Perception, verbal analysis, nonverbal analysis, decisioning by argumentation, listening, feedback, and interviewing all are strategies which have their place in one-to-many situations. Since these strategies have been reviewed in concise form before (see "Applying What You Know In New Ways" following Chapter 12), I will not review them here in detail, but the following will refresh your memory.

1. Perception: Understand that the perceptions of situations are personal, selective, inductive, context-bound, motivated, AND CAN BE CHANGED IF YOU FIND THEM UNJUSTIFIED.

2. Verbal analysis: Decide whether labels are used rationally or arbitrarily; know that the percieved meanings of verbal symbols vary; analyze the level of abstraction of troublesome symbols; avoid stereotyping; AND ADJUST OR HELP ADJUST LANGUAGE THAT CONTRIBUTES TO THE CONFLICT.

3. Nonverbal analysis: Isolate nonverbal communication that is troublesome, discover the meanings attached to such cues, compare common meanings to those meanings, AND ADJUST OR HELP ADJUST TROUBLESOME NONVERBAL COMMUNICATION.

4. Decisioning by argumentation: Phrase conflicts as claims with reservations and qualifiers, examine the support or evidence for the claims, AND SELECT THE CLAIM WHICH SEEMS BEST SUPPORTED.

5. Listening: Discover if you can any possible listening problems (DO NOT ASSUME THAT YOU UNDERSTAND), try to overcome the listening problem, discover the nature of the appropriate listening response, AND KEEP THAT RESPONSE IN MIND AS YOU TRANSACT.

6. Feedback: Make sure that the feedback is solicited (or at least welcome), descriptive, specific, focused upon modifiable things, and mutual. AVOID FEEDBACK GAMES.

7. Interviewing: Identify the goal of mediation; see if it can be aided by means of interviewing; pay attention to such things as timing and nonverbal communication; consider the goals of the other person; consider how the interview should begin or end, AND ADJUST THE TECHNIQUES AS THE SITUATION AND THE INTERVIEW EVOLVES.

Consider these strategies as you work through the following cases.

Case study a.   Yesterday, you and the boss (Ms. Hardy) met to discuss your yearly evaluation. You happen to be a sales representative and she did not seem to be terribly pleased with your progress. Today, you are handed this memo, which has gone to all personnel in sales:

From: L.J. Hardy

To: All sales personnel

Re: the employment of new sales representatives

It has come to my attention that we may be hiring new sales representatives. The exact procedures for this employment will be announced soon.

* * *

You finish reading the note, and you think, I wonder how displeased she really was yesterday?

Look at the case study from the standpoint of *perception*. What might have helped prompt the idea that your job might be in question? What might have motivated this perception? How might the memo have helped your recollection of yesterday's discussion to lead you inductively to that conclusion? In what way might the perception be completely unjustified? What about context?

Look at the case from a *verbal analysis* perspective. What does "it has come to my attention" *really* mean? What does it mean to YOU? If the new sales representatives will be *in addition to* those already employed, could the memo have been written more clearly? How?

Think about *feedback* skills. If you are that uncertain about how dissatisfied the boss is, what does that indicate about the clarity of her feedback? Do you think you should have asked for more feedback if the conflict was that troublesome? How has the interpersonal or intrapersonal conflict become a one-to-many conflict?

Case study b. Steve is in the office of the vice-president in charge of marketing, who is giving Steve an assignment to create a research project and presentation on new marketing media. The conversation goes like this:

V-P: So, if we can tap into some of these other media . . . .

Steve: Yeah, I see what you mean.

V-P: We will need a rather extensive research background for this. I would say probably . . . .

Steve: All I need is six weeks and the help of the staff.

V-P: Well, that's sensational. I would have thought that it would take three times that long, but if you think you can . . . .

Steve: I'll do it.

V-P: Do you need any more details?

Steve: Nope. I'll do the job.

The case seems exaggerated, but it is based upon a situation I observed as a consultant. The vice-president did not seem to care about Steve's abruptness, as long as the job was completed. Unfortunately, the task was not completed well—and the vice-president no longer thought Steve was sensational.

In terms of the *interview* this should have been an informational one, with Steve getting all the information he needed. It did not turn out that way. What are the questions that Steve could have asked?: How many people could he use for research? How much money could be committed to the project? For whom was the presentation to be made? None of these questions occurred to him. If they had, his presentation—if he had been allowed to make it—would have been better.

In terms of *listening*, Steve also had problems. What were they? How might listening skills have been applied as tools so that the problem of the presentation could have been handled better?

Case study c. Gail is speaking to a sorority gathering on "women in business." In an effort to identify with her audience, she dresses casually in jeans and a sweater. Unfortunately, her audience is dressed more formally for the occasion than she is. One of the points Gail wishes to make is that women in business must develop a good sense of appropriate dress. During the speech, she is interrupted by a member of the audience who asks her if she dresses like "this" at the bank.

Gail: No, of course not. I wear fashionable, but conservative clothes there.

Aud. Member: I was just wondering. You need to dress appropriately, huh?

Gail feels her audience slipping away from her on the basis of what she considers a silly issue.

From the standpoint of *nonverbal analysis*, it seems that Gail has made a mistake. What do you think the role of her appearance is in this situation? What meanings is at least one audience member attaching to her casual attire? How could both Gail and the audience member benefit from nonverbal analysis?

Look at the case from the perspective of *argumentation*. Gail was claiming that appropriate dress was important. Her own failure to dress appropriately made her uncomfortable. Yet the very fact that she had dressed inappropriately—and that at least some people reacted negatively to it—could have been used as evidence for her point. How? What might the embarrassed Gail have said to support the point she wanted to make?

In these cases, then, we have seen how strategies discussed earlier can be applied to problems in the one-to-many situation. The following chapters explore special strategies for the mediation of such conflicts.

17
SERIAL COMMUNICATION AS ONE-TO-MANY STRATEGIES

A new version of an old story: The president of the company tells the vice-president, "We are going to have to be more concerned with wasting the company's resources. We have spent thousands more dollars for supplies than we did last year. The busiest company cannot afford such expenditures—and we're not the busiest. I want us to make every effort to eliminate waste—everything from business forms to paper clips. Make sure your people are aware of the problem."

The vice-president tells his top managers, "We need to be more concerned with waste in the company. We've spent much more for supplies this year than last and we're not as busy as we should be. Make sure that everything from business forms to paper clips is being used wisely. Pass the word."

One of the managers tells her top supervisors: "We need to encourage more business this year—and we need to be more aware of waste. In particular, we need to be concerned with eliminating waste. Paper clips and business forms are top priorities."

One of the supervisors tells his foremen: "The word is out that we are concerned about new business, paper clips, and business forms. We need more of all of them. Let's try to eliminate waste."

Overheard at the coffee machine, "Hey, don't throw that away. Haven't you heard about the paper clip shortage?"

Stories like this have become traditional in studies of the problems of communicating through the organization. The stories all seem unrealistic until people get experience in actually trying to communicate in such situations. Communicating *through* the organization means that messages are passed from one person to another until everyone "knows what's going on." If organizations were not systems of people, the problems involved would not be so serious. A communicator actually could send his or her *meaning* to Person A, who would send it to Person B, and so forth. But organizations *are* systems of people. The president cannot send a meaning to the vice-president, who sends it to top-level managers, who . . . . Instead, the president must *symbolize his or her meaning in verbal and nonverbal messages* and hope that the meaning is re-created accurately. The vice-president has to do the same. In organizations, communication *must* flow upward, downward, and across the organization. In addition it probably *will* move diagonally, on the grapevine, and in a skip-level manner. This chapter is devoted to the discussion of how your communication *through* the organization—your *serial communication*—can be used for mediating organizational problems.

Basic strategies of using serial communication include: selecting your purpose, realizing sources of distortion, deciding how to communicate, deciding when to communicate, and using network interrelationships.

SELECT YOUR COMMUNICATION PURPOSE

One of the basic strategies of using serial communication involves your selection of a *purpose*. In your hectic life as a member of organizations, you will need to *send* messages through organizations. You *report* to your supervisor, you *confer* with someone on the same level as you, or you *get reports* from your subordinates. One of the first things you must do in using serial communication is to understand the main purposes of each of these types of communication.

In their excellent study of organizations, Katz and Kahn describe five major purposes for *downward* communication.[1] Higher-level members attempt to communicate about job instructions, job rationale, organizational policies and procedures, organizational goals—and also provide feedback. Each of these types of communication purpose is important.

Job instructions include any written or oral discussion about how someone is to perform a particular task. The instructions might relate to accounting duties, advertising methods, or almost anything else in the organization. Sometimes the job instructions are listed in *job descriptions* which are assigned to an employee. However they are communicated, one of the main purposes of downward communication is to re-create meanings about job instructions.[2] Frequently job instructions will be accompanied by *job rationales.* Job rationales explain *why* a particular job is important, why it needs to be done, or why it must be done in a certain way. Job rationales probably should always accompany job descriptions, so that employees have a greater sense of why they are doing what they do. Unfortunately, this is not always the case. Frequently, job instructions will be issued with no rationale, and the result is hostility among employees. They may feel that a task is make-work: an unimportant job done just to keep them busy. For that reason, communicating job rationales can be an extremely important goal of downward communication.

In an even more general sense, some downward communication deals with *organizational or corporate goals*. In order for whole systems of people—for organizations—to function well, everyone should be aware of the overall goals of the organization. People tend to work better and more efficiently when they know what's going on. Even the lowest-level employee needs to know something about the organization's broader goals.[3] These goals may be communicated by newsletter, by organizational brochures, or face-to-face communication. However the communication occurs, it is one of several basic types of downward communication.

A fourth sort of downward communication involves *policies and procedures*. Any organization must have a set of procedures for doing the various jobs of the organization. The organization must make clear its policies for salary increases, for promotion, for reporting, and so forth. Employees can function more efficiently if they are aware of the procedures which allow the organization to remain organized.

The final major purpose of downward communication is *feedback*. Employees should know something about job rationale and instructions, organizational goals, and procedures. They also must be told how they are fulfilling their responsibilities to the organization. Feedback from higher levels allows them to alter or continue their behavior—just as feedback generally helps people judge and adapt their behavior.[4] The feedback may come from job evaluations, company reports, or face-to-face discussions with supervisors. Regardless of how it is communicated, feedback is a primary type of downward communication.

Just as downward communication has several major purposes, upward communication serves specific functions. Communication from lower to higher levels in the organization can provide ideas and information to the organization, help make decisions, provide an outlet for dissatisfaction and grievances, and serve to check on understanding.[5]

First, upward communication can *provide ideas and information*. If the organization is seen as a system of people, it is reasonable that even the lowest-level employee may have good ideas or specific information. The people closest to the specific job being done may have ideas about how to do it better. The specialist in the organization may have information no one else has. Upward communication can be used to communicate the ideas and information throughout the organization. An open organization not only allows this type of participation; it encourages it. At times, awards are presented to employees who contribute valuable input to the organization.

Upward communication also can allow lower-level employees to *participate in decision-making* situations. Clearly, most decisions affecting the whole organization will be made at the top. This does not mean that the views and preferences of lower-level employees cannot be considered. Employees who feel that their input into the decision-making process is taken seriously may be more satisfied with their positions.[6] Groups, generally, like to feel that they have a hand in what goes on. The same is true of an organization of groups and individuals. The open organization takes advantage of all the sources of input, including that which comes up through the organization.

A third purpose of upward communication is to *air dissatisfactions and grievances*. When employees are unhappy with their jobs or the policies of the company, they *will* talk with someone. If they are not allowed to communicate to the organization or their superiors, they will talk with wives, husbands, neighbors, other employees—or strangers. Certainly not every employee can be completely satisfied. Not every complaint or grievance is justified. Still, employees should be allowed to communicate their feelings and complaints to the organization. Some problems may be solved by supervisors; some may have no solution, but can be explained to the employee. Whatever the result, communicating dissatisfactions and grievances to supervisors or through suggestion procedures is a major purpose of upward communication.

Finally, upward communication can serve as a *check for understanding*. The response of employees to policies, procedures, corporate goals, and so forth can serve to check whether misunderstanding has occurred. Feedback such as this can allow superiors to clarify their communication or to modify it. Upward feedback can provide the chief means of discovering mistaken interpretation of messages going through the organization.

Horizontal communication also has several major purposes, including procedure explanation, problem solving, organizational coordination, and information sharing.[7] In terms of *procedure explanation,* various parts of the organization may have established their own specific policies and procedures. The organization can function best if all parts of the organization are aware of these. Efficiency can be improved if the proper steps are taken or the appropriate forms are completed. In the same way, much horizontal communication is used to *coordinate the efforts* of parts of the organization. Any major project or task that the organization faces probably will need the efforts of several areas within it. When each area knows what responsibility it has for the project, the effort can become more efficient. Overlap and gaps in the project can be avoided by the effective use of horizontal communication.

In addition, some horizontal communication involves *problem solving*. The whole organization may face a common decision—or what one part of the organization does may create a problem for everyone else. Representatives from several parts of the organization may meet or communicate in written form for the purpose of solving problems. In the same way, representatives of different parts of the organization may communicate as a way of *information sharing*. Instead of facing a clear-cut problem, the task simply may be to pool information.

In addition to upward, downward, and horizontal communication, we have discussed communication that occurs diagonally, by the grapevine, or in a skip-level manner. Any of these types of communication may have the goal of doing whatever the other three types can do. They may occur because you as an employee feel you can communicate better with someone other than your supervisor. They may occur because channels seem to be blocked. Whatever the reason, diagonal, grapevine, and skip-level communication probably will occur.

In essence, then, there are certain basic purposes thay may be the goals of serial communication. One strategy in using serial communication for mediation is to be sure you are aware of the purpose of the message. It is not enough to "just send word down"; you should know what specific goal you hope to accomplish. It is not enough to "tell the boss"; you should know exactly what you hope to achieve. It is not enough to "meet with" Sharon from accounting and Joe from sales; you should know what your horizontal communication should accomplish. The discussion of purposes for the various types of serial communication may be relevant to your specific purpose. The task of selecting and knowing that specific purpose is left to you.

REALIZE SOURCES OF DISTORTION

Attempts to communicate serially in the one-to-many situation can make you aware of how messages are distorted in their path through the organization. Any consultant who has worked in business, government, or any other organization has heard the same questions asked: A vice-president wants to know why first-level supervisors fail to follow instructions; entry-level employees ask why the vice-president does not understand their problems; a manager in research wants to know why the manager in sales seems uncooperative. The list could go on nearly forever. The questions are similar because organizations are similar. Whatever their different natures, all organizations are composed of people. People have generally the same sorts of problems in trying to communicate through channels.

You as a communicator must realize first the sources of distortion in messages that travel through the organization. Some of these are created by the nature of communication. We have discussed the problems of using verbal and nonverbal cues to send the right message to another person or a group. The same symbols will mean different things to these other people, who engage in selective exposure, attention, perception, and recall or retention. The result of all this in interpersonal or group communication is that meanings will be avoided, ignored, misperceived, or forgotten. Whether these are the results of conscious or unconscious processes, the point is the same: communication from one person to another, or one person to a group is difficult.

Serial communication is even worse. When meanings have to be communicated through different levels of the organization, there is simply more chance of misperception and misunderstanding. Person B (who has avoided, ignored, misperceived, and misremembered parts of the message of Person A) now communicates the misunderstood message to Person C. On the basis of a further set of misunderstandings, Person C communicates with Person D, and so the process continues as the message moves upward, downward, across, diagonally, or in a skip-level manner. The process can be illustrated in the classroom when one student passes an oral message to another to another to another . . . until the message comes back to the first person. This game illustrates some of the problems of serial communication. The first person hardly recognizes the message he or she sent through the class. Is it any wonder that supervisors throw up their hands in desperation, saying, "No, that is *not* what I meant for you to do!" Some of the distortion in communicating through organizations occurs because of the nature of communication—and people.

Part of the distortion in serial communication has more specific causes. Organizations are not only systems of people. They are systems of people who work both for the organization and for their own benefit. All sorts of psychological factors can be related to the distortion of messages. Lower-level employees, for example, are often afraid to ask questions of supervisors: They do not wish to feel stupid. Sometimes lower level employees are fearful of presenting bad news to their superiors.[8] In either case, the result can be a distortion of messages. In the first situation, the result of failure to ask questions or to assess understanding is misunderstanding. In the second situation—the common fear of reporting unfavorable events or information—it is the supervisor who may fail to understand what is going on.

Other sources of message distortion are even more difficult to confront. Jealousy among co-workers and even between subordinates and supervisors may be a problem. Jealousy may be related to a desire to gain or to retain power and status. The supervisor may squelch the good ideas of an employee, or a lower-level supervisor may distort the messages of a higher-level supervisor. In either case, personal feelings of rivalry and jealousy may be a cause of message distortion. A manager in one area may be jealous of the progress made by a manager in another area. If these two are competing for the same sort of promotion, the rivalry based upon the desire for power may be extreme.

Another set of problems has to do with lack of information or motivation. The person who does not have the background for understanding a message, may pass along a misinterpreted idea.[9] Highly technical problems and information usually do not rise to the highest levels of the organization, but even somewhat technical messages can become distorted because someone somewhere does not have the background to understand the meaning of a message. Lack of information can be a problem, especially if the uninformed person is not *motivated* to communicate accurately. The unmotivated employee will see no reason to gather additional information or to ask for additional instructions. Lack of motivation can lead to a lack of effort in trying to pass on ideas and information accurately.

This discussion does not include all the sources of distortion in the serial communication process within an organization. The possible sources are as numerous as the relationships between and among its members. Rather, we have gained some insight into general sources of distortion. Once you know the purpose of your communication, you can prepare to deal—one by one—with the sources of distortion. A basic strategy of serial communication is to realize and confront sources of distorted messages.

DECIDE HOW TO COMMUNICATE

A third important strategy for mediation in the serial communication process is deciding how to communicate. Generally, you will have some choice as to the method of communication. You may have to decide whether to communicate orally or in writing. If you choose to put the message in writing, you may be able to use a memo, an in-house newsletter, a brochure, or a note on the bulletin board.[10] If you choose an oral message, you may have to decide whether to call a meeting, use a regularly scheduled meeting, set up an interview, or use some part of a casual conversation.

Contemporary thinking seems to be that organizations rely too much upon written communication. Face-to-face and oral communication allows for feedback, and avoids the problem of people not reading bulletins, memos, and so forth. However, written communication ensures that everyone involved receives the same verbal symbols—though perhaps not the same *meaning*. Written communication also has the advantage of providing a record that the message was passed through the organization. There are no rules to guide you in this matter. For any given type of communication, one or another method may seem best. In most cases, the decision should be made on the basis of the sort of message and the type and number of people who must receive the message. Eventually, the decision will be based on your experience. You may try one method and discard it in favor of another. Or, you try one method and continue to use it because it seems effective. You simply will need to analyze your purpose, the possible sources of distortion, and choose a method of communication. The feedback you receive from that attempt can begin to guide your choices in the future.

DECIDE WHEN TO COMMUNICATE

Timing can be crucial in communicating serially. If the message must be filtered through several or many levels in the organization, your message must be sent early. A message received too late may be almost worse than a message not received at all. In addition, there are psychological factors in timing. Feedback long after a situation has passed may be useless. Instructions about job performance may be disregarded if received too early, and disastrous if received too late when everyone is panicking. Communication cannot always be begun "when you get the time." Frequently, you will need to plan it carefully and with a sense of timing.

BEWARE OF THE INTERRELATIONSHIPS AMONG MESSAGES PRESENTED SERIALLY

This chapter should conclude with a warning about the interrelationships between and among serial messages. One of the general requirements of communicating in the one-to-many situation is that communicators should be *consistent*. Ethically, it seems to me that communicators should not tell their subordinates that they are slacking off while they tell their superiors the fine work that is being done in the area. Such inconsistency in the upward and downward communication means that someone is not receiving accurate messages. Ethically, that seems to me to be a problem. In practical terms, that sort of inconsistency is just as bad. Messages in an organization have a way of getting back around through informal channels. Inconsistencies may not be revealed through formal channels, but through informal channels. When inconsistencies are revealed to either subordinates or superiors, the effect upon credibility may be severe. Whether you use my ethical standard or not, you should realize how images of trustworthiness and goodwill may be damaged by inconsistent messages.

The one-to-many communication situation sometimes will involve serial communication. As a communicator, you should:

1. Determine your communication purpose or objective.
2. Realize the potential sources of distortion.
3. Choose what seems to be the best means of communication.
4. Take the timing of the message into consideration.
5. Take into consideration the interrelationships among the means of communication.
6. Use the various means of communication to complement, not contradict, your attempt at communication.

Together, these strategies can help you mediate the conflict between what you know (or accept) and what you want others to know (or accept). As practice in using these strategies, consider the following case studies.

Case study one: the memo.

From: G. H. Lerd, President
To: All Employees
Re: The Proposed Merger

> As all of you are aware, there are discussions underway regarding the merger of this company with Consolidated Box, Inc. The effect of the merger, if it occurs, is unclear at this point. One thing is clear: There will be a reduction of staff at this particular plant. Your immediate supervisors will fill in the details of the cutback.

The memo probably does more harm than good. The one bit of news is probably disheartening to people concerned about their jobs. In terms of timing, the message may have been sent too early: some of the effects of the merger are still unclear. The "reduction" of staff might mean one person, seven, or a hundred. The uncertainty in the memo will probably cause widespread activity on the grapevine. Just as important, the memo probably is not the best way to handle the information. Relying on future serial communication for transmitting information about details is a weakness: the details of the message are exactly what will be distorted most. Can you suggest better ways of handling the problem of getting this information to the company as a whole?

Case study two: what happened after the memo. Several days after the memo (Case Study One) was received about the merger, another memo stated that the cutback would affect only a dozen or so employees at the plant. By this time, however, newspapers had published accounts saying that the proposed merger would affect about one hundred and fifty employees. What the newspapers had not clarified was that the larger figure included staff changes in several plants in the state. In the absence of clarification, conversations like this were heard:

Jack: What do you think of the merger?
Mel: I'd like it better if I didn't think I'd lose my job. . . . Wow, two hundred people.
Jack: I heard it was only a hundred, fifty.
Mel: It doesn't matter does it if you're one of those hurt?
Jack: The whole place is talking about it. I guess the official number of a dozen is put out to keep everyone from panicking.
Mel: I guess. Well, see you around.

What President Lerd needed to consider is that in a situation where fears are high and information awareness is low, messages will become even more distorted than is usually the case. The problem was made worse by the conflicting newspaper stories. One of the things that can be done now is to create a detailed memo with all the information the company has—including an explanation of the newspaper accounts and acknowledgment of the rumors. If the newspapers and rumors have been dealing with erroneous information, some of the problem might be eased with a complete report sent directly (not through supervisors) to all employees.

The cases above illustrate some of the instances where effective serial communication can be used to mediate conflicts in the one-to-many situation. By choosing an appropriate kind of message at an appropriate time, and by taking into consideration message distortion and message interrelationships, some conflicts in the one-to-many situation can be mediated.

EXERCISES

1. Arrange the class in rows of five or six people. Have the first person in each row read a message (use a half page of a later chapter). Have the first person whisper the

message to the second person—without letting the second person read it. Have the second person whisper to the third, and so forth. When the message gets to the last person in the row, have the last person in each row leave the room to compare his or her message with those of the others. Have them arrive at a single interpretation of the message and reenter the room. Have them appoint a spokesperson who will relay the message orally back to the class. At this point, the instructor can read the original message to the whole class. Discuss the distortions, omissions, and additions to the message.

2. Choose another message from this book or some other source. This time, allow only one person to read the message. Pass the message from person to person until everyone has been given the message. Have the last person to receive the message present it orally. Reread the original message aloud. Discuss the problems of one person communicating to many *serially*.

3. Think of a rumor you have recently heard which has turned out to be false. Where did you hear it? Why did you believe it—or why didn't you believe it? If you can, track down the origin of the message—at least take it back as far as you can to the original source. (Note: I suspect you'll have trouble tracking it down; if so, what can that tell you about the grapevine?)

NOTES

[1] Daniel Katz and Robert Kahn, *The Social Psychology of Organizations* (New York: John Wiley & Sons, 1966).

[2] See Robert J. Mockler, *Management Decision Making and Action in Behavioral Situations* (Austin, Tx.: Austin Press, 1973), pp. 142–48.

[3] An interesting case study in which employees were allowed to participate in the creation of such goals is described in Wendell L. French and Cecil H. Bell, Jr., *Organizational Development* (Englewood Cliffs, N.J.: Prentice-Hall, 1973), pp. 12–14.

[4] For a discussion of how the criteria for giving constructive feedback are important in serial communication, see Ibid., pp. 161–62.

[5] See Katz and Kahn, *Social Psychology*.

[6] See Douglas McGregor, *The Human Side of Enterprise* (New York: McGraw-Hill, 1961), chap. 3.

[7] See Katz and Kahn, *Social Psychology*.

[8] For a discussion of these and other barriers, see Chris Argyris, "Interpersonal Barriers of Decision Making," *Behavioral Decisions in Organizations*, ed. Alvar O. Elbing (Glenview, Il.: Scott, Foresman, 1970), pp. 441–63.

[9] Even if background is not a problem, details almost surely will be omitted from messages. The phenomenon is called *uncertainty absorption*. See James March and Herbert Simon, *Organizations* (New York: John Wiley & Sons, 1958).

[10] For a discussion of these, see Normand Sigband, *Effective Report Writing* (New York: Harper & Brothers, 1960), pp. 371–93.

18
GENERAL STRATEGIES OF SPEAKING

Chapter 19 will deal with specific strategies for the presentational speaking situation. Chapter 20 will deal with specific strategies for the public speaking situation. Those chapters are based upon the belief that certain communication strategies can be valuable when you speak either to or for the organization. This chapter deals with various general strategies of communication that can help you with both presentations and public speeches. This chapter is based upon the belief that all *speaking* situations are alike to some degree. Because of that similarity, certain strategies can help you regardless of the sort of speaking you must do. This chapter will deal with strategies that relate to improving credibility, controlling anxiety, adapting delivery, supporting with visual aids, and adapting language.

IMPROVING CREDIBILITY

Whatever your speaking situation, you may be faced with the problem of low credibility. Credibility has to do with what other people think about you. Credibility is a matter of your audience's perception. The question is not whether you *are* trustworthy, dynamic, or competent. The question is whether your audience *thinks* you are a person of these qualities—or the other qualities discussed earlier. The problem of low credibility is not solved by you magically improving yourself. Specifically, the problem is one of improving your audience's perception of you. Research into credibility has not been able to provide anything like "Ten Easy Steps to Credibility." Perhaps research will never provide such a list. Speakers, topics, situations, and audiences all differ so much that general rules may be impossible. Yet, enough research and thought have been given to credibility that some suggestions for improving credibility can be made. These suggestions are merely suggestions.[1] They are not guaranteed to mediate your problems any more than other strategies. On the other hand, they are worthwhile to consider.

Low credibility, for example, might be related to your lacking *power* in some way. Few things can make you automatically more powerful. Perceptions of your power, however, can be changed. You may wish to tell your audience in a subtle manner about the support that you have for whatever you are saying. Are you being backed by the boss, by a department in the organization, or by the organization itself? If so, you may seem more powerful. There are other sources of perceived power. Do you have information that is valuable to the audience? Control of information can be perceived as power. Do you have experience that the audience can use for its benefit? Do you have solutions to problems your audience faces? Do you have special skills your audience needs? Do you have some *formal* control over members of your audience? The subtle indication of these sources of power does not make you more powerful, but may change your audience's perception of your power.

Credibility may also be related to the question of *dynamism*. The aggressive, enthusiastic individual simply may seem more credible. Make sure your audience knows you have taken an active approach to whatever your topic is. Have you done a sizable amount of research? Have you sought the advice of people? Have you actually looked for an answer or a solution? Finally, be concerned about your nonverbal activity during the speaking situation. That activity (which we call *delivery*) will be discussed later in the chapter.

Another factor in credibility is *similarity*. You may create a better impression of yourself by showing how you and your audience are alike. Do you share the same problems? Do you hold the same values? Do you have the same goals? Are you trying to solve the same problems? Your audience may realize that, in many ways, they are somehow like you. Research indicates that if that is what they think, your credibility may become higher with them.

Other factors of credibility relate to whether you are perceived as trustworthy in general or as a person of goodwill in this particular situation. Audiences may well trust speakers more who have had a continuing interest in the topic at hand. How long have you been concerned about the topic or problem? What have you done about it? In addition, they may trust more people who have had contact with them in the past. Have you been shown to be trustworthy on earlier occasions? When? How? What may be even more important is the factor of goodwill. Is this topic or problem important for the audience? What do they gain from the speech, the topic, or the solution? Are you interested in them and their needs—or you and your needs? Show them that you are speaking to somehow do them a good turn. Appeal to their interests, their values, and their needs. If you can do this, you may begin to be perceived as a person of goodwill.

Finally, your problem of low credibility with this audience may be related to their perceptions of your competence. In the speaking situation, you may need to explain your background and experience. You may need to describe the research that has gone into your speech or presentation. You may want to mention other sources or authorities who agree with your ideas. If you are using statistics or figures of some sort, you probably should explain the sources of this material. You should examine your topic and ask yourself, What makes me qualified to speak about this? Then analyze your audience and ask, What probably is the perception that these people have of me? Then ask yourself, How can I explain to these people why I am qualified to speak on the topic? When you have found answers to those three questions, you are better able to improve their perception of your competence.

A few additional points can be made about credibility-enhancing strategies generally. First, some of these credibility-enhancing strategies can be performed by other people. You may wish to be introduced to your audience by someone the audience already feels is competent. We call that technique *sponsorship*. In essence, you are presented or sponsored by a person of higher credibility. Or, you may want your audience to have *advance information* about you and the speaking task. Such information may include a short biography or a statement about what you have been doing about the problem or topic recently. Either of these approaches may improve your credibility without your having to say, Yes, I am trustworthy, competent, and so forth.

A second point about credibility-improving strategies is that they may be used badly enough to actually hurt your credibility. A person who speaks too much of his or her qualifications may seem to be boasting. The person who continually talks about how trustworthy he or she is may become suspect. For these reasons, I used the word *subtle* earlier. Your task is to improve your credibility without that becoming the major point of your message. Credibility building must be done with care.

Finally, you should know that improving credibility means changing the perceptions of *one* audience. Different audiences will be composed of different people—and their perceptions of you may differ. You must know your audience and try to build your credibility in its mind. In one situation, you may work toward improving the perception of trust. In another, your task may be to be more dynamic. In a third situation, you may need to emphasize your similarity and goodwill. No two situations will be exactly alike. Your credibility-improvement strategies must be tailored to the audience before you.

CONTROLLING ANXIETY

Frequently, *anxiety* is treated as a part of delivery problems, but I have decided to discuss this conflict in a special section: Everyone seems to feel anxiety, discomfort, or stage fright to some degree. The one-to-many communication situation may make you feel you are just that: one against the many. If you feel extremely high levels of anxiety, you may wish to find special help.[2] For most people, however, understanding performance anxiety can be a helpful step toward mediating this intrapersonal conflict which occurs in the one-to-many setting.

There are at least three levels of anxiety.[3] At the first level, you may experience an increased heartbeat, heavier breathing, and more perspiration. Those factors may or may not be noticeable to you. The human body automatically responds to challenging situations. Football players, actors and actresses, and speakers all have the need to get ready for their particular challenges. This level of anxiety probably should not concern you very much. In fact, you probably need this body readiness to perform your best.

A second level of anxiety occurs when you experience outward signs of tension. You may feel the perspiration. You may actually feel your heart beat more rapidly. You may experience a throbbing, twitching, or trembling in some part of your body. When I performed in college as a competitive orator, I regularly experienced a left leg that refused to remain stationary: it shook in a bothersome manner and was almost impossible to control. Whatever your personal outward signs might be, you probably will have one or several. The good thing about many of these outward signs is that they are invisible to the audience before you. You may be the only one who perceives them—as far as I know, no judge of oratory ever noticed my left leg. These outward signs may be bothersome, but they do not necessarily affect your speaking.

Only at the third level of anxiety should you be extremely concerned. At the third level, the audience is aware of the outward signs of your anxiety. The person who appears extremely nervous and anxious may be perceived as less-than-dynamic or less-than-competent. Credibility, then, is related to the problems of this third level. Anxiety may be no real problem (although you think it is) until your audience becomes aware of it.

The point of this discussion of levels of anxiety is to explain that your best strategy for anxiety is to *control* it, not end it.[4] Professional performers in sports and the theatre have traditionally testified that without anxiety, they could not do their best. The feeling is that you need to have your body in a state of readiness. You probably cannot end forever your anxiety—and maybe you should not want to even if you could. What you should do is to control the anxiety so that it works for you instead of against you. That sounds like an abstract and difficult task, but there are several specific strategies that may help you.

The most important strategy is to *be prepared* for the speaking situation. Plan the message as far ahead of time as possible. Do any necessary research. Analyze your audience and the situation as well as possible. Practice speaking as much as possible. Practice presenting the message as much as possible. Lack of adequate preparation can mean you have every right to be anxious and afraid. Make sure that you are prepared for the task at hand. Second, *consider the audience to be people.* Some speakers are given the advice, Look just above the heads of the audience—look at the back of the room. That seems to be bad advice for a number of reasons. Among other things, your audience will be able to tell what you are doing—and people usually want eye contact. In addition, there are benefits to be gained by realizing that there are *people* in front of you. They may be numerous, but they are still humans with the same general qualities you possess. When you realize that they are simply people who probably are sympathetic to you and the situation, you may become less anxious. Third, *concentrate upon your ideas* instead of upon how anxious you are. Pay attention to what you have to say and thoughts you have about the topic. After all, most speaking situations do not occur because people want to look at you and watch you squirm. Most situations arise because people want or need to hear what you have to say. Fourth and finally, *concentrate on communicating your message.* What are the meanings you want to re-create? What are the problems you must face in communicating them? How is your audience responding? I have found that my own students seem to relax and do a better job in the speaking situation as soon as they get a response from their audiences. When you find that your audience is alive, thinking, and interested in what you have to say, communication will seem easier—and more worthwhile. Concentrate upon communicating and transacting with that audience of other communicators.

The points just discussed are not magical ingredients for the solution to your anxiety. Some levels of anxiety are so high that therapy or training may be necessary. Still, for most people, anxiety may be controlled by doing the things suggested. You probably will find comfort in the fact that most people become anxious or nervous in the speaking situation. You should find even more comfort in the idea that your level of anxiety can be controlled. Remember to be prepared and to concentrate upon the communication of your ideas to those kindred souls out there.

ADAPTING DELIVERY

Speech delivery is a traditional concern among speakers. How do you deliver a speech or presentation so that it is effective? Delivery, more than anything else, is simply the nonverbal part of your message.[5] The question should be put, How do you control your nonverbal cues to make them consistent with your verbal message? The question is not easily answered. Delivering a speech is very different from delivering a package. There are few different ways to deliver a package to its destination. There are many ways of delivering a speech. You do not need rules for the delivery of the all-purpose speech. Instead, you need some understanding about how to *adapt* your nonverbal cues to your particular speaking problem. To more effectively use delivery skills as strategies for mediation, your nonverbal activity should be (1) credibility-enhancing, (2) communicative, and (3) appropriate.

Credibility-enhancing delivery

Anxiety, as we saw, is one factor of delivery which can hurt credibility. All the factors of delivery together, though, can aid credibility. In one sense, credibility is the personal force of a communicator. If this personal force were not important, *speaking* would make no sense at all. The speaker could just distribute copies of the speech and sit down. Yet there are many times when there is more to the message than words that can be put on paper. Part of the message—a large part of it—is the personal force of the speaker. Most ancient and modern communication scholars almost apologize for discussing delivery skills. After all, it would be better (they say) if audiences paid attention only to the verbal message; but audiences do pay attention to the delivery of a speaker. I suspect that one of the reasons they do is because of the judgments about credibility that are based upon delivery. Let me illustrate.

Power, dynamism, and competence, for example, are credibility factors we have discussed. Part of the image of *power* that an audience perceives in a speaker may arise directly from delivery. Does the powerful person speak uncertainly—or with force? Does the powerful person seem anxious or fearful—or confident? In the same way, much of the perception of *dynamism* probably is related to delivery. The dynamic person does not speak slowly and haltingly. The dynamic person speaks with enthusiasm and force. The dynamic person gestures freely and naturally, and feels confident enough to move the rest of his or her body effectively. In similar ways, delivery may help create the impression of *competence*. There is a difference between knowing information and sounding as if you know the information. The person who hesitates, pauses, and stumbles over words may not be perceived as knowledgeable about the topic. The competent speaker is both the person who knows something—and acts as if he or she knows something.

Other credibility factors include *trustworthiness and goodwill*. Some of the perception of these factors is related to sincerity and openness. From our earlier study of nonverbal communication, you know the importance of eye contact. People tend not to trust the person who cannot establish eye contact and maintain it. The person who pledges his or her concern for us and, at the same time, tells us nonverbally that he or she is uninterested in us creates a credibility problem. When the verbal and nonverbal cues communicate different things, the nonverbal is more likely to be believed. The result may be either that we totally distrust the person, or simply see him or her as a person of ill will. In either case, credibility suffers—in large part because of delivery problems.

Delivery, then, is not something that simply entertains the audience. Delivery skills are not important as a way of demonstrating how dramatic and oratorical you can be. Instead, delivery is a major way of establishing and maintaining perceptions of credibility. Part of the message of the speaker is the verbal message. At least as large a part of the message is the set of nonverbal cues perceived by the audience. The audience's favorable perception of these

General strategies of speaking

cues can help the overall acceptance of the message. An unfavorable perception may destroy credibility or at least not help it. The result may be lower levels of acceptance of your message.

One of the strategies of delivery is to use your knowledge of nonverbal communication. Review in Chapter 6 the information about the meanings that are often attached to nonverbal cues. Plan your delivery so that it will enhance your credibility.

Communicative delivery

The discussion of delivery and credibility is not meant to create *rules* of delivery. It is not so important that you plan when to raise an eyebrow or to gesture with your left hand. You should try to create a credibility-enhancing delivery, but perhaps the best way of doing that is to concentrate on communicating with your audience. Professors Bryant and Wallace have suggested ideas concerning a *psychology of delivery* that may be helpful to you.[6] Some of their ideas are: that delivery should not be a major focus for the audience; that the speaker should concentrate upon the meanings he or she wishes to communicate; and that the speaker should experience a *sense of communication* with the audience.

First, *the audience should not focus upon the delivery.* The focus of the audience should always be upon the ideas and information of the speaker. In short, you should not allow delivery to become a distraction. Delivery can become distracting if it is sloppily done. A monotonous voice, a nervous habit of scratching, too many *ahs* and *you knows*, and a frightened and frozen posture can all become distractions. The audience may be lulled to inattention by the monotone voice—or the voice that stays at the same speed or volume level. The audience may begin to absentmindedly count the scratches or the filled pauses. The audience may become as uncomfortable and anxious as the obviously frozen person before it. Poor delivery, then, can become a distraction from the message. Eloquent delivery may be just as bad. There was a time when the quality of a speaker was judged by the fluid gestures, the striking facial expression, and the dramatic rhythm and pause of the voice. There was a time when speakers learned the correct gestures by going into a large box and shoving their hands through different holes to learn the gesture-for-the-emotion. These times have passed. The speaker who finished a speech and is told how beautiful his or her voice is or how well he or she moves on the platform probably is a failure. The delivery that is too beautiful may distract the audience from the message. Ideas may be lost by the audience as they marvel at the voice, the body, or the eyebrow.

Good delivery is a natural expression of the body. It is not mechanical and it is not faked eloquence and grace. The audience should be affected by the message—and only indirectly by the nonverbal part of the message.

Second, according to Bryant and Wallace, *the speaker should concentrate upon ideas.* Try talking to a friend about the most exciting thing in your life—without gesturing, changing body position, or changing your voice and facial expression. Try discussing a serious and important idea with a friend—with dramatic gestures and exaggerated facial expression. I predict that you cannot do the first of those and that the second will make you feel foolish. When you talk to a friend, I suspect you will use nonverbal cues in a way that is consistent with your ideas and information. The task is easy; in fact, it is probably no task at all. The situation changes when you are in the one-to-many situation. Suddenly, you have all sorts of other things to think about: a grade or a promotion in the organization, your notes, the lectern or desk before you, and that sea of faces out there. With those things on your mind, the naturalness of delivery skills may become lost. You have to concentrate upon what you will do and how you will do it. The key to the mediation of this particular problem is for you to regain what you had in the conversation with the friend. Concentrate on your ideas, your feelings about them, and your information. Concentrating upon these may bring back some of the naturalness that has fled. You may find that, as you get interested in your ideas, your body takes over for itself. You may find that you will begin matching delivery with ideas in a surprisingly natural way. The speaker who stumbles through a speech may be the speaker with too many things on his or her mind. Once the speaker's ideas come alive to *him or her*, they may come alive to the audience too.

Third, *the speaker should experience a sense that the audience is made up of people who serve as communicators.* The audience is not something you are pitted against. It is not something that must be given something—in this case, a speech. Instead, the audience should be perceived as a partner in the communication process. The speaker should experience a *lively sense of communication* with the audience. These are people who are supposed to re-create your meanings. They can do this only if you let them. Do not speak *at* them. Do not act as if you are throwing out the speech, as you would a newspaper on their front porch. See them as people who are important to you. See them as people who must participate with you in the communication process. Speak to them, try to get them to understand, and watch for their feedback. If you begin to concentrate upon communicating to that group of people, you may find that your delivery becomes what it is when you talk with a friend: a way of communicating important ideas.

Appropriate delivery

Your delivery of the speech must be communicative and as *natural* as possible. Yet, *what is natural in one situation may not be natural in another.* Naturalness must be balanced by your concern for making your delivery *appropriate* to the situation. Rhetorical theorist and critic Kenneth Burke, has identified at least five parts of a *situation*. A situation is composed of:

an act: the thing that is done
an agent: the person who does the thing
a scene: the environment or surroundings of the act, including the audience
a purpose: the goal or intention of the agent
an agency: the means or instrument used by the agent to complete the act and achieve the purpose[7]

Good delivery means that the nonverbal parts of the message are *appropriate* to all these five factors.[8] Let us examine each.

First, your delivery should be adapted to the *act* or the thing you are doing. If you are speaking to protest something, your delivery perhaps should be more forceful than usual. If your speech is businesslike, you may have to soft-pedal some of your natural enthusiasm. If the speech is solemn and ceremonial, your delivery should reflect those qualities. There is really no such thing as the perfect speech delivery. Speech delivery is either more or less appropriate. One of the strategies of making delivery more appropriate is to match it with the kind of speech *act* you are performing.

Another strategy of making delivery more appropriate is to make sure your nonverbal behavior is appropriate to you as a speaker—as an *agent*. You are not exactly like anyone else. In normal conversation you do not act or sound exactly like anyone else. In the one-to-many situation, you will not gain much by trying to act and sound like your notion of the ideal speaker. You are not Patrick Henry or William Jennings Bryan. You are you. You can adapt to certain situations, or course, but you probably should not try to be someone you are not. If you are shy normally, you may have to liven up your voice and movement, but an exaggerated change in what you are comfortable doing may seem false and a put-on to an audience. Most speaking situations do not require you to be an actor or an orator. Most situations simply require you to communicate with your audience.

Third, make sure you adapt your delivery to the *scene*. Know what your speaking situation will look like. A large room may mean that you will have to speak more loudly or that your gestures and facial expressions will have to be somewhat exaggerated. A smaller room may mean you should lower your volume—and use completely conversational nonverbal symbols. A microphone may mean you will have to speak more slowly and more clearly. The point is simple: Make sure that the audience in your situation—whatever it is—can see, hear, and understand all the parts of your nonverbal message. That point is almost too simple. It may seem so obvious that you wonder why I make the effort to discuss it. The reason is that adapting to the scene may be much more difficult than you imagine. Even experienced speakers generally try to see the setting before their speech. They know from experience that knowing about adaptation and doing it are two different things.

There is another aspect of scene besides the physical surroundings. Part of what makes up the scene is psychological, and has to do with who the audience members are. Different audiences can turn the same setting into two different communication situations. Are the members serious and concerned? Fun-loving and carefree? Intellectual and sophisticated? Down-to-earth and good-natured? Angry and hostile? These various qualities of the audience will have something to do with how it evaluates your delivery, your credibility, and you. A wild and fun-loving audience may not appreciate a serious and dry delivery. A serious and concerned audience may not appreciate a casual and relaxed delivery style. Just as you should explore the physical setting for the speech beforehand, you should explore the nature of your audience. Then, you can use your knowledge of nonverbal cues as a way of adapting to your specific audience.

Appropriateness, however, is not only a matter of act, agent, and scene. In addition, your delivery should be appropriate to your *purpose*. Is your goal to entertain the audience, or to stimulate thought about something? Is the goal to persuade or to share some kind of information? After the speech, do you want the audience to be excited, calm and thoughtful, or in tears? These are not all the various goals you might have, but they do suggest the variety of purposes you may have. You must match the style of the delivery to the purpose. You hardly can expect to excite your audience if your delivery is boring and uninteresting. You cannot expect the audience to be thoughtful and concerned if your delivery has been relaxed and casual. Delivery skills can be one of your best tools for achieving your purpose—but only if the delivery is appropriate to the purpose.

Finally, your delivery should be appropriate to the *agency* or means of achieving the speech act. For our purposes now, the agency can be thought of as the speech itself. If your speech is technical and scientific, it will not be helped by a rapid and casual delivery. If your speech content is humorous and lighthearted, your delivery should be the same. In all these situations, the concern is for verbal and nonverbal consistency. Your language in the speech should be consistent with your silent, but visible, language. Make sure that your delivery is appropriate for the speech itself.

These five factors that we have discussed are not to be taken separately. Your delivery in any situation should be appropriate: appropriate to the act, to you as agent, to the scene, to the purpose, and to the speech as agency. No one can tell you exactly how to deliver a speech. There are no real rules. Yet, you can use your knowledge of nonverbal symbols to improve your delivery. In this section, we have discussed three major strategies of improving and controlling your delivery. First, concentrate on using delivery to improve and maintain credibility. Second, use delivery skills to actively communicate with the audience. Finally, adapt that communicative and credibility-building delivery. Make it appropriate to all the parts of the speaking situation. You will still need to practice your delivery skills. You will still need the guidance of a coach or classroom instructor. You will still need feedback from instructors and classmates. To better use all that help, you should use the strategies just discussed for improving delivery.

General strategies of speaking 261

SUPPORTING WITH VISUAL AIDS

If your conflict involves how to get others to know or to accept what you already know or accept, a *visual* demonstration may help you. Visual aids should be used in addition to other aids such as argumentation and delivery (which we have discussed) and language (which is the last topic in this chapter). The use of visual aids is often misunderstood by students, whose first reaction may be to *find* a visual aid rather than concentrate on *integrating* it with the total meaning of the speech. Speeches are essentially ideas that have been translated into verbal and nonverbal symbols. Visual aids are simply one of many sorts of ways of supporting, arguing, or developing ideas. *Visual aids should never become the major focus of the speech.*

There are several ways in which visual aids can become the accidental focus of the speech. For instance, you may choose your visual aid and then build the rest of the speech around it. The result may be that you yourself have little to say: It's all in the visual. A second sort of problem is illustrated by the student who overuses the visual aid. As he or she talks about it, the student looks at it and handles it constantly. He or she actually sets up communication with the visual—and forgets the audience. Another kind of problem involves the speaker whose visual aid is so interesting or striking that the audience's attention cannot be drawn away. An example of this problem is the snake lover who brings his or her boa constrictor to class. While the boa may be useful as a visual aid, frightened audience members may be able to think of little else but their own safety. A final sort of problem exists when the visuals are either so fantastically good and elaborate or so poorly done that they distract from the message. Just as extremes of delivery may be distracting, extremely elaborate or sloppy visual aids may become a problem for the speaker. In all the situations discussed here the problem is the same: somehow the visuals have acquired a life of their own—and they dominate the speech. Your speech is not supposed to explain your visual aids. Your visual aids are supposed to explain your speech.

The one apparent exception to this principle has to do with *demonstration* speeches. In class or in the real world, you may be called upon to present a speech demonstrating how something-or-other works or is made. In situations such as that, your response may be, Clearly, the visual aid in this case should be the focus. I disagree. Even in the demonstration speech, the thing or process being demonstrated is not the focus. How it works or how it is made is the focus. The thing or process should still be used to support what you *say* in the speech. If your audience remembers only what the object or process looks like, your speech has failed. The focus should always be upon the ideas you wish to communicate.

The discussion about visual aids so far has been negative. We have discussed what *not* to do, and the problems of allowing your visual aids to become the focus of the speech. Let us now turn to some more positive ideas. That discussion will involve answering three questions: What sorts of visuals can be used? When should visuals be used? How should visuals be used?

What sorts of visuals can be used?

Two of the kinds of evidence we discussed earlier were *objects* and *artifacts*. These terms can be used to describe visual aids. Actual objects, first, can be used as visual aids. If your speech concerns the advantages of one kind of detergent over another, you may wish to bring the actual objects. If the speech concerns the stringing of a tennis racket, you may wish to bring the necessary material. If your speech concerns gear ratios of a ten-speed bicycle, you may want to bring the actual bicycle.

In most situations, your speech will not concern something as simple and straightforward as the examples above. Usually, your task as a speaker will be more complicated. Because of that, most of the time you will find artifacts to be more useful. As visual aids, artifacts can be divided into several classes:[9]

Models: miniatures or mock-ups of an actual object. These may include scale models of wood, plastic, metal, or paper constructions, and so forth. (See Fig. 18.1.)

Pictures: actual photographs or drawings of an object, event, or person. These may be professionally taken photographs or snapshots; professionally drawn pictures, or simple line drawings. (See Fig. 18.2.)

Diagrams: simplified representations of processes or situations. These may be either elaborate or simple, and include the kinds of things used to introduce each part of this text. (See Fig. 18.3.)

Graphs and charts: visual illustrations or comparisons. These include bar graphs, line graphs, and pie charts. (See Figs. 18.4, 18.5, 18.6.)

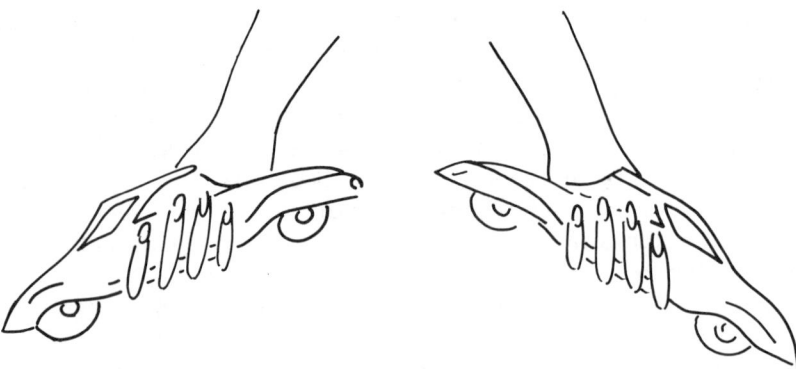

Fig. 18.1

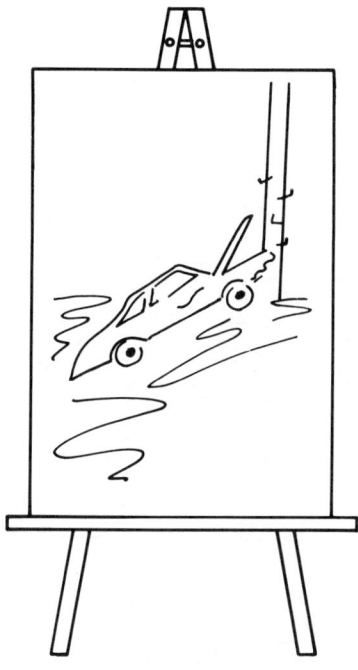

Fig. 18.2

Any of these artifacts can *take the place of* the actual object, event, process, or person. Each of these types should be familiar to you as you set about discovering the best support for what you have to say. In any particular situation, one or another of these types of visual aids may be most helpful to you.

Now that you know something about the types of visual aids that can be used, we may turn to the second question, When should visual aids be used?

When should visual aids be used?

Certain types of visuals should be used, for example, when the topic of the speech involves things which are *too large or too small* for the speaker to actually present. In a medical report, even microscopic bacteria may be presented in a blown-up photograph or a diagram. In a report on dam safety, photographs, drawings, or diagrams may be the best way to support the speaker's ideas and information.

Visuals are also useful when the topic involves something that is *illegal or inappropriate* in the speaking situation. A model of a handgun is preferable to the actual gun, which in university settings may be illegal. Diagrams or pictures of marijuana or opium-producing plants would make better (legal) visuals than the actual objects.

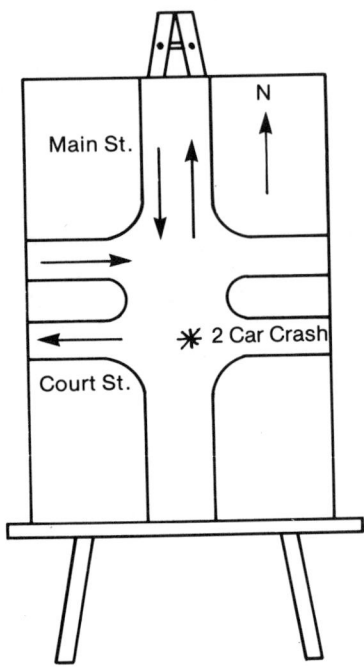

Fig. 18.3

Visual aids are also useful when *only the actual object will make the point*. Describing rock polishing may be difficult without rocks and the polisher. Demonstrating the merits of different brands of hand-held calculators may be difficult without the calculators themselves.

Visual aids also may be useful when the ideas expressed by the speaker are *too complex* to be expressed orally. In a financial report, the comparisons of inventories, costs, taxes, incomes, and profits would be highly confusing if done orally. Such reports, and other complicated topics, may require visuals such as diagrams and graphs.

Finally, visuals may be used when the materials to be covered in your speech are *too massive or too numerous*. Crime statistics, figures on energy users, and voting patterns are among the things that may need visual aids. While the specific point may not be complex, the figures may be large. One of the ways of allowing an audience to understand the ideas without all the specific figures is to diagram trends, comparisons, and relationships. There are, then, many occasions when visual aids are appropriate to support verbal messages.

There are also times when visual aids should *not* be used. You should not use a visual aid for the sake of using one. If the visual is not relevant and appropriate, your audience may be distracted trying to understand what you (and

General strategies of speaking

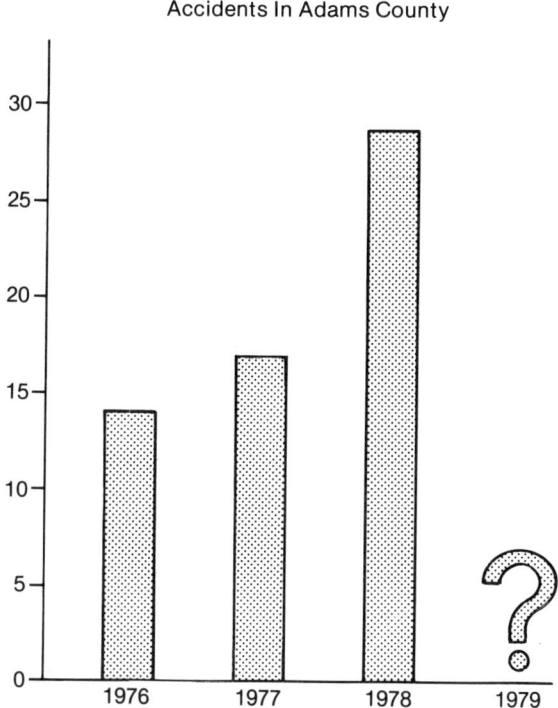

it) are doing. You should not use a visual aid simply to list the three major points you wish to cover. If there are only three main points, your audience can probably understand them without a visual aid. Similarly, a speech on the *history* of the bicycle does not benefit from the presentation of a modern bicycle: most people have already seen at least one. The point is that you should develop the ideas in your speech. Then and only then can you decide what visual aids you truly need for the speech. Visual aids are not magic, and having one does not necessarily help your speech. Make sure that your visual aids are constructive ways of supporting your ideas.

How should visual aids be used?

Our discussion of how to use visual aids may seem to be pointing out the obvious. Talking about using visual aids is easy. Using visual aids well is not. Take these guidelines for what they are: commonsense suggestions that you should put into practice.

First, make visual aids *large and readable.* Printing or figures that seem large and strange looking in a small room may be too small to be seen from where your audience will sit. Avoid using color combinations such as yellow

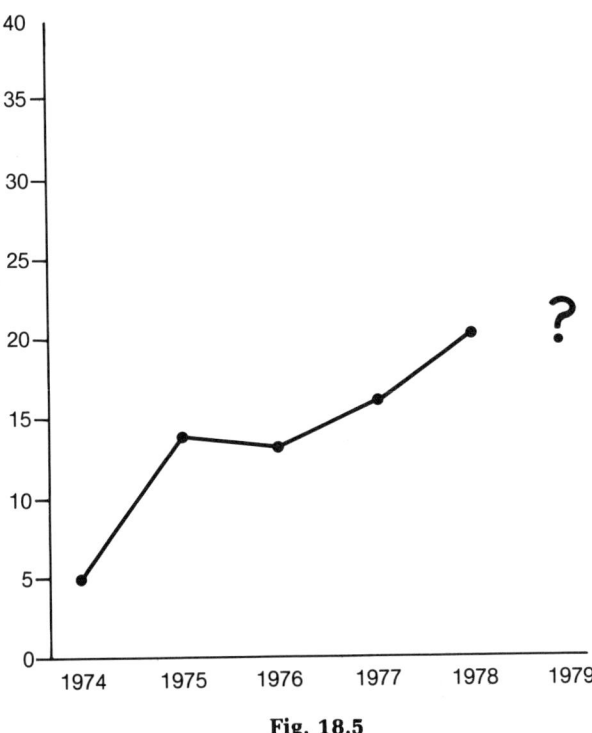

Accidents In Adams County

Fig. 18.5

print on white paper. Such combinations are visible in a small room, but they may not be visible to the audience. The best print is large, dark letters on very light or white paper or poster board. One of the worst mistakes you can make as a speaker is to have to say, "Well, if you could see the figures, what they say is . . . ." Make sure the figures, lines, and printing are all large and readable.

Second, make the visual aid *clear*. Label any parts of the visual that your audience should see. Print, rather than write cursively. Make sure that the relationships or comparisons or details of the visual aid are clearly explained. In general, your visual aid has failed if you have to say, "Well, this part over here is supposed to represent . . . ." Visuals should be clear.

Third, visuals should be *simple*. There is normally no limit to the number of visuals you can create and use. If the idea is a complicated one, you may wish to separate it into several points—each described in a different visual. You may need to use a combination of several types of aids. What you should not need to say to an audience is something like, "Now, the blue lines represent profits, the red is income, the black lines are the increase in inventories. Over in this other corner, the first diagram is . . . ." The visual should be immediately clear to your audience—or clear after a simple explanation. You can help yourself by keeping the visuals simple.

Accidents in Adams County by Major Cause

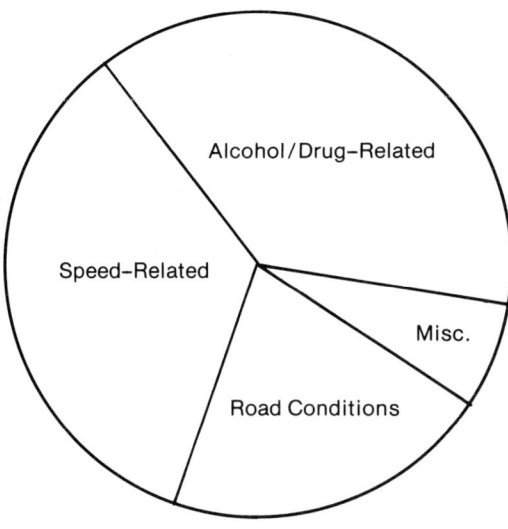

Figures: 1974–1978

Fig. 18.6

Fourth, use visuals to support *one idea at a time*. Do not show visuals until you plan to use them. When visuals are visible to an audience, its members will look at all there is to see. If you will not be getting to a point for some time, do not lead your audience astray by allowing an irrelevant (for now) visual to distract it. Similarly, once a visual is used, you should remove it and move on to the next idea or visual. If you fail to do this, the audience may attend to the "old" visual, waiting for you to return to it. Use your visuals to support only the idea you are concerned with at the time.

Fifth, *avoid distracting use* of the visual aids. You should never play with or fondle the visual aid. Use it, point to it when you need to, but do not absent-mindedly tap it or hold it. Do not be tempted to pass out material prior to the speech or during the speech. Whenever audience members have something to look at other than you, there is the danger that they will read it or study it at the wrong time. If the audience has the material to look at, they may get ahead of you, fall behind you, or look in the wrong place. In any of those situations, the result is the same. Your visual aid has become a distraction. Your visual is no longer supporting what you have to say. It is simply presenting a different message at the wrong time. Avoid allowing the visual aid to become this kind of distraction.

Sixth, *use the visual aid as you speak* to the audience. You should know the visual aid well enough to refer to it without losing contact with the audience.

You should beware of becoming so engrossed in the visual that you ignore your audience. Again, the idea is to have you use visual aids for support for what you are saying. Use them as you maintain good eye contact and fluent speaking.

Finally, and most importantly, *practice* using your visual aids. You can practice all of the earlier suggestions: Survey the room where you are to speak to find out how large and readable your aids should be. Study your visuals as you practice the speech. Are they clear and simple when seen from the back of the room? Do they support your ideas as you get to them? Are you familiar enough with them so that you can speak to your audience as you indicate the visuals? All these suggestions concern the things we have discussed.

There is still one other area in which you can practice. Practice how you will *handle* the visuals. Is there an easel? If so, how and when will you use it? If not, can you make one—or should you make your visuals "self-standing" with cardboard or wood? Some sort of easel is better than none at all. The easel will allow you to speak to the audience and point to the visuals simultaneously. Holding the visuals may prevent you from pointing to important aspects of them. Charts or graphs on a blackboard may be difficult to use without destroying eye contact. You will need to see your room ahead of time and discover the best way to handle your visuals. Practice your entire speech, so that you know how you will move easily and without distraction from one visual to another. Handling the visual aids well is crucial. Your hours of work preparing visuals will be for nothing if you have not made certain that they will be seen easily and effectively.

Guidelines for the use of visuals sound simplistic and obvious, and for that reason speechmakers often fail to take them into consideration—with disastrous results. Just as your words can be undermined by conflicting nonverbal cues and unskillful delivery, your visuals can have negative effects if not used well.

ADAPTING LANGUAGE

The language that you choose to use in the speaking situation is our final topic in this chapter. Though it is treated last, you should not assume that it is unimportant. Choosing a style of language is one of the most important parts of the speaking task. Obviously, without language, there can be no speech; yet *the language of your speech is not the speech itself.* Your speech is a communicative transaction—you just need language to engage in that transaction. The language you use, as we saw earlier, is one of the major ways of *symbolizing* what you *mean.* Language is important, not because it *is* your speech, but because it allows your meaning to be communicated.

Our discussion of nonverbal cues (delivery) did not reveal hard-and-fast rules for effective use. The same will be true about verbal cues (language). There are no always-effective rules for choosing the language that you will use in your speech, but you need to keep two important factors in mind. First, language in general should be nondistracting; and second, language should be appropriate.

Language should be nondistracting

Ideas and meanings are the most important parts of communication. Language (verbal symbols) is simply a means of helping the re-creation of similar meanings in the minds of other people. In general, language should not call attention to itself. It should not become the audience's center of attention. If the audience begins to focus upon the language you use, some of your meanings may be lost. *Nonstandard* language, for example, can distract an audience so much that some cannot pay attention to ideas and meanings. Nonstandard language would include slang and throwaway lines: "Like, you know, all you ... guys have had that problem dropped at your door, and well, you know what I mean, that can be a bummer." Highly pompous language can also be a problem. Consider this: "General Eisenhower, with judicious and politic endeavor, nurtured the paradoxical image of hero of the martial arts and archetypical pacifist." Highly technical language can also be seen as distracting jargon: "One of the concerns in deductive logic, of course, is that in the categorical syllogism, the major term is the predicate term of the conclusion and the minor term is the subject term of the conclusion. Obviously, the middle term must appear in both premises but not in the conclusion." Depending upon who you are and what you know, one, two, or all of these three examples may be the use of unfamiliar language. If that is the case—and if you are one of the audience members—the language does not help communicate. The language, in fact, becomes a distraction. You might become puzzled, offended, or angry. Whatever your reaction, it will create a distraction from the meaning of the speaker.

In general, the sorts of language problems I have discussed *are* problems, but there are exceptions to this statement. Senator Adlai Stevenson, who twice ran for President against Dwight Eisenhower, was known as an intellectual who used a sophisticated vocabulary. While this may have contributed to his defeats, stories are told about how his language won him votes. Some voters did not understand what he was saying, but they loved the language that he used. For some people, the unfamiliar language was an asset. As another example, former Vice-President Spiro Agnew had never been considered an overly intellectual person. Around 1970, however, he began making speeches which contained highly intellectual and unfamiliar language. Some of his opponents were an "effete corps of intellectual snobs;" others were "nattering nabobs of negativism." He became one of the most sought-after speakers of his time before he was forced to resign his office. A third example concerns speakers who must present technical or academic papers to professional or academic groups. In those situations, what you and I might call "jargon" is simply an acceptable and useful means of communication among people who use the terms every day. Finally, even slang may have its place in communicative situations. Certain audiences demand a relaxed, relevant (to them), and down-to-earth language style. In these sorts of situations, "standard American usage" may be a distraction.

The above situations are not common. They are exceptions to the general advice that slang, jargon, and overly-eloquent language will be a distraction for your audience. In most speaking situations, you will want your language to be a bit more formal and sophisticated than everyday conversation, and a bit less formal than the great works of literature. Good style, in general, is *elevated conversation*.[10] Your effort to create a clear and familiar language style is one of the most important strategies you can use for adapting language.

Language should be appropriate

You will find exceptions to the general principle just discussed. You will find that speaking situations demand different language styles. Perhaps the most important strategy of language use is to make sure that your language is *appropriate*. To describe appropriate language in the speech as *agency*, we can use Burke's ideas of *act, agent, scene,* and *purpose*.[11]

First, the speech language should be appropriate to the *act* you are attempting. An act of tribute to a dead hero demands elevated language—and so do graduation ceremonies, speeches of dedication, and so forth. An act of protest over something probably demands strong and forceful language. A speech of friendship and love should prompt a friendly conversational style.

Second, language should be appropriate to you as *agent*. Even though most situations require the elevated conversational style, you are who you are. If you try to use language that is strange and unfamiliar to you, you may fail. You may be uncomfortable with the language—and your discomfort may cause credibility problems. Try to make your language as clear and effective as possible, but do not attempt to sound like (you think) Patrick Henry sounded.

Third, your language should be appropriate to the *scene*. A slang-studded speech in an auditorium may sound silly because of the formality of the setting. High-flown phrases and elevated language may sound strange in a meeting of the company's task force. The audience, as well as the physical setting, is important. What is the audience like? How intelligent do you predict it will be? How educated is it generally? How familiar is it with the topic? How well do you predict it will listen? What are its interests and biases? What sort of language is it accustomed to hearing? What sort of language is it expecting? All these questions should be considered when you are selecting an appropriate language style, and all these questions relate to whether the language is appropriate to the scene.

Fourth and finally, your language should be appropriate to your *purpose*. If your goal is to inspire, your language perhaps should be exciting and vivid. If your goal is to stimulate thought about something, the best style may be one that is serious and fairly sophisticated. If your task is to entertain someone or improve public relations, you may wish to avoid technical or highly eloquent language. If your goal is to persuade, your language may need to be challenging, strong, and action oriented. Know what your specific purpose is, and then match your language to the goal.

In general—that phrase again—your language will be acceptable if it sounds like elevated conversation. Specifically, however, your language will be acceptable and effective if it is appropriate to the act, you as agent, the scene, and your purpose. Adapting language as a strategy of mediation means that your verbal cues are nondistracting and appropriate to the rest of your communication effort.

CHAPTER SUMMARY

In this chapter we have discussed some of the basic strategies of speaking to the organization or for the organization: these skills and strategies will be important to you.

We began by looking at ways to improve credibility as a strategy of mediation. Credibility problems, as we saw earlier, relate to a number of factors of credibility. We discussed how credibility may be improved in each of those areas. Next, we looked at the problem of controlling anxiety. Different levels of anxiety were discussed, and certain strategies of controlling anxiety were mentioned. Our attention turned to delivery skills—the nonverbal aspect of the speaking situation. Here, the relationship between delivery and credibility was examined. In addition to being concerned about credibility, delivery should be communicative and appropriate. We explored strategies of supporting speeches by discussing types of visuals, when they should be used, and how they best can be used. Finally, we discussed language. Verbal cues are a means of speaking; they are not the speech itself. Language should be nondistracting. In general, it should be elevated conversation; still, language must be appropriate to the act, to the agent, to the scene, and to the speaker's purpose.

The strategies discussed are like all the strategies examined in the text. They are not easily followed rules. Communication is complex and difficult and rules are not possible, but the strategies in this chapter can be of great help to you in mediating the important problems of speaking either to or for the organization. In Chapter 20, we shall explore specific strategies for public speaking—speaking *for* the organization. In the next chapter, however, we shall turn attention to strategies for presentational speaking—speaking *to* the organization.

NOTES

[1] Some of the ideas and concepts used here are based upon the research summary, Kenneth Andersen and T. Clevenger, Jr., "A Summary of Experimental Research in Ethos,"

Speech Monographs 30 (1963), 59–78. We shall relate these ideas specifically to problems in presentational and public speaking later.

[2] Frequently, departments of speech, communication, or psychology will provide services to help students with *extreme* performance anxiety. Your instructor will know or can find out if such a service is available to you.

[3] For an excellent summary of the research, see Theodore Clevenger, Jr., "A Synthesis of Experimental Research in Stage Fright," *Quarterly Journal of Speech*, 45 (Apr. 1959), 134–45.

[4] Control is important simply because of the nature of anxiety; in extreme cases, it is the anxiety which controls the speaker.

[5] See Richard E. Crable, "A Situational Approach to Purposeful Nonverbal Communication," *Exploration in Speech Communication*, ed. John J. Makay (Columbus, Oh.: Charles E. Merrill, 1973), pp. 299–314.

[6] Donald C. Bryant and Karl Wallace, *Fundamentals of Public Speaking*, 4th ed. (New York: Appleton-Century-Crofts, 1969), chap. 13.

[7] For a more complete discussion, see Richard E. Crable and John Makay, "Kenneth Burke's Concept of Motive in Rhetorical Theory." *Today's Speech*, 29 (Winter 1972), 11–18.

[8] Crable, "Situational Approach."

[9] A similar division of visual aids is found in Ray E. Nadeau, *A Modern Rhetoric of Speech-Communication*, 2nd ed. (Reading, Ma.: Addison-Wesley, 1969), pp. 145–57.

[10] See the discussion in Donald C. Bryant and Karl Wallace, *Oral Communication: A Short Course in Speaking*, 4th ed. (Englewood Cliffs, N.J.: Prentice-Hall, 1976), chap. 9.

[11] See Crable and Makay, "Kenneth Burke's Concept of Motive."

19
STRATEGIES OF PRESENTATIONAL SPEAKING

Strategies for speaking *to* the organization are based upon assumptions about the nature of presentational speaking. As we discussed in Chapter 16, presentations include your responsibility for (1) researching a particular organizational problem; (2) developing a solution in the form of a proposal for the organization to adopt; and (3) presenting the proposal to a group of active decision makers. You are likely to make presentations more often than public speeches, so strategies for the presentational situation are important to you and that present or future career.

Our discussion of presentational strategies will include: creating the proposal, analyzing decision makers, organizing for reasoning, preparing for the presentation, and adapting to the process.[1]

CREATING THE PROPOSAL

Presentations focus upon proposals. Proposals are created in much the same way as problems are solved by small group task forces or committees. In fact, company proposals are normally the result of cooperative work among several or many individuals. When the proposal is presented, however, it may well be given by a single person—perhaps you.

The creation of a proposal involves four highly important tasks. Normally, a person or an area of the organization will be charged with the responsibility to research a problem and to make a presentation to the organization. The first task is to *analyze the responsibility*. The responsibility may be to propose a new plant site, to propose a new accounting system, to suggest a new hiring procedure, or to create a new employee evaluation system. Whatever the nature of the responsibility, the first step is to understand it completely. What are the guidelines—that is, what is the organization hoping to do? How much time can be allowed for the research and development of the proposal? How much of your company time will be set aside for the task? How much money can the organization spend for the research? Will there be other people who serve as staff? If so, how many and who are they? If not, how much support can you expect from the usual pool of employees? All these questions are among the things that must have answers before the presentational task is understood.

The second step is to *research the problem*. You may have to do this alone, you may have a special task force, you may have the help of the members of your regular department—or you may be able to hire a professional research company. *How* you do the research will depend upon the available money and help. *What* you research depends upon the nature of the problem. *Where* you research depends upon the time allowed, the nature of the problem, and your creativity. *When* you do the research depends upon how crucial the problem is. *How much* research you do depends upon your previous knowledge, your (and others') skills, and probably a bit of luck. The importance of your research cannot be overestimated. Certain parts of the organization and your own career may depend a good deal upon how thorough you are.

The third step is to *analyze all the research material and information*. Here your previous knowledge of argumentation is important. Treat every bit of information as a claim. Test it to see if it is acceptable by looking at the *evidence*. How qualified must the claim be; are there reservations? What are the acceptable claims? Which are not acceptable? Use the tests of information in Chapter 14. Be sure you have confidence in the information you have—even if that means doing further research to "plug the holes" in what you know.

Finally, *arrive at a proposal that will best solve the problem*. Since the creation of the proposal probably will be at least partly a group effort, the decision-making strategies in Chapter 14 will be important. You have already been made aware of the problem and you have analyzed it. Now, establish standards for the solutions, consider the possible solutions, and compare the solutions with your standards. Select your proposal as the best, most defensible solution to the organizational problem.

At this point, the steps in creating the proposal have involved strategies you know and skills you possess. The next strategy in presentational speaking is analyzing decision makers. Who are they? How do they think? How will you persuade them? Those are among our concerns in the next section.

REASONING AND PERSUASIVE ANALYSIS

The audience for the presentation probably will be a fairly small group of decision makers. As we saw earlier, they may be higher in status than the speaker.

They probably will be an active group since they are knowledgeable and sincerely interested in the problem to be faced. One thing more: They probably will be familiar to the presentational speaker. This audience probably will be composed of members of the organization. They may not be people you work with every day, but they will not be total strangers.

What all this means is that you as a presenter can take advantage of your knowledge of who these people are and how they think and reason. Specifically, you have a better chance of being a successful presenter if you know (1) how these people make decisions and (2) what their attitudes are toward aspects of the problem and your proposal.

Reasoning analysis

Argumentation, as we have dealt with it, involves the presentation and examination of claims and reasons. To have a proposal accepted, you must engage in argumentation. You must present claims about what you feel is the best proposal, then attempt to give good reasons for adopting the proposal. The catch is that there is no such thing as a *good* reason. People attach the label *good* to reasons that *make sense* to them.[2] A friend of yours may say he or she is going into law because of "the money and status that lawyers have." Your response may be, "Well, money and status are not that important to me.... They are not reason enough to study law." In another situation, a friend may spend hours studying for a test that you think will be easy. When you ask your friend why he or she is studying, the reply may be, "The prof. said it would be hard." You may begin studying more seriously for the test. The professor's remark is reason enough for your change. In these examples, neither money, status, nor a professor's comment is a *good* reason. They only become good reasons because someone attaches significance or importance to them. When you ask someone to accept a claim, you are asking him or her to accept the reasons for it as *good enough*.

Without analyzing your decision makers, you will have no idea what will be a good enough reason for them to accept your proposal. You may present what seems to you to be a good reason—a reason built around what you think is good evidence. Yet, your decision makers may reject the evidence and the reason. The result may be that the proposal is rejected also. Your strategy in the presentation is not just to present good reasons, but to present reasons that your decision makers will *think are good*.

What you must do, then, is to find out how the individuals in this fairly small group think and how they reason. What are the sorts of things that they, as individuals, consider to be good reasons? With a mass audience of millions of people, the task would be impossible. With a small group of decision makers, the task is not only possible; it is necessary. There are three basic levels of decision-maker analysis that you can use strategically.

First, you can use the idea of *field-related standards* of judging good reasons.[3] Different professions, different types of businesses—different *fields*—will consider different things good reasons. If the presentation is to members of the Art Center, the standard of attractiveness or beauty may be important. A good reason for something may be because that something is more attractive, more pleasing, or more beautiful. In law, precedent is an important standard for the good reason. If proposals are presented as being consistent with earlier decisions or earlier procedures, that may be reason enough for the proposal. In business, generally, the good reason may be the reason which is most profitable. In banking, a reason might have to relate to safety and security in order to be good. The point is that different fields in general will consider different things as good reasons. Part of your task is to present good reasons for the proposal—good as judged by your field.

Second, you must take *group standards* into consideration. As noted earlier, one of the characteristics of groups is that they develop a group climate. The group climate may include *habits* of thinking or *norms* of decision making. Your group of decision makers may have served as a group long enough to develop a *pattern* of decision making or a group standard for evaluating reasons. You can use these standards to your advantage. Talk with group members, secretarial staffs, and others who have worked with the group on earlier proposals. Research decisions that the group has made in the past. Is there a pattern emerging? Do they respond to the same sorts of things time and again? Do they consistently accept and reject the same sorts of ideas? The process of analyzing group standards is easier to discuss than to do; yet your success in creating good reasons for the group's decision may depend upon your knowing the standards that the group typically uses.

Finally, your group will be small enough for you to concentrate on *individual standards* of judgment. Who are the opinion leaders—that is, who has the power to affect the other group members' decisions? What do these people demand in a good reason? As you talk with the members, their staffs, and others about group standards, learn about individual biases and prejudices. Do certain people consider good reasons to be economical, or progressive, or pretested? Do they consistently reject "new fangled" ideas and "wild-eyed" schemes? How do they reason? If there are no clear leaders, then discover the same things about individual members. As important as field-related and group standards may be, people still must make decisions personally. Since they do, you can find out enough about their individual standards to use them in the presentation.

The three-step strategy of reasoning analysis may not always be difficult, but it is almost always time-consuming. Your task, though, is not to avoid effort but to have your well-thought-out proposal accepted by the group. In order to do that, reasoning analysis is an excellent and efficient strategy of mediation.

Persuasive analysis

The reasoning analysis we have just discussed has to do with how people think and reason. It involves discovering the standards that people use when they

Strategies of presentational speaking

must examine reasons. These general reasoning processes are made more complex because people have various specific attitudes toward the problem and your solution. Another strategy of analysis is to gain and use insight into the attitudes of the group. The goal of this is not successful argumentation, but rather successful persuasion.

Although there are other ways of understanding persuasion, persuasion in the presentational situation can be viewed as *changing attitudes*. An attitude can be considered a *readiness to respond* to a situation or object.[4] In order to have a proposal accepted, you must overcome any attitudes opposing your solution, and develop positive attitudes toward the proposal. The most practical help in doing these things may be your understanding of what the attitudes of the members may be. You can then attempt to modify any attitudes that are inconsistent with your proposal.

First, you can try to understand the attitudes that decision makers have toward the problem and the proposal. That information can be gained in your earlier discussions with group members, staffs, and others in the organization. You will need to know how group members feel about the problem and the possible solutions—including the one you are going to present. This may not be as difficult as it sounds. The problem you have been working with probably is important. It is important to the organization and to individual members of the organization. In short, people will already have feelings and attitudes about the problem and the possible solutions. In addition, decision makers typically will not be secretive about their attitudes. A problem that results in a presentational assignment probably will have already been a subject of discussion. Group decision makers will have already stated opinions—or at least, it is likely that they will share their feelings with you if you talk with them. When group members are reluctant to discuss their attitudes, you may still discover information from co-workers or others in the organization.

Once you have discovered what the attitudes are, you must face an additional problem: attitudes can be resistant to change. An attitude will be more or less difficult to change depending upon its nature, how it was learned, and so forth. To change attitudes, you should be aware of the kinds of things that make attitudes resistant to change. Brembeck and Howell have provided a useful summary of what they call *sources of resistance to attitude change.*[5] Your effective use of this knowledge of resistance to attitude change can be an important strategy of mediation in the presentational situation.

Brembeck and Howell's discussion of sources of resistance to attitude change suggests the following ideas:

1. Attitudes that are developed early in life and have been held for long periods of time are more resistant to change.
2. Attitudes that have been successfully held and/or rewarded and reinforced are more difficult to change.
3. Attitudes that are of strong personal concern are difficult to change. *Ego-involvement* means that someone has a *personal stake* in the attitude.

4. Attitudes that have been expressed publicly are more resistant to change. When people have gone on record in support of something, they are reluctant to change position.
5. Attitudes are more resistant to change if the attitude is seen as a *central* attitude: related to other attitudes and beliefs.
6. and 7. Attitudes are more resistant to change if the change seems inconsistent either with a person's *logic* or a person's *experience.*
8. Attitudes are more resistant to change if the change is called for by a low credibility source.
9. Attitudes may be more difficult to change if a strong fear appeal is used; arguing for a change on the basis of strong threats or references to what might happen may backfire.

The topic of persuasion is complex and detailed. The full discussion of it goes beyond the scope of this text. Yet, your knowledge of *what* your group's attitudes are and *why* they may be resistant to change can be of great help to you. Certain strategies can be suggested which will give some idea about how attitude change can be attempted.

If the attitude was developed early and has been reinforced, you may want to acknowledge the worth of the attitude. You may wish to admit that the attitude has been justified—until the present time. You may want to show how situations have changed which demand different attitudes. You may want to show how the new attitudes are desirable and how they will be rewarded.

If the attitude has strong ego-involvement or if members of the group have gone on record in favor of the attitude, your task may be more difficult. You may be able to show how a different attitude is more desirable, or you may be able to show that the change in attitude is not so drastic a change. Members of a group may have gone on record in support of the existing policy, but they may also be on record in support of progress, efficiency, and so forth. Try to relate this change of attitude to different attitudes that are also a matter of record.

If the attitude is considered a central issue, you may need to show that a change in attitude does not destroy a whole series of other beliefs. Perhaps the attitude change is only a small change, or a change that is still consistent with most other attitudes already established. Perhaps the change you are suggesting is actually more consistent with other attitudes and beliefs that members have.

If the attitude change is seen as inconsistent with members' experience or their sense of logic, you may need to reexplain what you are suggesting. You may need a great deal of evidence in order to show how the change is both logical and rational—and how it makes sense. You may need to build a strong, carefully organized presentation aimed at making the proposal seem like a sound, commonsense solution to your group of decision makers.

Finally, you may need to avoid strong fear appeals and to enhance your own credibility. We have already discussed credibility-improving strategies, but you should pay attention to fear appeals. Even though you are convinced that the future of the organization depends upon the proposal, you may have to be subtle in your statement of the belief. People often tend to avoid or to repress fearful ideas. Your goal is to present a well-reasoned argument for the proposal—not to frighten your decision makers into acceptance.

Persuasive analysis, then, means that you attempt to learn about attitudes that relate to the problem and to your proposal. Once you learn of the attitudes, you can try to understand why they may be resistant to change. Then and only then, can you develop arguments that can overcome that resistance to attitude change. Persuasive analysis can be an important strategy of mediation. Persuasive analysis provides a way of dealing with specific attitudes that must be changed. To illustrate the value of persuasive analysis, let us assume that you have had the responsibility of researching the problem of accounting procedures in the organization. You feel strongly that a "first-in/first-out" method is best; your conflict involves how to get the company as a whole to change its accounting procedures by accepting your idea. One way of approaching the problem is this:

> . . . and let me say that the task has not been difficult. The first-in/last-out procedure is simply silly by today's standards. No one else is still using it—and for good reason. By moving to the new approach, we will need, of course, a complete shakedown of the company's accounting procedures. But let me make myself perfectly clear, the future of the company rests on this decision. . . .

That would be one way of approaching the presentation, but it violates most of what we know about persuasive analysis: It ridicules the company and the people who have supported the old system; it neglects the fact that the company has prospered under the old system; it presents the change as even more central to the company than it probably is; and it uses strong fear appeals with regard to the company's future. Much the same thing could have been said in a more persuasive manner:

> . . . Surely, we all know that the old approach has served us well in the past; our company has become a leader in its field. The reason we have remained a leader, partly, is that we as a company have changed with the demands of the situation. The situation now seems to suggest a change—a change which can be activated systematically, with little perceivable effect upon the company. The first-in/first-out approach can help us remain a leader in the field. . . .

The differences between the approaches are great—and important. As we saw earlier, reasoning analysis provides a way of dealing with methods of making decisions. Reasoning and persuasive analysis together can provide good guides for understanding your decision makers.

ORGANIZATION AND REASONS

Once you have the proposal firmly developed and your decision makers analyzed, you can begin to consider ways of *organizing* the presentation. In general, the process of organization is how you create an understandable sequence of ideas and information. In speaking, you cannot afford to "throw out" material randomly. You must put the material into some kind of order that will make sense to both you and the decision makers.

In speaking generally, there are many different types of organization. In presentational speaking, however, there are several types of organizational *patterns* which will be most useful. These various types all have three things in common. First, they are *patterns that have something to do with problem solving*. Second, they are *patterns that involve comparisons*. These two factors are important. The presentational situation will always be a problem-solution situation—and for every problem, two or more solutions are always possible. The different solutions may be all new (new plant site A is compared with B, C, and D). Or, the solutions may be a comparison between or among the old and new (present procedure A is compared with new procedures B, C, and D). These types of patterns also have a third thing in common: They are a *means of reasoning or argument*. Organization in the presentation may be helpful because it shows that you are well-prepared and knowledgeable about the problem. Organization may help your presentation be clear, understandable, and memorable. Organization in the presentation is most important because it is a strategy for you to use in arguing the worth of your proposal. In short, the patterns to be discussed are *problem-solving patterns* that you use *for comparisons* so that *you can argue* the merits of your proposal.

One method of organizing your presentation is by *criterial reasoning*.[6] Your proposal probably is the result of a problem-solving process in which you have established criteria and then matched solutions with the criteria or standards. Your proposal is the one that best met the standards. You can use this kind of criteria-solution comparison for organization:

> Our research group and those of you who helped with the project were concerned that the solution to the situation be fairly uncomplicated, economical, pretested in other companies, and possible to do with our present staff. I wish at this time to show how each of the proposed solutions met or failed to meet these standards . . . .

Obviously, the solution you are presenting will emerge as the winner when solutions and standards are compared. This is no accident. The reason that you are proposing the solution is because your research and problem solving have indicated that your proposal is best as judged by these standards.

A second method of organizing your presentation is *comparative advantage* reasoning. With this sort of organization, you begin by stating the possible solutions—including perhaps the possibility of making no change. Then, you list the advantages and disadvantages for each possible solution. In the end, you demonstrate how the proposal you are presenting presents the most or most important advantages, and the fewest or least important disadvantages:

> Research by the group and conversations with some of you have indicated that there are four potential alternatives to the problem. I want to demonstrate the implications of choosing each of these solutions—in essence, let's look at the advantages and disadvantages of each of the suggested alternatives....

Obviously again, the proposal you are presenting will emerge the winner in this comparison of advantages and disadvantages.

A third important method of organization is *residual reasoning*. Residual reasoning means that you analyze all the potential proposals in order to demonstrate that the proposal you suggest is the *only one left* that seems workable. Your strategy here probably will be to emphasize the disadvantages of all the proposals except your own. You will need to be fair, of course, since some members of the group may know nearly as much about the problem as you do. Still, if you have selected a proposal carefully, you may have made the selection not because it was the one with the most advantages, but because it had fewer disadvantages. If that is the case, you may want to use the residual method of reasoning:

> Our research group and those of you who have helped us feel that there are several possible alternatives for the problem we face. We have explored all aspects of the proposed solutions, and it does seem to be the case that the one which has fewest major problems is the one which I shall urge you to accept. Plant site A, for example, has the severe problem of poor transportation in the area....

The result of this pattern of reasoning is that the group is confronted with one solution that has the fewest or no major problems. The proposal you present is the one that's left after the others have been rejected.

The specific method of organization you use may be a combination or variation of the three discussed. Your selection of the organizational pattern should be based upon your evidence, the way your decision makers seem to reason, and the sorts of attitudes you must change. Organization, then, is not only for clarity. It is also important as a major mediational strategy for your persuasive and argumentative speaking.

PREPARING FOR THE PRESENTATION

In the previous chapter, we discussed general strategies of speaking. Some of these strategies can be stated more specifically to help you in the presentational situation.

Strategies of improving credibility and controlling anxiety have been discussed. In the presentational situation, adequate preparation is your best tool. You will have to appear to be—as well as be—a knowledgeable, trustworthy member of the organization. A good impression created as you talk with group members beforehand can be helpful. A supportive introduction by an organizational executive may be appropriate. Certainly, you will need to have done extensive and intensive research on the problem. All these can help with your credibility—but the confidence you receive from having done a good job may be the key to controlling anxiety. The group is there to hear you and to work with you until a decision is made. You must focus upon them and how your proposal can be best communicated. If you are prepared to do so, anxiety may be easier to control.

Verbal and nonverbal speaking skills were discussed as *delivery* and *language use*. In the presentational situation, you constantly must be aware that you are *talking with* a group, not *speaking to* an audience. Normally, your delivery and language will need to be businesslike and as close to standard practice as possible. Exaggerated gestures and lack of movement altogether are two extremes you should avoid. Your group will be a group of decision makers who are all experts of some sort. Yet, not every one of your members will be an expert in everything you discuss. Technical language should be at levels that you are sure all members will understand. The keys to adapting delivery and language are basically the same. They depend upon analysis of the room for the presentation, the assignment you have, and the people who must make the decision.

The topic of visual aids also has special importance in the presentational situation. Your research may have spanned months of time and hundreds of sources of information. Your tasks are to condense material and to create comparisons between and among proposals. To do those things, you will almost certainly have to rely upon charts, graphs, drawings, and so forth. Each visual can present some comparison that you need to make. The illustrated comparisons can make your arguments for your proposal more clear. They can also make the comparisons come alive and be more dramatic, as well as more memorable. Presentations may be scheduled for an hour or two, and that will seem like a long time. That time, however, will include discussion between you and group members. You will find that your task includes condensing and (visually) dramatizing your ideas. Using visual aids for that purpose may be a highly important strategy.

The presentation requires specific applications of the general strategies of speaking. Your preparation for the presentation should be guided by the need for these applications.

ADAPTING TO THE PROCESS OF PRESENTATIONAL SPEAKING

All this discussion of preparing for the presentation should not make you think that the presentation is a static or one-way communication situation. Your decision makers probably will be an active group who are generally knowledgeable and concerned. You can expect them to take their task of decision making as seriously as you do the task of presenting the proposal. The presentational situation can be more effective and satisfying if you keep the following strategies in mind.

First, expect questions and discussion. Assume that part of your time will be spent "away" from your carefully organized and rehearsed message. You probably will need to answer questions, provide more details, and so forth.

Second, invite questions and discussion. I suspect such an invitation will be unnecessary: the decision makers have done this before. Still, the invitation to ask questions or to make some ideas known may improve the decision makers' image of your competence, openness, and concern—factors related to credibility.

Third, have as much back-up information and material as possible. Answering questions or explaining ideas may require more information than you have planned to put into the presentation. Your decision makers may already understand what you have said, so repeating the same material probably will not help. You need to be ready with more information, more statistics, and perhaps even other visual aids. Some of this may never be used, but your strategy should be to be ready for anything.

Fourth, answer questions effectively. That means a number of things. Make sure you understand the question—restate it if you wish to make sure you are about to answer the right question. Answer the question at the time asked if at all possible. Sometimes, the question might be best answered if put off until later in the proceedings. That, however, may be dangerous. The question is asked because a decision maker wants to know something at this point. The delay in answering may be worse than eventually coming to it, as you have planned. Feel free also to seek information from other members of the group. Though the presentational situation is a one-to-many situation, it is also a group effort. Answer the question if you can, but get help from other members of the group for a question more "in line with Ms. Smith's expertise." Answering questions in the presentation should be approached as much like answering questions in conversation as possible.

Fifth, make sure that no questions, answers, or discussion take you on long digressions from the point you wish to make. If their discussion or your response has taken you away from your point, get back to the main point as soon as possible. The transactions of the group are meant to help, not stop your presentation.

Finally, use the verbal transactions of the group in the ongoing presentation. If you have answered a question earlier than you had planned, you can refer to the answer or someone's response as you make the point again. If you have received information during the presentation from group members, use it to argue your point. Using the transactions of the group has a two-part advantage. First, it may help clarify your arguments and persuasive strategies. Second, it may help members of the group feel that the presentation has been more than a one-person show.

Transacting effectively in the process of the presentation may require as much thought and practice as preparing for the presentation. The effort you give to adapting to the process of presentation, however, may be one of the strengths of your effort.

CHAPTER SUMMARY

This chapter has been a discussion of specific strategies for the presentational situation. We began with a concern for creating the proposal, which involves basic decision-making techniques. Next we examined the strategy of decision-maker analysis. The good presenter uses both reasoning analysis and persuasive analysis in order to build his or her presentation. As much as possible is discovered about the way the listeners make decisions, and about the attitudes that must be altered if the proposal is to be accepted. That analysis is important when you begin to organize a problem-solving message which uses comparisons for argumentation and persuasion. We looked at criterial reasoning, comparative-advantage reasoning, and residual reasoning. Any of these might be best for the particular situation you face.

Next, we analyzed how the general speaking strategies of credibility building, anxiety control, delivery skills, language use, and visual aids can be tailored to the presentational situation. Finally, we looked at various strategies of adapting to the process that is the presentation. The presenter must be prepared to adapt to and to use questions, opinions, and discussions by group members.

In sum, the chapter has dealt with specific strategies of presentational speaking—of speaking *to* the organization. When the conflict is between what you know and accept and what the organization as a whole knows and accepts, strategies of presentational speaking can be invaluable to you. Remember to:

1. Create the proposal.
2. Analyze decision makers in terms of:
   A. Reasoning
   B. Persuasion
3. Organize the presentation by:
   A. Criterial reasoning
   B. Comparative-advantage reasoning
   C. Residual reasoning
4. Prepare for the presentation.
5. Adapt to the presentational process.

These strategies can be helpful to you in the presentational speaking situation.

EXERCISES

1. Presentational speaking is not normally discussed in basic communication courses—but my consulting work tells me it should be. You may want to discover the

frequency of presentational speaking for yourself. Search out people you know who are managers, supervisors, or officers in businesses, government, hospitals, and so forth. Find out how often they are called upon to give a public speech. Match that number with the number of times that they are called upon to give a presentational speech. You may be surprised to find that what they call *talks, briefings, sales pitches,* and the like are what we are calling presentational speeches.

2. If you can discover someone you know who regularly or on occasion makes presentations, see if you can get permission from the person (or others) to observe one. Remember that these presentations are usually given in conference rooms, meeting rooms, and so forth. Do not expect to see one presented to the public.

3. Examine your own occupational goals—or at least your field of study. In your field, whether it be economics, management, biology, music education, or anything else, there will be research to be done and problems to be solved. Select a problem to attack, and prepare a presentation. Depending upon the wishes of your instructor, you may want to have your class audience play the roles of decision makers in your particular field. However you decide to do it, remember you are asking your audience for acceptance of your proposal (NOTE: This is a fine example of a time to MAKE your communication class relevant to your major area, job, or job goal. Do not hesitate to use experts from outside class in the preparation of your presentation.)

4. Select a problem in your major area or a problem related to your job or job goal. Instead of organizing the presentation in *one* way, try to organize it in several ways. Refer to the section, "Organization and Reasons" in this chapter while you work. What differences in effectiveness do you see? Do you see that one organizational method may be better in a particular situation than others?

NOTES

[1] An excellent longer treatment of presentational speaking is William S. Howell and Ernest G. Bormann, *Presentational Speaking for Business and the Professions* (New York: Harper & Row, 1971).

[2] The discussion of reasons developed here is indebted to the writing of Stephen Toulmin. See Stephen Toulmin, *Reason in Ethics* (Cambridge, England: Cambridge Univ. Press, 1968), pp. 70–71; and Stephen Toulmin, "Reasons and Causes," *Explanation in the Social Sciences,* ed. M. Berger and F. Cioffi (Cambridge, England: Cambridge Univ. Press, 1970), p. 4. Also, see the discussion in Richard E. Crable, *Argumentation as Communication: Reasoning with Receivers* (Columbus, Oh.: Charles E. Merrill, 1976), pp. 190–99.

[3] The topic of *fields* is more than merely *occupational* fields although this latter is what is important here. For discussions of standards and fields, see Stephen Toulmin, *The Uses of Argument* (Cambridge, England: Cambridge Univ. Press, 1969), chap. 1. See also Crable, *Argumentation,* 200–201 and 209–214.

[4] Gordon W. Allport, "Attitudes," *Handbook of Social Psychology,* ed. C. Murchison (Worcester, Ma.: Clark Univ. Press, 1935), p. 810.

[5] Winston L. Brembeck and William S. Howell, *Persuasion: A Means of Social Influence,* 2nd ed. (Englewood Cliffs, N.J.: Prentice-Hall, 1976), pp. 151–52.

[6] The methods of organization discussed here are borrowed from my experience in intercollegiate debate—such debates always involve the persuasive handling of a proposal or *policy.*

20
STRATEGIES OF PUBLIC SPEAKING

Lieutenant Tom Holmes is a detective with the New York Police Department. He has been invited to speak to a junior high school gathering about vandalism. The precinct in which Lt. Holmes works has been developing a program of incentives to try to help curb vandalism. The program is designed to soft-pedal the punishment aspect, and instead emphasizes prevention. Rewards have been set up for assistance in vandalism prevention. This will be the first public statement about the program.

Mrs. Hendricks has just been elected president of the local teachers' union. At a meeting of the Rotary Club—a civic organization—she has been asked to discuss the role of unions in contemporary education.

John Scott is a banker from a medium-sized western town. This year's winter has brought an unprecedented amount of rainfall to the community. The rainfall has caused flooding and mud slides which have resulted in millions of dollars of property damage. At a meeting open to the public, three speakers are scheduled: a local insurance executive will discuss the role of insurance companies in rebuilding; a local contractor will discuss the role of the construction industry; and John will discuss the role of bankers and finance organizations.

In all of these different settings, people face situations that need mediation: Lieutenant Holmes wants to make his world better by gaining the acceptance of the new program; Mrs. Hendricks wants to bridge the gap between what she knows about unions and what the average citizen does; and John Scott wishes to head off some of the panic created by local property losses. Though their exact goals are different, their need for mediation can be met by the same sorts of general strategies. All of them can benefit by knowing how to use public speaking for the mediation of conflicts.

In some respects public speaking is more difficult than presentational speaking. When you speak *to* the organization, some things are given; some things are already decided. The audience is already determined and your task is clearly labeled persuasive. The presentation will be a proposal-centered message that is either accepted or rejected by a small group of the organization's members. The public speech—the speech presented *for* the organization—may provide you with more uncertainty and more flexibility. In this chapter, we shall examine four major strategies: analyzing the audience, creating the specific purpose, organizing the speech, and adapting general speaking strategies.

ANALYZING THE AUDIENCE

Audience analysis is different from *decision-maker* analysis in the presentational situation. The audience for a public speech may be dozens, hundreds, or thousands of times larger than the decision-making group in the presentational setting. The methods that are effective in the presentation probably will not work for the public speech. You will not be able to analyze each individual member of the audience. Since you will not know most or any of the members of the audience, you need to rely upon other methods of analysis.

Demographic variables

Demographic variables are the basic means of audience analysis. Demographic variables include:

1. The number of people you will be addressing.
2. The setting for the speech (such as an auditorium, a large conference room, a dining hall, a football stadium, and so forth).
3. The sex division of your audience, and whether it is predominately male or female.
4. The age spans and age distributions of the audience.
5. The educational level of the audience.
6. The affiliations of your audience, including (but not limited to):
   a. religious groups
   b. political parties
   c. social clubs or societies

Strategies of public speaking

   d. civic organizations
   e. professional or occupational groups

A number of things must be said about demographic variables. First, sometimes you will not be able to know beforehand some or most of this information. You may have to rely upon secondhand information from others—or upon your own guesses. Second, even if you have the above information, be careful not to overestimate its importance. Demographic variables can be misleading. All men, for example, do not like the same things and respond in the same way; neither do all women. People of the same age may differ greatly; not all Republicans are alike; and so forth. Third, remember that demographic variables may be best used *in combination* to discover something about the audience. You may get a clear picture of an audience made up of retired university professors who are members of a Grey Panther group, the American Progressive Party, and Common Cause. But what about the audience of businesspeople who belong to the American Conservative Party, who have a group subscription to *Playboy*, and who have served terms in the Peace Corps? The examples, of course, are exaggerated, but the point is that combining variables allows you to detect consistencies and inconsistencies in your audience. The combined variables help you avoid stereotyping your audience too excessively. Fourth, many audiences will be highly varied. They may be of both sexes, all ages, various political persuasions, and so on. Even that disturbing conclusion can be helpful: At least you will not adapt your speech to one particular age level or sex.

Psychological variables

Your audience analysis must take into consideration factors other than demographic ones. What are the attitudes, beliefs, biases, and prejudices of the audience? The demographic variables may help somewhat, but again, demographics lead to stereotyping which may or may not be accurate. Normally, there are people who can tell you something about the audience's psychological variables: the person who arranges for the speech, club or group officers, or civic leaders. You may consult them, and perhaps you will even have the opportunity of speaking with some members of the audience during a luncheon or before the speech.

What may even provide a better clue to the psychological variables in the audience is the task you have been given. Are you supposed to challenge, confront, entertain, improve the image of the organization, or inform? What sort of speech is the audience anticipating, a lighthearted statement, a technical discussion, a sales job, a financial statement, or what? Normally, you will not be asked to "make a speech;" you will be asked to "make a speech on . . . ," or a speech "that will . . . ," or a specific kind of speech. What the audience expects from you can provide perhaps the best idea of what task lies ahead of you. These expectations and desires may be just as valuable to you as the demographic variables you have discovered.

CREATING THE SPECIFIC PURPOSE

In presentations, the speaker's purpose is generally the same: to have an audience of decision makers accept a proposal. The proposal may vary, but the goal is clear. In public speaking, the situation may be less clear. The *specific purpose* you select will both guide your preparation and lead your audience to respond in the way you wish. In short, *the specific purpose is a statement of what you want your audience to do, be, or know after your speech.* Arriving at a specific purpose requires a number of steps. You must consider the audience, yourself as a speaker, the general purpose, possible topics, and organizational guidelines.

The audience and you

How you want the audience to respond depends much upon its members—what they are like and what they want from the speech. Your audience analysis will have already provided that information. Next, you need to think about the relationship between you and the audience. What are you an expert in, or what is it about you that has made you the selected speaker? What does the audience know about you—if anything? What is expected from you? How can you provide what is expected? What kind of speech are you comfortable presenting? What have you experienced? What do you know? What can you do to mediate the differences between what you and they think, do, or feel?

General purpose

Next consider your general purpose. On the basis of your analysis of the audience and you, what is the general goal of the speech? Is it persuasive, informative, challenging, entertaining? What general response do you wish to elicit?

The handling of topics

The topic of the speech must be created. Normally, the speech will concern some aspect of your expertise. It usually will concern something you and your organization are doing, thinking about, involved in, committed to, fighting against, or identified with. Your specific topic will be chosen from a series of things that might be discussed. You will wish to take into consideration the nature of the audience and what it desires from you. You will want to think about the educational and age level of the audience, and its members' various affiliations.

Perhaps as important, you will need to *narrow* your topic so that you can discuss whatever it is in the time allotted. Public speeches are normally fairly short because of the situation, the number of speeches, or the audience's attention span. Of all the things you could discuss, what can you discuss easily and satisfactorily in *this* situation? If your specialty is medicine and particularly cancer research, the following *narrowing process* might be used:

> First idea: Cancer and the Human Body
> Narrowed to: Cancer and What Seems to Produce It
> Narrowed to: The Causes of Skin Cancer
> Narrowed to: Skin Cancer and the Sun's Rays

Only this last narrowing may be appropriate for the time you have. Any of the other narrowings might be too broad for you to cover adequately. If this last narrowing is too broad; if your speech is to be made before a professional group already knowledgeable about skin cancer and the sun, you may need to narrow the topic to the specific effect of the sun in relation to atmospheric conditions, precautionary measures, and a particular type of skin cancer. There are no real rules for narrowing a speech. The guideline simply is to narrow the chosen topic until it can be discussed adequately with your audience.

Organizational guidelines

One of the main factors to be considered in creating the specific purpose is the set of organizational guidelines which may confront you. Since virtually all public speakers are speaking *for* some kind of organization, the organization may decide some of your questions for you. You may be given a very specific task to perform for the organization as you speak. You may be expected to establish goodwill between the organization and the audience; you may be expected to persuade the audience toward the beliefs of the organization; or you may be expected to describe some aspect of the organization. At the very least, you probably will be expected to speak so that no erroneous or unfavorable impressions are created concerning the organization. The guidelines from the organization may be specific or general, direct or indirect, but they will exist. You normally will be free to speak for the organization only if you follow the existing guidelines set by the organization.

Factors in selecting the specific purpose

Though the factors used to select the specific purpose have been dealt with in a particular order, there is no *correct order* in which to consider them. In a particular speech, your general purpose may be given to you either by the organization or by the representatives of the audience; or your specific topic may be assigned. Organizational guidelines may be more or less clear. The point is that all these factors need to be considered. The order in which you consider them will vary.

Selecting the specific purpose

On the basis of the factors we have discussed, you should select the specific purpose. What do you want the audience to do? How do you want it to respond? Those questions can only be answered by taking into account you, your audience, the general purpose, the organizational guidelines, and the topic you will discuss. With a narrowed topic such as "Skin Cancer and the Sun's Rays," and a particular audience, your specific purpose might be to persuade audience members to protect themselves against cancer-causing sun rays. It might also be to have the audience understand how the rays of the sun can cause skin cancer. The specific purpose—the response you want from the audience—must somehow be decided. The specific purpose allows both you and the audience to know what the speech is supposed to do.

ORGANIZING THE SPEECH

In organizing the public speech, you can use any of the patterns we discussed with regard to presentations, but certain public speaking patterns can be used as well. Public speaking patterns have more variety because public speeches are not limited (like presentations) to the advocacy of a proposal. A list of public speaking patterns follows.

The *topical* pattern means that you arrange your ideas into groups that somehow make sense. If your speech is about the services of the dean of student's office, your organization might include:

I. Vocational advising
II. Personal counseling
III. Testing services
IV. Special-problems counseling (minority affairs, older students, veterans' affairs, and so forth.)

Any of these topics may be treated in any order, but to make sense of the services, you might wish to divide them that way.

The *spatial* pattern means that you discuss ideas on the basis of location, usually using geographic areas. In a speech about student services, you might divide ideas spatially:

I. Services at counseling offices
II. Services at department offices

Strategies of public speaking

   III. Services at the health center

Or:

   I. Student services at Purdue University
   II. Student services at Indiana University
   III. Student services at Wabash College
   IV. Student services at Depauw University

A third pattern of organization is the *cause-effect* method. Here you would describe a certain problem and then look at the causes of it—or look at causes and then at effects. In a speech about student services, you might use the following:

   I. Causes of student problems
       A. Lack of counseling
       B. Lack of experience
       C. Lack of motivation
   II. Effects of the student problems
       A. Poor grade averages
       B. High drop out rates
       C. High rates of academic expulsion

The organization above is a cause-effect pattern. To use an effect-cause pattern, points I and II simply would be reversed.

Another organizational pattern is the *problem-solution* method. As you might expect, a problem is described and a solution suggested. In using a problem-solution approach, you can use the patterns that relate to presentational speaking, or you can use the reflective-thinking model used in group decision making. If you used this last, your speech about student services might be described as:

   I. Awareness of the problem: Did you know that students face all sorts of problems, including . . . ?
   II. Definition of the problem: Student problems are basically . . .
   III. Analysis of the problem: The factors that contribute to the problem include . . .
   IV. Criteria for the solution: Solutions to student problems must be . . .
   V. Comparison of the standards with the solutions: The best solution would seem to lie with the office of student services since . . .
   VI. Implementing the solution: So, I urge you to make use of the office of student services. All you need to do is . . .

Generally, speakers are advised to have no more than four *main points* in a speech, so you may wish to combine, for example, the definition and analysis steps in the speech outline. Other adaptations may also be helpful: If your analysis of the problem leads you to believe that there are *several* good solutions to general student problems, you may use the same general outline as above, but list several possible solutions. If your audience is already aware of the problem, or if it already understands the nature of the problem, certain steps in the pattern may be left out, or just mentioned in passing. In any case, the goal of the problem-solution pattern is the goal of all organizational patterns: the clear expression of what you have to say.

In terms of *introductions* and *conclusions,* the public speaker again has more flexibility than the presentational speaker. The presenter probably will begin almost immediately with his or her material. The public speaker, however, may need an introduction that will:

1. Enhance credibility (the speaker may state briefly his or her qualifications and concern for the topic and audience).
2. Establish identification (again, a credibility factor, but this concerns specifically the idea of *perceived similarity* between speaker and audience).
3. Introduce the speech (this can be considered a warm-up to channel the audience's thoughts toward the topic).
4. Gain attention (this means attention specifically toward the topic—an attention-getting introduction that is irrelevant to the speech misses the point). THIS STEP SEEMS MOST IMPORTANT.

In order to accomplish all those things, a speaker may introduce a speech with a variety of openers, including:

1. An appropriate quotation: Ben Franklin once said . . .
2. A startling fact or statement: One of every ten persons in this room will die before the age of fifty because of . . .
3. A story or illustration: Last Wednesday evening, I was walking through a dark alley when suddenly . . .
4. A joke or humorous story: My father used to tell about this coon hound who used to bark at the sun rather than the moon. Well, this dog got so bad that . . .
5. A rhetorical question—a question for which you really expect no answer: How many of you have ever felt so depressed and angry that you . . . ?

The introduction should truly begin your speaking effort. You should develop your speech first, and then create a way of introducing what you have to say.

The conclusion of the speech should accomplish several things. Depending upon your specific purpose in speaking, the conclusion should:

1. Add the feeling of finality to the speech. (A "thank you," a "that's about it," or a "are there any questions?," is not necessary if the speech has truly come to a finish.)

Strategies of public speaking 297

2. Summarize the main points. (This should be brief, but it may aid the audience's understanding and retention.)
3. Reemphasize the purpose of the speech; and/or
4. Tie the speech together as a whole message. (Here, relating the conclusion to the introduction may add a sense of completeness to the speech.)

The conclusion of a speech can be handled in almost any way that is consistent with the speech as a whole. Yet, there are some basic and traditional strategies for concluding a message, including:

1. A simple summary of main points: The new parking garage will be more attractive, more economical, and more efficient than other solutions to the parking problem. The new parking garage should have the support of all of us.
2. A challenge to the audience: Clearly, the decision about using drugs is yours to make. But I urge you to have the courage to avoid making a decision that may affect the rest of your life.
3. A rhetorical question: You will soon be in the position to elect one of the two candidates. Which one will you want to have representing you?
4. A concluding story or illustration: Bill smoked for twenty years. When he became convinced that smoking would shorten his life he quit once and for all. I agree with Bill: If he could do it, anyone can do it.
5. A closing quotation: One of the reasons that the new gasoline tax seems to be a solution that is too good to be true is because it is. It looks good from the outside, but the oil companies, not you, will benefit. It is still true today that, "All that glitters is not gold."

Your conclusion, as well as the introduction, should probably be created after the rest of the speech. Only then can the conclusion help the overall goal of achieving the speech's specific purpose.

Introductions and conclusions are actual parts of the speech. They are not simply ornaments that you hang onto the beginning and the end of the speech. There are no rules that say which is the best sort of introduction or conclusion—just as there are no rules that say which sort of an organizational pattern is best to use. Analyze your audience, your topic, your purpose, and the speech itself. Then and only then can you arrive at an appropriate and effective means of total organization.

ADAPTING GENERAL SPEAKING STRATEGIES IN PUBLIC SPEAKING

We have found that public speaking situations are more varied than the presentational situation. Unlike the presentation, the public speech might be on almost any topic related to your expertise and the nature of the organization. The audience for such a speech might be almost anyone. Because of these differences, you as a public speaker have more flexibility in choosing purposes and organizational patterns. The varieties of public speeches also mean that you will have greater flexibility in adapting the general strategies of speaking discussed earlier.

In terms of verbal and nonverbal skills, you must choose language and a delivery style that is appropriate for the specific audience, topic, and situation. Visual aids may or may not be used, because the public speech may not demand, for example, that you condense months or weeks of detailed research. Credibility-building strategies should depend upon your audience, topic, and situation. In all these areas, your task is to analyze your audience and to adapt to the needs of the situation.

More specifically, the public speech allows for more flexibility in how you handle your information. The presentational speech nearly always will be extemporaneous—you will speak from notes. The public speech may or may not be extemporaneous. Certain speeches will be given from manuscript: you write the speech word-for-word and then read it, making few or no changes. That sort of delivery requires a well-written speech and practice in reading it. In addition, the speech may have to be *impromptu*. Without warning, you may be called upon to say a few words about the organization or one of its major projects or programs. Impromptu speaking requires an experienced speaker who is also extremely knowledgeable about all aspects of the organization. In even rarer situations, a speaker may be called upon to present a *memorized* speech. The memorized speech requires much work in preparation, and a great deal of practice so that it does not sound memorized. Even though some speeches will be manuscript, memorized, or impromptu types, most public speeches given *for* the organization will be extemporaneous. For that reason, developing your skill in giving the extemporaneous public speech should be of highest concern.

CHAPTER SUMMARY

In this chapter, we have examined specific strategies of public speaking. We dealt first with the problems of audience analysis that face public speakers, including demographic analysis and the analysis of psychological variables. Next we looked at the factors that should guide the selection of a specific purpose. Our last major topic was the question of organization in the public speech. Various patterns of organization were discussed and introductions and conclusions were examined and illustrated. The final task of the chapter was to note how general speaking strategies could be adapted to the public speaking situation. With an understanding of these various topics—together with your knowledge of general speaking strategies—you should be prepared to speak *for* the organization. You should be prepared to use strategies of public speaking when you need to mediate the differences between the knowledge, action, or

Strategies of public speaking

beliefs of your organization and what the *public* thinks, does, or feels. To accomplish this mediation, you can:

1. Analyze your audience in terms of:
   A. Demographic variables
   B. Psychological variables
2. Create the specific purpose.
3. Organize the speech by a pattern of:
   A. Topic
   B. Space
   C. Cause-effect
   D. Problem solution
4. Introduce and conclude the speech effectively.
5. Adapt general speaking strategies.

By using these strategies effectively, you can begin to be able to use public speaking strategies as a means of mediating conflicts in the one-to-many situation.

EXERCISES

1. In introducing "Organizing the Speech" in this chapter, I noted that you could use any of the types of organization discussed in the chapter on presentational speaking, as well as others that usually are not used for presentations. The patterns discussed in terms of presentations are basically *problem-solving* patterns. What relationships do you see between them and, say, the reflective-thinking pattern discussed in this chapter? Can you see how any of them might be beneficial in creating certain types of speeches on problems?
2. Begin working on a speech topic of your choosing. Now, assume that you are going to give the speech ideas four different times: to a group of fourth-graders, a group of senior high school students, a meeting at a local social/civic club, and at a program for senior citizens.
   a) How might you create different *specific* purposes?
   b) How might your language use be affected?
   c) How might the length of the speech be affected?
   d) How might you change the nature of the introduction?
   e) How might you change the nature of the conclusion?
3. Take the same speech topic or choose a different one. Create at least *three different* ways of organizing the speech. Do you see the relationship between organizational pattern and specific purpose? Do you see that different patterns of organization may call for different introductions and conclusions? Does this help you see the advantage of creating conclusions and introductions last?
4. Choose a speech or several speeches from a recent issue of the periodical, *Vital Speeches.* Analyze the speech in terms of the reported audience, the specific purpose, the narrowing of the topic, the introduction, the organizational pattern, the language used, and the conclusion. What strengths do you see? What weaknesses do you detect? Are there suggestions you would have liked to make to the speaker(s)?

5. Attend a local public speaking situation. Analyze the speaker in terms of delivery. In addition, analyze the speech in terms of the points listed in exercise 4. What strengths or weaknesses do you see—and hear?
6. Select a topic for a *public* speech. Assume that your class is the public—or, depending upon your instructor's wishes, have the class play the role of the audience you are envisioning for the speech. Create and present a five- to eight-minute public speech, following the guidelines suggested.

PART 6

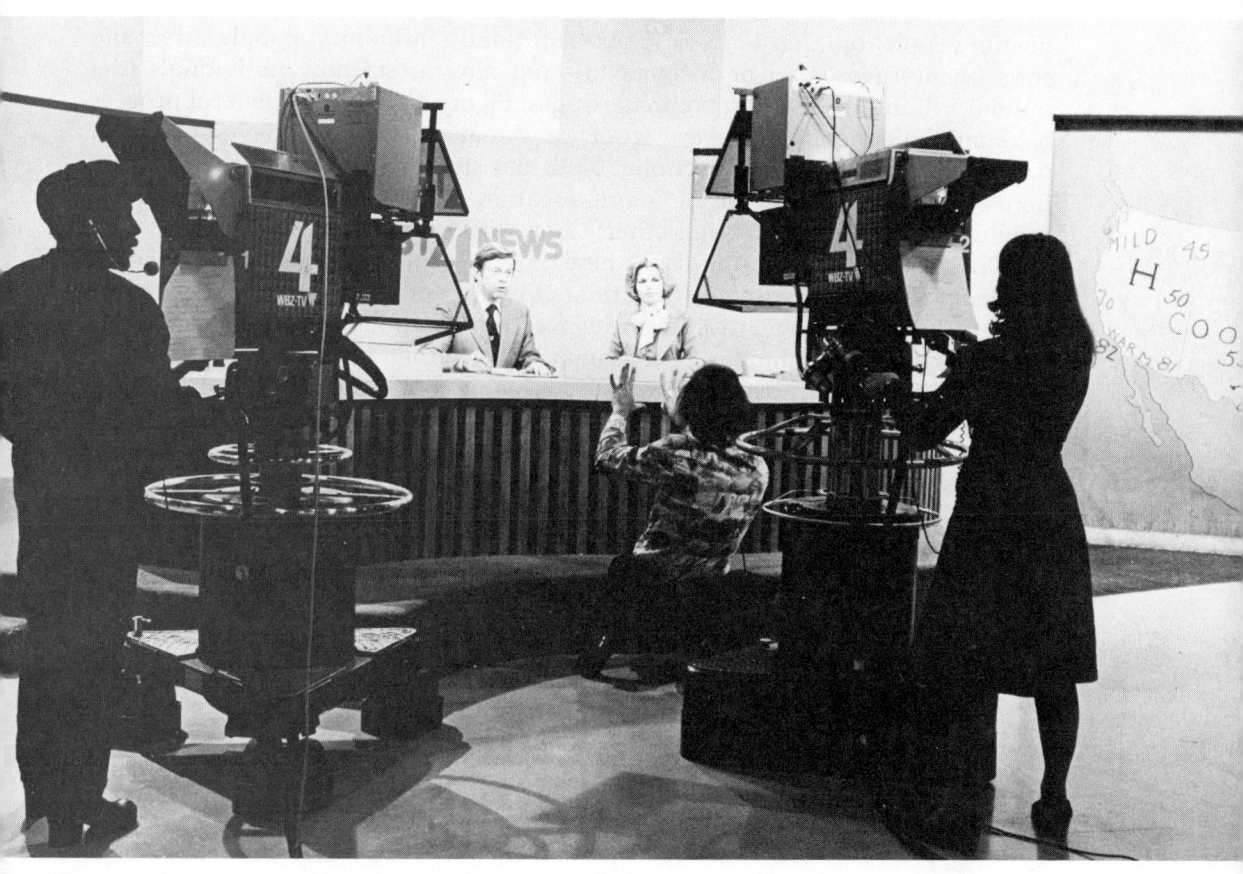

INTRODUCTION

The mass media play an important role in your life—and your personal problems. Media messages may influence your attitudes, values, knowledge, images, and beliefs, and a multitude of other factors. Media messages are not communicated simply, but by organizations such as newspapers, television and radio networks and organizations, and book and film companies which make high-level decisions and gather information, stories, ideas, and so forth. Media messages are further affected by lower-level *gatekeepers:* reporters and so forth who *screen* messages and may be directly responsible for transmitting them.

Furthermore, messages are picked up and screened by influential (non-media) people: *opinion leaders.* These informally influential people affect the sorts of messages read or listened to—and may affect how individuals (the public) will interpret and react to messages. Figure 1 shows the general process as communication progresses from raw material to well-developed and distributed messages to the public. Note the similarity between the diagram here and the diagram of serial communication. Note also that members of the public may interact with each other. Consider Fig. 1.

The mass media present some new as well as some old problems. These problems will be discussed as they relate to your personal conflicts in Chapter 21. In Chapter 22 we will discuss strategies for mediation in the mass media setting. Look at Fig. 1. Chapter 21 is primarily concerned with conflicts involved when messages are transmitted by media organizations (the thin lines). Chapter 22 will be more concerned with how you can mediate some conflicts by using feedback (the heavy lines) effectively. Together, the chapters give you some introduction to conflicts and strategies in the mass media setting.

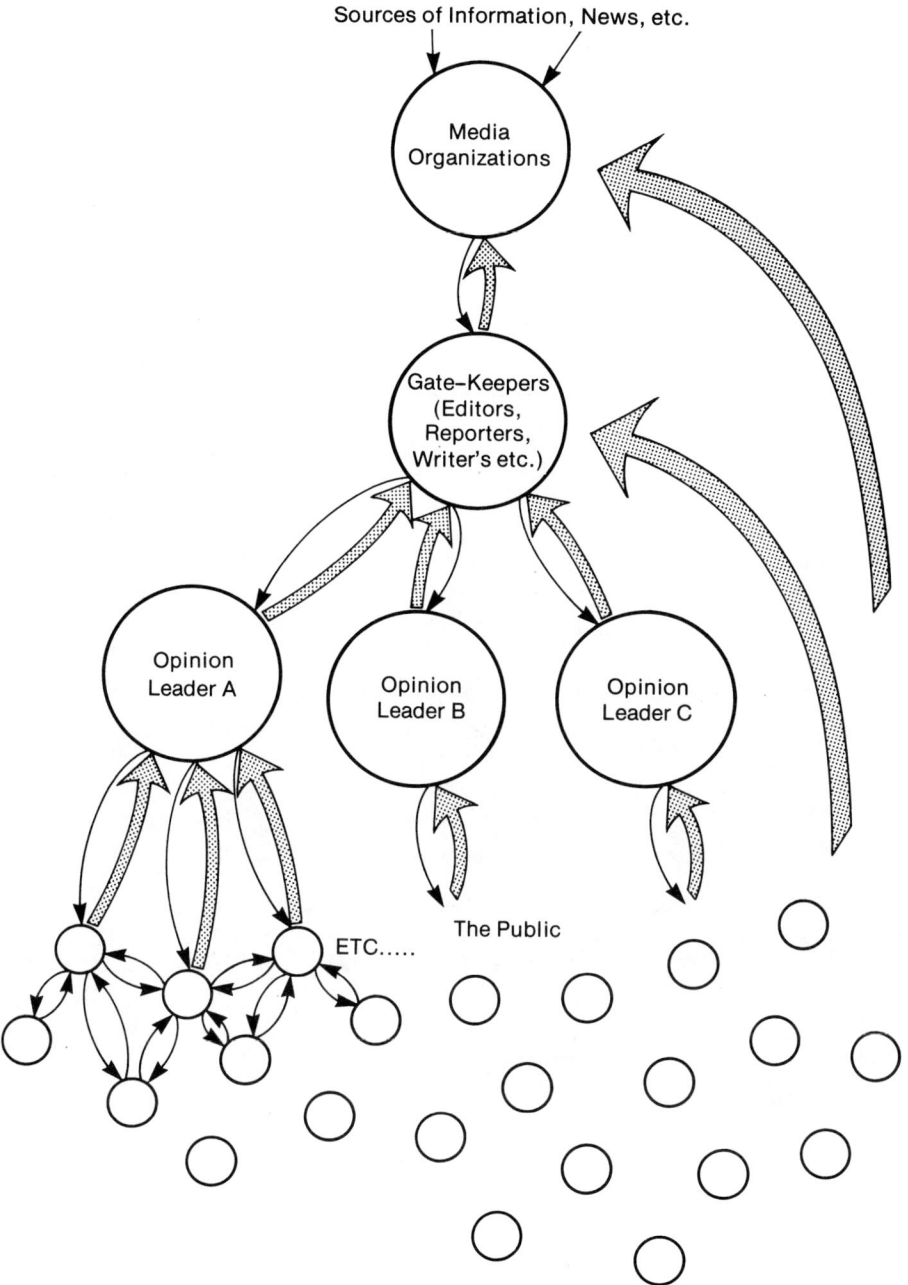

Fig. 1 The mass media setting

21
MASS COMMUNICATION CONFLICTS AS PROBLEMS

Early humans, at best, communicated in no more complicated situations than the one-to-many setting. While messages may have been handed down through many people to many people, the *oral tradition* was not mass communication, but a rough form of serial communication. The messages *presented* by the ancient Greeks and Romans were not mass communication, but public speeches. With the discovery and use of writing, *mass* communication still hardly existed. With the invention of printing, and an increase in literacy, *mass* communication finally was possible. Whole groups of people finally could receive a simultaneous message. From this point on, mass media became an important part of the human environment.

The mid-1900s, however, has brought a new situation. Mass media no longer are *a part of* the environment. As media critic Marshall McLuhan has argued, the media *have become* an environment.[1] We live in a world of messages that tell us what to know, what to think, what to do, what to look like, what to believe in, and what to smell like. The discussion of mass media here is not an afterthought—even though it appears last in the text. The mass media present an environment or context for understanding better everything that we have discussed prior to this chapter. To understand yourself, the other person, and the groups and organizations that surround *you*, you must understand the mass media that surround *them*. The 800 to 1,500 messages (many of them from the mass media) that confront the average person during the day cannot be ignored.[2]

This chapter could not possibly explore all there is to say about the mass media. The chapter is intended to explore mass media problems as conflicts that affect you. I will begin with a general treatment of various *types of influence* transmitted through the mass media. The rest of the chapter will be concerned with mass media problems: the problem of potential effects, the problem of monopolized channels of communication, problems of responsibility and control, and the problem of interrelated media.

TYPES OF MEDIA INFLUENCE OR EFFORTS

Mass media, of course, include television, magazines, movies, newspapers, and radio. Mass media also include less traditionally studied means of communication such as billboards and bumper stickers. These varied communication media are not always successful in their communication efforts—any more than you are. Still, the mass media may affect your personal life in a number of ways. There are several traditionally recognized types of media influences.

Mass media messages, first, may be related to *actions you are asked to take*. Every second fall and certainly every fourth fall, the media become full of political announcements: Candidates want you to vote—if not campaign—in their behalf. The national military forces constantly urge citizens to enlist with them. The utility companies urge you to save fuel and energy. Evangelists and ministers try to bring about your conversion. Charities ask you for support and donations. Public service organizations ask that you give up smoking, get more exercise, establish fire escape plans for your home, and prevent drunk drivers from being on the road. Then, of course, there are commercial advertisements in all the mass media. These messages try to persuade you to buy, lease, or rent the right almost-anything. Your actions are a major media concern.

Mass media also present messages aimed at affecting your *attitudes about something*. Print and electronic messages urge you to adopt tolerant attitudes toward other races. Religious organizations ask for understanding among the religions of the world. Other organizations ask that you adopt positive attitudes toward humanity and brotherhood in general. In addition to attempting to change your attitudes about people and things, some messages seek changes in your *images of something*.[3] Major oil companies want you to consider them "pioneers" in ecology—instead of destroyers of the environment.[4] Tree-using companies such as those in the paper industry want to be known as tree-growing companies. The National Guard—after its use in the sixties to put down demonstrations—wants to be known as helper in time of snow, flood, or tornado.

The efforts to change action, attitudes, and images are not usually easily separated. Companies, politicians, and so forth, may try to change *images* as a way of changing *attitudes* in order to affect your *action*. In some cases, these efforts may be in different messages; in others, they may be in the same message. However they are attempted, changes in action, attitudes, and images are some of the types of media influence.

Another group of media influences has to do with knowledge of one kind or another. Your *contemporary knowledge* of current events undoubtedly is affected by news from various media: on television, on radio, in the print media. These media "cover the news" in different degrees of detail and depth—from the superficial coverage of evening television news to in-depth analysis in the *Washington Post*. Other media messages are aimed at providing exposés or more *sensational and unique stories* in the news. The messages vary from the undocumented *National Enquirer* to the well-done "newsmagazine" shows on television. Other types of messages are aimed at improving your *general and personal knowledge* of the world. Specials (often seen on public television) about scientific achievements, explorations, and animal life are among these efforts. Finally, your *social knowledge* is the goal of some media efforts. Specialized magazines, newspaper magazine sections, and special television programs improve our understanding of life styles, other cultures, other nations, and the people around us.

A third category of media messages is almost wholly aimed at *entertainment*. Often this entertainment is culturally worthwhile: television versions of the great plays, novels, and short stories; radio coverage of concerts and operas; printed stories and poetry; work by new artists. More frequently, the entertainment is pure escapism: cop shows, situation comedies, and variety shows; recorded music over radio; "pulp" novels and collections of stories; and movies based on violence, sex, fantasy—or a combination of all three. Entertainment is a major type of media effort.

I suspect you are already aware of the types of media efforts and influences you face each day. Our review of these forces is designed to help you appreciate the theme of the rest of the chapter: How can media problems become personal conflicts?

THE PROBLEM OF POTENTIAL EFFECTS

One of the main conflicts in mass media is *how much* and *how* you are affected by mass media messages. The research into media effects has produced many more questions than answers. My goal here is not to attempt to describe that research. Instead, I want to indicate some of those areas in which media *may* affect your life. Sex and violence, for example, are popular topics of media research. Some researchers hypothesize that violent comic books, stories, and especially television shows encourage violence in youngsters. Some people argue that violent heroes prompt youngsters to imitate their behavior. Similarly, some believe that exposure to pornography or erotica may encourage or discourage deviant sexual behavior. The questions about sex and violence portrayed in the mass media center on *cause and effects*. The answers have not been found, although there are people who have decided the issue for themselves.

More generally, some people are concerned that the mass media affect *cultural and personal norms*. Do the media present life as it is, was, could be, or should be? It can be argued that shows such as the long-running "All in the Family" encourage *or* discourage bigotry and prejudice. It may be that shows such as the old "Leave it to Beaver" or "Father Knows Best" (still being re-run today in some areas) teach *only* white, middle-class values. Should they teach something else? Do magazines and movies that include bank-robbing, gambling, gun-slinging heroes and heroines encourage antisocial behavior and values?

The mass media have also been studied to learn if they provide unrealistic *expectations* about human situations. Surely, everyone cannot be the ideally sensual man or woman. What happens when people learn that not all problems can be solved by a dramatic and all-knowing father or mother? What happens when people of low income see that everyone (on television) has two cars, a large house, and money to burn? Some researchers are convinced that people seeing unrealistic things in the media want those same unrealistic things. And, of course, not every "three sons" has Fred MacMurray as a father.

There is also concern that media—particularly the news media—present slanted or biased versions of the news and the world. It is often argued that commentators are politically too liberal. Certainly, some stories are reported and some are left out. In a way, the media create *their reality* for us to believe. Even attitudes toward the organizations you belong to or work for can be affected by national and local news and analysis. Editors and reporters have to select stories from the hundreds available. How well they select is, in large part, a matter of their perceptions.

There are excellent texts which explore these issues in great detail.[5] What you should understand for our purposes is that a major source of conflict in the mass media concerns effects. Very little is known absolutely about the potential effects of the media, but you do not need research findings to know that you personally do not always find media messages compatible. If the media have become our environment, how does this environment affect you?

THE PROBLEM OF MONOPOLIZED CHANNELS

The question of potential effects is important because the media sometimes have no competition for their messages. It is difficult to talk back to your television, radio, magazine, or newspaper. There is no citizen's voice that speaks with as much force as NBC, CBS, and ABC. There is frequently only one newspaper in an area: Who is there to balance it? The media seem to many to have a monopoly on the channels for communication. That situation will seem desirable to those people who agree with what is being said or written, but to those who disagree the monopoly seems unfair and unhealthy.

THE PROBLEMS OF FREEDOM AND CONTROL

Freedom of speech and freedom of the press are jealously guarded in the United States. The monopoly of the mass media could be controlled by local, state, or federal agencies—and to some degree it is. Control may mean that certain freedoms of expression will be lost. Absolute freedom may mean that the media are responsible to no one. They can say, do, and print exactly what they want. Control and freedom, then, are factors which somehow must be balanced. Some messages are already controlled. Products must not present false and misleading claims. People cannot be slandered. Candidates for political office must be given equal time to gain access to the media—particularly important in television. The amount of commercial time during television programming is limited by regulation. Obviously, we do not live in a nation where the media enjoy complete freedom.

Conflict arises when some people want more freedom of expression and others want more control. The question becomes how to balance the concerns for freedom and control. Should the federal government control the media more? Should state or local agencies have the power to censor certain types of programs? The questions are difficult, and the answers are continually being investigated. The regulation of the mass media is a major source of conflict.

THE PROBLEM OF MEDIA INTERRELATIONSHIP

Most of us probably spend little time worrying about the conflicts just discussed. To some, the issues may seem to be those abstract, distant things that really don't affect them. Unfortunately, conflicts in the media affect everyone—directly and indirectly. Mass media researchers long ago abandoned the belief that information is "injected" directly into the public by the mass media. Instead, media messages are *filtered* through *gatekeepers* (editors, producers, newspeople, and so forth), through *opinion leaders* (high status and influential people *in your opinion* such as, perhaps, community leaders, supervisors at work or the clergy), and through various levels of other people. This phenomenon was previously discussed as *serial communication*.

Our intrapersonal communication is affected by what we see, hear, or read. Our relationships with others may involve what we have heard, read, or seen in some mass media message. Attitudes and expectations in the small group setting may be influenced by mass media messages. What we think of our churches, our clubs, our schools, and our employers may be affected by mass media messages and effects.

All communication media are interrelated in a modern nation; they make up the media environment in which we all live, and which we cannot afford to ignore. The mass media affect directly or indirectly almost everything we say, do, or think about. Few of the problems you confront will be direct conflicts with mass media, yet many of your personal and interpersonal problems may be related to their indirect influence.

This chapter is not meant to prepare you to understand all the problems and effects of mass media, but to point out that the media are involved with issues of fairness, effects, and so on. *Some of these issues will become your personal conflicts.* When they do, your goal will not be to solve all the country's problems with the media, but to react to your conflicts in a constructive way. The next chapter is devoted to communication strategies that will help you to cope with the mass media conflicts you experience.

NOTES

[1] For an interesting and readable introduction to the thinking of McLuhan, see Marshall McLuhan, "Understanding Media," *Contemporary Theories of Rhetoric: Selected Readings,* ed. Richard L. Johannesen (New York: Harper & Row, 1971), pp. 273–87.

[2] For the figure, I am indebted to Professor Steve Robb of the Department of Communication, Purdue University. The estimate is based upon a variety of estimates by others in the field.

[3] For a detailed discussion of *images,* see Kenneth E. Boulding, *The Image: Knowledge of Life and Society* (Ann Arbor, Mich.: Univ. of Michigan Press, 1969).

[4] For an example of *image-manipulation,* see William R. Brown and Richard E. Crable, "Industry, Mass Magazines, and the Ecology Issue," *Quarterly Journal of Speech,* 59 (Oct. 1973), 259–72.

[5] Two excellent texts are Robert D. Murphy, *Mass Communication and Human Interaction* (Boston: Houghton Mifflin, 1977); and, Steven H. Chaffee and Michael J. Petrick, *Using the Mass Media: Communication Problems in American Society* (New York: McGraw-Hill, 1975).

22
STRATEGIES FOR MASS MEDIA CONFLICTS

When mass media present problems for you personally, you may wish that you had some means of mediation. Actually, problems involving the mass media are somewhat like conflicts in other settings. Some problems probably are impossible to solve. Other problems can be mediated by using certain strategies of communication. This chapter is devoted to describing several sorts of strategies for mediating conflicts related to the mass media. In approaching such problems, you will need to (1) be both fair and critical of the media; (2) realize that the media can be held responsible; (3) realize that you can affect the media; and (4) realize the interrelationships among communication strategies.

BEING CRITICAL; BEING FAIR

It may be true that "There's a sucker born every minute," but it is also true that "You cannot fool all the people all the time." One of the best guides to use in mediating media-related problems is to *be critical* of what you see, hear, or read. My seven-year-old son, Bryan, after watching a commercial for a "new, fantastic, miracle product," will say, "I don't believe that." I suspect that you are even more skeptical of everything that is reported or discussed in any mass medium. There have been too many "miracle products" that do not work; too many costly "free trips" to Arizona; too many news stories that turn out to be different from the first report; and too many contests without winners. Scattered research confirms what you probably already know: people are critical of some of those mass media messages. Still, for everyone who is careful and critical, there is someone who buys a worthless product, who gets a loan to pay for a free vacation, and who believes a false news story. In dealing with mass media, be *skeptical:* critical, but fair.

One of the basic strategies of using communication to mediate your personal conflicts with mass media messages is criticism. By *being critical,* I do not necessarily mean *reacting unfavorably.* Criticism simply means you carefully analyze what you see, hear, and read. Strategies learned earlier can help you with your criticism. Listening well and carefully can alert you to subtly-misleading messages. Adapting listening skills to your reading activity is not difficult. Your knowledge of verbal and nonverbal analysis can be helpful in discovering *intended* meanings. Your understanding of perception can help you understand why the reporter, the advertiser, the politician, or you, believe what you do. Your understanding of argumentation can be of help. Treat what you see, hear, and read as claims—things that should be supported by more evidence before you believe them. Understand what the claim is—or is supposed to be. Use the strategies for information analysis in Part 4 of the text to analyze the information you receive. In short, you now have the tools that you need for being critical of mass media messages.

You should balance your criticism of the media with *fairness.* We see television shows and movies that cost millions of dollars to produce. We read newspapers, books, or magazines that are the products of perhaps hundreds of people and months of preparation. It is easy to assume that because of the people, time, and money used, mass media messages must somehow be perfect and flawless. In fact, media messages are created by people, and are just as likely to be inefficient or biased as your messages are. Media messages are even more difficult to communicate than your messages—the problems are as numerous as the thousands of people involved in sending and receiving them. Mass media communication—like all communication—is difficult, often frustrating, and sometimes in error. Do not expect more from the media than you do from people generally—some of whom are involved in the media.

REALIZE THE MEDIA'S RESPONSIBILITY

Human beings generally are *responsible* and *accountable* for what they do. Communicators generally are responsible for what they say, do, or write.[1] In the same way, the mass media are held responsible for the messages they *send.* If fact, because these messages often reach millions of people directly (and millions more indirectly), the mass media have a greater responsibility than other communicators and means of communication. You may have influence with one, several, or dozens of people. What you do and say may either be helpful or harmful to them in different ways. Mass media messages, though, may affect millions of people in ways we discussed in the last chapter. The complete control of the mass media would be a terrible attack upon freedom of speech. So, while the mass media realistically cannot be controlled, they can be held responsible for the messages they present.[2]

REALIZE THAT YOU CAN AFFECT THE MASS MEDIA

One of the chief means of holding the media responsible for what they communicate is the public's reaction to the messages. Newspapers, magazines, and publishers cannot stay in business without people buying their products. Radio and television programs cannot be aired without sponsors—and sponsors have withdrawn support in the past because of public reaction. Movies that do not draw the public will not be used as models or patterns for forthcoming movies. In short, mass media depend upon the support of masses of citizens.

Keeping the media responsible to the public directly and indirectly is a major solution to the problem of balancing freedom and control. In the mid-seventies, groups of citizens began a major war against violence in children's television. Whether that war succeeds is still a question. Still, probably few Americans (and no network executives or advertisers) are unaware of the issue. Films that contain violence, explicit sex, obscenity, and so forth have been traditional targets for citizen's groups. Citizen reaction—and the threat of government regulation—has resulted in a coding system that rates (primarily) the amount of sex in movies. The citizens who have effected these changes are like you and me. Not all of them have been rich, famous, and powerful—although that helps. Many simply have been people who perceived that their own lives and the lives of their children were affected by the mass media. They have taken steps to hold the media responsible for their messages. In certain areas, they have been successful; in certain other areas, the fight goes on. They have proven that citizens can affect the mass media.

REALIZE THAT STRATEGIES OF MEDIATION INTERRELATE

Many citizens' efforts to affect the mass media do not involve using mass media themselves. The mass media, as we discussed earlier, sometimes have a monopoly on mass media channels. Typically, the citizen does not have access to his or her newspaper, television station, or magazine. Strategies aimed at mediating mass media-related problems do not have to involve the use of mass media. You can use non-mass media channels to react to mass media messages. Reactions to the mass media can involve individual, group, or organizational strategies.

Individual strategies include the ever-popular letter to the editor. Most newspapers and many magazines provide a means for people to respond to what they have read. This sort of opportunity means that the channel of communication is not entirely monopolized. You as a citizen can have nearly the same audience for your reaction as the original message had.[3] Local television stations frequently air responses to their news, commentaries, or programming. Some allow citizens to tape their comments for replay during the news or during a special time set up for that purpose. With advances in cable television, the letter-to-the-editor kind of response may be even more exciting. Time allotted to citizen feedback or response may be enlarged; channels devoted to citizen discussion and response may be included in future facilities.[4]

Personal letters also are a means of reacting to conflicts related to the mass media. Well-written, businesslike letters can be sent to your representative or senator. In my interviews with members of congress, they frequently have surprised me with their tabulation and knowledge of the responses they get from "the folks back home." Letters of the same sort may be sent to local or state Better Business Bureaus or consumer organizations such as Common Cause. While not media-controlling bodies, these organizations do have influence and the power to report media activities. A more powerful group for radio and television-related problems is the Federal Communications Commission in Washington, D.C. All television and radio stations are licensed "in the public interest." That means that the stations must *prove themselves worthy* of a license renewal. In the past, the renewal was automatic. Now, however, the FCC does examine "all the evidence" related to how well the station has served the public interest—and the evidence includes letters from people like you. Relatedly, letters may be sent to the attention of station managers. When licenses are reconsidered, stations must produce a file of the responses they have received from citizens. I suspect that letters marked "Carbon copy to FCC" guarantee that the letters are in fact filed. Letter writing, then, can be an effective means of mediating your personal problems with the media.

Informal contacts with individuals, groups, and organizations can also help your efforts. You can share your concerns—whatever they are—with other individuals in what amounts to a persuasive interview. You can voice your concerns in social, civic, and professional groups. You can present your views in a public speech to civic clubs and gatherings. You may succeed in starting a neighborhood or community grapevine of concerned citizens who share your views. Your face-to-face communication efforts can be an important part of your overall strategy of mediation.

Group strategies can be an effective help in mediating your personal problems. An aroused group of people concerned about something-or-other can become the audience which invites political, religious, or civic speakers to share and publicize your views. Group letters (individually written and created) may affect congressional activity, FCC action, or local investigations. Group visits to local newspaper, television, and radio stations probably are not common, but they might be effective if all else fails. Finally, group strategies are effective simply because more people—many of whom will belong to other groups—can "spread the word" faster and more effectively than you could alone. If you experience conflicts related to the mass media, you may wish to consider either using a group already formed or creating a new group. Group communication strategies may be your key to mediation.

Finally, *organizational strategies* can be used to mediate media-related problems. Organizations will be composed of individuals and various established groups, so organizational mediation can be attempted in the ways already discussed. Your organization may share your feeling that conflict exists—or your organization may feel itself involved in conflict. In either situation, the existence of an organization probably means that you have access to more money and more methods of reaction to mass media messages. Organizations, for example, have the ability to generate media attention. A company can react to unfavorable news stories by announcing new equipment aimed at making their organization more efficient, cleaner, or better. Companies sometimes can make news by announcing a new plant, new management, new procedures, or just changes. In addition, individual teachers, executives, medical personnel, and so forth can make official appearances at club meetings, civic affairs, and fundraising events. Finally, most organizations of even moderate size have professional public relations areas, people, or departments.[5] These may be labeled as the *public relations department,* the *public information service,* the *community information agency,* or any other title. Whatever the title, public relations people are involved in basically one task: the creation of favorable images for the organization. People involved in this task may use image-related advertisements like the commercials for the "tree-growing company." They may prepare and distribute information about the organization. They may write news items for the local newspaper or provide information for the national or statewide news services (such as Associated Press). They may be in charge of newsletters, pamphlets, or brochures. Not all of these efforts, of course, are aimed at mediating problems related to the mass media. The point is, however, that organizations may have an array of specialized tools that *can* be used for mediating such problems.

Your life, then, can be affected by conflicts involving the mass media and you, your group, and your organizations. The mediation of these conflicts sometimes can be accomplished with communication strategies. You can begin your efforts to mediate those problems by being both critical and fair. You should realize that the mass media can be held responsible for their messages—and that you can affect the mass media. You can use your general knowledge of communication strategies to understand the conflict you feel. To make the incompatible situation more as you want it to be, you may use individual strategies, group strategies, or organizational strategies. Some combination of efforts may help you react to your media environment. You are not completely helpless when you experience mass media-related conflicts.

Marshall McLuhan has said that the "medium is the message," meaning that the ideas you receive from the media are based more upon the *form* than the *content* of the media messages. McLuhan has also created several puns on the phrase. The "medium is the mass-age," for example, illustrates the relationship between messages and the size and complexity of the society. He has also said that the "medium is the mess-age" which may reflect some of the confusion in a large society bombarded by messages. Finally, though, he has argued in various places that the "medium is the massage." The media "reach out" and "rub" you—sometimes the wrong way. The hundreds of daily messages you experience are intended to change you, mold you, improve you, or take advantage of you. With global media transmission, the world has become what McLuhan calls a "global village." We "know" what's going on in India, Peru, and around the corner; just as important, people of the global village know us. There seems at times very little privacy in the village—a situation that can make us personally experience even greater conflicts with the media environment. Yet, we are not entirely helpless in that environment. In this chapter we have discussed certain strategies with which you can attempt to mediate some of those conflicts you experience in the mass media setting.

EXERCISES

1. As a class or in groups, discuss which (if any) of the potential effects or actual problems in mass media most concern you as individuals. Second, have each person who voices an opinion describe the kind of thing he or she is doing to mediate that conflict. Finally, (especially if you find that no one is doing anything) discuss how the strategies in this chapter might have some influence on the mediation of the conflict.
2. As a class or in informal groups outside class, watch the three major evening news programs. Assign at least one (or more) groups to each network. Keep track of the stories presented, in the order of presentation. What was said about each story? How much time was given to each story? Later, the class as a whole should compare the information obtained. Given the idea that many people watch only one of the network programs, what different perceptions of the world might they get if they listened and watched ABC, CBS, or NBC?
3. Use the procedures above, but compare newspapers (local or national) that are available in your area. Look especially at page one: What is the headline? What are the featured stories? How much space is devoted to each? Compare your findings.
4. Check the letters-to-the-editor section of any newspaper for a given week. Is there any pattern of certain issues you detect? Check the editorials for the same week. Are there relationships between the two features?

NOTES

See, for example, Richard E. Crable, "Ethical Codes, Accountability, and Argumentation," *Quarterly Journal of Speech* (64) (Feb. 1978), 23–32.

[2] For an in-depth discussion, see Jerome A. Barron, *Freedom of the Press for Whom?* (Bloomington, In.: Indiana Univ. Press, 1973).

[3] See Keith P. Sanders, *What are Daily Newspapers Doing to Be Responsible to Readers' Criticisms?*, ANPA News Research Bulletin No. 9, November 30, 1973.

[4] An excellent discussion by a former FCC Commissioner is Nicholas Johnson, *How to*

Talk Back to Your Television Set (Boston: Little, Brown, 1967). Johnson's discussion covers a wide variety of topics, including many alluded to in the rest of the chapter.

[5] For an interesting discussion, see Ben Bagdikian, *The Information Machines* (Stanford, Ca.: Stanford Univ. Press, 1964).

INDEX

Anxiety:
  controlling, 254–255
  levels of, 254
Argumentation:
  as mediational strategy:
    group, 168
    interpersonal, 110–112
    intrapersonal, 79–85
    one-to-many, 234
  defined, 79
  elements:
    claims, 79–80
    evidence, 80
    qualifiers, 81
    reservations, 81
    warrants, 80
  group, 192–194
  reasoning analysis, 277–278
Attitude:
  persuasion and, 279
  sources of resistance to change, 279–281
Audience analysis, 276–281, 290–292

Behavior, 33–34
Brainstorming, 190

Channel (or medium), 15
Choice, 19–20
Chronemics, 64, 70–71
Climate, factors, 101–102
Communication:
  as mediation, 6
  defined, 14
  elements of a model, 14–18
    channel (or medium), 15
    conceptual screens, 14–15
    feedback, 15
    interference, 15–16
    messages, 15
    people, 14
    system, 16
  features, 12–14
    intent, 13
    meaning, 12
    process, 12
    re-created, 13

Communication (cont.)
- symbols, 13
- transaction, 13
- feedback, 15
- interpersonal (defined), 91
- miscommunication and, 13
- patterns in organizations, 224–227
- perception, 19 (see also Perception)
- phases or sub-processes, 19–21
  - choice, 19–20
  - interpretation, 19
  - reception, 19
  - symbolization, 20
  - transmission, 20
- receivers, 15
- senders, 15
- settings, 7–8

Compatibility:
- defined, 4
- helpful and dysfunctional, 5

Conceptual screens, 14–15

Conflict:
- defined, 4
- helpful and dysfunctional, 5
- types, 4

Conflicts:
- group, 153–165
  - climate, 160–161
  - decision-making, 161–163
  - dysfunctional roles, 163–164
  - participation, 155–158
  - people-task balancing, 158–160
- group participation, 155–158
  - intra/interpersonal, 156
  - membership, 158
  - representation, 157–158
  - status, 156–157
- interpersonal, 91–106
  - ethics, 103–106
  - perception of others, 92–94
  - relationships, 97–103
  - roles, 94–97
- intrapersonal, 29–36
  - behavior, 33–34
  - information, 32–33
  - roles, 31–32
  - selves, 29–30
  - values, 34–35

mass media:
- interrelated media, 309
- monopolized channels, 308
- potential effects, 307
- responsibility and control, 308–309

one-to-many:
- presentational speaking, 230–231
- public speaking, 231–232
- serial communication, 228–230

people-task balancing:
- leadership/membership, 160
- personal/group goal, 159–160
- task/interpersonal, 159

Conformity, 161 (see also Compatibility)
Consensus, 162, 176
Creativity, 189–192
Credibility:
- delivery and, 256–257
- factors of, 225–226
- improving, 251–252

Decision-making (see also Argumentation):
- as mediational strategy in group, 183–197
- group, 161–163, 183–197
  - creativity, 189–192
  - information analysis, 184–186
  - reflective thinking, 186–189
- quality vs. acceptance, 177–178

Delivery:
- defined, 155
- factors in good, 256–260
- styles of, 298

Demonstration speeches, 261
Diagonal communication, 226, 242–243
Downward communication, 224, 240–241

Ethics:
- defined, 103
- ethical standards, 104–105
- ethical standards applied, 105–106
- humans and, 103–105

Ethos (see Credibility)

Feedback:
- as mediational strategy:
  - group, 170

Index

interpersonal, 125–126
one-to-many, 234–235
defined, 15, 126
games, 133–135
interpersonal relationships and, 128–133
purposes of, 126–128
specific strategies, 130–132
trust/risk cycle and, 127

Games:
feedback, 133–135
group gaming, 173–179
Grapevine communication, 226, 242–243

Haptics, 64, 69
Horizontal communication, 224, 242

Information analysis, 184–186
Information processing, 32–33
Intent, 12
Interference, 15–16
Interpretation, 19
Interviewing:
as mediational strategy:
group, 170–171
interpersonal, 139–147
one-to-many, 235
characteristics, 140
defined, 140
general strategies, 144–145
questions, 142–144
neutral, leading, loaded, 143
open, closed, 142–143
primary, secondary, 143
probes, 143–144
types (by purpose), 140–142

Kinesics, 64, 67–68

Language and verbal self-analysis:
as mediational strategy:
group, 167
interpersonal, 109
intrapersonal, 53–60
one-to-many, 234
factors, 54–57
abstraction, 56
arbitrary and rational, 55
labeling, 54–55

perception and, 56
stereotyping, 57
Language use:
good, 269–271
jargon, 269–270
nonstandard, 269
symbolizing and, 268
Leadership, 205–207
styles, 206
Listening:
as mediational strategy:
group, 169–170
interpersonal, 115–123
one-to-many, 234
interpersonal problems and, 116–118
responses, 118–120

Maintenance roles, 203–204
Mass media:
affecting, 315
criticism and fairness, 313–314
influences, 306–307
interrelated media, 315–317
responsibility, 314–315
Meaning, 12
Mediation:
communication and, 6
communication settings and, 7–8
counseling and, 6
defined, 4
methods, 5–6
physical acts and, 5
rhetoric and, 6
spiritualism and, 5
Medium (see Channel)
Messages, 15
Metaphors (see Synectics)

Nonverbal self-analysis:
as mediational strategy:
group, 168
interpersonal, 110
intrapersonal, 63–75
one-to-many, 234
Nonverbal symbols:
defined, 63
functions of, 66
meaning and, 64–65
meanings, common:

Nonverbal symbols (*cont.*)
  chronemics, 70–71
  environmental factors, 70–72
  haptics, 69
  kinesics, 67–68
  objectics, 70
  oculesics, 69–70
  physical appearance, 72
  proxemics, 68–69
 types, 64

Objectics, 64, 70
Oculesics, 64, 69–70
Organization (in speeches):
 conclusions:
  purposes, 296–297
  types, 297
 introductions:
  purposes, 296
  types, 296
 patterns of, 282–283, 294–296
 reasons and, 281–283
Organizations (businesses, etc.):
 patterns of communication, 224–227
 roles in, 204–205
 systems and, 227–228
 variables in, 218

Patterns of serial communication, 224–227
Perception:
 as mediational strategy:
  group, 166–167
  interpersonal, 108–109
  intrapersonal, 41–49
  one-to-many, 234
 characteristics:
  active, 42
  context-bound, 45
  inductive, 44–45
  motivated, 45–46
  personal, 46–47
  selective, 43–44
 defined, 19
 described, 41–42
 of others, 128–133
 of self, 128–133
 selection:
  selective attention, 43
  selective exposure, 43
  selective interpretation, 43–44
  selective retention, 44
Persuasion:
 attitudes and, 279
 persuasive analysis, 278–281
Presentational speaking:
 adapting to, 284–286
 analyzing decision-makers, 276–281
  persuasive analysis, 278–281
  reasoning analysis, 277–278
 as mediational strategy, 275–286
 assumptions of, 230–231
 conflicts in, 231
 creating the proposal, 275–276
 organizing for reasoning, 281–283
 preparation, 283–284
Process, 12
Proxemics, 64, 68–69
Public speaking:
 as mediational strategy, 289–299
 audience analysis, 290–292
  demographic variables, 290–291
  psychological variables, 291–292
 presentational speaking and, 231–232
 purpose:
  defined, 292
  factors in, 292–294
 styles of delivery, 298

Questions (*see* Interviewing: questions)

Reasoning analysis, 277–278
Reception, 19
Re-created meanings, 13
Reflective thinking, 186–189
Relationships:
 conflicts of:
  climate, 101–103
  dominance, 100–101
  liking/distance, 97–98
  similarity, 98–100
 types:
  complementary, 100
  symmetrical, 100–101
Rhetoric, 6
Risk-taking, 127, 161
Role enactment, 201–208
Roles:

Index

conflict, 94–97
conflicting and compatible, 31–32
constructive, 201–208
  leadership, 205–207
  maintenance, 203–204
  organizational, 204–205
  task, 202–203
defined, 31
dysfunctional, 163–164
formal/informal in organizations, 224–227
group, 163–164, 200–208

Selectivity, human (see Perception: selective)
Self:
  actual, 29
  desired, 30
  feared, 30
  metaperceptions, 30
  perceived, 30
  self-acceptance, 36–38
    as-is self, 36–37
    becoming self, 37–38
  self-rejection, 36
Self-fulfilling prophesy, 46
Serial communication:
  as mediational strategy, 239–247
  conflicts, 228–230
  purposes of:
    diagonal, 242–243
    downward, 240–241
    grapevine, 242–243
    horizontal, 242
    skip-level, 242–243
    upward, 241–242
  sources of distortion, 242–245
  timing, 245
  written/oral, 245
Skip-level communication, 226–227, 242–243
Small group communication:
  characteristics, 154
  defined, 153–154
  gaming, 172–179
  types (by purpose), 154–155
Speaking (see Public speaking; Presentational speaking)

Speaking strategies for mediation, 251–271
Strategies of mediation:
  group:
    consensus/win-win gaming, 173–179
    decision-making, 183–197
    role enactment, 201–208
  interpersonal:
    feedback, 125–136
    interviewing, 139–147
    listening, 115–123
  intrapersonal:
    argumentation, 79–85
    language and verbal self-analysis, 52–60
    nonverbal self-analysis, 63–75
    perceiving, 41–49
  mass media, 313–318
  one-to-many:
    general speaking, 251–271
    presentational speaking, 275–286
    public speaking, 289–299
    serial communication, 239–247
Symbolization, 20
Symbols (defined), 13
Synectics, 190–192
System (in communication), 16

Task roles, 202–203
Transaction, 13
Transmission, 20

Upward communication, 224, 241–242

Values, 34–35
Verbal symbols (defined), 53–54
  (see also Language)
Visual aids:
  as support, 261
  how to use, 265–268
  kinds of, 262–263
  when to use, 263–265
Vocalics, 64, 71

Win-win strategy, 175–177